D1384409

# PRINCE WILLIAM

Center Point
Large Print

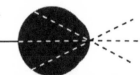

**This Large Print Book carries the
Seal of Approval of N.A.V.H.**

# PRINCE WILLIAM

## THE MAN WHO WILL BE KING

## Penny Junor

CENTER POINT LARGE PRINT
THORNDIKE, MAINE

This Center Point Large Print edition
is published in the year 2013 by arrangement with
Pegasus Books.

Copyright © 2012 by Penny Junor.
Revised epilogue opyright © 2013 by Penny Junor.

All rights reserved.

The text of this Large Print edition is unabridged.
In other aspects, this book may vary
from the original edition.
Printed in the United States of America
on permanent paper.
Set in 16-point Times New Roman type.

ISBN: 978-1-61173-842-1

Library of Congress Cataloging-in-Publication Data

Junor, Penny.
 Prince William : the man who will be king / Penny Junor. — Center Point
Large Print edition.
  pages cm
 Previously published: New York : Pegasus Books, 2012.
 ISBN 978-1-61173-842-1 (library binding : alk. paper)
 1. William, Prince, Duke of Cambridge, 1982–
  2. Princes—Great Britain—Biography.  I. Title.
 DA591.A45W555455 2013
 941.085092—dc23
 [B]
                                                                2013027549

For Marlene, Max and Oscar

# CONTENTS

# INTRODUCTION

His mother was an icon, 'the People's Princess', whose shocking, violent and early death plunged the nation into grief that bordered on hysteria and brought the monarchy perilously close to the end of the road. His father is one of the most controversial figures of the age and the man who will one day be King. Having written biographies about both the Prince and Princess of Wales, and followed them on and off for the last thirty years, the opportunity to write about their eldest son, Prince William, was irresistible. I find him one of the most interesting, remarkable and, whatever one's view of the monarchy, important young men of his generation. One day he will inherit the throne of the United Kingdom. He will be Head of State, Supreme Governor of the Church of England, Colonel-in-Chief of the Armed Forces, and possibly Head of the Commonwealth. His face will be on our coins and our stamps; he will have little power but incalculable influence; he will represent the nation to itself and be the ultimate symbol of stability in a world of rapid change.

Although he is second in line to the throne, and may not accede for a couple of decades or more, this character is key to ensuring the institution has a long-term future. The Queen, his grandmother, celebrating her Diamond Jubilee, has been a remarkable sovereign and is deservedly and universally loved and admired. Sadly, the same cannot be said for the Prince of Wales. The very public breakdown of his marriage and subsequent remarriage to the woman Diana blamed for her unhappiness, divided the nation and undermined almost everything the Prince had achieved in the last forty years. He has worked relentlessly to improve life for the less privileged in our society and to ensure that the earth is a safe and sustainable place for future generations. His dedication to duty has been unflinching but his approval rating among the public has never fully recovered.

Opinion polls commissioned by newspapers asking whether the throne should skip a generation when the Queen dies suggest that a high percentage of the population would favour this outcome. According to these polls some people go further and think the Queen should abdicate so William could inherit the throne while he is young. These proposals are as realistic as fantasy football and fail entirely to understand how hereditary monarchy works. As the old refrain so aptly runs, 'The King is dead, long live the King', and when the Queen does come to the end of her life and, therefore, her reign, her son and heir, Charles, will become King, provided he is sane and fit when the time comes. Any engineering of the system is out of the question.

I happen to believe he will be a very good King and I hope that public opinion will change. He has had bad press for most of his adult life and been unfairly judged. However, he will always be a man whose lifestyle and interests are far removed from those of the general public. This was not a problem sixty years ago when his mother came to the throne, although she is considerably less extravagant than Charles. But ours is a different and far less forgiving age. Deference and respect for all our institutions, not just the monarchy, has long gone. Usefulness and value for money have become all important. If it is to survive in the long term, the monarchy needs to be relevant and in tune with ordinary people. Paradoxically, Charles is very much in tune with the man in the street, more so than most politicians, and has a natural rapport with young and old, rich and poor— though this isn't the general perception. As the former Prime Minister Sir John Major says, 'The most important thing for the monarchy is that they aren't seen to be curious creatures drafted in from Planet Windsor and who have nothing in common with and no relevance to the way most people live their lives.'

William, with his less plummy voice, chinos and easy, jocular manner, is someone they can immediately relate to. He has more of his father in him than you might think, but also plenty of his mother's impish humour and warmth. He also has the advantage of an almost normal upbringing, which his father never had. He knows how the rest of us live, knows what it's like to get cash out of a hole-in-the-wall, peel potatoes and cook coq au vin. His father wouldn't know where to begin.

William plays polo and follows rich men's pursuits, but he also loves rugby and football and plays a mean game of pool. There's no denying he's privileged and that most of his friends are wealthy, but he wears it very lightly; there is no trace of the arrogance that so often goes with the public school, hunting, shooting and fishing set. He is remarkably humble for a man in his position, modest and self-deprecating—laughing at himself is not only an endearing trait but also a very effective icebreaker when talking to strangers. And in our celebrity, body-perfect, youth-obsessed age, he ticks all the boxes.

He is also Diana's son. That alone makes him special. For so many people she was the beautiful fairytale Princess, the angel of mercy who, despite her own suffering and sadness, reached out and gave solace to others. They loved her with an alarming intensity, and they love the son who keeps alive her looks and so many of her mannerisms.

The first fairytale had an unhappy ending. Now there is a new Princess and a new story. Catherine Middleton is reminiscent of Diana, and she's another gift for the fashion industry, but she has the advantage of a stable background and a good education; and, unlike Diana, she had a long, hard look at the bizarre world William inhabits before agreeing to join him there. This love story is the genuine article, and William knows that it can't disappoint. This union must be as solid, supportive and companionable as his grandparents' marriage.

'If you want to understand William,' says one of his friends, 'his relationship with the Middletons is the beginning and end of it. He likes them, they're happy and they're nice, straightforward people.' And the fact that they are not blue-blooded is a bonus. For too long the Royal Family has been associated with the aristocracy and the upper classes.

William is fiercely protective of Kate. He saw what happened to his mother and has seen the pain and torment his father has suffered by attempting to be open and honest. He will not make the same mistakes. He is determined to keep his private life private, as his grandmother has done. He will give his time, his talents, his energy and his enthusiasm to the country, but he won't give his soul. His father allowed work and duty to all but take over his life. William will make sure he keeps enough time aside for himself and for his family.

This steely determination to create the life he wants, and to be in control of it, is possibly the most noticeable effect of his home life as a child.

While the world pruriently read about the War of the Waleses in newspapers and magazines, he lived through it. The woman killed so tragically, whom millions mourned, was his mother. As one of his friends says: 'Imagine what it must have been like to live through the s**t of his childhood: the divorce, the acrimony, the shame of it all being played out in public, his mother's *Panorama* interview, then she's dead. His father's mistress hanging around, then moving in. It makes you shudder. Even if you were living on a sink estate, you'd feel sorry for your neighbour if they'd gone through that.'

What is interesting is how he came through it so apparently unscathed. If home *had* been a depressed sink estate, you would expect him to be badly damaged, a loner maybe, an addict, a drop-out. Being rich offers no protection either; the scions of some of the oldest and wealthiest families in the land have gone disastrously off the rails. William didn't even come close.

He would be superhuman if he didn't have demons. But he keeps them to himself; he is one of the most intensely private people you could meet. There are subjects he doesn't talk about. If asked, the shutters come down and those that know him well know better than to ask. It's a survival mechanism in a world where everyone wants a piece of him. On the outside he shows no sign of being anything other than a cheerful, grounded, well-adjusted human being, happy in his own skin, open, confident and content. At the very least he could be excused for turning his back on the people he blames for killing his mother. He never has. He has come through the experiences of his childhood and adolescence a strong and resolute character, but with vulnerabilities like everyone, and a wariness of strangers, but a great capacity to love. His close friends are a small and tightly knit group; they go back a long way. They are loyal and protective; they like him for who he is and don't care that he's an HRH. As one of them puts it, 'He's someone you'd like to have alongside you in the trenches.'

'I think it's a complete misconception,' the Duke of Edinburgh once said, 'to imagine that the monarchy exists in the interests of the monarch. It doesn't. It exists in the interests of the people.' William would like nothing more than to be an ordinary man. As a teenager, he wanted to be a gamekeeper. Now, between Royal duties, he's flying search and rescue helicopters, which he loves, and living with Kate in a small farmhouse in Wales. They have no staff, and in his ideal world there would be no palaces or motorcades. But he was born to do this job, and sooner or later, in the interests of the people, he will give up his personal preferences and do it full time.

He has strong views about the way he will do it. Monarchy must constantly evolve to remain relevant and his ideas imply no criticism of his grandmother, they are merely a reflection of today's world. He does nothing unless he is convinced it is worthwhile; he is not a celebrity putting in appearances for the sake of publicity, and one of his greatest concerns is that he will be confused with one. Many years ago, emotionally drained by a visit to a premature baby unit at the hospital where he was born, he turned to his Private Secretary and said, 'I have no idea why people want to talk to me but as long as they do, and it seems to make them happier, then let's please do more.'

A recent survey said Prince William was the most influential man in the world after President Obama. His stock could not be higher, but people in Britain have a short shelf-life; prime ministers don't last more than a few years before the public wants a change. We have a culture that values youth over age. His challenge will be to find a way of changing that, of bypassing celebrity and maintaining a clear focus on his objectives, and of sustaining public interest for the rest of his life—without forfeiting his soul.

# BEGINNINGS

There had been months of speculation in the press about where Diana's first baby would be born. According to the tabloids, she and the Queen were locked in argument; the Princess of Wales wanted to have her baby in hospital but the Queen insisted the heir to the throne should be born at Buckingham Palace, where her own four children had been delivered.

Like so many royal stories over the years it was not quite true. Diana was under the care of Mr George Pinker, the Queen's Surgeon-Gynaecologist—better known to the young mothers of west London as one of the senior consultants at St Mary's Hospital in Paddington. A delightful man, he'd been delivering babies there for twenty-four years, including those of the Duchess of Gloucester, Princess Michael of Kent and Princess Anne. There was never any doubt—or disagreement—about where this baby would be born. It would be delivered in the safety of a private room on the fourth floor of the Lindo Wing, with everything on hand in case of emergency.

So Prince William, who came into the world at three minutes past nine on the evening of Monday 21 June 1982, was the first direct heir to the throne to be born in a hospital. It was the first of many firsts for the healthy, 7 lb 1½ oz little boy, who genealogists declared would be the most British monarch since James I and the most English since Elizabeth I. He was 39 per cent English, 16 per cent Scottish, 6.25 per cent Irish and 6.25 per cent American. The remaining 32.5 per cent was German. To his parents he was quite simply the best thing that had ever happened to them.

When news reached the wider world that Diana had been taken to St Mary's at five o'clock that morning, people flocked to the hospital, clutching Union Jacks and picnics, and set up camp in the street outside, just as they had for the wedding almost exactly a year before. Undaunted by the pouring rain they waited excitedly, transistor radios on, bottles of bubbly at the ready, and when news of the birth finally came, the cry went up: 'It's a boy! It's a boy!' Corks popped, to cheers and roars of delight and stirring rounds of 'For she's a jolly good fellow' and 'Rule Britannia'.

Heading home to Kensington Palace a couple of hours later, Charles was greeted by about five hundred well-wishers and a host of journalists. He looked exhausted but flushed with excitement and pride. He had been with Diana throughout and would later tell friends about the thrill of seeing his son born, and what a life-changing experience it had been. 'I'm obviously relieved and delighted,' he said as the cameras flashed. 'Sixteen hours is a long time to wait.' And then, in typically philosophical mode, he added, 'It's rather a grown-up thing, I find—rather a shock to the system.' 'How was the baby?' someone asked. 'He looks marvellous; fair, sort of blondish. He's not bad.' When asked if he looked like his father, he added, 'It has the good fortune not to.' As for names, he said, 'We've thought of one or two but there's a bit of an argument about it. We'll just have to wait and see.'

There were no crowd barriers outside the Lindo Wing and as people pushed in on Charles, the better to hear his answers, a woman suddenly lunged forward, flung her arms around the new father and kissed him firmly on the cheek, leaving a smudge of bright red lipstick. 'Bloody hell,' said the Prince with a wry smile, 'Give us a chance!' The crowd loved it and burst into song, like football supporters: 'Nice one Charlie. Give us another one!'

As he slipped into a waiting car he appealed for quiet so that mother and baby could get some well-deserved rest. They had not been disturbed at all; their room on the fourth floor faced the opposite way. It was the other new mothers in the wing whose rooms overlooked the road he was concerned about.

Crowds had also gathered outside the gates of Buckingham Palace, where a self-appointed town crier was hoping to be heard above the noise of car horns and general merriment. At 10.25 p.m., in traditional style, the official announcement was posted on the gates. 'Her Royal Highness the Princess of Wales was today safely delivered of a son at 9.03 p.m. Her Royal Highness and her child are both doing well.' It was signed by Dr John Batten, head of the Queen's Medical Household, Dr Clive Roberts, the anaesthetist, Dr David Harvey, the royal paediatrician, and Mr George Pinker.

The proud father was back the next morning at 8.45 a.m., by which time the police had brought in barriers to keep the enthusiasm less physical. Frances Shand Kydd, Diana's mother, and her elder sister Lady Jane Fellowes, arrived about half an hour later. They left full of excitement. 'My grandson is everything his father said last night,' said Mrs Shand Kydd. 'He's a lovely baby. The Princess looked radiant, absolutely radiant. There's a lot of happiness up there.' The Queen was the next visitor. She arrived clutching a small present shortly before eleven o'clock and left twenty minutes later looking jubilant. The last familiar face to arrive was that of Earl Spencer, Diana's father, who had survived a massive brain haemorrhage three years earlier and was universally admired for having valiantly walked his youngest daughter up the long aisle of St Paul's Cathedral the previous July. He left the hospital repeating over and over, 'He's a lovely baby.'

Charles commented that his son was 'looking a bit more human this morning'. Diana was well and recovering her strength and the baby 'was in excellent form too, thank goodness.' They were in such good form that in the afternoon mother and 'Baby Wales' went home. Diana was looking flushed and a little fragile, but also radiant. It had been a normal birth, albeit induced, relatively pain-free, thanks to an epidural spinal injection, and the baby, wrapped in a white blanket for the journey home, was breast-feeding well. Charles was carrying him as they came through the doors of the hospital, but soon handed him carefully to his mother. They smiled for the cameras and crowds, said their goodbyes to the staff who had come to see them off, and were whisked away by a waiting car.

It was unusual for a first-time mother to leave hospital so soon. Thirty years ago it was common practice to stay for five to eight days after the birth, but Diana's home circumstances were rather special. As well as daily visits to Kensington Palace from Mr Pinker and Dr Harvey, she had the reassurance of a maternity nurse living in for the first few weeks while she established a routine. Sister Anne Wallace had previously worked for Princess Anne when her two children, Peter and Zara Phillips, were newborn.

Charles was overjoyed to have a family and quickly mastered the art of bathing the baby and nappy-changing. He had wanted children for years and was always quietly envious of his friends' cosy domestic arrangements. Just days after the birth he wrote to his cousin Patricia Brabourne, 'The arrival of our small son has been an astonishing experience and one that has meant more to me than I could ever have imagined. As so often happens in this life, you have to experience something before you are in a true position to understand or appreciate the full meaning of the whole thing. I am so thankful I was beside Diana's bedside the whole time because by the end of the day I really felt as though I'd shared deeply in the birth and as a result was rewarded by seeing a small creature which belonged to *us* even though he seemed to belong to everyone else as well! I have never seen such scenes as there were outside the hospital when I left that night—everyone had gone berserk with excitement . . . Since then we've been overwhelmed by people's reactions and thoroughly humbled. It really is quite extraordinary . . . I am so pleased you like the idea of Louis being one of William's names. Oh! How I wish your papa could have lived to see him, but he probably knows anyway . . .'

Her papa was Lord Mountbatten of Burma, the Prince's great-uncle, killed by an IRA bomb while setting out on a fishing trip off the coast of Ireland in August 1979. Patricia had also been in the boat, as had her twin fourteen-year-old sons, her husband, her mother-in-law and a local boy. Only she, her husband and one of the twins survived, all with terrible injuries. Mountbatten was the Prince's 'Honorary Grandfather'; he had been a mentor and friend and closer than any other member of his family; closer perhaps than anybody at all. His murder in such appalling circumstances had left the Prince completely grief-stricken.

It was almost a year after his death that Charles met Lady Diana Spencer, as she then was, at the house of mutual friends near Petworth in Sussex. He had just had a dramatic bust-up with Anna Wallace, the latest in a string of girlfriends, some more suitable than others. It was July 1980. They had met a few times before, but until that evening, Charles had never seen Diana as a possible girlfriend; she was, after all, twelve years younger than him, and when they'd first met he had been going out with her elder sister, Sarah. It was at Althorp, the Spencer family home in Northamptonshire, and Diana was a fourteen-year-old home from school. She was now nineteen, and while their hosts tended the barbecue, she and Charles sat side by side on a hay bale chatting. Charles brought up the subject of Mountbatten's murder.

'You looked so sad when you walked up the aisle at Lord Mountbatten's funeral,' she said. 'It was the most tragic thing I've ever seen. My heart bled for you when I watched. I thought, "It's wrong, you're lonely—you should be with somebody to look after you."'

Her words touched him deeply. He was lonely; he had lost the only person he felt understood him, the man who had been grandfather, great uncle, father, brother and friend. He had struggled so hard to hide his emotions on the day of the funeral, knowing how much his father disapproved of tears in a man.

On the evening he heard the news, he wrote in his journal, 'Life has to go on, I suppose, but this afternoon I must confess I wanted it to stop. I felt supremely useless and powerless . . .

'I have lost someone infinitely special in my life; someone who showed enormous affection, who told me unpleasant things I didn't particularly want to hear, who gave praise where it was due as well as criticism; someone to whom I knew I could confide anything and from whom I would receive the wisest of counsel and advice.'

It was ironic that Diana's sensitivity about Mountbatten was what triggered Charles's interest in her as a future bride, since the old man would almost certainly have counselled against the match. He would have applauded Diana's sweet nature, her youth, her beauty, her nobility and her virginity (important for an heir to the throne at that time), but he would have seen that the pair had too little in common to sustain a happy marriage.

He might also have seen that, despite the laughter and the charm, she had been damaged by her painful start in life, that she was vulnerable and needy. And he might have recognised that the Prince, with his own vulnerability and insecurity, would be the wrong person to cope with such a complex personality.

In his absence, there was no one who could offer advice of such a personal yet practical nature. His relationship with his parents had never been sufficiently close. There is no question that they loved their eldest son, but theirs is a family of poor communicators with a surprising dearth of emotional intelligence. He was brought up by nannies and had minimal contact with his parents, who were away for long periods during his childhood. As a little boy, there were occasions, friends remember, when his mother would sit Charles on her knee at teatime and play games with him, but she didn't spend hours in the nursery (intimidated, they say, by the authoritarian nanny), and signs of overt affection stopped altogether as he grew older. His father was equally sparing with his affection. He was rough with Charles, baffled by a child who was so emotional and sensitive. According to witnesses, he often reduced him to tears. As a result, Charles was frightened of his father and desperate to please him, but was always left feeling that he was a disappointment.

Mountbatten, older, perhaps wiser, and with time on his hands in his retirement, saw that his great-nephew was in need of help and took the teenager under his wing for some much-needed understanding and direction. He criticised him on occasion, most notably for his selfishness, but he also made him feel he was loved and valued— something his parents had never managed to achieve. Where his father had cut him down, no doubt in an effort to make a man of him in the traditional mould, Mountbatten built up his confidence, listened to his doubts and fears. He rebuked him when he felt he had behaved badly, but overall he provided encouragement and praise. He was a sounding board for some of his more outlandish ideas, and a shoulder to cry on when things went wrong. He had been, in short, a good parent to Charles and his death was devastating.

Charles was lost and rudderless without him. He knew he had a duty to find a wife and to produce an heir, but his love life was a mess. He had pursued and fallen for a series of women, but the one he really loved and felt comfortable with was Camilla Parker Bowles. He had first fallen in love with her in the early 1970s when he was in the Navy, and her long-term boyfriend, Andrew, was stationed in Germany. She was then Camilla Shand and they enjoyed a happy time together but he felt he was too young and too uncertain to suggest marriage. When she announced her engagement to Andrew, just a few months after Charles took to the high seas, she broke his heart. He wrote forlornly to Mountbatten that it seemed cruel that 'such a blissful, peaceful and mutually happy relationship' should have lasted no longer than six months. 'I suppose the feeling of emptiness will pass eventually,' he added.

Her marriage, however, proved less than perfect and, while her husband pursued his Army career and other women, she was left alone in the country with their two children. Charles and Camilla's friendship resumed. It was still mutually rewarding, but it could never progress to anything more. The Prince of Wales had been weaned on the story of the abdication and how the previous Prince of Wales' obsession with Wallace Simpson, a twice-divorced American, had wreaked mayhem and nearly brought the monarchy to its knees. Camilla would always be close to his heart but he knew he had to find love and a wife elsewhere.

Less than seven months after their conversation on the hay bale, when Diana had touched him with her concern and empathy, Charles asked her to marry him. The amount of time they had spent alone during that period was minimal; they scarcely knew each other, but his hand had been forced by the combination of the press and poor communication.

He invited Diana to join him and his friends

and family at Balmoral Castle, the Queen's home in the Highlands of Scotland, where they traditionally stay during the summer. She was sweet and unsophisticated, bubbly and funny and everyone at the Castle that summer adored her. She was unlike anyone he had ever known and her interests and enthusiasms seemed to match his own.

She seemed like the answer to his prayers. Someone he could love, who was young enough to have no sexual past for the press to rake through, who would understand his world and be the perfect partner with whom to face the future. She was from the very top drawer of British aristocracy; as her father said at the time, 'The average family wouldn't know what hit them if their daughter married the future King . . . But some of my family go back to the Saxons—so that sort of thing's not a bit new to me . . . Diana had to marry somebody and I've known and worked for the Queen since Diana was a baby.'

What he didn't mention was that four of his Spencer ancestors were mistresses to English Kings in the seventeenth century; three to Charles II and one to James II, and the beautiful Georgiana, Duchess of Devonshire, daughter of the 1st Earl Spencer, was the talk of the nation in the eighteenth century and counted the future George IV among her many conquests.

While the women of the family frolicked with

Kings and Princes, the Spencer men became courtiers, and Althorp, the family estate in Northamptonshire, must have had more royal visitors over the centuries than any other private house in Britain. Spencers have lived there since 1486, accumulating a fortune, historically from sheep farming, and filling it with fabulous works of art. It is now home to the 9th Earl, Diana's brother, Charles, to whom the Queen is god-mother.

Johnny Spencer, then Viscount Althorp, had been an equerry to both George VI and the Queen before his marriage in the 1950s. He was educated at Eton and Sandhurst and until he moved to Northamptonshire on his father's death in 1975, he had rented a house from the Queen on the Sandringham estate, in Norfolk, where Diana lived until the age of fourteen. Park House was just across the park from the big house, and sometimes Diana and Prince Andrew, who were contemporaries, played together during the Royal Family's regular stay at Sandringham over the New Year. There were links on her mother's side of the family too. Her maternal grandmother, Ruth, Lady Fermoy, was a friend and lady-in-waiting to Queen Elizabeth the Queen Mother.

On paper she was the perfect match, but in reality the vulnerable Diana was anything but perfect as a bride to one of the most complex men in the country.

# BEHIND CLOSED DOORS

Diana's father was thirty-two when he married Frances Roche. She was eighteen; while her ancestry couldn't compete with his for nobility, and is positively murky in patches, it did add a little colour to the picture, as well as some Scottish, Irish and American blood. The royal connection was comparatively new. Diana's grandfather, Maurice, the 4th Baron Fermoy, became friendly with George V's second son, Bertie, then Duke of York, when he and his wife moved to Norfolk. They played tennis together and their wives shared a passion for music; Ruth Fermoy, née Gill, an Aberdeen girl, was an exceptionally gifted pianist who'd been studying at the Paris Conservatoire under Alfred Cortot when they met. They moved from house to house in Norfolk until George V offered them Park House on the Sandringham estate (where Johnny and Frances later lived). Thus the Fermoys and the Yorks became neighbours and the friendship was sealed.

Frances was born there on the day George V died in 1936. It's said that the news of her arrival was rushed across the park to Sandringham House where he lay gravely ill and that Queen Mary told him of her birth before he died that evening. When Bertie acceded as George VI after the abdication of his elder brother, Edward VIII, the friendship continued. During the war, Bertie and Maurice used to play ice hockey together against visiting American and Canadian troops on the frozen lakes at Sandringham, and Maurice was out hare shooting with Bertie the day before the King died in February 1952. After Maurice died three years later, Ruth became a lady-in-waiting to the Queen Mother, and they remained close until Ruth's death in 1993.

Johnny and Frances met at her coming-out ball at Londonderry House in Park Lane. He was supposedly already engaged to Lady Anne Coke of Holkham Hall, eldest daughter of the Earl and Countess of Leicester, and there was a sharp intake of breath in aristocratic drawing rooms when he ditched her for Frances Roche. The Queen is said to have tried to distract him by taking him with her on a tour of Australia for six months as Master of the Household, but after seeing the daily flow of letters between them, she gave him permission to go home and prepare for the wedding.

They married in Westminster Abbey in 1954. It was the society wedding of the year, attended by fifteen hundred guests, including the Queen, the Queen Mother, Prince Philip and Princess Margaret. 'You are making an addition to the home life of your country,' the Bishop of Norwich had declared prophetically, 'on which above all others, our national life depends.' Who could have guessed that their fourth child would be the mother of a future King?

Their first child, Sarah, was born in Northampton in March 1955, nine months after the wedding, and was christened in Westminster Abbey with the Queen Mother as one of her godparents. They had started out in a rented house in Rodmarton near Cirencester, where Johnny was studying at the Royal Agricultural College, but by the time Sarah was born they were living in a cottage on his father's estate at Althorp. His father was a difficult man, and it didn't help that Frances refused to kowtow to him. It was a relief all round when, after the death of Lord Fermoy later that year, Ruth suggested that Frances and Johnny take over Park House. It was a large family home with ten bedrooms, extended servants' quarters and garages.

Their second daughter, Jane, was born in King's Lynn in 1957, and this time the Duke of Kent was a godfather. Two years later Frances was pregnant again and, on 12 January 1960, gave birth to a boy—the all-important son and heir—in her bedroom at Park House. They named him John but, tragically, he lived for only ten hours.

Frances plunged into depression after her baby's death. Her marriage had not turned out to be the blissful union she had imagined. Johnny, who, as an older man, had seemed the embodiment of sophistication and excitement, had settled comfortably into monotony and middle age, while she was still just twenty-four, full of sparkle and wanting more from life.

More to the point, behind closed doors he was not the mild, kindly gentleman that his wide circle of friends and neighbours thought they knew. To them he was affectionate and witty, an entertaining addition to any gathering. In the privacy of his own home, he was altogether more physical and frightening. His mother, Cynthia, had put up with years of abuse from the 7th Earl and Frances endured the same. It clearly ran in the family.

Today there are refuges for women who are victims of domestic violence and the subject is often spoken about, but even today those women, even if they do seek help, often choose to stay with their abuser, believing that in some way they are to blame. In 1960, there was no help to be had and no real understanding of the scale or severity of the problem. Had she been able to confide in anyone, they would probably not have believed her; not have believed that such a thing was possible in a man so well bred and so well connected.

So Frances continued to live with Johnny and to keep trying for the boy that she knew he so desperately wanted.

Later that year she became pregnant again, and

on Saturday 1 July 1961, Diana was born at Park House. She weighed 7 lb 12 oz and was hailed by her father as 'a perfect physical specimen'. She was christened at Sandringham church and was, ironically, the only Spencer child not to have a royal godparent.

In May 1964, the long-awaited boy arrived. The relief and excitement were palpable, and at Althorp flags flew in celebration. Charles was christened in grand style in Westminster Abbey, with the Queen a godmother.

Diana was not quite three when Charles was born. She was a happy little girl, secure in the cosy routine of nursery life. But in later years, she looked back and convinced herself that her own birth had been nothing but an inconvenience. Her parents had longed for a boy; ergo, she was unwanted. It was a belief that ate away at her and which she could find no reason to refute.

Life at Park House was typical for a family of their social standing. There were fewer staff now, but they knew their boundaries and the cook would no more change a nappy nor the nanny boil an egg than they would step uninvited beyond the swing door that separated staff from family.

The children lived in the nursery wing consisting of three bedrooms, a bathroom and a large nursery, all on the first floor. Their upbringing was very traditional and as a result they were scrupulously polite and well mannered. A governess came to teach them every morning and in the afternoons they went for a walk in the park or to tea with the children of neighbouring families or shopping in the nearby village with their mother.

There were bicycles and a pony called Romany and their birthdays were always celebrated with parties for their friends; and the Spencer fireworks display on 5 November was a great event in the social calendar. All the local children came and Johnny, as master of ceremonies, let off an arsenal of rockets, whizzers, bangers and squibs, while everyone warmed themselves with sausages around the bonfire.

Kept busy in this way, on the surface the family appeared united, and the children might not have noticed the unhappiness that prevailed beyond the swing door. It must have been a great shock when their mother told them she was leaving home in the autumn of 1967. She explained why but she feared that only the elder children, Sarah and Jane, who had just started boarding school, understood. She had fallen in love with another man, Peter Shand Kydd, and grasped the opportunity to escape her loveless marriage.

Johnny was also shocked. He was possibly the last person to see it coming, but the staff, who heard the ferocious rows, were not surprised and none of them condemned her—indeed one of the housemaids went with her to London as a cook. Condemnation came from the one person Frances might have looked to for support; her own mother, Ruth. She was a snob and was so appalled that her daughter should leave the son of an earl for a man 'in trade'—albeit a millionaire—that the pair didn't speak to each other for years.

Initially, Frances took the younger children and their nanny to live with her in London, and she had every expectation that when her divorce came through she would keep them all. But things didn't go according to plan.

Peter Shand Kydd was also married with children and his wife soon divorced him for adultery, naming Frances as the other woman. Frances then began proceedings against Johnny on the grounds of cruelty, which he contested and was able to bring as witnesses some of the highest names in the land. Her case collapsed and he divorced her for adultery. In the bitter custody proceedings that followed, Ruth gave evidence against her daughter, claiming Frances was a bad mother. Custody of all four children went to Johnny. Frances was allowed to see them only on specified weekends and for part of the school holidays. She must have been grief-stricken.

Diana, just six when her mother left, was far too young to understand the complexities of the adult world. In her mind the matter was simple: her mother didn't want her, therefore she must be worthless.

'It was a very unhappy childhood,' she told

Andrew Morton, the author to whom she famously unburdened herself when her own marriage was falling apart. 'Always seeing my mother crying . . . I remember Mummy crying an awful lot and . . . when we went up for weekends, every Saturday night, standard procedure, she would start crying. "What's the matter, Mummy?" "Oh, I don't want you to leave tomorrow." '

Another early memory was hearing Charles sobbing in his bed, crying for their mother. She told Morton that she began to think she was a nuisance and then worked out that because she was born after her dead brother, she must have been a huge disappointment to her parents. 'Both were crazy to have a son and heir and there comes a third daughter. "What a bore, we're going to have to try again." I've recognised that now. I've been aware of it and now I recognise it and that's fine. I accept it.'

She learned to accept all kinds of difficult emotions. Shortly before Diana's fourteenth birthday, her grandfather, the 7th Earl, died and the family was uprooted from Norfolk. She had to leave the comforts of Park House, her friends and everything she had grown up with for the impersonal grandeur and loneliness of a stately home in Northamptonshire, a county nearly a hundred miles away. With the new house came a formidable stepmother. Her father's marriage in 1976 to Raine, Countess of Dartmouth, the forceful daughter of the romantic novelist Dame Barbara Cartland, caused terrible upset in the family. None of his children liked her and they resented the way she took over Althorp, reorganised it and starting selling off its treasures.

Three years later her father collapsed in the estate office at Althorp with a massive cerebral haemorrhage that no one expected him to survive. He lay in a coma for four months, while his children awaited the news they dreaded. Just as he was beginning to pull through he developed an abscess on the lung and was again close to death. He was saved by a new drug that Raine discovered in Germany. The Spencer children all acknowledged that she had saved their father's life, but her conduct did nothing to endear her to them. She guarded him like a hawk during those months in hospital and gave instructions that no one, not even his children, was allowed to see him.

# TRAGIC MISMATCH

That June evening in 1982, while the first photographs of the day-old Baby Wales were being broadcast on television and the morning newspapers were building their front pages around him, Charles and Diana went home to Kensington Palace full of hope that a baby would work its magic and bring them closer together.

Their marriage was not yet a year old but already there were serious problems that must have been as distressing as they were apparently insoluble. Within days of announcing their engagement, the Diana who had captivated the Prince of Wales had changed from a happy-go-lucky teenager into a volatile and unpredictable stranger. Charles was mystified and had no idea how to deal with it. The engagement had happened far too early in the relationship—after only a few months—and well before either of them could know whether they were making the right choice. When asked in their televised engagement interview whether they were in love, he had famously and agonisingly said, 'Whatever in love means,' while she, quick as a flash, said, 'Of course!'

The Royal Family has an important relationship with the media. The institution of monarchy might have disappeared years ago had the media not been interested in the comings and goings of the Family and thereby kept alive the public's interest. But it is true, nonetheless, that media pressure on Charles to find a bride and the constant intrusion before and after the marriage played a significant part in its breakdown.

A lot has been written about the Royal couple's relationship over the years, by me as well as others, and Charles and Diana both gave differing accounts of it, but since it formed the bedrock of

William's childhood, and explains much about the man he is today, it needs to be retold. So does the part the media played in it, because it was the mistakes of thirty years ago that gave William the determination to make sure that when Kate Middleton was no more than a girlfriend, she was spared the worst of what his mother had to endure.

While staying at Balmoral in the summer of 1980, Diana was spotted by the late veteran royal correspondent, James Whitaker, then working for the *Daily Star*, whose binoculars were shamelessly trained on Prince Charles while he fished for salmon in the River Dee. Scanning the bank, Whitaker saw a girl he hadn't seen before, sitting under a tree keeping the Prince company. Whitaker was with his photographer but Diana kept her back to them and neither got a view of her face. All they knew was that Charles had a new girlfriend—and they had a scoop.

It wasn't long before they worked out who she was and where she lived, and from that day until the engagement was announced five months later, she had no privacy. Photographers camped outside her flat in Fulham, cameras flashed at her, following her wherever she went. Reporters fired questions at her whenever they saw her; they raked through her rubbish, posed as neighbours, anything to get a scrap of information. She handled it well and at times seemed quite pleased;

she said good morning politely to the journalists she recognised, called them by name, and inadvertently posed in a see-through summer skirt at the kindergarten where she worked. It was intrusive, aggressive and at times frightening.

In the midst of all this there was an incident involving the Prince of Wales on the royal train, which had stopped at sidings in Wiltshire for the night. The *Sunday Mirror* was tipped off that a blonde woman, matching Diana's description, had driven up from London, boarded the train and spent the night, the implication being that she had slept with Prince Charles. The paper contacted Diana for confirmation and, although she denied having been there, the editor was so convinced it was true he published the story anyway.

The result was an immediate and furious reaction from the Queen's Press Secretary, the late Michael Shea, who normally let inaccuracies, even of this sort, pass. He demanded a retraction, calling the story 'total fabrication'. A letter to *The Times* from Diana's mother soon followed, appealing for an end to it all. 'In recent weeks,' she wrote, 'many articles have been labelled "exclusive quotes", when the plain truth is that my daughter has not spoken the words attributed to her. Fanciful speculation, if it is in good taste, is one thing, but this can be embarrassing. Lies are quite another matter, and by their very nature, hurtful and inexcusable . . . May I ask the editors of Fleet Street, whether, in the execution of their jobs, they consider it necessary or fair to harass my daughter daily from dawn until well after dusk? Is it fair to ask any human being, regardless of circumstances, to be treated in this way? The freedom of the press was granted by law by public demand, for very good reasons. But when these privileges are abused, can the press command any respect, or expect to be shown any respect?'

Sixty MPs tabled a motion in the House of Commons 'deploring the manner in which Lady Diana Spencer is treated by the media' and 'calling upon those responsible to have more concern for individual privacy'. Fleet Street editors met senior members of the Press Council to discuss the situation. It was the first time in its twenty-seven-year history that such an extraordinary meeting had been convened, but it did nothing to stop the harassment.

It was against this backdrop that the Duke of Edinburgh wrote to Charles. He told him he must make up his mind about Diana. It was not fair to keep her dangling on a string. She had been seen without a chaperone at Balmoral and her reputation was in danger of being tarnished. If he was going to marry her he should get on and do it; if not, he should end it.

If only father and son had been able to discuss the situation face to face, instead of relying on letters, everyone might have been saved years of unhappiness. Charles, mistakenly, took it as an ultimatum to marry and, even though there were serious doubts in his mind about his feelings for Diana, he knew that everyone else seemed to love her, and therefore he did as his father asked. He confessed to a friend that he was in a 'confused and anxious state of mind'. To another he said, 'It is just a matter of taking an unusual plunge into some rather unknown circumstances that inevitably disturbs me but I expect it will be the right thing in the end . . . It all seems ridiculous, because I do very much want to do the right thing for this country and for my family—but I'm terrified sometimes of making a promise and then perhaps living to regret it.'

He sought the advice of his beloved grandmother, the Queen Mother, who was enthusiastically in favour of the match. She was as enchanted by Diana as everyone else, and she was the granddaughter of her lady-in-waiting, Ruth, Lady Fermoy. The Queen gave no opinion, but almost everyone else whose views he canvassed thought Diana was the ideal bride. The only words of caution were to do with how few interests they had in common, and one friend was worried that Diana was a little bit in love with the idea of becoming a Princess but had no real understanding of what it would entail.

As Patty Palmer-Tomkinson, one of the Prince's

oldest friends, who was staying at Balmoral with her husband in the summer of 1980, told Jonathan Dimbleby, the Prince's authorised biographer: 'We went stalking together, we got hot, we got tired, she fell into a bog, she got covered in mud, laughed her head off, got puce in the face, hair glued to her forehead because it was pouring with rain . . . she was a sort of wonderful English schoolgirl who was game for anything, naturally young but sweet and clearly deter-mined and enthusiastic about him, very much wanted him.'

No one who spent time with her during the next six months—not Charles nor any of his friends or family—suspected she was anything other than Patty described, because Diana was good at hiding her feelings and keeping the hurt buried deep inside. No one spotted that she was in any way more complicated than she seemed, far less that she was suffering from any sort of incipient mental illness.

The people who did know, kept quiet. A month before her death in July 1993, when the marriage was in ruins and their public feuding at its height, Ruth, Lady Fermoy, told the Prince that she had known Diana was 'a dishonest and difficult' girl and wished she had screwed up her courage to tell him he shouldn't marry her. Even Diana's father, who died in 1991, said before he died that he had been wrong not to say something to warn Charles. They both knew that Diana had been badly affected by the traumas of her childhood and that in marrying her, Charles was taking on an almost impossible task.

# THE ROOT OF THE PROBLEM

The cracks began to show when Diana was removed from her bustling flat in Fulham, which she shared with three young friends, to a suite of rooms at Buckingham Palace. It must have stirred up memories of the painful move from Park House to Althorp, only this time she was among strangers and it wasn't so easy to seek out the kitchen staff for company. The contrast could not have been more extreme, and while everyone within the Palace was kind to her, and went out of their way to be helpful, they were no substitute for her teenage girlfriends.

As one of them said, 'She went to live at Buckingham Palace and then the tears started. This little thing got so thin. She wasn't happy, she was suddenly plunged into all this pressure and it was a nightmare for her.'

'Is it all right if I call you Michael, like His Royal Highness does?' Diana asked Michael Colborne, a friendly father figure who was the Prince's right-hand man and with whom she shared an office.

'Of course,' he said.

'Will you call me Diana?'

'No,' said Colborne. 'Certainly not. I appreciate what you've just said, but if it all works out you're going to be the Princess of Wales and I'll have to call you Ma'am then, so we might as well start now.'

He wasn't being unkind, he was simply being truthful. She was joining a traditional, formal and hierarchical institution and, however close they came to members of the Family, courtiers never allowed themselves to believe that they were anything other than servants. The adjustment was hard for a young girl who had spent hours sharing confidences with the kitchen staff at Althorp.

Who knows how she imagined life would be with Charles? She had never watched a couple play happy families. Her role models were probably taken from magazines and the idealised plots of the Barbara Cartland romantic novels she had grown up with. She certainly hadn't expected that marriage would leave her feeling so lonely.

But she was marrying a man who was already heavily engaged in royal duties. Almost every day took him to a different part of the country. Immediately after her arrival at Buckingham Palace Charles had left for a five-week foreign tour, organised long before their engagement. His diary was set six months in advance and there was no room for manoeuvre; any cancellation, he knew, meant letting people down and he was too conscientious to even contemplate it. Whatever he might have wanted privately, duty and discipline were second nature to him; he had been brought up to respect both, whereas Diana had never had occasion for either. She was charm personified and had excellent manners—she would have written and sealed a thank-you letter to a dinner party host that same evening before their heads had touched the pillow—but she had never stuck with something that she found hard going.

Charles was thirty-two years old and he longed for a happy and companionable family life with children that so many of his friends had; but his lifestyle was well established. He worked hard and he played hard—hunting and shooting in the winter, polo and fishing in the summer; he had a close, if curious, family who traditionally spent high days and holidays together; and when he wasn't working or with family, he had a wide circle of friends whose company he enjoyed.

He imagined that Diana would fit into his world without his having to change. He assumed that she would like his friends as much as he did, enjoy his country pursuits, share his passion for gardening, opera and old churches and be happy to settle down companionably with a good book and some classical music. He imagined that because she was so young she would easily adapt and fit into everything that royal life demanded.

But she didn't. Despite having been brought up

in the country, she was only nineteen years old and, not surprisingly, was far happier in the city. She hated horses and had no interest in taking part in field sports. Like most teenage girls she read trashy novels and magazines rather than literature and philosophy; she listened to pop rather than classical music (although she came to appreciate it and always loved ballet) and would much rather have spent a day gossiping over lunch with a friend, shopping or watching a good film than digging and weeding or sitting on a hillside with a sketch pad.

Charles had little experience of putting himself in other people's shoes and was surprisingly naive. He didn't see that Diana might have a problem with his former girlfriend remaining in his circle of friends. As he saw it, he had chosen Diana as the one he wanted to marry and his romantic involvement with Camilla was over. It never crossed his mind that Diana might be suspicious that they were still involved or that he loved Camilla more than her. Finding a gold bracelet he had bought for her on Michael Colborne's desk was, in Diana's mind, all the proof she needed. It had a blue enamel disc with the initials GF, which stood for Girl Friday, his nickname for Camilla. Diana was convinced the entwined letters stood for Gladys and Fred, the names she thought they called each other and felt nothing but 'Rage, rage, rage!' It was, however, one of several pieces of jewellery he had bought for special friends as a means of saying thank you for having looked after him in his bachelor years.

Diana told Andrew Morton she had felt like 'a lamb to the slaughter' as she walked up the aisle at St Paul's Cathedral on their wedding day in 1981. Her sisters, Sarah and Jane, have told friends they will always feel guilty for not helping her when she said she wanted to back out at the eleventh hour. Either way, there is no doubt that when the world thought they were witnessing a fairytale and celebrated with abandon, both Charles and Diana knew that something was amiss.

The honeymoon was hardly an intimate getaway *à deux*. After three nights at Broadlands, Lord Mountbatten's former home, where Charles had entertained previous girlfriends, they cruised the Mediterranean on the royal yacht *Britannia*, along with a crew of 256, a valet, a Private Secretary and an equerry. During the day Charles would sit blissfully immersed in a Laurens van der Post book, while Diana, according to him, dashed about chatting up the crew and the cooks in the galley. They would have seen a happy-go-lucky girl who made them all laugh. But Diana confided to friends that physically the honeymoon was a disaster, and beneath the cheerful exterior the old feelings of rejection were bubbling away. There ᴗre fearsome rows and rages and tears, and during the final stage of the honeymoon, spent at Balmoral stalking and fishing with family and friends (not many people's idea of a honeymoon), Diana had lost so much weight that Charles arranged for her to see a psychiatrist in London. Even her fingers were noticeably thinner; her wedding ring no longer fitted and had to be made smaller.

The medical profession's understanding of eating disorders is imprecise even today. Thirty years ago, when Diana first displayed symptoms, most people had never heard of anorexia or bulimia.

As Diana said herself, 'All the analysts and psychiatrists you could ever dream of came plodding in trying to sort me out. Put me on high doses of Valium and everything else. But the Diana that was still very much there had decided it was just time; patience and adapting were all that were needed. It was me telling them what I needed. They were telling me "pills"! That was going to keep them happy—they could go to bed at night and sleep, knowing the Princess of Wales wasn't going to stab anyone.'

Prince Charles was dumbfounded. He hadn't the faintest idea what was the matter with the beautiful wife who was wasting away before his very eyes and who was so troubled. At one time she was so thin he thought she was going to die and he thought he must be responsible, that marriage to him was just too awful or that he had destroyed her by bringing her into his bizarre way of life. He spoke to no one about the difficulties they were experiencing, but gradually became increasingly depressed and despondent.

The condition often affects fertility but clearly not in Diana's case, and she discovered she was pregnant on the second day of their tour of Wales, in October.

On the rain-sodden streets she was a star, a complete natural, her smile and her warmth brightening up the dull day, and the people who had waited hours for a glimpse loved her; but back in the car or the train she collapsed in tears saying she couldn't face another crowd.

It was ever thus. The public face was so very different from the one that Charles had to support and cajole and encourage in private. She needed constant reassurance, constant attention, constant love; but the mood swings were violent and unnerving. She went from cheerful and funny to brooding and sobbing, or furiously angry and screaming, in the blinking of an eye. Many were the times she cut herself until she bled profusely; and there were other instances of self-harm. She said herself that she had once hurled herself at a glass display cabinet and another time thrown herself down a flight of stairs. These were classic symptoms of the bigger problem, but thirty years self-harm was little understood and almost never spoken about.

Charles had no idea how to cope; he did everything she asked: he got rid of loyal staff whom she said she didn't like, gave away the faithful dog she couldn't stand, and stopped seeing the friends she neither liked nor trusted. Nothing he did seemed to make Diana happy, and, not knowing what more to try, as often as not he simply walked away, which only exacerbated her feelings of isolation and abandonment.

And while the birth of William initially brought fantastic elation, it didn't last.

# BABY WALES

William's arrival in the world could not have come at a better moment. Britain was in triumphant mood; the Falklands War, which had brought people together in a way not seen since the Second World War, was over. An end to hostilities was formally declared the day before his birth.

Victory restored national pride, and brought huge relief, not least for the Royal Family, on a personal as well as professional level. Prince Andrew's life had been on the line along with all the other servicemen and women. He was a Royal Navy helicopter pilot with the aircraft carrier *Invincible* and, like everyone with a son or brother in the war, they had lived in fear of bad news. His scalp would have been a fantastic propaganda coup for the Argentinians. The Cabinet had wanted him to be moved to a desk job for the duration of the war, but Andrew had insisted on being allowed to do the job he was trained for and the Queen and Duke of Edinburgh supported him.

So when the Task Force had set sail from Portsmouth on 5 April, leaving emotional scenes on the quayside, Prince Andrew had been amongst them. The Prince of Wales became preoccupied by what was happening on the other side of the world; partly as heir to the throne, partly because he was Colonel-in-Chief of two of the regiments, and not least of all because he worried about his younger brother. Yet Diana was so deeply turned in on herself by then that she couldn't share his anxiety and seemed to positively resent his focus being on the Falklands instead of her.

Before the war, few people in Britain had even heard of the Falkland Islands. They were eight thousand miles away in the South Atlantic, barren, windswept, and largely populated by sheep; but they had been British for 150 years, and when Argentina, which had long disputed their ownership, took them by force in April 1982, Margaret Thatcher, then Prime Minister, took the country to war to reclaim them. It was the first time that modern communications and television brought the shocking reality of war into people's living rooms.

Throughout the remains of the summer the ships made their way home to Portsmouth, each one returning to a hero's welcome; and photographs and snippets of news about the new royal baby did nothing but enhance the country's temporary sense of wellbeing.

A week after the birth, the baby's names were announced. He was to be William Arthur Philip Louis—with William never to be abbreviated, according to Buckingham Palace, to Will, Willie or Bill. See how long that lasted. The choice of William was, as his father explained, 'Because it is not a name that now exists in the immediate family.' The last Prince William, Charles's cousin, Prince William of Gloucester, a keen pilot, had been killed ten years earlier in a plane crash. He was just thirty.

His namesake was christened on 4 August, the Queen Mother's eighty-second birthday, in the Music Room at Buckingham Palace, dressed in the lace christening gown that had first been worn by Victoria's second child, the future Edward VII. Dr Robert Runcie, then Archbishop of Canterbury, conducted the service using the Lily Font—and water from the River Jordan in the Holy Land, which was a custom dating back to the Crusades. The ceremony began at noon, followed by a champagne lunch in the State Dining Room for the family and sixty guests, including George Pinker and the nurses who had attended William's birth. The cake, again in keeping with tradition, was the top layer from Charles and Diana's wedding.

The choice of godparents showed a strong bias towards Charles's side of the family. Only one, Natalia, the twenty-three-year-old Duchess of Westminster, was Diana's choice and age—they had been childhood friends. The others were Lady Susan Hussey, one of the Queen's ladies-in-waiting, who had known Charles since he was a child; Sir Laurens van der Post, the seventy-five-year-old South African explorer and writer; and three relatives—Constantine, former King of the Hellenes, Lord Romsey, who was Lord Mountbatten's grandson, and Princess Alexandra, the Queen's cousin and one of the most popular members of the Royal Family, to whom Charles was especially close.

Despite being swaddled in oceans of antique lace for his baptism, and having such a distinguished roll call of grandparents, godparents, friends and relations, William's early years were remarkably normal and informal. For all its history and grandeur, Kensington Palace was a comfortable family home. George III had converted it into apartments for the Royal Family and grace and favour apartments for the Royal Household.

Diana's elder sister, Jane, had married Robert Fellowes, who was then Assistant Private Secretary to the Queen, so they were neighbours. Their first child, Laura, was a year old when Charles and Diana moved in. Princess Margaret was another neighbour, and initially a staunch supporter of Diana. Prince and Princess Michael of Kent, whose children were slightly older than William, had an apartment in the palace, as did the Duke and Duchess of Gloucester with their three children.

Numbers 8 and 9 were entirely refurbished and redecorated before Charles and Diana moved in, and although a uniformed butler would open the door to visitors, inside it was like any smart, privately owned townhouse. It was not large by royal standards; it had three reception rooms (one housing a grand piano), a dining room, three bedrooms, including a master suite, and on the top floor a nursery suite plus rooms for the staff. The décor was the work of Dudley Poplak, a South African designer Diana's mother had recommended and who had known Diana since she was a child. He ensured that the furnishings were elegant but cosy, a comfortable mixture of antique and modern, with pretty fabrics and wallpapers. The hall and stairway were carpeted in fresh lime green and pink with a Prince of Wales feather design running through it.

After the first few weeks, Anne Wallace, whose

speciality was newborn babies, was replaced by Barbara Barnes. Aged forty-two, she had spent the previous fifteen years working for Princess Margaret's friends, the Hon. Colin and Lady Anne Tennant. She was not a formally trained nanny, didn't wear a uniform, liked the children she looked after to call her by her first name and had a good sense of humour. Her style was exactly what Diana wanted and reinforced the sense of normality that she insisted would be the hallmark of William's childhood. She didn't want him to be seen and not heard, or banished to the nursery, and she certainly didn't want anyone thinking they might take her place as his mother.

But Diana didn't know how to be a mother. She adored William, and Harry when he came along two years later—there is no doubting her all-consuming passion for them both and the love she showered on them—but she had never been successfully mothered herself and therefore had a skewed view of motherhood.

She continued to suffer bouts of depression—compounded by postnatal depression—and self-loathing from which the only release was to cut herself, to the alarm of all those around. At times, Barbara Barnes must have wondered who needed more looking after, mother or baby. As Diana said herself of that time, 'Boy, was I troubled. If he didn't come home when he said he was coming home I thought something dreadful had happened to him. Tears, panic, all the rest of it.' Always in the back of her mind were the feelings of loss and abandonment she had experienced as a six-year-old and the fear that it would happen again.

Her mind became a cauldron of jealousy. She imagined Charles with Camilla Parker Bowles, whom she knew he had loved and was afraid he still did love. He was crass in his handling of the situation. Unable to put himself inside the head of an insecure twenty-year-old, he kept a photograph of Camilla in his diary, which, inevitably, fell out in front of Diana; and he wore gold cufflinks on his honeymoon that had been a gift from Camilla. 'Got it in one,' she said. 'Knew exactly. "Camilla gave you those, didn't she?" He said: "Yes, so what's wrong? They're a present from a friend." And, boy did we have a row. Jealousy, total jealousy . . .'

The rows were tumultuous and terrifying but they were only half the story. There were good times too, which were precious. When she was feeling happy and confident, Diana was pure delight. She was funny, carefree and impish and there were days when the house resounded with laughter. Friends remember going to lunches when she and Charles would giggle and joke throughout. Others remember arriving to go to the theatre with them one evening and Diana saying to Charles, 'Come on, let's go and say goodnight to the children—I'll race you to the top of the stairs!' The pair of them then ran up the stairs and collapsed at the top in a heap of laughter.

KP, as Kensington Palace was known, was not the grandest house that the heir to the throne might have lived in, but the idea was that it would be a London bolt hole. The master plan was that they would base themselves at Highgrove, the country house Charles had bought near the Cotswold town of Tetbury in Gloucestershire in 1980. He was never happier than in the country, and although the house had one or two security drawbacks—like a public footpath running through the garden—and was neither very large nor architecturally imposing, Charles fell in love with it and it has remained one of the greatest pleasures in his life. And while he set about creating a garden, he gave Diana a free rein to do up the inside of the house, for which she once again turned to Dudley Poplak.

Although not palatial, Highgrove did have four good reception rooms, nine bedrooms, six bathrooms, a nursery wing and staff accommodation. While outside there was a big stable block with room for ten horses, a lodge, a farm manager's house, a couple of farm cottages, farm buildings and a dairy.

But what he really fell in love with were the trees and the parkland surrounding the house, which he felt had 'a particularly English feel' and he developed an instant passion for a 200-year-old cedar tree, just feet from the west side of the house.

The garden swiftly became Charles's passion. He sought the help of a family friend, Lady Salisbury, known as Mollie to her friends (mother of the 7th Marquess), who designed, amongst others, her own garden at Hatfield House in Hertfordshire. She was a legendary plant expert and garden wizard, and was much amused some years later that, having gardened without the use of chemicals since 1948 and been written off as a crank, she was suddenly fashionable. She taught the Prince almost all he knows about landscaping and horticulture and as they dug, plotted, measured and planted side by side, many of her ideas rubbed off on her eager student.

But there was another influence on Charles in his conversion to organics, Miriam Rothschild, a scion of the famous banking family, whose passion for bugs, butterflies and wild flowers was second to none. The influence on the Prince of both women was profound.

The sadness was that while Charles became ever more immersed in his creation, of which in the early days Diana kept a photographic record, Highgrove soon lost its charm for her and she increasingly chose to stay away, preferring to be in London.

# DOWN UNDER

Early in 1983, when William was nine months old, Charles and Diana set off for their first foreign tour together—six weeks in Australia and New Zealand. In another break with tradition, they took William with them, prompting stories in the press that they had done so against the Queen's wishes, which was not true. But they did defy the custom that no two heirs to the throne should travel in the same plane together. And so with William, Nanny Barnes, an entourage of twenty staff and a mountain of luggage, the royal party arrived to a rapturous reception.

William, with his own little entourage of Personal Protection Officer, nanny and chef, spent the first four weeks of the trip safely installed on a sheep station called Woomargama in New South Wales, while the rest of the country went into a frenzy that verged on hysteria over 'Lady Di', and wanted to know every last detail about her infant son. They turned out in their thousands to see her, and as she and Charles zigzagged their way across the Continent, she was treated more like an A-list celebrity than a member of the British Royal Family. Waving flags and clutching gifts, they were desperate to catch her eye, shake her hand, touch her coat, engage her in conversation or in some way feel they had claimed a bit of her; and they were much more vocal and demanding than the Welsh had been when she and Charles toured the Principality the year before.

Once again, it was obvious that Charles was no longer the star. He had never particularly sought the limelight, but like all members of the Family he was used to it, and to find himself eclipsed after thirty-four years was painful. Proud though he was that so many people seemed to love Diana, he had never expected to play second fiddle to anyone other than the Queen. In Wales, the murmurs of disappointment when the people on one side of the street realised they were getting Charles and not Diana were faint; Down Under, they were unmistakable.

Returning to Woomargama every so often between engagements to see William was a blessed release. As Charles, always a prolific letter-writer, wrote to friends, 'I still can't get over our luck in finding such an ideal place. We were extremely happy there whenever we were allowed to escape. The great joy was that we were totally alone together.'

To Lady Susan Hussey he wrote, 'I must tell you that your godson couldn't be in better form. He looks horribly well and is expanding visibly and with frightening rapidity. Today he actually crawled for the first time. We laughed and laughed with sheer, hysterical pleasure and now we can't stop him crawling about everywhere. They pick up the idea very quickly, don't they, when they've managed the first move.'

In New Zealand they all stayed together at Government House in Wellington, where William experienced his first photo call. In the garden, dressed in an embroidered romper suit, with bare legs and feet, he swiftly demonstrated his newfound skill and set off across the carpet that had been laid out for the trio to sit on, stopping only when his father grabbed him. As Charles proudly wrote to his friends the van Cutsems, 'William now crawls over it [Government House] at high speed knocking everything off the tables and causing unbelievable destruction. He will be walking before long and is the greatest possible fun. You *may* have seen some photographs of him recently when he performed like a true professional in front of the cameras and did everything that could be expected of him. It really is encouraging to be able to provide people with some *nice* jolly news for a change!'

After a polo match the next day, Charles was presented with a miniature polo stick for William. 'I suspect the first thing he will do with it is to chew it,' he said, 'the second thing will be to hit me sharply on the nose but I hope in twenty years' time he will be galloping up this field, with me in a Bath chair on the sideline.'

The pleasures of William aside, it was a long and gruelling tour, and Charles was worried about

Diana. She found the crowds terrifying and was exhausted much of the time. In another letter home he wrote, 'I do feel desperate for Diana. There is no twitch she can make without these ghastly, and I'm quite convinced mindless people photographing it . . . What has got into them all? Can't they see further than the end of their noses and to what it is doing to her? How can anyone, let alone a twenty-one-year-old, be expected to come out of all this obsessed and crazy attention unscathed?'

Everyone was worried about what the media obsession with Diana was doing to her. There were photographs of her in newspapers almost every day—and often she hadn't even seen the photographer. In one picture she was inside the house at Highgrove, evidently taken with a powerful lens from across the park. Her face had become a money-spinner for them all. An exclusive picture on the front page for any one of them, no matter what the caption, meant a huge hike in circulation for that newspaper. Inside, any story, however trivial, however true, excited comment, but after the initial honeymoon period when Diana could do no wrong, she began to wobble on her pedestal. The columnists that would heap praise on her one day were just as likely to hurl brickbats the next. She read every last word of it obsessively, and was as buoyed up by the praise as she was depressed by the criticism.

Before William's birth, the Queen had taken the unusual step of inviting the newspaper editors to Buckingham Palace, where Michael Shea, her Press Secretary, appealed to them to stop harassing her daughter-in-law and to allow her private life to be private. Diana couldn't go anywhere without being photographed; she couldn't even go to the village shop to buy some wine gums. After the briefing, the editors were ushered into an adjoining room for drinks with the Queen and the Duke of Edinburgh. The editor of the *News of the World*, who had obviously been pondering on the matter of the wine gums, asked why Diana hadn't simply sent out a servant to buy them for her. 'That,' said the Queen, 'is the most pompous suggestion I've ever heard.'

For a while most of the editors did stop buying the photos that came from the paparazzi, but it didn't stop the commentary and speculation, and it didn't help with Diana's fragile and at times volatile condition.

As William was to discover more than twenty years later, to achieve any kind of real privacy, you had to do more than appeal to the better nature of the press.

# A NEW ARRIVAL

Within weeks of returning home from the Antipodes, the Wales family was off again to conquer Canada, this time using the royal yacht *Britannia* as a base. The 'Lady Di' mania was every bit as alarming as it had been in Australia and New Zealand. While Charles looked ever more dispensable by her side—and collected tributes on her behalf from disappointed fans— she took the country by storm.

Her outfits were more dazzling, she attended more ceremonies, concerts and parades, planted more trees, held more hands and won more hearts. What people seemed to go crazy about, in Canada as much as everywhere else she went, was that she seemed so approachable. No one would have dreamed of lunging forward to touch, far less kiss, the Queen or even Princess Anne, but Diana looked sweetly vulnerable and waif-like and her friendly style struck a chord with the crowds. She did common-sense things, like squatting on her heels to talk to children or to people in wheelchairs so as to be at their level, and if someone dropped something in front of her, she would bend down to retrieve it for them. She had youth, beauty, glamour and a lightness of touch, which had never been seen in the Royal Family before.

It was a winning combination that was rapidly turning her into a superstar that no one in the Royal Household had any idea how to handle. Diana was becoming intoxicated by the adulation. Wherever she went, she was the centre of attention and she could see that with no more than a coquettish tilt of the head or a teasing laugh, men, and women too, fell like ninepins in her thrall. The adoration of strangers in some curious way made up for the vacuum she felt in real life and in her marriage.

Away from the cameras and the cheering she struggled with feelings of emptiness and depression and her moods continued to swing violently. Having tried everything in his power to help, Charles had run out of ideas and of sympathy. As he felt the chill of being outside the spotlight, the old feelings of insecurity and inadequacy that had haunted his youth came back with a vengeance. He didn't understand what went on inside her head, or what he had done to incite such vitriol. The more he retreated into himself, the more she raged against his absences and lack of concern and the more she convinced herself that his friends were conspiring behind her back.

Her suspicions were completely unfounded, and Charles had spoken to no one about their difficulties, but her obsession ate away at her and corroded what little was left of their relationship. He became uncharacteristically moody and prone to violent outbursts of temper that he unleashed on his most loyal and trusted staff; people like Michael Colborne, who had been with him in the Navy and who had tried so hard to help Diana, were being lambasted for spending too much time with her. Gone was the man Colborne had known in his bachelor years, a man thirsty for life, who was ready to have a go at anything and everything, who worked hard and drove himself hard, but who was fun to be with. The joy seemed to have gone out of his life and the serious side to his nature, which had always been there, appeared to have taken over.

Early the next year Diana became pregnant again, 'as if by a miracle', she would later say—and on 15 September Prince Harry was born. Charles was again with her throughout, and the next morning brought William to see his new brother. Diana would later say that for six weeks before his birth she and the Prince were closer than they had ever been, or ever would be. 'Then suddenly as Harry was born it just went bang, our marriage, the whole thing went down the drain.' She claimed it was because Charles was disappointed the baby was another boy, and a redhead. 'Something inside me closed off.'

Those around them at the time say that if Charles was disappointed he showed not the slightest trace of it. He appeared to be thrilled to have another son, saying, 'We almost have a full polo team,' and was again overwhelmed by the miracle of childbirth.

But there was going to be no miracle cure for the marriage. Diana was spared the chronic postnatal depression she had suffered after William's birth, but the bulimia was bad, as were her mood swings, and her demands were increasingly unrealistic. She insisted that Charles spend more time with the children and sent a note to Edward Adeane, their Private Secretary, saying that in future her husband would not be available for meetings in the early mornings or evenings because he would be upstairs in the nursery with William. Adeane, a bachelor with no children, and a courtier of the old school, was dumbfounded. Mornings and evenings were the two moments in their normally hectic day when they had time to go through vital briefings.

As his relationship with Diana deteriorated, the Prince became temperamental and depressed and hugely demanding of everyone around him. He cut back on his engagements and spent many a contemplative hour digging the garden at Highgrove or riding hard, pushing himself physically to the limits. And having cut his closest and oldest friends out of his life, he became isolated in his misery.

The press was quick to notice that he was slowing down. They had calculated that in the same three-month period, Prince Charles had carried out fifteen engagements while Princess Anne had done fifty-six, Prince Philip forty-five and the Queen twenty-eight. Meanwhile he seemed to have plenty of time for polo. They were calling him work-shy and lazy. His father told him to pull his socks up. Prince Philip had no time for the soul-searching his son seemed engaged in and less time for men minding the babies.

Charles, who had been plagued ever since he came out of the Navy by the feeling that he had no real role in life, was becoming more spiritual and philosophical by the day and his interests were turning towards the alternative and controversial.

This wasn't the first time that he'd stepped outside the royal mould—or found his father unsympathetic. Back in 1972, he had been moved by a radio interview, which opened his eyes to what life was like for young people in deprived areas; many of them turned to crime in the absence of families or other support. Some scribbled thoughts on the back of an envelope about how he might help, and his severance pay from the Navy, formed the basis of the Prince's Trust, which is now the UK's leading youth charity and as mainstream as it is possible to be. It has given a leg-up in life to well over half a million eighteen- to thirty-year-olds, and spawned many other initiatives, but social deprivation is a highly political topic and one, therefore, which is highly controversial for the heir to the throne to be involved in.

By the early 1980s, he was straying into ever more dangerous waters. He was invited to convene a conference at Windsor for leaders in the business community to meet leaders of the black community. It was one of the most significant advances in race relations ever made, but it could have gone terribly wrong. At the same time, he was sending shock waves through the hallowed corridors of the Royal Institute of British Architecture and the British Medical Association with speeches that were sharply critical and in turn brought an avalanche of criticism on the Prince's head.

Edward Adeane did not approve and thought the Prince should curb his words and confine his activities to safer, more traditional areas. Colborne supported Charles every inch of the way, telling him to forget what previous Princes of Wales had done: these were the 1980s. There was a social revolution going on outside the Palace gates, a whole generation of young people who needed his leadership and he should stop feeling sorry for himself and go out and do it.

It was a fractured and unhappy Household and that July, Colborne, who had been a Chief Petty Officer with Charles in the Navy and who was one of the few people who dared tell him what he thought, handed in his notice. He had been with the Prince for ten years and would have walked over red-hot coals for him. He had also grown very fond of Diana and felt sorry for her, but he'd had enough of being caught in the crossfire between the two of them and being the one on whom his boss took out his anger and frustration.

The Prince of Wales has many strengths, but he has never happily put up with people around him who disagree with him; Colborne was an exception, and because their relationship went back to the Navy, he could get away with it. His relationship with his Private Secretary was another matter, and with such divergent ideas on what he should be doing with his life, it was only a matter of time before the Prince and Edward Adeane came to grief. The day after Colborne left, the two men had a blazing row and Adeane resigned.

It was an opportunity for Charles to look for a successor beyond the military and the diplomatic service, whence most royal courtiers came. He instructed a head-hunter, and the man chosen to take Adeane's place was a 13th Baronet from the City, who was as surprised as he was flattered to have been selected. Sir John Riddell, from an old Northumberland family, had no experience of the Royal Family and therefore no pre-conceptions about how things should be done. A successful investment banker of fifty-one, he was delightfully gentle, humorous and unassuming. He was married with a young family, of much the same age as William and Harry—therefore deeply sympathetic to the draw of the nursery.

# HIS ROYAL NAUGHTINESS

When the time came to choose a first school for William, Charles and Diana opted for Mrs Mynor's in Chepstow Villas, Notting Hill, where Sir John Riddell's youngest son was a pupil.

Dressed in clothes he had chosen himself (essential for a good mood)—a checked shirt, red shorts and a striped jumper—and accompanied by both parents, William arrived for his first day in September 1985. He was three years and three months old and went into the lowest year group, which was called Cygnets. No heir to the throne had ever been to school at such a young age. Charles had a governess until shortly before his eighth birthday, and when he went to school he became the first heir ever to have done so. But Diana wanted William to mix with ordinary children from the earliest age and be treated like a normal child.

The only difference between him and his classmates that day was that a bank of photographers, reporters and TV cameras were waiting on the pavement outside the school to record this historic moment in the life of the nation's favourite three-year-old. It was to be their one and only chance. Charles and Diana had written to the editors of every national newspaper asking that William be allowed to come and go in peace thereafter. The exception was the Christmas play.

As a friend told Diana's biographer Sarah Bradford, 'William was in the school play. He was very little, probably three and a half . . . all dressed up in a little nativity outfit. And there was this huge bank of photographers all on ladders. And everyone was shouting out "William, William, William!" It must have been terrifically difficult for a child that age to understand.

'I asked her once, what do you do about that? And she said she had had to say to him: "You are going to go to school today and there's going to be all these people who want to take your picture and if you are a good boy and you let them . . . then I'll take you to Thorpe Park next week."'

Charles and Diana had already done some groundwork with the media. They had held a series of lunches at Kensington Palace and invited the editors one by one. My father, Sir John Junor, then editor of the *Sunday Express*, was one of them and was duly flattered to have been asked to advise them on public relations. Over plums from the garden at Highgrove, the conversation turned to the catalogue of untrue and hurtful stories that had appeared in the press. As he later wrote in his memoirs, 'Looking slightly tremulous . . . she poured out to me her resentment about the way in which it was suggested in newspapers that she was influencing her husband and turning him against shooting and hunting. Prince Charles broke in. "I'm angry about that too. Because my wife is doing nothing of the kind. My wife actually likes hunting and shooting. It is I who have turned against it."'

My father left profoundly smitten by the Princess, who kept in touch over the years, recognising she had a powerful ally. He was not the only man to become putty in her hands.

By all accounts, William was quite a handful. Until Harry's arrival he had been the centre of his parents' universe, and like most first children who are indulged—as only first children can be—he was not best pleased to be supplanted by a demanding baby who was picked up and fussed over every time he cried. His mother nicknamed him 'Your Royal Naughtiness' but was mostly amused by his cheekiness. At Mrs Mynor's he quickly became 'Basher Wills' or 'Billy the Basher'. His father had been rather cowed and insecure as a small boy and found it hard to make friends. William was the opposite. He was a confident and happy child, not to say irrepressible, and was more than capable of standing up for himself. Staff remembered him being very popular with the other children and for 'his kindness, sense of fun and quality of thoughtfulness'.

On a snowy January day in 1987, at the age of four and a half, he moved on to Wetherby School, also in Notting Hill, where he spent the next three years in preparation for boarding. His first day—this time dressed in a grey and red uniform, with short trousers, long socks and a cap—was again marked by a melee of media in the street and dozens of clicking cameras. Although not a daily occurrence, they were becoming a familiar part of life and William, eager to race up the steps to be with his schoolfriends, was frequently tethered by his mother and made to wave or to smile.

She always tried to take him to school before her day's engagements, and often stopped off at her local Sainsbury's to buy him and his little brother Twiglets or some other treat on her way home afterwards—'I know they're not good for them,' she'd say, 'but they do love them.'

However, most of the childcare fell to Barbara Barnes. She was the constant and consistent figure in their lives and inevitably a very close bond formed between them. Although the apartment at Kensington Palace was far less formal than any of the other royal residences, the children lived in the nursery and, according to the Princess's Private Secretary, Patrick Jephson, their domain under the eaves on the top floor was almost a court in its own right. There were bedrooms, bathrooms, playrooms, a kitchen and a dining room. In addition to Barbara, there were part-time nannies, policemen and a shared driver, all of whom operated a routine of school runs, parties, shopping and trips to the cinema. The children didn't always have the run of the house, but usually came downstairs before bedtime.

The house was an office as well as a home. Both the Prince and Princess had meetings and lunches with staff or advisers or charity executives, and it was not unusual for the Prince in particular to hold meetings in the evenings. Stephen O'Brien, then chief executive of Business in the Community, and his colleague Cathy Ashton were sitting in the Prince's study waiting for him to arrive one evening when Diana burst through the door. 'I'm sorry,' she said, 'I'm looking for William. It's bedtime so he's vanished. Will you give me a shout if you see him?' They were left wondering how one might give the Princess of Wales a shout, when squeals of laughter from above solved the problem.

Roger Singleton, then director of Barnardo's, arrived for lunch one day, bearing a large green plaster frog. It was a gift from a group of physically handicapped children at a school in Taunton that Diana had visited the previous week in her capacity as president. As Singleton was ushered through the front door, William and Harry came bounding down the stairs and instantly began clamouring for the frog. It was too heavy for either of them to carry alone, so William went racing off up the stairs, excitedly yelling to his mother that a frog was coming, while Harry, who refused to be parted from it, staggered up the stairs with one small hand resolutely on the frog's bottom and the other tightly clutching Singleton's free hand.

Another visitor who unexpectedly encountered William was Bob Geldof, the habitually dishevelled musician and human rights activist. He was at Kensington Palace for a meeting with the Prince, when William appeared and, cross that his father was busy, said, 'Why do you have to talk to that man?'

'Because we have work to do,' said his father.

'He's all dirty,' said William.

'Shut up, you horrible boy,' said Geldof.

'He's got scruffy hair and wet shoes,' said William, undeterred.

'Don't be rude,' said Charles, mortified as only parents of tactless small children can be. 'Run along and play.'

'Your hair's scruffy too,' said Geldof as a parting shot.

'No, it's not,' said William. 'My mummy brushed it.'

Geldof doesn't relate whether Diana heard the exchange but if she did, the chances are she would have found it funny. She was good at providing the love and the hugs for her boys and she enjoyed playing games, but she was sometimes more like a big sister than a mother to them. William's antics made her giggle and she let him see that they did, which undermined any discipline he was getting from anyone else. Yet on other occasions, instead of giggling, she would smack him, which must have sent a confusing message to the child. Barbara Barnes meanwhile was told she must never smack the children and never even raise her voice to them if they misbehaved. If things reached an impasse between the nanny and her charges and they ran to mummy to complain, as often as not, Diana would side with the boys, thus entirely undermining Barbara's authority.

In the absence of any real discipline from Diana—or the Prince of Wales, who was a similarly soft touch—William tended to get his way in most things and inevitably pushed the boundaries further and further. He became so noisy, cheeky and unruly that the Queen, who was a very loving grandmother and normally reticent about interfering in such matters, let it be known that William's behaviour was not acceptable. The final straw came when William was a pageboy at Prince Andrew's wedding to Sarah Ferguson in 1986. After dragging his cousin Laura Fellowes up the aisle, he fidgeted throughout the ceremony, rolled his order of service into a trumpet, scratched his head, covered his face with his fingers, poked his tongue out at Laura, and left the Abbey with his sailor hat wildly askew. He may have been doing what any four-year-old might, but not many other four-year-olds were of such public interest.

By contrast, Prince Harry was a timid, shy little boy, overshadowed and bossed about by his big brother. But all that soon changed. Harry became the extrovert, the risk taker, the naughty boy, and William became more circumspect and pensive, his early confidence perhaps less certain.

# HIGHGROVE

The Prince of Wales's plan that the family should base themselves in Gloucestershire never worked. Diana wasn't an outdoor person at heart and the country, filled as it was with dogs, horses and mud—and her husband's unbridled enthusiasm for it all—bored her. For him, it was an oasis of peace after the endless merry-go-round and exhaustion of royal duties. He spent as much time as he could there, often on his own—in as much as the Prince of Wales, with a team of courtiers, round-the-clock PPOs (Personal Protection Officers) and domestic staff, is ever on his own. Diana and the boys, meanwhile, based themselves in London, and once William started school in Notting Hill, they stayed at Highgrove only at weekends and during the school holidays.

But the boys adored it, and after a week cooped up at Kensington Palace the weekends couldn't come fast enough. They sometimes drove with their mother but more often travelled with Barbara Barnes, their PPOs and the rest of the nursery team. There was so much more freedom for them there. It was the perfect environment for noisy, energetic and inquisitive small boys—plenty of space to roar around and lots of places to explore.

They had their father's Jack Russells, Tigga and Roo, to play with, there were ponies to ride, ducks on the pond, cows and sheep in the fields and chickens running about in the yard. There were woods and hay lofts and, when it was warm enough, a heated outdoor swimming pool. They had a climbing frame on the lawn and a swing, and they could grow their own vegetables from the little patch of garden their father had set aside for them.

Charles has often said that if he hadn't been a Prince he would be a farmer. His passion for the countryside and its conservation is legendary. He also firmly believes that it is only possible to lead by example—one of the many beliefs he has passed on to his sons, so when he first became interested in organic agriculture in 1982, he realised he had to do it himself. He would never be able to persuade farmers to give up chemicals unless he himself had tried it and proved it was viable. So when a farm with 710 acres near Tetbury came up for sale two years later, the Duchy bought it and employed David Wilson as manager. Gradually they converted the land to Soil Association standards and started not only experimenting in organic production, but using it as a showcase for all the Prince's ideas about the countryside, conservation and the environment. Over the years it has become an impressive example of best-practice farming and a thriving business.

But for William and Harry, as they were growing up, it was simply a good fun place with every sort of farm animal; and tractors, combine harvesters and exciting machinery. Whenever the Prince drove over there in a Land Rover, which he did at least once every weekend, the boys would want to go with him. David and his wife, Caroline, had sons of much the same age as William and Harry and the boys would muck about while their fathers talked shop, or they would go with Charles and inspect the animals and wander about the fields and hedgerows. There was great excitement if they spotted a buzzard circling, or a hare running across a field, or a fox. Charles was thrilled to watch their interest in the countryside developing. It was important to him that the boys should see nature at work and that they should understand and respect the natural order. He wanted them to see how food is produced, how animals are reared and to learn the value of good husbandry of both land and livestock.

Teaching them manners was a struggle—as it is

with most lively little boys—but William's godfather, King Constantine, says that Charles always treated them like young adults. He didn't force them to do anything but would explain and reason with them; and William, who was bright, exhausting and extremely wilful, would have stretched the patience of a saint at times.

One bitterly cold winter's day when he and his father went to the farm together, William, aged four, arrived without any gloves. He had refused point blank to wear them. He hadn't been out of the car long before he began to grumble that his hands were cold. Eventually he started to cry. 'I told you to bring some gloves,' said Charles, 'and you wouldn't listen, so shut up.'

Diana never joined them on those visits to the farm. Unless the weather was glorious and she could swim in the pool, she preferred to be in London and, as the years went by, she saw less and less of Highgrove. And the less she enjoyed it, the less she hid her antipathy. She cut a lonely figure walking around the grounds listening to music through earphones, or curled up on a sofa watching a film, reading magazines or telephoning her friends. Her friends were her lifeline, although they sometimes, inexplicably, went out of favour. And many were the times she would suddenly cut short the weekend, sweep up the children and take them back to London early on a Sunday afternoon, much to the Prince's dismay.

Charles revelled in the time he spent with the children, particularly at Highgrove, and was never happier than on the rare weekends when the nanny was off and he was needed for nappy-changing and bathing. He had been a doting elder brother to Princes Andrew and Edward, and was a popular godfather to many of his friends' children. He never tired of reading stories to the boys and was good at making them laugh. He would pull silly faces and put on strange Goonish voices, never remotely embarrassed about making a fool of himself. They loved spending time with him but it was always in short supply since he was frequently called away to work.

There was no clear dividing line for Charles between work and play, office and home. Every day was a work day. Even those when he was ostensibly on holiday, or went hunting or played polo, some part of the day would be taken up furiously writing memos or with paperwork, speechwriting or letters. Even on Christmas Day, when the whole extended family would be together at Sandringham, the Prince would find time to fire off memos to his staff or to the people who ran his charities to tell them about some great idea he had had or someone he'd met who might be useful; his mind was never still. Private secretaries and press secretaries yo-yoed up and down the motorway from London, papers arrived daily, and he held meetings with advisers and experts in every field as he expanded his knowledge on the myriad subjects that fascinated, excited and troubled him.

Thus Highgrove was as much an office as a home, and while the children had the run of the gardens, most of the house for most of the time was out of bounds. They lived in the nursery on the top floor, as they did in London, and generally ate all their meals with the nanny rather than with their parents. Their other constant companions and playmates were their PPOs, who had guns discreetly tucked under their clothes. Knowing of no other life, it seemed perfectly normal.

The nursery at Highgrove was like another self-contained flat, with bedrooms, bathrooms, sitting rooms, play rooms and a kitchen, although their meals tended to be delivered on a tray from the main kitchen downstairs, cooked by the homely figure of Mrs Whiteland, whom Charles had inherited from the previous owners. He had bought the house from Maurice Macmillan, MP, son of the former Conservative Prime Minister, the late Lord Stockton, and Paddy and Nesta (better known as Mrs Paddy) Whiteland had worked for the family for nearly forty years. Mrs Paddy was cook and housekeeper and her husband, Paddy, who was something of a legend locally, was groom and general factotum. They instantly took to the Prince, and he to them, and the boys gravitated to Mrs Paddy's side in the kitchen, bringing in eggs that they'd found in the barn and chattering away about all they'd been up to in London.

In his book about Highgrove, the Prince said one of the most crucial and persuasive factors in buying the property was the presence of Paddy, 'one of the most inimitable Irishmen I have ever come across . . . A former prisoner of war of the Japanese, he can only be described as one of "Nature's Gentlemen". Meeting him for the first time, you invariably came away (a considerable time later!) feeling infinitely better. Once met he is never forgotten. His rugged features and twinkling eyes are one of the most welcoming features of Highgrove and his Irish stories are famous . . .'

Mrs Paddy sadly died in 1986, when the children were still small, but Paddy worked on until cancer took him in 1997 at the age of eighty-five, and he was as much a part of Highgrove for William and Harry as the furniture. He was a grandfatherly figure, who had a way with horses, and who captivated the boys with his tales of country lore. Charles described him as 'one of the most loyal people I have ever met . . . also one of the best and truest of individuals', and he looked after him and paid for his care to the end.

Banishment to the nursery was no hardship for the boys; it was customary in aristocratic families and, besides, William adored Barbara Barnes. Every morning when he woke up he would go and climb into bed with her before they both got up for breakfast. He might then go and sneak into bed with his mother for a second cuddle of the day. His mother would always be his mother, but he had an undeniably strong and loving bond with his nanny too. It was hardly surprising. She was the one who was always there: she comforted him when he fell and hurt himself, reassured him when he woke in the night, distracted him when he was upset, battled with him and managed his tantrums, read to him, deciphered his childish chatter and answered his endless questions. She did everything a mother would and loved him as a mother would.

It was, after all, what she had been hired to do; what every good and caring nanny does. The homes of the aristocracy are filled with retired nannies who live on with the family long after the children have grown up. They are loved like family and are no threat to the mothers they help or stand in for—they are simply another anchor in the child's support system. But Diana's old insecurities began to surface. She didn't consider what removing Barbara would do to William; here, she thought with the selfishness of a child. She wanted a hundred per cent of his affection, just as she wanted a hundred per cent of her husband's. She had lost the latter battle, but she could fix the former. Giving the flimsiest of reasons, she showed Barbara Barnes the door.

The irony is that in suddenly cutting Baba, as he

called her, out of the four-year-old's life, Diana was inflicting on her son the same painful feelings of loss and bewilderment that she herself had struggled with when her mother suddenly disappeared from her life at the age of six.

William understood nothing of his mother's insecurities and had no comprehension of why Baba had gone. Had he, perhaps, been so naughty he had driven her away? Once she was out of the house, she was out of his life and Diana entertained no contact. Barbara was invited to his confirmation ten years later because Charles recognised she had been an important part of his life. William never forgot her either. Barbara Barnes was one of the most important names on the guest list at his wedding twenty-five years after she vanished from the nursery.

Two other nannies followed, Ruth Wallace and Jessie Webb, but neither stayed for more than two or three years. Finally Olga Powell slipped seamlessly into the role. She had been deputy to all three nannies, in place since William was six months old, and remained with him until his mother's death in 1997. Both boys stayed in touch with her after her retirement and, in her eighties, she was another prominent name on the wedding-guest list.

But something died in William the day his beloved Baba left; he became less outgoing, less trusting, less inclined to make himself vulnerable.

# THE BEGINNING OF THE END

In 1998, more than a year after Diana's death, I wrote a book that attempted to discover the truth about the relationship between the Prince and Princess. I called the book *Charles: Victim or Villain?* because I wanted to determine, if possible, which of the two he was. Had he caused Diana's problems, as she had suggested in her famous *Panorama* interview, by his obsession with Camilla Parker Bowles, or had Diana gone into that marriage already damaged and Charles had returned to Camilla Parker Bowles because he couldn't cope with her erratic behaviour? Had he, in short, been a villain, or was he as much of a victim as Diana?

The conclusion I came to, after talking to many of the key people in their lives during this period, was that there were no villains.

While Charles sank into ever deeper depression, mystified by Diana's mood swings and his inability to make her happy, she embarked on a series of love affairs which were each as unfulfilling as the last. Charles, meanwhile, started seeing those friends that he had ostracised at Diana's insistence. Now back in the fold, they were deeply concerned about how their friend had changed in the intervening years, and feared he might be close to thoughts of self-destruction. He had said nothing about the difficulties of his relationship and had been loyal to Diana to the nth degree, but they guessed that if anyone could help restore his spirits it would be Camilla, whose own marriage was less than fun, and Patty Palmer-Tomkinson put them in touch. Charles and Camilla had not seen each other to speak to since his engagement, except once, on the occasion when he gave her the famous bracelet, and the only telephone call was with the news that Diana was pregnant.

At first they wrote each other long letters, then there were phone calls and after several months they met at the house of their mutual friend; and eventually the relationship became physical. Camilla became his lifeline; she made his spirits soar, although it was a long climb back from the abyss. She was a sympathetic ear, someone who understood and cared about him—and crucially believed in him—and the only person to whom he felt he could speak openly and honestly without for a second doubting she would keep his trust. Yet there was a lightness in the friendship too, and an easiness; she was on the same wavelength, she had the same sense of humour, loved the same things and shared the same interests. Her marriage to Andrew was a sham; although she was deeply fond of him, and remains so, he had been unfaithful to her for years.

Whatever Diana might have imagined, and

whatever she accused her husband of when she spoke to Andrew Morton, Charles did not commit adultery, as he said to Jonathan Dimbleby, 'until his marriage had broken down irretrievably', and he did not sleep with Camilla on the night before his wedding, as Diana claimed he did. He may have weaknesses in his character, but Charles has never been dishonourable. If anything he has been too honest for his own good, unable to tell the white lie that would have harmed no one and prevented the emotional tsunami. He was racked with guilt about Camilla, little knowing about Diana's own infidelities, which had begun years earlier.

Once Diana realised that Camilla was back in the picture, she went into meltdown, and any pretence of proper married life became impossible. They could barely tolerate being in the same room as each other, let alone under the same roof, as everyone who worked for them was painfully aware. The curse of royalty is that there is no privacy and no clear distinction between work and play, public and private. There were blistering rows, tears and hysterics, rage and fury, all heard to some degree by everyone who was hapless enough to be in the house. Kensington Palace was small and badly soundproofed but not even the Cotswold stone walls at Highgrove were enough to keep the poison from pervading the house—and as time passed it was increasingly out in the open.

Greeting one of his staff in full uniform one morning before setting off on a formal engagement, the Prince said, 'You only have one medal. We'll have to do something about that.' Whereupon the Princess, following Charles down the stairs, said, 'Yes, but at least he earned his.'

Such moments were uncomfortable for everyone, but the sarcastic remarks weren't reserved for the Prince. Members of the Household often found themselves in the firing line too. As one of them said, 'I would have given up all the flowers, all the niceness if only we could have avoided the sheer bloody-minded sarcasm, the silences, and sending to Coventry that went with it.'

It was a lottery what kind of mood both bosses would be in. The Prince, always demanding but normally friendly, polite and businesslike, was prone to unnerving temper tantrums. They quickly passed and although he didn't always apologise, he thought no more about it. The Princess was deadlier. In a good mood, she was a veritable angel and couldn't do enough to help people, be they strangers, staff, family or friends. She would send their mothers flowers on their birthdays, give them presents and open her heart to them. That could turn on a sixpence, and if she got it into her head that someone was plotting against her, or being disloyal, or she simply no longer liked having them around, they found themselves out in the cold; cut dead. Members of staff lost their jobs, friends were cut adrift without a word and even her own mother endured long periods of estrangement from Diana.

Arguably, the only people Diana consistently loved were William and Harry. She would repeatedly say, 'They mean everything to me.' Her love for them was almost obsessive and it was possessive; as if she was afraid that if she didn't demonstrate it, with treats and hugs, or verbalise it, they might not be aware of it. She couldn't leave them to be quietly confident of her love for them, as they were of their father's. Another of her favourite phrases to the children was, 'Who loves you most?' She told her biographer Andrew Morton: 'I want to bring them up with security, not to anticipate things because they will be disappointed. That's made my own life so much easier. I hug my children to death and get into bed with them at night. I always feed them love and affection. It's so important.'

No one knew better than she how painful and upsetting it had been for her as a child to see her mother cry when her parents' marriage disintegrated; and to hear her brother call out for their absent mother in the night. She knew precisely how sad and insecure it made her feel.

Yet now she was a mother, she seemed unconcerned that William and Harry should see her tears and witness her distress—in just the same way as she had witnessed her own mother's. William, being older, was more aware, and almost took on a parenting role. She spoke about running into her bathroom in tears one day, after an altercation with Charles over the Duke and Duchess of York's separation, and William pushing paper tissues under the closed door, saying, 'I hate to see you sad.' William was only ten.

The reality was Diana was not always as warm and demonstrative in private as she was in public—and she wasn't the only one who handed out the laughter and the hugs. Away from the cameras, the boys saw the extremes of her moods as clearly as everyone else and were often quite frightened and bewildered by them. When a friend once suggested it was unwise to have hysterics in front of Prince William, who was then in a cot, Diana said he was too young to notice, and anyway, he would 'have to learn the truth sooner or later'.

Her attitude to their learning the truth was much the same when it came to her lovers. Several men had come and gone from her life after Harry's birth, but there was one, James Hewitt, whom she seems to have loved very deeply. During the five years of the affair, he was part of William and Harry's lives too. Hewitt was a charming, good-looking young officer in the Life Guards, one of the regiments that form the Household Cavalry, which traditionally guards the Sovereign and the Royal Household. He was a brilliant horseman and, as it turned out, a first-class cad, but their affair lasted longer than any other.

They first met in a corridor when she flirtatiously admired his uniform. They met again at a party in St James's Palace in 1986 when she asked whether he would teach her to ride. Riding lessons at his Windsor barracks swiftly turned into a love affair, and he later revealed that she seduced him. As she confessed so publicly on *Panorama*, it was all true. 'Yes, I adored him. Yes, I was in love with him. But I was very let down.'

During their affair he was a frequent visitor at Kensington Palace but also at Highgrove, when the Prince was away. Diana would invite him for weekend parties and allot him a bedroom across the corridor from her own, where she slept in a four-poster bed. Once everyone else was asleep, he would creep into her bed for the night, returning to his room before the rest of the house was awake. This ruse fooled no one, except perhaps William and Harry, who slept in the nursery above. Like their mother, they thought the world of Hewitt. He represented everything that small boys admire. He took them to his barracks and dressed them in little army uniforms he had specially made and let them climb all over the tanks and other armoured vehicles at Windsor. He joined in pillow fights and read them their favourite bedtime stories. He gave them riding lessons on their ponies, and took them and Diana to stay with his mother at her home in Devon.

He always insisted he hadn't tried to take the place of their father, but he evidently bonded with them and both boys seemed to enjoy their time with him. Maybe what they enjoyed, subliminally, was seeing their mother happy.

When he went to the Gulf in 1991, after Britain's invasion of Iraq, Diana wrote him long, loving letters, which could so easily have fallen into the wrong hands. She watched the TV news avidly, with Harry beside her, fearful that he might be killed. When he returned home safe the following year and grew ever more besotted with her, she ended it in her usual way by refusing to take his calls.

In what Diana saw as a devastating betrayal of trust, Hewitt wrote a book, *Love and War*, about their affair when it was over. He had been cut to the quick when she ended it, but recalled the happy times he'd spent with William and Harry and said they had 'appeared to have the time of their lives.'

Hewitt was a redhead like Harry and a rumour persisted in the wake of the affair that Harry was Hewitt's son. It was untrue—he and Diana didn't meet until Harry was two years old—yet it persisted and there are some who still ask the question today. Dates aside, Harry has the Spencer family colouring and his father's and grandfather's green eyes. He is a Windsor through and through—or, as Diana used to call him, 'My little Spencer'.

Their father turned a blind eye to what was going on. As he wrote in one letter, 'I don't want to spy on her or interfere in her life in any way.' But she didn't have the monopoly on love towards their sons. He had been brought up to keep his emotions hidden from public display but it didn't mean he didn't have those emotions or couldn't show them.

Away from the cameras, he was every bit as loving as Diana, but in a different way. He would fool around with the boys, kick a football and have a rough and tumble. They share the same silly sense of humour and are great practical jokers, as Diana was too—also talented mimics. They loved going to polo matches with their father or to follow the hunt. They also loved watching him shoot, and were not yet in their teens when they first picked up a gun themselves, taught by the gillie at Balmoral, Willie Potts, from whom they also learnt to cast for salmon. Charles built them a massive tree house in a holly tree at Highgrove, wittily known as Holyroodhouse, after the Palace of Holyroodhouse, the Queen's official residence in Edinburgh. But as well as the *Boy's Own* stuff, they weren't afraid to hug and kiss—even in their teens.

Charles never invited Camilla to the house when the boys were there, but William, at least, as the elder and Diana's confidant, will have known about her existence. Her name was never far from Diana's lips—she called her 'The Rottweiler'—and it was frequently accompanied by vitriol or by tears. It was a lot for a child to handle.

Even if his parents had tried to remain civil in front of him and his brother, it would have been impossible for two such sensitive children not to have sensed the tension and notice the absences. Even the press noticed those. At the end of the summer of 1987, one newspaper calculated that Charles and Diana had spent one day together in six weeks.

They had long stopped sleeping in the same room. They saw their own friends, did their own things and lived largely separate lives. The only times they came together and affected a show of unity were at family gatherings that Diana couldn't get out of, joint engagements and the children's school events—most memorably the Wetherby's sports days where, for a couple of years running, Diana triumphed in the mother's race. Having kicked off her high heels and run like a gazelle, she made Charles look churlish and stuffy as she badgered him to run with the fathers, only to demonstrate what he knew at the outset, that running was not his forte.

Yet during these years in the mid- to late-1980s,

when their private lives were so disastrous, they were in many ways a formidable double act.

The Prince had established himself as a controversial figure and although some people were bemused by his stance on various issues from architecture to complementary medicine, many of his speeches had struck a chord with the public, as the hundreds of letters that arrived in his office made clear. The Prince's Trust had begun to see impressive results in helping young people make a start in life; he was busily importing ideas from America to help solve inner-city problems through his involvement with Business in the Community, and he was making big waves on the environmental front.

Diana, meanwhile, looking ever more glamorous and delighting the fashion industry, was making it clear that she had more to offer than her looks. She had taken on unglamorous causes like drug abuse, marriage guidance and AIDS, and was proving to be quite unparalleled in her ability to charm, communicate and empathise with ordinary people.

Abroad, they were a sensation on every trip—in Australia, America, the Gulf States, Italy, Japan, the reception was rapturous. At home the combination was never more successful than as joint patrons of the Wishing Well Appeal for Great Ormond Street Children's Hospital. The target was £30 million in two years and in well under that time, they had helped raise £54 million with a further £30 million promised by the government.

No one saw what went on behind closed doors, and those that did, who knew that both Charles and Diana were seeing other people, never thought for a moment that this might imperil the marriage. Okay, it wasn't happy, but it wasn't the first aristocratic marriage to find a way of accommodating differences.

At that time, Charles had an office in St James's Palace but he had no press office of his own and relied on the team at Buckingham Palace. Their concern was how to manage the runaway success of the royal couple. They felt the need to pace it; not to allow too much exposure, not to allow them to give too many interviews, not to let too much light in on the mystery of monarchy. They were well aware that members of the Royal Family were not like normal celebrities, whose popularity would wax and wane. They had to keep the popularity going for a very long time, maybe twenty or thirty years. Unlike politics or show business or any other career in which fame and popularity are a measure of success, the monarchy is a long-term game. There is no stepping out of public life when the going gets tough, no retreating into anonymity or even retiring at sixty. The work goes on remorselessly and the exposure with it, and as every celebrity knows, the greater the adulation, the faster it can disappear. The danger was if they had too much too quickly they wouldn't be able to sustain it.

It is the dilemma that William's team grapples with today.

# A GIANT SLEEPOVER

William was eight when he started boarding school at Ludgrove, on 11 September 1990. Both parents were there to deliver him in a show of family unity, and the media were there in force to record it, but in reality they had come from different directions. Diana had driven William to Wokingham from London; Charles had travelled up from Gloucestershire. They rendezvoused down the road from the school, and drove the last mile or so together in the Prince's Bentley. They were greeted by the headmasters, Gerald Barber and Nichol Marston, and Gerald's wife, Janet.

Whatever their differences, they were united in their choice of school for William, and it couldn't have been a more successful one. Ludgrove was as close to a home environment as a school could be. It was a small, family-run private preparatory school in the Berkshire countryside, set in 120 acres, with everything boys between the ages of eight and thirteen could possibly dream of. There has been a tradition of two headmasters working in tandem with their wives. Simon Barber and his wife Sophie and Sid and Olly Inglis are in post today and running it along much the same lines as Simon's grandfather did when he moved the school from Cockfosters to the present site in 1937.

It was not a homely environment by accident. Their view is that home is the best place for a small boy to be, but every child has to be educated, so why not educate them in an atmosphere that feels as much like home as possible? As Simon Barber says, 'Yes, some miss home but when they're busy, all together, all doing the same thing, full boarding, they have such fun. And if they are homesick, there's a massive support network from their own peer group and the adult population.'

William was homesick, like many children leaving the nest for the first time, and found it hard to settle. He was also anxious about the rows at home and the uncertainty, but there were mortal fears as well. His father had recently had a bad fall on the polo field and been rushed to hospital with his arm badly broken in several places. After a second long and complicated operation, Diana had taken William and his brother to visit him at the hospital. It was a shock to see his strong and dependable father in a hospital bed. His anxiety about his father aside, William was leaving the calm of the nursery and everything that was familiar to him, and leaving his mother too, while knowing of her unhappy state and just how much she would miss him. Every day she wrote loving notes to her 'Darling Wombat', which he kept safely locked inside his tuck box.

The Barbers were aware of the situation and while treating him no differently from the other boys in their care, they kept a particularly watchful eye. Janet is a naturally warm and affectionate woman and was like a mother to everyone; she referred to them as 'my boys'—and when she meets an old Ludgrovian today, of whatever age, she still thinks of him as one of hers. She had an encyclopaedic memory—as did her husband—and knew everything about each one of them. She was quick to notice if something was amiss or if a boy was unhappy; and if something was wrong, she quickly stepped in to sort things out or to support and help him through it, just as she would for her own son.

Boys come to the school at eight and for the next five years build friendships and support systems that last a lifetime. The Barbers liken the eight-year-olds to a collection of stones with edges that are thrown into a bag together. Their aim is to round off the edges so that by the time the boys move on to their next schools at thirteen, the stones all sit comfortably together. Empathy and tolerance are what they aim for, teaching the boys to get on with one another and to notice when someone is unwell or feeling down.

This nurturing environment is particularly

valuable when home life is volatile. As Simon explains, 'The continuity offers wonderful stability for the few from broken homes. They know where they are, they come back every Sunday with everybody else. They haven't got the concern about what's going on at home because they can immerse themselves in what's going on here. It can be easier to be here than at home with all the anguish.'

It was, as one child remarked, 'Like having a giant sleepover.'

There is certainly no shortage of fun things to do. The school has a nine-hole golf course, cricket pitches and practice nets, football pitches, squash courts, Eton fives courts, four tennis courts and a swimming pool. There is a music block, a sports hall, and the old milking parlour houses ceramics, art and carpentry. The pupils make camps and dens in the woods, and in the summer sleep out occasionally on the golf course and have sing-songs around the camp fire. For budding horticulturalists, there are little plots where each boy can grow his own flowers or vegetables. And to remind the boys that there is a world outside, newspapers are delivered daily and current affairs discussed every morning with a test every Saturday. There were many occasions during those years when the Barbers had to pretend the papers hadn't been delivered—they didn't want William to see the stories of Charles and Diana's failing marriage that filled the front pages.

One memorable story involved William himself. A group of boys had been playing around on the putting green when one of them swung his club and accidentally hit William on the head. He was briefly concussed and, according to one of the boys, he fell to the ground with blood pouring from a gash in his head. His detective went into a spin. The last bit of the story is certainly true. The school nurse carried William to the main building and planned to take him to the sanatorium and send for the doctor. His PPO stepped in and insisted that an ambulance be called, which it duly was, and William was taken to the local Accident and Emergency Department at the Royal Berkshire Hospital in Reading. Diana was having lunch at San Lorenzo, one of her favourite restaurants in London, when she heard the news; Charles was at Highgrove and said of that moment, 'My heart went cold.' Both of them dashed down the motorway to meet at the hospital. By the time they arrived, William was sitting up in bed looking one hundred per cent. 'He was chatting away,' said Charles. 'Then I knew he was going to be all right.'

The doctors, however, were more guarded, and decided to transfer him to a special brain unit at Great Ormond Street Hospital for Children. Diana travelled with William in the ambulance; Charles followed in his Aston Martin, which his mother had given him as a twenty-first birthday present and which William borrowed on the day of his wedding.

Tests showed that William had a depressed fracture of the skull, and later that evening he had an operation to relieve the pressure on his brain and to check for bone splinters. Diana stayed at the hospital and held his hand as he went under the general anaesthetic. Charles, having been assured by the surgeons that there was no need for him to stay, went to the Royal Opera House at Covent Garden where he hosted a group of visitors from the European Commission in Brussels. It was a long-standing engagement and he felt, given the surgeon's assurances, it was unnecessary to cancel.

The press didn't see it that way, and Charles was roundly condemned as an uncaring father, while Diana was the saintly mother. To make matters worse, her friend James Gilbey, of whom more anon, let it be known that Diana thought Charles was a bad and selfish father who would give up nothing for his children.

# A VERY PUBLIC WAR

The golf club incident was not the only occasion when William found himself in the middle of a marital game of one-upmanship. And it was no coincidence that the public were firmly of the view that Diana was a model mother and Charles a cold and absent father, out of touch with the modern world.

When the boys were with their mother, they were photographed having fun, hurtling down water shoots at funfairs, laughing and looking like ordinary little boys. When their father was in the picture, they were more likely to be looking immaculate in suits and ties at family gatherings, with the Queen and Queen Mother, attending church services or the traditional New Year pheasant shoots. Diana was also seen as the one introducing the boys to the thrill of skiing, knowing when she booked the holiday and alerted the press that Charles would be otherwise engaged.

Both Charles and Diana were avid skiers and he had promised the boys he would take them. He was looking forward to watching them put on their skis for the first time and discover the excitement of the mountains. But there was a disagreement about where to take them. Charles wanted them all to go to Klosters in Switzerland.

It was his favourite resort, but it had been the scene of a tragic accident three years earlier when his friend Major Hugh Lindsay was killed by an avalanche that narrowly missed the Prince and badly injured Patti Palmer-Tomkinson. Diana, understandably, didn't want to go back to a place filled with such terrible memories. Without resolving the impasse, she quietly booked a holiday for herself and the boys, with a few other friends, in the pretty Austrian resort of Lech during William's half-term in March 1991. The dates clashed with a large shooting party Charles had arranged at Sandringham and he couldn't let down his friends at short notice.

This was not the only time she made plans for the children or changed pre-existing plans. As Patrick Jephson, her Private Secretary at the time, wrote in his memoir, *Shadows of a Princess*, William and Harry's 'theoretical potential as pawns in the Waleses' game of rivalry was loudly decried on all sides, but it did not stop it happening. The Prince was perhaps slow to recognise the value of being seen to be introducing the boys onto the public stage—or, more likely, he jealously guarded their privacy. His wife, on the other hand, suffered few such inhibitions . . .'

William's first official public appearance was a prime example. There had been no discussion in advance and no agreement that William would be taken out of school on St David's Day, 1 March 1991, and flown to Cardiff, the capital city of Wales, to attend a service in Llandaff Cathedral. Indeed, the agreement between them was that the children would not be made to undertake public engagements until they were older. But without telling anyone in the Prince's office, Diana quietly organised it.

It would have been a political and public relations disaster for the Prince of Wales's eldest son (and in all probability, the future Prince of Wales) to make his first visit to the principality without his father, yet it was by sheer chance that his Private Secretary discovered the Princess's arrangement. Luckily he was able to reschedule the Prince's day so that it looked like a family outing.

A far greater disaster was looming, which was to upset William more than anything so far and was the beginning of a series of acutely difficult years. During the summer of 1991, when he turned nine, Diana embarked on her life story. Speaking into a tape recorder at Kensington Palace—which found its way, via an intermediary, to the journalist Andrew Morton—she described her marriage. After ten years she wanted the world to know just how unhappy she was, and she wanted the world to know why. The result was an explosive book which took the Prince and his staff completely by surprise and was as damaging to him, the Queen and the institution of monarchy, as it was hurtful and humiliating.

In the weeks before publication in June 1992, *Diana: Her True Story* was serialised in the *Sunday Times*. The first instalment appeared under the headline, 'Diana driven to five suicide bids by "uncaring" Charles.' It went on to talk about her bulimia, her husband's indifference towards her, his obsession with his mistress, his shortcomings as a father, and the loneliness and isolation she had felt for so many years, trapped in a loveless marriage within a hostile court and a cold and disapproving Royal Family. The book had a compelling authority and many of the Princess's closest friends and family members were openly quoted and thanked in the acknowledgements. For example: 'James Gilbey explains: "She thinks he is a bad father, a selfish father, the children have to tie in with what he's doing. He will never delay, cancel or change anything which he has sorted out for their benefit. It's a reflection of the way he was brought up and it is history repeating itself. That's why she gets so sad when he is photographed riding with the children at Sandringham. When I spoke to her about it she was literally having to contain her anger because she thought the picture would represent the fact that he was a good father whereas she has the real story." '

Diana swore she had not been involved, leading Robert Fellowes, the Queen's Private Secretary (also married to Diana's sister, Jane), to appeal to Lord McGregor, chairman of the Press Complaints Commission, who issued a tough statement condemning the serialisation as an 'odious exhibition of journalists dabbling their fingers in the stuff of other people's souls in a manner which adds nothing to the legitimate public interest in the situation of the heir to the throne'.

Diana's response was to visit Carolyn Bartholomew, one of the most quoted sources in the book, after first ensuring the press cameras would be there, and put on a very public display of affection for her old flatmate. Robert Fellowes immediately offered his resignation but the Queen refused it.

Several people already suspected Diana was the principal source. Patrick Jephson, for one, had been puzzled by a conversation just before publication when she had asked him whether the charity Turning Point might be able to cope with a sudden donation of some tens of thousands of pounds (her share of the spoils), but he didn't know for sure and his loyalty was to his boss. Also, some obviously well-sourced stories had been appearing in the *Sunday Times*, such as the dismissal of Sir Christopher Airy as Private Secretary to the Prince of Wales. Airy had been selected to take over from Sir John Riddell in 1990 but had not been a success. His end came at Highgrove one afternoon when Diana was at the house, and she was one of a handful of people who could have known what happened. When the story ran, the Prince's office was a very unhappy place, with no one knowing who they could trust as various leaked stories appeared in other newspapers.

What puzzled them most was that much of the book was accurate in many respects. There were stories that only Diana and very few others could have known about, and memos leaked that nobody else could have seen. But most of the stories had a spin, which made them not quite as anyone else present remembered.

For example, there was a memo which, according to Morton, Richard Aylard (who took over as Private Secretary when Airy left) had written to the Prince of Wales following the public condemnation of his behaviour when William cracked his skull, encouraging him to be seen in public more frequently with his children. 'At the conclusion of his missive,' said Morton, 'he [Aylard] heavily underlined in red ink and printed in bold capitals a single word: "TRY".'

What really happened was that the Prince had sent Aylard a memo saying William and Harry wanted to do a few things with their father and could Aylard please look in the diary and pick out a few engagements that would be suitable for the boys. Aylard wrote back with three or four suggestions, including a trip to a naval ship, and said that the next step was to speak to the Princess to make sure she was happy with the plans. It would be best, wrote Aylard, if the Prince could speak to her about it himself. Failing that, he would speak to Patrick Jephson. Charles sent the memo back, annotated in red pen—and he was the only person in the office allowed to use red ink. Against the suggestion that he should speak to his wife, he wrote 'I will TRY!'

Charles kept a dignified silence, even when he knew for certain that Diana had been involved in the book. He didn't attempt to defend himself or correct the facts. Despite all the years of provocation, he has never publicly criticised Diana. His friends were itching to weigh in on his behalf but he was adamant he wanted none of them to get involved. Some did as he asked, others couldn't bear the sense of injustice. The War of the Waleses was under way and the newspapers delighted in it as their circulations rose, particularly those Diana was personally briefing. She was a master tactician, oblivious, or so it seemed, to the effect it had on her children, particularly on William, who was old enough to take in what was going on.

There was only so much the Barbers could shield William and Harry from, but the boys at Ludgrove did what they do best when their friends were in trouble: they formed a loyal and protective ring around them and kept their minds on other things.

# ONE TAPE AFTER ANOTHER

No one imagined that things could get any worse after Morton's book but in just a matter of months the *Sun* newspaper published the transcript of a flirtatious thirty-minute telephone conversation between Diana and James Gilbey. It was rapidly picked up by every other newspaper and media outlet, and the particularly prurient could dial a *Sun* telephone hotline and for 36p a minute, hear the tape for themselves. He called her 'Darling' fourteen times, and 'Squidgy' or 'Squidge' fifty-three times, which led to the scandal being dubbed 'Squidgygate'. Amongst the endearments Diana talked about how her husband made her life 'real, real torture', and described a lunch at which the Queen Mother had given her a strange look. 'It's not hatred, it's sort of interest and pity . . . I was very bad at lunch and I nearly started blubbing. I just felt really sad and empty and thought, Bloody hell, after all I've done for this fucking family.'

After her sense of triumph with the book (although she did later say she regretted having done it), this was less welcome. However, according to her PPO, Ken Wharf, 'Diana raised the subject with me in a fairly light-hearted way—the fact that it had reached the front page of a national tabloid newspaper.' She had even listened to the tapes on the *Sun*'s hotline. 'When I asked if it was her, she said, of course it was.' Charles, the boys and the Queen were less amused, and the institution was again brought into disrepute. The recording had been made late at night on New Year's Eve in 1989 when Diana was on a landline at Sandringham and Gilbey in a car parked in Oxfordshire. A radio ham in Oxford picked it up, but it was always thought the recording might initially have come from GCHQ, MI5's listening post in Cheltenham, Gloucestershire.

The foreign tour to Korea three months later was always going to have been tricky. At first Diana tried to duck out of it, but the Queen intervened and persuaded her she must go, so go she did, but it proved to be the final straw. The press were only interested in the marriage, and since neither the Prince nor Princess could exchange a civil look let alone a civil word, the media were hovering like vultures just waiting for the final death throe.

It came soon enough, when Diana yet again used the boys to outmanoeuvre her husband. There had been a long-standing arrangement to host a private shooting party at Sandringham together on the weekend of 20 and 21 November, which was the Ludgrove exeat. The weekend had become something of a tradition and Charles had invited the usual sixteen friends with their children for what should have been a relaxing and jolly time for everyone. Harry was now at Ludgrove too, and both he and William were looking forward to a trip to Sandringham, which was a boys' paradise, and to seeing their friends. Both of them loved shooting.

Less than a week beforehand, the Prince discovered that Diana had decided not to come to Sandringham and was planning to take the children to stay with the Queen at Windsor instead. According to Jephson, she had looked forward to the weekend with a mixture of anger and dread. 'They're all *his* friends,' she complained. 'I'm going to be completely outnumbered.'

Her instincts were probably right; most of his friends took his side in the marital war, and now that they had Morton and Squidgygate in their armoury, it could have been a very uncomfortable weekend. Charles spoke to his mother who spoke to Diana who swiftly said that if she couldn't go to Windsor then she would take the boys to Highgrove instead. She refused a plea from the Prince who asked, if she was determined to stay away, that she should let the boys go to Sandringham by themselves. On the advice of her lawyer, she wrote a careful letter of explanation in which she said that she felt the atmosphere at Sandringham would not be conducive to a happy weekend for the children. Nor could she be sure that he would not expose them to guests whose presence would be unwelcome to her (by whom she meant Camilla). Charles finally lost it. The farce had to end.

Thus on the afternoon of 9 December 1992, John Major, then Prime Minister, stood at the dispatch box in the House of Commons before a packed but silent House and read aloud the following statement: 'It is announced from Buckingham Palace that, with regret, the Prince and Princess of Wales have decided to separate. Their Royal Highnesses have no plans to divorce and their constitutional positions are unaffected. This decision has been reached amicably and they will both continue to participate fully in the upbringing of their children.'

Julia Cleverdon, chief executive of Business in the Community, who had worked closely with the Prince of Wales for ten years and was with him in Holyhead that day, first knew of it when reporters shouted, 'Give us a statement, Charlie.' Later, he told her about the separation, and she says that in all the years she'd known him, she had never seen him look so miserable.

Coincidentally, 20 November was the date of a devastating fire at Windsor Castle, while the Queen, who spent much of her childhood there, was in residence. The fire started accidentally when a curtain that had been touching a spotlight burst into flames in the Private Chapel. Fortunately no one was hurt but it raged for fifteen hours and caused millions of pounds' worth of damage to what is the oldest of royal residences and the only one that has been in constant use since William the Conqueror selected the site for a fortress after his conquest of England in 1066. These events and more were what led the Queen to declare 1992 an 'annus horribilis'.

William and Harry had been told about the separation in advance. Charles and Diana had gone to Ludgrove—where Harry had joined William in 1992—and first explained the situation to the Barbers, so that they were prepared to support and reassure the boys in the days and weeks that followed. Then, in the homely surroundings of the headmaster's sitting room, they broke the news to William and Harry. William's rather grown-up response was to hope that they would both be happier now. He let more of his feelings be known, perhaps, in a letter to his trusted nanny Olga Powell. She wrote him a very personal letter back consoling him about the impending separation.

The Households were swiftly divided. Diana took sole possession of Kensington Palace and kept the two senior butlers, Paul Burrell (who was later prosecuted for stealing her belongings after her death) and Harold Brown. Charles took butler number three, Bernie Flannery. The Prince and Princess were careful to keep photographs of each other in their homes for the sake of the boys. The office at St James's Palace, which they continued to share, remained much the same. There was talk of warring factions, but the two teams were surprisingly united and continued to work together to co-ordinate diaries, particularly over arrangements for the children.

But as is the way with wars, when one side loses ground another side surges forward. After Diana's embarrassment it was the Prince's turn. For a man jealous of his privacy, the publication in the *Daily Mirror* in January 1993 of his own intimate late-night telephone ramblings with Camilla was the ultimate humiliation. Even Diana, while enjoying a little *Schadenfreude*, was embarrassed on his behalf. The tape was eleven minutes that could be distilled into one: the heir to the throne's wish that he could always be with the woman he adored and musing on the possibility of turning into a tampon to achieve it.

The puritanical outburst that followed, what was immediately dubbed 'Camillagate', verged on hysteria and was out of all proportion. An alien would have concluded Britain was a nation in crisis. There were lurid headlines and cartoons, wide condemnation of the Prince, questions about his fitness to be King and, in the mounting fever, demands from Cabinet ministers that the Prince give up Mrs Parker Bowles.

How this ridiculous rambling demonstrated that Charles was not fit to be King was a mystery. It was the sort of idiotic conversation with crude jokes that many lovers might have when entirely alone at the dead of night. All it demonstrated was that the Prince had found in Camilla what he had so much hoped for with Diana. They clearly had a loving, friendly, familiar relationship with no suspicion or tension or jealousy. She was fun, she was sexy and giggly and pulled his leg when he was angry or sounding pompous, but she didn't criticise him or put him down. She was interested in him: she boosted his ego, bolstered his confidence and made no demands on him. She wanted to hear about his work, read his speeches and listen to his plans and ideas. She was happy when they could be together but understanding when that wasn't possible. It was clear she was a friend as well as a lover and shared many of his enthusiasms.

No one has ever determined who made the recordings but Charles and Camilla worked out that it was a compilation of several conversations held over several months around Christmas 1989—shortly before Diana was being listened into—but, curiously, like Diana's, they weren't published until much later.

Before investigations into either record began, the Home Secretary, Kenneth Clarke, told the House of Commons 'There is nothing to investigate . . . I am absolutely certain that the allegation that this is anything to do with the security services or GCHQ . . . is being put out by newspapers, who I think feel rather guilty that they are using plainly tapped telephone calls.' An interesting theory in the light of Prince William's discovery that his was one of several mobile phones being hacked into, which led to an avalanche of claims against the Murdoch empire.

The Prince of Wales was furious that his phone had been illegally bugged and deeply annoyed that the press should have published the tape. He was also miserable that he had managed to drag the monarchy through the mire yet again, and devastated for Camilla, who was bombarded with hateful letters and accused of breaking up the royal marriage. He was humiliated beyond words and it required huge courage to step out of the car on a visit to Liverpool the following day, not knowing what kind of reception to expect from the crowds. As it was, there was not one single snigger or catcall and no evidence that people had stayed away.

But his greatest fear was for William and Harry, and also for Camilla's children, Tom and Laura Parker Bowles, who were a few years older. They were all at school and children, he knew, could be horribly cruel. He was terrified about how they would cope.

Yet again, the Barbers worked overtime to keep the most lurid headlines out of sight and to support William and now Harry. The school had had the children of high-profile parents through their doors before and scandals in the press were nothing new, but nothing before or since could have compared with the upsets that these young boys had so far had to handle.

# A TOUGH CHOICE

With every episode, the bold, confident, cheeky boy was becoming more muted, while his brother, the quiet, subdued one, still too young to fully understand what was going on, appeared to blossom. It was becoming clear that William was taking onto his young shoulders the burden of responsibility for his parents' wellbeing and happiness.

He saw the newspapers and the television news, witnessed the sarcasm and shouting, felt the corrosive atmosphere, but because he loved both his parents, his loyalty and emotions were torn down the middle. Fortunately, they were not the only providers of care in his young life and it was perhaps the stability that came from the other people around him that prevented him from careering off the rails when everyone else seemed to be hell bent on self-destruction.

One of these people was a ditzy young aristocrat called Alexandra Legge-Bourke, known as Tiggy, whose mother, Shaun, and aunt, Victoria, were both ladies-in-waiting to Princess Anne. Tiggy was taken on as an aide to Richard Aylard, but swiftly moved sideways as a female presence in the boys' life and to act *in loco parentis* when, under the terms of the separation, they were with Charles but he had commitments elsewhere. It was a magical appointment. Tiggy was twenty-eight and a bundle of fun, something between a loving, liberal mother and a slightly wild big sister. She was a nursery school teacher who had a delightful rapport with children of all ages and temperaments, whom she called her Tiggywigs. She said of her royal charges, 'I give them what they need at this stage; fresh air, a rifle and a horse. She [their mother] gives them a tennis racket and a bucket of popcorn at the movies.' William and Harry took to her like ducks to water but their mother once again grew frightened that she was being usurped.

Meanwhile, another crisis was brewing. The veteran writer and broadcaster, Jonathan Dimbleby, had spent two years working on a double project: a television documentary about Charles and a biography, which he had managed to persuade the Prince to authorise. He was given unrestricted access to the archives at St James's Palace and at Windsor Castle, where an entire floor is filled with documents and memoranda accumulated over the last four decades. 'I have also been free to read his journals, diaries and many thousands of the letters which he has written assiduously since childhood,' Dimbleby wrote. 'Not only have

I drawn heavily from this wealth of original material but I have been free to quote extensively from it. Nor has the Prince discouraged past and present members of the royal Household from speaking to me; likewise, at his behest, his friends and some of his relatives have talked about him openly at length, almost all of them for the first time.'

Both were timed to coincide loosely with the twenty-fifth anniversary of his Investiture as Prince of Wales, in July 1994. What began as an innocent and well-intentioned exercise had unimaginable consequences and was ultimately responsible for Camilla's divorce from Andrew Parker Bowles, terrible ructions within the Royal Family, Diana's devastating *Panorama* interview, Richard Aylard's departure and the fiercest controversy yet about the Prince's fitness to be King. William was twelve and deeply affected by it.

The documentary was called 'Charles: the Private Man, the Public Role'. It ran for two and a half hours and attracted fourteen million viewers, many of whom understood for the first time what the Prince actually did when he wasn't playing polo. But what most people remembered about the film ran to no more than three minutes.

Dimbleby asked Charles about his infidelity: 'Did you try to be faithful and honourable to your wife when you took on the vows of marriage?'

'Yes,' said the Prince, and after a brief and rather anguished pause added, 'until it became irretrievably broken down, us both having tried.'

When asked about Camilla he said she was 'a great friend of mine . . . she has been a friend for a very long time.'

At a press conference the next day, Richard Aylard, who had overseen the project, confirmed that the adultery to which the Prince had confessed was indeed with Mrs Parker Bowles.

His reasoning was sound enough, even if the results were not. The question had to be asked because after the Morton book, the taped phone calls and everything else that had gone before, it was the only thing the public was interested in. How he should answer it was a tough choice. The Prince could have refused to answer, but that wouldn't have stopped the paparazzi who followed him and Camilla and made their lives so difficult. He could have lied but that was morally unacceptable, and if and when the paparazzi did catch the two of them together, he would be shown to be a liar. Or he could tell the truth, which he did, naively believing that the public would understand that he committed adultery only after the marriage had irretrievably broken down.

'NOT FIT TO REIGN' ran the *Daily Mirror* headline, and other front pages took a similar tone.

Diana went down to Ludgrove to talk to the

children. As she said in her *Panorama* interview, 'I . . . put it to William particularly, that if you find someone you love in life you must hang on to it and look after it, and if you were lucky enough to find someone who loved you then one must protect it.

'William asked me what had been going on and could I answer his questions, which I did. He said was that the reason why our marriage had broken up? And I said, well, there were three of us in this marriage and the pressures of the media was another factor, so the two together were very difficult. But although I still loved Papa, I couldn't live under the same roof as him, and likewise with him.' In answer to what effect she thought her explanation had on Prince William, she said, 'Well, he's a child that's a deep thinker and we don't know for a few years how it's gone in. But I put it in gently, without resentment or any anger.'

It was Dimbleby's book that followed in the autumn, simply called *The Prince of Wales*, or more precisely its serialisation in the *Sunday Times*, which did the most damage. Inevitably sensationalised and cherry-picked, it gave the impression that Charles was a whinger whose parents had never shown him any affection, that he had loved Camilla for most of his adult life and never loved the wife his father had bullied him into marrying.

The Prince no doubt thought it would be a good vehicle for delivering his message about the serious issues that consumed his time. Instead it turned into an own goal of staggering proportions. His parents were left hurt by the portrayal Charles gave of his childhood and bemused that he should have agreed such access. And Andrew Parker Bowles felt honour-bound to formally bring his marriage to Camilla to an end. They were divorced the following January and he married his long-term girlfriend.

Sir John Riddell was amazed that his advisors had ever allowed it to happen.

'They released Jonathan Dimbleby and the Prince of Wales on to the Scottish moor together at 9.30 and they came back breathless and excited at 4.30; and when you go for a very exhausting walk with anybody—if you went with Goebbels—after a time the blood circulates, the joints ease up, the breath gets short—you'd pour out your heart to anyone, even Goebbels. Jonathan Dimbleby's charms are huge so the Prince of Wales gave him all that stuff about how unhappy he was when he was a boy—the Queen never spoke to him, the Duke of Edinburgh was beastly to him—and it very much upsets them.

'Everyone was told this book would finally show what a marvellous person he was; and people were bored out of their wits by Business in the Community and the Prince's Trust; they wanted to know about their private life. We're interested in who they're going to bed with, except we got rather bored by that because we couldn't keep up with it.'

And just as the excitement over one book started to wane, there was another hot on its heels. James Hewitt, having licked his wounds, decided to tell the writer Anna Pasternak about his five-year love affair with Diana. *Princess in Love* hit the bookshelves in September 1994. The Queen can't have been the only person wondering what revelations would dominate the headlines next in this battle between the Prince and Princess of Wales—and which of them could inflict the most damage on their two sons.

The answer wasn't long in coming.

# THE PLAYING FIELDS OF ETON

On 6 September 1995, Prince William arrived at Eton College, probably the most famous public school in the world, having successfully passed his common entrance exam. It was a big leap from the cosy surroundings of Ludgrove, and it had a whole new and contrary vocabulary to learn: a 'school' was a class but more commonly called a 'div', a teacher was a 'beak', homework was called 'EWs', 'chambers' were elevenses, and the smart outfit he wore, marked with his name and laundry number, was called 'formal change'. For lessons the next day he would be in 'school dress', black tailcoat, waistcoat, a stiff white collar with a paper tie and pin-striped trousers, which were apparently adopted to mourn the death of George III in 1820.

Once upon a time, having the right name was enough to guarantee a place in this bastion of privilege, but while that was no longer true when William joined the school, it had no shortage of boys with their own grouse moors and salmon rivers, two or three houses and a brace of Range Rovers. Be that as it may, the education and the quality of the teaching staff, the academic and sporting facilities and the opportunities it provided were second to none. It also boasted three theatres, two concert halls, two major libraries, an intranet and computer terminals in every boy's room.

Charles and Diana delivered him to the school together, along with Harry, in a public display of smiles and family alliance. As well as the daunting prospect of being a new boy in a new school that was almost ten times the size of the old one, William was also aware that everyone would be curious about him and that everyone would know what was going on in his family. On top of that he had the press cameras to cope with and the inevitable anxiety about leaving his parents. It was more than the average thirteen-year-old had to handle on his first day at a big school.

Despite their differences, Charles and Diana were united in their choice of this next school for William, and in their choice of house master, the most significant adult in every Eton boy's daily life. Just as Gerald and Janet Barber had been key in seeing William through uncomfortable times at Ludgrove, Dr Andrew Gailey, who presided over ALHG (houses are known by the house master's initials) proved to be another exceptional figure, whose support of William through the next five years, and beyond, was nothing short of heroic. An Irishman with a good sense of humour (vital, particularly when Harry joined his brother three years later), he is a historian and has written numerous books on Anglo-Irish relations. It was a case of the right man being in the right place at the right time.

The town of Eton and the school are interwoven and many of the buildings and shops in the High Street are owned by the school. At the top of the High Street, a footbridge across the River Thames links Eton with Windsor, and thereafter, Windsor Castle, the Queen's main residence. William would often walk to the Castle to have tea with Granny and Grandpa, braving the local youth, who used to take delight—and still do—in duffing up anyone they suspected of being Etonian. In the past boys were only allowed into Windsor in 'formal change'; now, they are only allowed across the bridge if they are *not* wearing any sort of uniform. Teenagers in jackets and ties are about as inconspicuous as zebras in a pride of lions.

In stark contrast, when the Prince of Wales was at school he didn't see any of his family for months on end. At the Duke of Edinburgh's insistence, he was sent to Gordonstoun in the north-east of Scotland, hundreds of miles from everyone and everything that was familiar. It was a Spartan regime, including runs before breakfast and cold showers, and he was profoundly unhappy there. He would never have let William suffer the same fate.

While the scholars, or Collegers, inhabit College and eat in the most magnificent room in the school, the rest of the boys, known as 'Oppidans', are distributed between twenty-four boarding houses scattered about the town, typically with fifty other boys, ten to a year group. But unlike most schools of its type, there are no dormitories. Every boy from day one has a study bedroom of his own, which changes every year as he moves up the school.

There are many idiosyncrasies that set Eton apart but one of the most obvious is that day-to-day life is more akin to a university regime than a school. From the age of thirteen, boys have to manage their own time. They can choose whatever extracurricular activities they want—and there is every conceivable extracurricular activity on offer. The only requirement is that lessons and tutorials are attended and that their work is completed and handed in on time. There is an unexpected amount of freedom, but plenty of sanctions for boys who misuse it.

Several weeks into the Michaelmas term, every new boy had to take a Colours Test, set by the older boys. It was supposedly to ensure that they had learned their way around the school and had mastered the vocabulary. In reality it was an alarming initiation ritual, and if any boy slipped up they were made to sing the Founder's Prayer in Latin while standing on a table, and any boy who was seen to falter was dragged onto the floor and bashed with cushions.

Although always referred to as ALHG, the real name for Dr Gailey's building was Manor House. It is situated in the centre of the school, next to School Library and 'the Burning Bush' (an elaborate wrought-iron street lamp). Like all the boarding houses, it has two separate doors, the Boys' Door, leading into the boys' living area, and the door to the Private Side, where the house master lives with his wife and family, if he has one. Dr Gailey was married with a young daughter, but the wives, unlike at Ludgrove, have no role as far as the boys are concerned. Each house employs a woman known as a Dame (except in College where she is called Matron), whom the boys address as 'Ma'am'. She looks after the physical welfare of the boys and deals with laundry, administration, catering (in those houses with dining rooms) and domestic issues. William's Dame was Elizabeth Heathcote, said to be 'a bit firm but very nice'.

Security was an obvious issue in a school as spread out as Eton, and where townspeople and boys intermingled so freely. The grounds stretch to four hundred acres and include a rowing lake. Many of the classrooms are similarly spread out and to reach them boys must cross public roads and walk through narrow pedestrian passages between buildings.

The school took William's security very seriously. When a boy idly sitting at his bedroom window spotted William walking down the street, he thought it would be funny to point a laser pen at him. Seeing the red dot homing in on its target, William's PPOs immediately thought he was a sniper. The boy found himself looking down the barrel of a much more serious weapon—and, rumour had it, was soon looking for a new school.

Every boy was visible to the outside world on a daily basis, yet because the school had such a long history of educating children of the rich and famous, including Princes from other parts of the world, the arrival of the Queen's grandson was not entirely out of the ordinary. It didn't take long for people's curiosity to fade and he was soon treated like any other boy, both at school and in the town, and that was possibly William's salvation. Boys and locals alike became surprisingly protective; a few tried to make money out of the new arrival, offering items of 'William's' uniform to gullible tourists, but on the whole they would question anyone hanging around with a long lens and never give truthful answers when quizzed about William.

Sports played a major part in his life at Eton. Boys are divided into two groups during the summer: those who choose to row are called wet bobs; those who play cricket are dry bobs. He chose rowing, but swimming was where he excelled. Eton has an Olympic-sized indoor pool and William was the Under-16 60-m Freestyle champion in his second year. A year later he won both the Senior 50-m and 100-m Freestyle competitions and later broke the school 50-m record (in 27.94 seconds). He also took up sub-aqua diving, which became a major enthusiasm, and played on the school water polo team.

On land, he played all the major sports for his House, except cricket. These included football and rugby in the Michaelmas Half, hockey and rowing in the Lent Half and athletics, rowing and tennis in the Summer Half. He also played rugby for the 3rd XV until he broke a finger badly, which required an operation. Thereafter, he concentrated on the Field Game and the Wall Game, two hybrids unique to Eton. (It's said that the only other place these games have been played is Ford Open Prison.) Both games are a type of football, but of the two, the Wall Game is the least explicable. Two teams of sweaty boys covered in mud form a 'bully' or a scrum up against a high red-brick wall and push against each other, endeavouring, I am told, to free the ball. It rarely happens; goals are scored every hundred years on average, and if the scrum moves more than a couple of feet in either direction it's considered an exciting match.

William's other great interest was the Combined Cadet Force, which he joined in his first year in the sixth form. His father came to watch the CCF Tattoo on College Field in the summer of 1999, when William won the Sword of Honour for the top First Year Cadet.

But possibly his greatest achievement was being elected a member of Pop, bestowed on the best-liked and most successful boys in the final year. (There are only nineteen members.) It used to be a debating society but today it consists of prefects elected by their peers, and with the title they receive all sorts of privileges including the right to wear wing collars, white bow ties, spongebag trousers and colourful waistcoats of their own choice. William had several, including one with the design of the Union Jack.

# THE QUEEN CALLS TIME

Inquisitive tourists, even devious journalists, were comparatively easy to keep at bay during William's five years at Eton, but it was far more difficult to protect him from what was going on beyond Eton and its curious customs. No sooner had his smartly polished shoes hit the forecourt of Manor House than his mother's love life was once again all over the newspapers—and there was no chance of pretending there had been a problem with the newspaper delivery in a school the size of Eton, full of bright and inquisitive teenagers.

This time the man in question was the England rugby captain, Will Carling, whom Diana had met while working out at the Chelsea Harbour Club gym in south-west London. She was obsessive about exercise (a classic symptom of bulimia) and trips to the gym formed part of her early morning routine. Like most boys, William was mad about rugby and Will Carling was a hero; at twenty-two he had been the youngest England captain, and the most successful. William had watched him play and met him several times with his mother. He was a regular visitor at Kensington Palace, and the boys were thrilled when he had given them each a rugby shirt. Discovering there was more to his mother's friendship with Carling must have come as a shock.

It was also at the Harbour Club, in 1990, that Diana had met Oliver Hoare, Carling's predecessor in her affections. Like Carling, he was married, but his wife was more long-suffering than Carling's. She put up with their affair for four years, only threatening to divorce him when the press exposed it. When he chose his marriage over Diana, the Princess bombarded his Household with phone calls: up to twenty a day, three hundred in all, many of them silent. After the Hoares reported the calls, a police investigation discovered that many of them were traced to Diana's private number at Kensington Palace.

Carling's wife was not as tolerant as Diane Hoare. Although he never admitted an affair, Julia Carling, a pretty, blonde and feisty television presenter, was convinced that it was more than friendship. The marriage ended in a bitter, protracted and very high-profile way. And although there was no proof of adultery, the public, who had followed the story closely in the tabloids, were left in no doubt that Diana had been instrumental in the break-up.

Having always been portrayed in the media as the victim, and been sustained by the love of her public, it was an uncomfortable sensation for Diana to feel the chill wind of disapproval. But it didn't last long—she had something much bigger waiting to detonate.

On 20 November 1995, a large proportion of the

nation sat glued to their television sets in disbelief as Diana gave the performance of her life. The rousing *Panorama* theme music played over glamorous shots of the Princess, and as it faded we saw her walking up the aisle with Charles on her wedding day, which the voice of journalist Martin Bashir dramatically reminded us 'was the wedding of the century . . . but the fairytale wasn't to be. Tonight on *Panorama*, the Princess of Wales . . .'

After shots of the iconic kiss on the balcony, with the roaring and cheering of the crowds, Diana was revealed in Kensington Palace and the mood was very different. Sitting forlornly on a chair, occasionally pausing to recover her composure or wipe away a tear, HRH the Princess of Wales told Bashir about her marriage, her in-laws and life after separation.

Looking pale and vulnerable, with heavy black kohl lining her eyes, head to one side and slightly tilted down, she talked about her feelings of isolation and emptiness, of being a strong woman, a free spirit. She talked about her bulimia, her self-harming, her cries for help. She talked about the Prince's friends who waged a war in the media against her, indicating that she was 'unstable, sick and should be put in a home'. She talked about his obsession with Camilla, and 'the enemy' that tried to undermine her—her 'husband's department', jealous that her work got more publicity than his.

She admitted to the telephone conversation with James Gilbey, and that she had made calls to Oliver Hoare, but denied there were three hundred. She also confessed that she had been unfaithful to her husband with James Hewitt, whom she had adored, and that she had been devastated when his book came out 'because I trusted him, and because . . . I worried about the reaction of my children . . . and it was very distressing for me that a friend of mine, who I had trusted, had made money out of me.' She said that when the books arrived in the bookshops 'the first thing I did was rush down to talk to my children. And William produced a box of chocolates and said, "Mummy, I think you've been hurt. These are to make you smile again."'

Had she forgotten, as she told that story to an audience of over twenty million people, that William was thirteen years old and in his first term in a new school?

The most memorable moment of the broadcast was her simple description of what had destroyed her marriage. 'There were three of us in this marriage,' she said, 'so it was a bit crowded.'

The most damaging remarks, however, were reserved for her husband, though couched in velvet. She had been devastated, she said, when she heard on the news that he had disclosed his adultery to Jonathan Dimbleby, but she had admired his honesty, which for someone in his position was 'quite something'. When asked whether the Prince of Wales would ever be King or would wish to be, she said, 'being Prince of Wales produces more freedom now, and being King would be a little bit more suffocating. And because I know the character, I would think that the top job, as I call it, would bring enormous limitations to him, and I don't know whether he could adapt to that.'

And for the final thrust to the heart, when asked if, when he came of age, she would wish to see Prince William succeed the Queen rather than his father, she said, 'My wish is that my husband finds peace of mind, and from that follows other things, yes.'

No one beyond the *Panorama* team knew what was in the programme. It had been filmed and prepared in total secrecy and announced at the last minute. The BBC governors had not even been told for fear they would pull it. And although she hadn't been able to resist telling Patrick Jephson, her Private Secretary, that she had done an interview, she refused to tell him what it was about. 'It's terribly moving,' she said. 'Some of the men who watched were moved to tears. Don't worry, everything will be all right . . .'

But when the opening credits rolled at 9.30 p.m., Jephson was not alone in knowing it wouldn't be all right. He resigned as a result of the interview and so did her Press Officer, Geoff Crawford.

Everyone else, friends, courtiers, family, were left speechless. It had been pure, brilliant theatre, as those who knew her recognised. She had again made their private war public and chosen to punish Charles in the most damaging way possible. But the Prince wasn't the only one who was damaged. Did she not think about how her boys would feel when they saw the film, or what taunting schoolmates might say? She had struck right at the heart of the monarchy, which was not just about the Queen and the Prince of Wales. It was the throne that William would one day inherit.

According to Ingrid Seward, who spoke at length with Diana before her death, when Andrew Gailey heard that an interview was about to be broadcast, he telephoned Diana and told her it was imperative that she come to the school and explain to William face to face what she was intending to do. She refused, asking, 'Is that really necessary?'

The next day he phoned again and insisted that she come to see her son. She agreed reluctantly but the meeting lasted no longer than five minutes. She told William that the programme would contain nothing controversial and that he would be proud of her. Before he had a chance to ask any embarrassing questions she left.

He watched it in Andrew Gailey's study and was deeply upset, as any child, watching one parent assassinate the integrity of the other, let alone talk about their infidelity, would be. He was angry and incredulous that his mother could have done such a thing.

The Queen called time. Her principal concern was for William and Harry and the effect all of this public bickering was having on them. After consulting with the Prime Minister and the Archbishop of Canterbury, she wrote formally and privately to her son and daughter-in-law asking them to put the country out of its uncertainty and to divorce as early as could practicably be done.

It was the following year before a settlement was reached. In the intervening months the war continued and the newspapers continued to report it. On what Diana called 'the saddest day of my life', she put out a premature and unauthorised statement to the press. 'The Princess of Wales,' it said, 'has agreed to Prince Charles's request for a divorce. The Princess will continue to be involved in all decisions relating to the children and will remain at Kensington Palace with offices in St James's Palace. The Princess of Wales will retain the title and be known as Diana, Princess of Wales.'

The Queen was furious and, having kept well out of all previous spats between her son and daughter-in-law, immediately issued a response. 'The Queen was most interested to hear that the Princess of Wales had agreed to the divorce. We can confirm that the Prince and Princess of Wales had a private meeting this afternoon at St James's Palace. At this meeting details of the divorce settlement and the Princess's future role were not discussed. All the details on these matters, including titles, remain to be discussed and settled. This will take time. What the Princess has mentioned are requests rather than decisions at this stage.'

When the divorce was finally settled in July 1996, by two top-weight lawyers—Anthony Julius, from the well-established firm Mishcon de Reya, acting for the Princess, and Fiona Shackleton from the royal solicitors, Farrer and Co., acting for the Prince—Diana received a generous financial package thought to be worth more than £17 million. Negotiations could not have been more difficult or more acrimonious, but the Prince had always intended to be generous. They retained equal access to William and Harry and equal responsibility for their upbringing. Diana was still to be regarded by the Queen and the Prince of Wales as a member of the Royal Family and would carry on living in Kensington Palace, but her office would be there rather than at St James's Palace. The one detail in the settlement that was widely perceived as petty was that Diana was stripped of the title Her Royal Highness. It was the Queen's decision, not the Prince's, and in public relations terms it turned out to be a blunder, as her brother made so painfully clear in his eulogy at Westminster Abbey a year later.

When she asked William if he minded her losing her royal status, he replied, 'I don't mind what you're called—you're Mummy.'

# OUTSIDE THE GILDED CAGE

Many years later, when William first started to visit the Middleton family home in Berkshire, one of the things he most loved about them was that they were normal. They lived in a comfortable, spacious but unremarkable red-brick house with no armed policemen at the gate, and no butlers. They could come and go as they pleased without being photographed, they could take the dog for leisurely walks across the fields with no PPOs on their tail, meet locals for a pint or two in the pub at the weekend, or visit friends without the building having to be swept for security risks first. And they clattered about in the kitchen and sat down to chatty, friendly, family meals together.

This scenario, taken for granted by most people in Britain, was something William never experienced at home. There were no intimate family meals when he was growing up—the closest he came to it was in the nursery.

Diana had also craved the normality of a happy family life—which she had never had either—but she found it, vicariously, with her friends. She and the boys would be folded into other families and became involved in the everyday to and fro. Diana would arrive with huge bunches of beautiful flowers and, while entertaining everyone with dirty jokes and tales out of school, she would set to, unloading the dishwasher, chopping onions, peeling potatoes, laying the table and doing all the ordinary things she never did at home. 'They can feel imprisoned in palaces,' says one friend about royal life. 'It's like living in a gilded cage.' She is also convinced that this is why William is so determined to keep staff to a minimum in his own Household and to cling to normality for as long as he can.

Lady Annabel Goldsmith (after whom the eponymous London nightclub is named) has a large Queen Anne house on the edge of Richmond Park, full of barking dogs and on Sundays full of her large, colourful family. Hers was one of several homes into which Diana and the boys folded comfortably and frequently. She had known Diana's parents long ago but didn't meet Diana until 1989.

As Annabel wrote in her memoirs, 'Sunday lunch at Ormeley remains an institution . . . The lunch itself is usually chaotic. There is a huge sideboard in the dining room and all the food from the first course through the main course and the pudding is laid out buffet style and everyone helps themselves. Lunch is eaten so fast that Diana started to time us. "Right," she would say, "today was an all-time record. Fifteen minutes!"

'She would ring and ask if I was going to be at home and if she could come and join me. She would land like a butterfly, have lunch and dart off again, sometimes bringing the boys with her, sometimes not. She would drive herself down . . . dash through the back door often clutching a present, greet the staff who all loved her, try to evade the mass of dogs yapping at her feet and settle down to amuse us . . . Her repartee became an essential part of these Sunday lunches, interrupted occasionally when she vanished to the kitchen to do the washing up.'

The two women, despite the difference in their ages, became good friends. As she wrote, 'Although I felt she responded more to my surroundings than to me personally, I think she did regard me as something of a surrogate mother.' Diana would say, 'William's like a caged tiger in London, can he come down?' Lady Annabel's youngest son, Ben, was also at Eton and she would sometimes collect the two boys on a Sunday morning and drive them together, with William's PPOs in the car behind trying to keep up.

Friendships for Diana were often as inconsistent as everything else in her life. The closest, warmest and most loyal of friends, like employees, could suddenly find they'd been dropped without the slightest inkling of what they had done to deserve it. Phone calls stopped, everything stopped; some people heard from her again a year or so later, while others never did. Annabel Goldsmith wasn't one of them, so William and Harry weren't suddenly cut off from the friends and welcome they'd come to enjoy at Ormeley. It was harsh for them to be suddenly deprived of others.

After the separation, Diana had nowhere in the country to take the boys other than to the houses of her friends. Keeping them amused in London, where they were all so instantly recognisable, was more difficult now they were older. Their outings to theme parks, cinemas and burger restaurants were a great way of bringing normality into their lives but there was a limit to how many they could visit. So while she didn't much like the country herself, she knew how much the boys did. The solution seemed simple. She would ask her brother for a cottage on the Althorp estate, which he had inherited after their father's death in March 1991. She knew exactly the one she wanted; it was the Garden House, far enough from the big house to cause him and his family no nuisance yet safely enough within the grounds to afford her and her children privacy.

Diana's relationship with her family was as volatile as with her friends, and Charles, the 9th Earl, turned her down. He had inherited the £85 million estate with two hundred-odd cottages and farmhouses, but said that he didn't want the media circus that her presence would attract. The real reason only came out in the Burrell trial (of which more later) after her death, when a letter Charles had written to his sister was produced. He had felt hurt, like so many others, that she had cut him out of her life. Friends say she was very upset. The relationship, sadly, was never fully repaired and the boys missed an opportunity to get to know their uncle.

Their country home remained Highgrove, where Tiggy would be in charge. Tiggy was miraculously uncomplicated compared to their parents. She had a healthy, 'jolly hockey-sticks' approach to most of life's problems and very little sense of self-preservation. Both boys adored her, although the bond is probably closest between her and Harry. She went everywhere with them, on half-term and summer holidays, on skiing holidays, on trips to join the rest of the Royal Family at Sandringham and Balmoral. She took them to and from school and to and from Kensington Palace. At Highgrove, she helped them load their ponies into trailers and took them to gymkhanas and shows and pony clubs and to polo lessons and to tea with their friends. She took them shopping, rabbit shooting, and drove across the countryside with them after the hunt. They went fishing and climbing and go-karting. She told them jokes and laughed at theirs, watched the same videos and listened to the same music.

Tiggy was never a threat to Diana—a child's love for its mother is as strong a bond as can be found on this earth, however good or bad she may be. Tiggy was simply an affectionate, effusive, demonstrative, confident, overgrown tomboy, who put a hundred and ten per cent into the job she was paid to do and probably would have done it for nothing. If their father told them to go to bed, they would ignore him or wheedle him round. If Tiggy told them to, they would call her a 'bossy Old Bat' but go. But Diana, with her old insecurities, once again felt threatened. She started a rumour that Tiggy and Prince Charles were having an affair, 'proof' of which was an innocent, and very public, kiss on the cheek on the ski slopes. It was hardly surprising since he had known Tiggy's parents for most of her life—and she is the sort of generous, big-hearted girl who gives everyone hugs and kisses.

The hate campaign, which involved a series of disturbing messages left on Tiggy's answering machine, culminated at the Lanesborough Hotel in Knightsbridge in 1995. It was the combined staff Christmas lunch party, which the Prince and Princess continued to attend together even after their divorce. Tiggy had recently been in hospital for a minor operation, and before everyone sat down, Diana allegedly sidled up to her and whispered in her ear, 'So sorry about the baby'.

The implication that she'd had an abortion was unmistakable. Tiggy reeled in shock and disbelief and Michael Fawcett, the Prince's valet, took her home, while the party continued in high spirits, ending in a rather drunken crazy-foam fight. No one seemed to be enjoying it more than Diana. A letter from Tiggy's lawyers arrived four days later, and although she never received the apology she demanded, she let the matter go.

Diana continued to obsess about Tiggy, who in her mind had taken over from Camilla in her ex-husband's affections. She appeared to have come up with the fanciful idea that Camilla was just a smoke screen and that the real woman he loved and wanted to marry was the nanny. When she discovered that Tiggy (now only working part-time since the boys were at school for much of the year) had helped Charles with the invitations to William's confirmation, in March 1997, she went through the roof. She threatened not to go to the service herself if 'that woman' was going to be there.

What should have been a joyous and spiritually meaningful occasion for Prince William turned out to be another family nightmare.

On arrival at Eton every boy has to sign the school register and state their religious denomination. William was not the first small boy who had to ask his father what denomination he was, although he was the only one who will one day become the church's Supreme Governor. He had been a regular churchgoer all his life and there were weekly chapel services at Ludgrove, as there were at Eton, but, like most small boys, it was a routine he had never thought too much about. Confirmation was another routine he went into with most of the other Anglicans in his year. They all went to classes with the college chaplain, the Reverend T.D. Mullins, but while they were confirmed in College Chapel, he was confirmed separately at St George's Chapel, Windsor Castle.

Sir Laurens van der Post had died a few months earlier, but all five of William's remaining godparents were there, as were the Queen, the Queen Mother and both his parents, who, unusually, arrived for the service in one car with the Prince driving, Diana sitting beside him and William and Harry in the back. After the service, the group posed for an official photograph, and Ian Jones, who was attached to the *Daily Telegraph* and had been photographing the family for nearly ten years, was invited to take it. He was given three minutes, and owes the success of the picture to the Queen. The seating plan was a delicate matter, which he left to the Palace, but when he looked through the lens of his camera he realised that the second row was standing too far back. As he wrestled with the protocol of addressing several

Royal Highnesses, a few Your Majesties and many Lords and Ladies, the Queen looked behind her and said, 'Come on, come on, all move forward or you'll all be out of focus.' Then turning to Ian she said, 'You see, I know a thing or two about photography!' It had a wonderfully relaxing effect on the whole group and when Ian was finished, the Queen said, 'Is that it? That's very good. Snowdon [the professional photographer once married to Princess Margaret] always takes thirty minutes.' It was the first time in four years that the Wales family had posed together—and it was to be the last.

Tradition dictates that the Archbishop of Canterbury presides over all matters spiritual relating to the Royal Family, but Charles, a deeply spiritual man with views that are as firm about religion as they are about everything else, wanted his old friend and Cambridge contemporary, the Bishop of London, the Right Reverend Richard Chartres to conduct the service. Unlike Archbishop Carey, Chartres was a traditionalist who, like Charles, abhorred the 'happy clappy' evangelical wing of the Church and stuck firmly to the sixteenth-century Book of Common Prayer.

Tiggy was not among the forty members of the congregation. The Duke of Edinburgh was excusably away on a foreign tour, but another sad and glaring omission was William's grandmother, Frances Shand Kydd. Diana was going through a phase of not speaking to her mother and had chosen not to invite her; in fact, she was asked to invite forty people and invited no one. When asked why she was not there, Frances had said, 'I'm not the person to ask. You should ask the offices of William's parents. I don't want to talk about it.' Instead, she placed a notice in the newsletter of Oban Cathedral (she had recently converted to Roman Catholicism), which read, 'For my grandson William on his confirmation day, love from Granny Frances.'

William's love for his mother would never be diminished; in his eyes she was and remains the perfect mother; but he was not blind to her behaviour and as a teenager beginning to make his own judgements and to step away from the parental yoke, he must have found some of her antics embarrassing and hard to handle, particularly when they caused evident pain to people he loved. He also disliked profoundly the media attention that she courted.

But when it came to choosing who to invite to the Fourth of June, Eton's equivalent of speech day, William asked Tiggy and told his parents that he didn't want them to come. Tiggy arrived with William's friend, William van Cutsem, bearing a wonderful picnic and plenty of drinks.

When it was over, William went home to his mother for half-term, and found her in tears. She was distraught that he wanted Tiggy to be at the

Fourth of June and not her, and as was her way, swiftly let the media know her feelings.

A month later, after the end of the summer term, Diana took William and Harry plus their two PPOs—at her request, she no longer had one herself—on holiday to the South of France. She had been invited by Mohamed Al Fayed, the wealthy Egyptian owner of Harrods department store, to spend some time with him and his family in St Tropez. William wasn't thrilled to be going back to that part of the world: they had had a disastrous holiday on the French Riviera the previous summer when they had shared a villa with Fergie, the Duchess of York, and his cousins, Princess Beatrice and Eugenie. The paparazzi were everywhere and William spent most of his time hiding indoors.

Al Fayed promised total privacy. He would collect them from Kensington Palace in his private helicopter, take them to his home in Surrey for lunch with his family, then his private Gulfstream 4 jet would take the entire party to Nice, where they would pick up a private yacht for the last leg of the journey to St Tropez. There they would alternate between his sumptuous villa on the coast, which was closely guarded, and his boats, including the newly acquired £14 million yacht, *Jonikal*.

On the third day Diana was spotted on board Al Fayed's 1912 teak schooner by a paparazzo who sold his picture to a Sunday tabloid. For the rest of the holiday the whole town was crawling with photographers. Their principal interest was the burgeoning romance between Diana and Al Fayed's eldest son, Dodi.

Diana was on the rebound. For two years she had been having an affair with Hasnat Khan, a Pakistan-born heart surgeon, whom she'd met while visiting a friend at the Royal Brompton Hospital. She spent time with him at his small flat in Chelsea and he became a regular visitor to Kensington Palace. Friends say she was very much in love with him and wanted to marry him; she even contemplated converting to Islam and moving to Pakistan. But he ended it just weeks before she went to France. As he told his father, 'If I married her, our marriage would not last for more than a year. We are culturally so different from each other. She is from Venus and I am from Mars. If it ever happened, it would be like a marriage from two different planets.'

She made a point of introducing him to William, who, like most children of divorced parents, never much enjoyed meeting her lovers. Harry was always more relaxed about it, but William didn't really want to know. According to Diana's friend Rosa Monckton, 'She told Prince William in particular more than most mothers would have told their children. But she had no choice. She wanted her sons to hear the truth from her, about her life and the people she was seeing, and what they meant to her, rather than read a distorted, exaggerated and frequently untrue version in the tabloid press.'

That same tabloid press, it must be remembered, to which Diana herself incessantly fed stories and most of the time, they compliantly ate out of her hand. She was in regular contact with the *Daily Mail*'s good-looking reporter, Richard Kay, ringing him just hours before she died; and she had invited most of the tabloid editors to lunch at KP where she had been hugely indiscreet. On at least one occasion, William joined them.

However, not even Diana was immune to the British delight in bringing down to size the people they have hoisted onto pedestals. When she went back to St Tropez on her own with Dodi a couple of weeks later and the two were photographed entwined on his father's yacht, it was too much for the commentators.

'The sight of a paunchy playboy groping a scantily-dressed Diana must appal and humiliate Prince William,' wrote the late Lynda Lee-Potter, doyenne of columnists, in the *Daily Mail*. 'As the mother of two young sons she ought to have more decorum and sense.'

'Princess Diana's press relations are now clearly established,' wrote Bernard Ingham, Margaret Thatcher's former press officer, in the *Express*. 'Any publicity is good publicity . . . I'm told she and Dodi are made for each other, both having more brass than brains.'

And Chris Hutchins, in the *Sunday Mirror*, wrote, 'Just when Diana began to believe that her current romance with likeable playboy Dodi Fayed had wiped out her past liaisons, a new tape recording is doing the rounds of Belgravia dinner parties. And this one is hot, hot, hot! I must remember to take it up with Diana next time we find ourselves on adjacent running machines at our west London gym.'

Charles, like everyone else at court, was very concerned about Diana's love affair with Dodi. Not because he didn't want her to be happy but because Mohamed Al Fayed was a controversial figure. Long denied British citizenship, he had tried relentlessly to ingratiate himself with the establishment. What could be a better two-fingered salute to them now than to pair his son off with the former Princess of Wales? Or what better trophy to show off to the world than a photograph of him on his yacht with the Queen's grandsons? He didn't keep his delight under a bushel.

William and Harry didn't enjoy their holiday. They hadn't particularly taken to Dodi Fayed, nor cared much for the glitzy lifestyle, and they hated the publicity. William and his mother had a terrible row; Harry got into a spat with Mohamed Al Fayed's youngest son, Omar; and Fayed's heavies had attempted to give their PPOs brown envelopes stuffed with pound notes. The whole trip had been extremely uncomfortable.

It was with huge relief that they flew back to England to spend the remainder of the holidays with their father, their grandparents and other members of the Royal Family. After a lunch for the Queen Mother's ninety-seventh birthday at Clarence House, they joined *Britannia*—a far cry from *Jonikal*—for her last-ever cruise of the Western Isles before being decommissioned. Then it was Balmoral and the peace of the Highlands and a month doing all the countryside things they loved best.

But first they had to endure a couple of photo calls with their father. Sandy Henney, the Prince's Press Secretary, had promised editors that she would give them good pictures of the Princes and in return they would not use paparazzi shots. She then had the unenviable task of organising the photos: one for the daily papers, the other for the Sundays. 'The first one, William did not want to do it,' she recalls. 'It's not true to say that he didn't like the press after his mother died; he didn't like them before that. The three of them were at a particular cabin on the banks of the River Dee and they were going to walk down along the shore. William had his dog, Widgeon, the sister of Hercules, Tiggy's dog. I said, "All you have to do is come down to the shore and walk along. I promise you the press are not going to shout questions—they're too frightened to (joke). All you have to do is throw a couple of stones in the river, or whatever."

'The dog saved the day. William was throwing sticks for him and you could see Harry was egging his brother along. The Prince of Wales is just the master because he's lived with it all his life, but the reluctance is there. A week later we did one for the Sunday papers at some weir. I was wracking my brains. So I said to Tiggs, "Have you got any ideas?" And she said, "Christ no, let's go out in one of the jeeps with Harry." And he was hanging off the back of the jeep like kids do and he said, "I've got a couple of ideas. How about doing this one, this one and this one." I said, "Not sure that would work, Harry." "I've got another idea," so off we go. The third idea was brilliant, it was all Harry's. There was a salmon ladder in the river. "Okay Harry, how are you going to make this one work?" "Well, William and I can run down here . . ." and Tiggy's up there with a fag, and Harry's clambering down and I'm thinking, Oh my God, we're about to lose Number Two, and he came up and he said, "Right that's what we're going to do." And I said, "Well done, Harry, that's going to work. Now you've got to sell it to your father and your brother" and bless this kid's heart; what was he, eleven? Coming up twelve? He briefed the Prince, my boss. I had the radio and we were on the other side of the weir with the press and I said, "Right," to the police, "get them to get out of the car and walk down and Harry will take it from there"; and you could see him directing his father—you couldn't hear because of the noise of the weir—but Harry directed the whole thing and it worked. He was brilliant.'

# TRAGEDY IN PARIS

The first call alerting the Royal Family to Diana's accident, less than three weeks after that photo call, came through to Balmoral at one o'clock on the morning of Sunday 31 August 1997. Later that day, William and Harry had been due to fly to London and Tiggy Legge-Bourke had, as the Queen said, 'by the grace of God,' just arrived to accompany them. The holidays were almost over and Diana was flying back from Paris to spend the last few days with the boys, as she always did before the start of the new term.

The call came through to Sir Robin Janvrin, then the Queen's Deputy Private Secretary, who was fast asleep in his house on the estate. It was from the British ambassador in Paris, who had only sketchy news. There had been a car crash. Dodi Fayed, with whom Diana had been travelling, had been killed, although there was no confirmation. Diana had been injured but no one knew how badly. Their car had smashed into the support pillars of a tunnel under the Seine. It had been travelling at high speed while trying to escape a group of paparazzi in pursuit on motorbikes.

Janvrin immediately woke the Queen and the Prince of Wales in their rooms at the Castle. He then phoned the Prince's Assistant Private Secretary, Nick Archer, who was in another house on the estate, as well as the Queen's equerry and PPOs. They agreed to meet in the offices at the Castle, where they set up an operations room and manned the phones throughout the night.

Meanwhile, in London, the Prince's team were being woken and told the news, ironically, by the tabloid press. The first call to Mark Bolland, the Prince's Deputy Private Secretary, came at the same time as the Embassy was on to Janvrin. It was from the *News of the World*. Having had a very good dinner, Bolland let the answering machine take the call and it was only when he heard the voice of Stuart Higgins, then editor of the *Sun*, saying something about an accident that he picked up the phone. Higgins had the same story as the Embassy. Higgins then rang Sandy Henney, the Prince's Press Secretary, who had just hosted a 40th birthday dinner for her sister-in-law. His call was closely followed by one from Clive Goodman from the *News of the World*. Bolland alerted Stephen Lamport, the Prince's Private Secretary, and within minutes the lines between London and Scotland were buzzing.

Plans were underway to get the Prince on a flight to Paris as soon as possible to visit Diana in hospital, when the Embassy rang at 3.45 with an update. It was left to Robin Janvrin to ring the Prince and let him know his plans would have to change. 'Sir, I am very sorry to have to tell you, I've just had the ambassador on the phone. The Princess died a short time ago.' She had sustained terrible chest and head injuries and lost consciousness very soon after the impact and never regained it. She was treated in the wreckage of the Mercedes at the scene for about an hour and was then taken to the Pitié-Salpêtrière Hospital four miles away, where surgeons fought for a further two hours to save her life, but in vain.

The Prince's first thought was for the children. Should he wake them or let them sleep and tell them in the morning? He was absolutely dreading it, and didn't know what to do for the best. The Queen felt strongly that they should be left to sleep and he took her advice and didn't wake them up until 7.15; but while they were sleeping, he sneaked into the nursery and removed their radios and televisions from their rooms, in case they woke up early and switched one of them on. William had a difficult night's sleep and woke up many times. He knew, he said, that something awful was going to happen.

There was much discussion about how Charles was going to get to Paris to bring home Diana's body. She was no longer a member of the Royal Family, therefore it was not automatic that a plane of the Queen's Flight should be made available. 'What would you rather, Ma'am,' asked Robin Janvrin, 'that she come back in a Harrods' van?' That clinched it: 'Operation Overlord' went into action, a plan that had been in existence for years but never previously needed—the return of a body of a member of the Royal Family to London. There was a BAe146 plane earmarked for the purpose, which could be airborne at short notice from RAF Northolt.

At 10 a.m. it was in the air with the Prince's London team—Lamport, Bolland and Henney—on its way to Aberdeen, via RAF Wittering in Rutland, where it collected Diana's sisters, Lady Sarah McCorquodale, who lived nearby, and Lady Jane Fellowes. Charles had telephoned Robert Fellowes, who had broken the news to Diana's sisters, and they both wanted to travel with him.

He decided that this was not a trip for the children and so they stayed at Balmoral with Tiggy. When he saw their mother's body, laid out in a coffin which had been flown to Paris earlier in the day, as part of Operation Overlord, he was glad he'd left them behind; it would have been too distressing for them. Paul Burrell, Diana's remaining butler, had flown out earlier and dressed her but her head had been badly damaged in the crash and her face was distorted.

Diana's sisters and Charles stayed with the body for seven minutes. The girls left sobbing; Charles, his eyes red and his face racked with pain, stopped for a moment to compose himself, then, as someone watching remarked, 'Went from human being to Windsor', as nearly fifty years of training ensured he would. A small crowd was waiting in the corridor, most of them hospital staff whose hands he shook and thanked sincerely for everything they had done. And when he heard that the parents of the sole survivor of the crash, Al Fayed's bodyguard, Trevor Rees-Jones, were at the hospital, he immediately said he must talk to them.

On the flight home, with the coffin draped in the maroon and yellow of the Royal Standard, the Prince wanted to know what arrangements had been made at the other end. It had been an emotional and moving drive through Paris where thousands of people thronged the streets, their heads bowed in silence. He was told who would be among the welcoming committee at Northolt, which included Tony Blair, the Prime Minister, and that the Princess would be taken to the mortuary in Fulham, commonly used by the Royal Coroner.

The Prince put his foot down. 'Who decided that?' he said. 'Nobody asked me. Diana is going to the Chapel Royal at St James's Palace. Sort it. I don't care who has made this decision. She is going to the Chapel Royal.'

It was sorted out in a series of heated telephone conversations from the plane, and when they touched down at Northolt the rest followed seamlessly. Diana's sisters travelled with the body to the Chapel Royal and Charles took a flight back to Balmoral to be with William and Harry.

It was only as the hearse and its entourage crawled down the A40 and into west London that the enormity of what had happened began to dawn on the Palace staff. The motorway, the bridges and embankment—and when those ran out, the roads and pavements—were full of cars and people who had come to watch and weep as Diana's coffin passed by. Tributes had started pouring in from all over the world, and flowers were being laid at the gate of every building with which Diana was associated.

This, they realised, was going to be unlike anything anyone had ever seen before.

# THE WEEK THE COUNTRY WAITED

How the Prince of Wales broke the news to his sons and how they reacted will remain between the three of them, though the memory of it will no doubt haunt him until the day he dies. Suffice to say that in a lifetime spent comforting the bereaved and being steadfast in the face of tragedy, nothing could have come close to the pain of that moment. Any parent who has ever had to tell their unsuspecting children that the woman who gave them life will never be coming home will share his pain. Just as any child who has been sat down by a red-eyed, tear-stained father and told their mother is dead will identify with William and Harry. The gut-wrenching shock, the terror, the disbelief, the impossible concept that the mother they adore will never again light up the room with her laughter, never again hold her arms wide for a reassuring hug, never again ruffle their hair . . . will never again *be* there is too much to absorb.

And for Charles too. For all the difficulties and exasperation and anger he sometimes felt towards his ex-wife, she was the mother of his children and as such he had always loved her and continued to worry about her. They had even started talking civilly again since their divorce, and she had been much more reasonable. She was always in his prayers. His faith runs deep and has always been an important part of his make-up. He will have drawn on it on that terrible day and no doubt used it to comfort his children. He firmly believes in life after death and sees death as 'the next great journey in our existence'; a mystery and a painful parting but not something to fear. As he once said at a Macmillan Fund anniversary, 'The seasons of the year provided for our ancestors a lesson which could not be ignored; that life is surely followed by death, but also that death can be seen as a doorway to renewed life. In Christianity the message is seen in the mystery of resurrection, and in the picture of Christ as a seed dying in the ground in order to produce the new life that supplies bread, and sustenance.'

Diana also believed in life after death. She frequently consulted mediums and clairvoyants; and she was quite certain that her paternal grandmother, Cynthia, Lady Spencer, who had died in 1972 when Diana was a child, kept guard over her in the spirit world.

William, newly confirmed, will also have had his faith to draw on; he too, will have understood that life on earth is just the beginning and that death is no more than a temporary separation from those we love. But no amount of belief can take away the agony of loss, the hollowness, the numbness, the inevitable rewind of last conversations, last thoughts, last memories, the what ifs, the words left unsaid and the guilt.

That morning at Balmoral everyone's focus was on William and Harry and how best to help them get through the day and handle their feelings of loss. They were surrounded by a loving and supportive and probably rather inspirational group of people and both boys were very close to their grandparents. Their grandmother has always found grief difficult to handle, but the Duke of Edinburgh will have been a pillar of strength to them both. His early life was punctuated by loss. By the age of seventeen his mother had been admitted to a mental asylum, his father had virtually disappeared from his life, one of his sisters and her entire family had been killed in a plane crash and his guardian and favourite uncle had died of cancer. For all his bluff exterior, he understood grief.

William said he wanted to go to church 'to talk to Mummy', and Harry and he were as one, so the Queen took the boys and the rest of the family to the little kirk at Crathie, where she is a regular Sunday morning worshipper while at Balmoral. For those who have been brought up with religion in their lives, as they all had, there is something deeply comforting in the traditional ritual and language of a church service.

The secular media didn't see it that way. They were outraged that Diana's children should have been taken to church—one newspaper called it a public relations exercise—and they were even more outraged that the minister should have made no mention of the Princess in his prayers. And they blamed the Queen for it. The Reverend Robert Sloan, rightly or wrongly, had decided it might be less upsetting for Diana's sons if he didn't mention her name. 'My thinking,' he told reporters, 'was that the children had been wakened just a few hours before and told of their mother's death.' What irked the media the most was that not one member of the Royal Family displayed so much as a wobbling chin on their outing to church.

Diana's death was perceived as a national tragedy and in a week that saw the most unprecedented (and to some, entirely incomprehensible) outpouring of public grief, the nation, encouraged by the media, wanted to see and hear from the Queen. At every other national disaster, she or a member of her family were the first to visit, the first to offer words of commiseration and comfort, and to be present alongside ordinary people, doing what royals do best, spearheading national sentiment, representing the nation to itself. And yet, in this greatest hour of need, there was no sign of them. And there was no indication that they were as grief-stricken as the rest of the country. In the remoteness of the Scottish Highlands, wrapped up in the needs of two fragile young boys, and pulling together as a family, their antennae for the mood elsewhere in the country were not functioning as they normally do. The Queen, rationally but mistakenly, viewed it as a private tragedy and decided her priority was her grandsons. And in human terms, who is to say she was wrong?

The Prime Minister, Tony Blair, got it right. That Sunday morning he paid a moving tribute to Diana that entirely caught the mood of the nation. His voice cracking with emotion he said, 'I feel like everyone else in this country. I am utterly devastated. We are a nation in a state of shock, in mourning, in grief. It is so deeply painful for us. She was a wonderful and a warm human being. Though her own life was often sadly touched by tragedy, she touched the lives of so many others in Britain and throughout the world, with joy and with comfort. She was the people's Princess and that is how she will remain in our hearts and memories for ever.'

Whatever the psychological and sociological explanations for the nation's reaction to Diana's death might be, there was not only grief but also anger on the streets of London. Some of it was directed at the tabloid press, for paying huge sums of money for paparazzi photographs (conveniently forgetting that if the tabloid-reading public didn't buy the tabloids there would be no paparazzi). Some of the anger was directed at the

Royal Family, so clearly out of touch and anachronistic in modern Britain; and the rest was directed at Charles. One of his first thoughts on hearing the news of Diana's death was that he would be blamed, and he was right. Had he loved her instead of his mistress, they said, this would never have happened. They would still have been married and Diana would never have been racing through the streets of Paris with Dodi Fayed. Yet at the same time others were leaving tributes to the lovers outside Kensington Palace. 'To Diana and Dodi, together for ever' was a common message.

While William and Harry had been with their father, Diana had gone back to the South of France and she and Dodi had spent the previous nine days on *Jonikal*. The photographs of them entwined were what had led the columnists in London to sharpen their pens. On their way back to London, they had stopped in Paris for the night, where Dodi's father owned the Ritz hotel, and also an apartment. The accident happened as they were being driven from one to the other. In an attempt to fool the paparazzi, a decoy car had sped away from the front entrance of the hotel, while Dodi and Diana left from the back, but they were soon spotted and a chase ensued.

No blame was ever levelled at Dodi, or even his father, who had provided the car. It was his employee, Henri Paul, the chauffeur, who had been driving well over the speed limit when he hit the Alma underpass. None of them had been wearing seat belts, and Paul was killed at the wheel. An eighteen-month French judicial investigation concluded that it was he—and not the paparazzi—who was to blame for the crash. He had a cocktail of alcohol, anti-depressants and traces of a tranquillising anti-psychotic drug in his blood and should never have been behind the wheel of a car that night.

In the meantime Mohamed Al Fayed did nothing to stop rumours that the pair were about to announce their engagement—and there were (false) rumours that Diana was pregnant. He also shared his own private theory about the crash with the media. It was, he suggested, a conspiracy cooked up by the Duke of Edinburgh and the British security services to assassinate Diana so that she would not marry Dodi, because such a marriage would have given William, second in line to the throne, a Muslim stepfather. All these allegations and more would be dealt with in subsequent enquiries and inquests.

But for the time being, there was a funeral to be arranged and a public relations disaster to be averted, one which threatened the very existence of the monarchy.

# YOU CAN'T
# READ ABOUT THIS

The family was getting news of the mood in London, and advice from every quarter—politicians, friends, historians and VIPs from all over the world—and the newspapers were screaming at them to come back to the capital: 'They're up in bloody Scotland' was the common cry, or 'They should be here. Those children should be here.' The absence of a flag flying at Buckingham Palace became another focus for anger. While flags were flying at half mast all over the country, at the Queen's official London residence there was nothing; just mountains of flowers piling up outside. 'Show us you care,' demanded the *Express*. 'Your subjects are suffering, speak to us Ma'am,' said the *Mirror*. 'Where is our Queen? Where is her flag?' shouted the *Sun*.

It was a problem of protocol. The only flag that flies at Buckingham Palace is the Royal Standard and only then when the sovereign is in residence, and it never flies at half mast because, technically, the sovereign is never dead: the instant one dies, another succeeds—'The King is dead, long live the King.'

The people didn't give a damn about protocol. They wanted to see some feeling, some indication that the Royal Family was affected by the death of the Princess. There had been none, and this most elementary of gestures, the lowering of a flag, had not been observed. To the press and to the nation this embodied everything that was irrelevant and out of touch about the monarchy in the 1990s, and stood in stark contrast to the warmth and compassion of the Princess. It caused a furious row internally and in the heat of the moment it was suggested that Sir Robert Fellowes might 'impale himself on his own flag staff'. Eventually, the Queen was persuaded and on the Thursday a Union flag was raised to half mast.

While the headlines ranted and the leaders thundered, entire forests were devoted to the saintliness of the Princess, and for those papers that had been attacking her just days before for her antics in the Mediterranean, it involved a dramatic U-turn. 'She was the butterfly who shone with the light of glamour which illuminated all our lives', said the *Express*; 'A comet streaked across the sky of public life and entranced the world', said the *Times*, and the *Daily Mail* called her 'A gem of purest ray serene.'

The Prince of Wales, via Stephen Lamport, was getting graphic updates on what was happening on the streets from Sandy Henney, his Press Secretary. 'You can't read about this,' she said, 'you can't even see it on television. There is real hatred building up here, and the public is incensed by your silence.' But, although some were urging him to make a statement, Charles recognised that he was not the one to take the lead. On the Tuesday, the *Daily Mail* headline read, 'Charles weeps bitter tears of guilt', printed above a photograph of him taken some months before. The Royal Family was appalled and from that morning onwards they stopped putting the newspapers out on display at the Castle. He knew that any public expression of sadness from him would be a red rag to a bull, but as the days went by and the anger mounted, and his mother's advisers still saw no need to put on a public display of emotion, he became more forceful.

He also realised that the boys needed to be prepared for what awaited them when they went back to London—the mountains of flowers and tributes, the crowds, the emotion—and asked Sandy to come up to Balmoral to speak to them, as he often did, when there was something confrontational or difficult to impart. A week or so before, he had asked her up to Birkhall, the Queen Mother's home on the Balmoral estate, where Charles himself often stayed, to speak to William.

The Prince did not, however, ask Sandy to Balmoral in order to talk the boys into walking behind the cortège at the funeral, as Alastair Campbell claimed in his diaries, *The Blair Years*. The Prime Minister's former spin doctor believes that the Prince was frightened that if he walked without William, he might be attacked by members of the public. His theory is that Sandy persuaded the Princes that their mother would have wanted them to do it. Initially, he said, William's hatred of the media was so great that he refused to talk to anyone about taking part in the funeral, and saw walking as appeasing the media.

'At no time,' Sandy says, 'was there ever a question of using the boys as a barrier against possible reaction from the public towards my boss. But there was genuine concern as to what reaction the public might have to the Prince of Wales—and indeed any member of the Royal Family from a highly emotionally (some may say irrationally) charged public. The boys talked about walking with the cortège to close members of their family and only those they trusted, and no one they talked to at that time would ever speak to a third party about what the children said.' I think Mr Campbell might be that third party she's referring to.

Sandy needed to explain to the boys the extraordinary scenes they could expect to see on the streets of London. 'I was going up and down these queues of people [waiting to sign the books of condolence at St James's Palace],' she remembers, 'and I couldn't believe what I was hearing, the things they were saying about the Queen and the Duke and the Prince. It was verging on hatred for this family.' She was as loyal an advocate of the institution of monarchy as you could hope to find and like most of the people who have worked for the Prince of Wales, she was devoted to him and passionate about his children.

She took them aside and said, 'Mummy's death has had the most amazing impact on people. They are really sad because they loved her very, very much and they miss her, and when you go down to London you will see something you will never, ever, see again and it may come as a bit of a shock. But everything you will see is because the public thought so much of your mummy, it is the sign of their grief for your loss. We want you to know about it so you will be ready for it.' She asked if they wanted to ask any questions and there were many but they were all to do with why she was telling them this, why people were behaving in this way. Harry was the one with the curiosity; William was very quiet and contained.

Later, Sandy was up in the tower at Balmoral, where letters were pouring in by the thousand. 'Harry arrived with Tiggs and said, "What are you doing?" I explained that all of these people wanted to say how sorry they are that your mummy's dead and that they're thinking of you.

' "Can I open some?" said Harry, snatching up some envelopes. "Of course you can. Go on, help yourself." ' She was a motherly figure, with no children of her own, but stepchildren, and she was the perfect person for the sensitive task of coaxing the boys out of their shell. She had worked for their father, and known both boys for four years, but because of Diana's suspicion that everyone who worked for 'the other side' would betray her or let her down, she hadn't had much to do with them. 'Sad,' says Sandy simply. 'Our view [meaning Alan Percival, her predecessor] was that if you let one of them down, you let the children down, but more importantly, you let the institution down.'

William was no longer a young boy, but not yet a man; it was a difficult age. He didn't speak to Sandy about his feelings or his mother, and she never saw a tear; he appeared to internalise the grief, just as he had internalised so much in his life already. He never allowed much of himself to be exposed in all the years she worked with him, from the age of eleven to eighteen, and he was always more guarded than his brother. He was always someone who seemed to be dealing with whatever situation arose in his own way.

'I think he has an innate sense of self-protection,' Sandy says, 'and wouldn't have answered questions about his mother even if I'd asked him. He'd have been polite. He's a politician that man, he can charm people. If you ask him a personal question he will be as honest as he wants to be but you will never get down, thank God, into the real root of William, because that's how he protects himself.'

The day the flag appeared on the roof of Buckingham Palace the family ventured out of the gates of Balmoral for the first time since the day of Diana's death. William and Harry expressed a desire to go to church again so the Prince took the opportunity to give them a small taster of what awaited them in London. The funeral was just two days away. There were hundreds of flowers and tributes, but nothing compared to those that had piled up outside Kensington Palace, where there were said to be a million bouquets and goodness knows how many teddy bears and other offerings, 1.5 metres deep in places. There were almost as many outside Buckingham Palace.

About sixty members of the press were waiting outside the gates of Balmoral that day, a crowd for the Highlands, yet they uttered not a single word as the Queen, the Duke of Edinburgh, Peter Phillips (who had flown up to be with his cousins), the Prince of Wales and his sons stepped out of their cars to look at the flowers and the tributes. The only sound to be heard, apart from the clicking of the camera shutters, was the voices of the royal party. It was the first time in the five days since their mother's death that the country had seen Diana's boys. It was a touching scene. All three Princes, father and sons, were visibly moved by what they saw and taken aback by the messages attached to the bouquets.

'Look at this one, Papa,' said Harry, grabbing

hold of his father's hand and tugging him down. 'Read this one.' Captured on film, the gesture was surprising, if not shocking. The Prince of Wales did seem to have a heart after all. He actually held his son's hand, something no one could ever have imagined before. And he seemed to have aged.

Of all the criticisms Diana threw at the Prince during their bitter war of words, the one that hurt the most was that he was unfeeling and cold. It was patently untrue, as anyone who has seen Charles with his children knows very well. Diana knew it too, and later regretted her words.

The sight of the Prince of Wales and his sons did much to soften the public mood, and when the Queen made a surprising live television broadcast that Friday evening before Saturday's funeral, the mood softened further. The fact that it was only the second time during her reign that she had broadcast to the nation other than at Christmas— the first being during the Gulf War—made it an additionally impressive gesture.

'Since last Sunday's dreadful news we have seen throughout Britain and around the world an overwhelming expression of sadness at Diana's death.

'We have all been trying in our different ways to cope. It is not easy to express a sense of loss, since the initial shock is often succeeded by a mixture of other feelings: disbelief, incomprehension, anger—and concern for all who remain.

'We have all felt those emotions in these last few days. So what I say to you now, as your Queen and as a grandmother, I say from my heart.

'First, I want to pay tribute to Diana myself. She was an exceptional and gifted human being. In good times and bad, she never lost her capacity to smile and laugh, nor to inspire others with her warmth and kindness.

'I admired and respected her—for her energy and commitment to others, and especially for her devotion to her two boys.

'This week at Balmoral, we have all been trying to help William and Harry come to terms with the devastating loss that they and the rest of us have suffered.

'No one who knew Diana will ever forget her. Millions of others who never met her, but felt they knew her, will remember her.

'I for one believe that there are lessons to be drawn from her life and from the extraordinary and moving reaction to her death.'

The Queen's words possibly prevented a revolution.

# THE ENVELOPE

The country might have been angry at the Queen's decision to keep her family in Scotland, but those days spent in the peace and solitude of the Highlands were a godsend to William and Harry.

The boys were the priority and Balmoral was the most sensible place for them to be—far away from prying eyes and long lenses. It is the spiritual home of the Royal Family, where the boys had spent happy summers every year of their lives. It is the place where the Queen instinctively feels relaxed and at ease, where she adopts an informality that is not seen in any of her other residences. They love it there, and in that week when their entire world turned upside down, it offered balm to their broken hearts. The hundreds of acres of heather and wild, craggy moorland, lochs and rivers offered everything they needed; they could go for long walks—as William did for the first two days—he went for long, long walks alone. They could go fishing, stalking, riding, or go-karting; there were picnics and barbecues, when their grandparents did the cooking and everyone mucked in. They were surrounded by all the most important and familiar people in their lives. It was the best possible environment for them both. They could be kept busy or they could be given the space and time to talk, to reminisce, to ask questions and begin to take in the enormity of what had happened. And to prepare for their mother's funeral and another traumatic day.

The funeral was another tinderbox. The Spencer family wanted a small, private funeral, with which the Queen was inclined to agree. The Prince of Wales wanted nothing less than a full royal funeral at Westminster Abbey. As they watched the public reaction intensify, the Spencers came round to his point of view but Charles Spencer wanted to be the only one who walked behind the cortège. The Prince disagreed; he also wanted to walk as a mark of respect to Diana who, after all, had been his wife for fifteen years; and he wanted the boys to walk with him if they so chose. He felt intuitively it was something they should do for their mother and that it would aid the grieving process. Downing Street, meanwhile, wanted a 'People's Funeral' with the public marching behind the coffin.

There was a bitter exchange on the telephone between the Prince of Wales and Earl Spencer in which the Earl hung up on his ex-brother-in-law. Over dinner on the Friday night, when the whole Royal Family was together at Buckingham Palace, the Duke of Edinburgh settled the argument by saying he would walk too. In the end, the three men and two boys all walked together. William had the reassurance of being safely between his father and grandfather.

It was a long walk from St James's Palace, where they joined the cortège, to Westminster Abbey, with every bite of the lip and tremble of the chin exposed to the word's media and the millions of people who had flocked to the city to be there and witness the atmosphere of a unique day. Hundreds had aimlessly walked the streets all night or held candlelit vigils in the parks—even Diana's mother had walked quietly among the mourners, her grief unimaginable. Some brought sleeping bags that were soaked through by torrential rain the afternoon before. No one minded. The sun shone brightly and the anger and slightly menacing atmosphere of the days before were gone. Emotions were still very raw but there was laughter as well as tears. United in their loss, strangers spoke to strangers, as they had seventeen years before when the Royal Wedding had united them in celebration.

They lined the route and filled the streets and the parks, where giant television screens had been erected. The mood was electrifying. People threw flowers as the cortège passed, some cried, some wailed. It was an ordeal that called for huge courage from William and Harry, and they did their mother—and their nation—proud. They walked slowly and steadily, struggling at times to hold back tears, but their composure never wavered, until they were inside the Abbey when at times the music, the poetry and the oratory were too much for them. But by then the cameras were off, forbidden to focus on the family. Both boys displayed a maturity beyond their years, which touched everyone who saw it.

It was an ordeal for their father too. He was desperately worried about whether they would cope with being on such very public view when the day was already going to be difficult enough. There was also the thought that he might be attacked or booed. He knew that many of the people weeping for Diana blamed him; but his fears were unfounded.

The funeral was immensely moving and a masterpiece of organisation, the British monarchy doing what it does best: the precision timing, the military professionalism, the ceremonial pageantry, but mixed with a refreshingly human touch so perfect for Diana—the combination that William winningly reproduced for his wedding day in the same place fourteen years later. Tony Blair read 1 Corinthians 13 and Elton John sang a specially rewritten version of 'Candle in the Wind'.

The most heartbreaking element of the whole day, however, was the white envelope, propped into a bouquet of white freesias, that sat on the top of Diana's coffin with the single handwritten word: MUMMY. Sandy had foreseen that the boys might want to write a note. 'I remember ringing Tiggy. "The boys are going to put some flowers on their mother's coffin?" "Of course." "And they're going to write a note aren't they?" "Yes." "Right, could you do me a favour? Please make sure that whatever they say is in an envelope." "Okay. Why?" "Because one of the first things the cameras are going to do is zoom in on their words."'

Their privacy was fortunately protected, but no

one could protect them from Charles Spencer, their uncle, whose harsh and bitter words marred the day.

'Diana was the very essence of compassion, of duty, of style, of beauty. All over the world she was a symbol of selfless humanity . . .' he said in his tribute. 'Someone with a natural nobility who was classless and who proved in the last year that she needed no royal title to continue to generate her particular brand of magic . . .

'She would want us today to pledge ourselves to protecting her beloved boys William and Harry from a similar fate, and I do this here, Diana, on your behalf. We will not allow them to suffer the anguish that used regularly to drive you to tearful despair.

'And beyond that, on behalf of your mother and my sisters, I pledge that we, your blood family, will do all we can to continue the imaginative way in which you were steering these two exceptional young men so that their souls are not simply immersed by duty and tradition but can sing openly as you planned.'

It was a shocking kick in the teeth, on the day their mother was buried, to the people that William and Harry, now motherless, loved most: their father and their grandparents who were sitting just a few feet away from him in the Abbey.

There was gentle applause from a few of those sitting inside the Abbey, but he was loudly cheered by the thousands listening on the sound relay outside. And, I can only conclude, he was also cheered by the millions more watching the funeral service on their television sets at home. I was interviewed by ITN, at their temporary studio at Canada Gate, next to Buckingham Palace, where I had listened to the tribute, and was asked what I thought of it. I said I had every sympathy with the Earl, who was clearly distraught by the loss of his sister, but I thought it very inappropriate: this was neither the time nor the place to say the things he said. The switchboard at ITN was instantly jammed with angry callers and the producer was told to get me out of the studio right away.

What offended the Prince of Wales most was being forced to sit and be lectured about parental responsibility by a man who'd had a disastrous marriage of his own and who had brought his latest mistress to the funeral.

While Diana's coffin was driven slowly to her ancestral home in Northampton, past thousands of spectators on the roadside, the Prince of Wales, William and Harry and the Spencers all made the journey in the Royal Train to the private burial service on an island in the middle of a lake. She had said she wanted to be interred in the family crypt at Great Brington, but it was deemed that the small churchyard in the village would be unable to cope with the number of visitors. There are some, however, who believe that her body was, in fact, quietly placed alongside her father's and that of her beloved grandmother, Cynthia, at Great Brington.

Having denied Diana the cottage she asked for on the estate for fear of the media attention it would attract, it seems ironic that Charles Spencer should have turned Althorp into a Mecca, with the old stable block fashioned into a permanent exhibition called 'Diana: A Celebration', and for £30 for a family ticket, the world and his wife are welcome to visit.

In the aftermath of the funeral, Earl Spencer was feted for his speech and the Prince of Wales criticised for having forced his sons to walk behind the cortège. Sandy Henney very nearly came to blows with Stuart Higgins, editor of the *Sun*, over his refusal to believe it was the boys' own choice. 'When she died, the country may have lost a Princess but two young boys had lost their mum and I'll never forget saying to Stuart, who I actually like a lot, "Who is anyone, to tell those boys what they should do? I'm sick of this, Our Princess has died." Their MUM has died; they should choose where they walk. All this nonsense of the children being forced to protect Charles. Right up until the last minute when the boys decided to walk behind the coffin, there was a plan that if they couldn't do it—entirely their choice—I would go, take them from the Prince's apartment at St James's, across to Clarence House and they would go to the funeral with their great-grandmother. It was their choice and it angered me because everyone was deciding what should happen to their mum.'

## GETTING ON WITH THE DAY

Charles took William and Harry home to Highgrove after the funeral. No one could have better understood the pain they were going through than he, and he will have been able to draw on his own experience as they struggled to make sense of all that had happened in the last week. He had never lost a mother, obviously, but he had endured the loss of the man he called his 'honorary grandfather' and the memory of that dark time, and the feelings of loss that never go away, were all too familiar to him. Charles was not a child when it happened, but Lord Mountbatten's murder was as sudden and violent as Diana's and Charles had taken a long time to come to terms with it.

He was grateful that Tiggy was there to help keep their spirits up and to deal with all the last-minute back-to-school chores. She was a vital ingredient in the mix of sensitive and supportive people the boys had around them at that time; likewise their PPOs, who were one hundred per cent trustworthy, had known them all their lives and were like older brothers. And there were those from the Prince's private office, particularly Sandy, who supported them professionally. The staff at Highgrove ensured that life carried on as normal, except that no newspapers were brought into the house. Since Diana hadn't lived at Highgrove for some years, her absence from it was not a constant reminder.

From the very start, both boys appeared to be in remarkable control. With school starting just a few days later, they were soon enveloped in their academic and sporting routines; the Barbers taking care of Harry at Ludgrove, and the remarkable Andrew Gailey keeping a close watch on William at Eton. The presence of his grandparents across the bridge was another crucial factor. He became particularly close to the Queen, but also to his grandfather, and their weekly conversations were a source of comfort and inspiration.

Another important person who came into their lives after their mother's death was Mark Dyer, an ex-Welsh Guards officer, whom colleagues describe as a Captain Hurricane figure. He was taken on as a male Tiggy. He and Tiggy, who were old friends, were partners in crime and were as devoted to the boys as the boys were to them, but again it is Harry who has the closer bond. Mark had worked as an equerry to the Prince of Wales when the children were younger, and Charles had asked if he could come back to help them through this difficult period. 'He was a rugby player, a good egg,' says one of the Prince's team. 'He's a very straightforward, hard-drinking, hard-living adventurer, and a great soldier. He was also somebody the Princes could relate to at that age; and they remembered him from their childhood when he'd shown them guns and tanks and things and taken them rock climbing. The press thought he was a bad influence but he did a bloody good job for them. He had huge integrity, and he was around when they needed advice that didn't come from their father.'

But what probably helped the boys more than anything was having each other. They are such very good friends and so close that even today, the people who work for the Princes find it hard to think of them as separate entities. It is a closeness brought about in part because of their unique situation. They grew up not knowing who they could trust, who to attach themselves to, who would be there next week, who would be gone. They were unnerved by the shouting of photographers and the lurid headlines and stories about their mother and father. They had no shortage of love but life was full of uncertainties. What they could be certain of was each other; and long before their mother's death, the early sibling rivalries and irritations were gone and they came to rely on each other, almost to parent each other. There was no one else who knew what they knew, who had heard what they'd heard, seen what they'd seen, felt what they had felt. After Diana's death, the bond between them was their lifeline and they clung to it. And despite being the younger, Harry, the more adventurous and outgoing of the two, was as much a support to William as the other way round.

On the Monday after the funeral, Tiggy took both boys out to follow the Beaufort hunt on foot. On seeing them arrive at the meet, Captain Ian Farquhar, who as Master had known the boys and their father for as long as they had been living at Highgrove, went over to them and, speaking on behalf of the entire field, said very simply, 'It's good to see you, sirs. I just want you to know that we are all very, very sorry about your mother. You have our deepest sympathy and we were all incredibly proud of you on Saturday. That's all I'm going to say, and now we're going to get on with the day.'

'Thank you,' said William. 'Yes, you're right. We all need to get on with the day.'

Whether by nurture or nature, both boys had the Windsor ability to keep their emotions hidden. William, in particular, as a teenager, had been embarrassed by some of his mother's public outpourings. By contrast, he had watched his father and the way he conducted himself so stoically, no matter what disaster had befallen him; and his grandmother, whose neutral expression is legendary. The Duke of Edinburgh, another stoic, had been dismayed by Charles's tears when Lord Mountbatten died, and ever eager to win his father's approval, he has scarcely let an eye well up publicly since. Behind closed doors he is a deeply emotional man who is easily moved to tears—and also to laughter. And behind closed doors the Queen is a delightfully astute and funny woman who inspires utter loyalty and utter devotion.

Stoicism, fortitude, self-restraint; all these very British qualities that the Windsors hold so dear are now outdated. But they are the qualities that have made the Queen such a universally loved and admired sovereign. We like the fact that after sixty years on the throne, we still don't know anything about her. We know that she likes dogs, pigeons and horses and that she rides without a hard hat. We know nothing about her politics, her faith (except in broadest outline), her fears or foibles. And because we don't know what she thinks or how she behaves in private, we can't disagree with her or disapprove. We can't take exception or offence as we can with politicians, churchmen, broadcasters, businessmen, footballers and leaders in every field, but we can't take against the Queen. Of course there will be those who ideologically disagree with the institution, but that is different. And usually, even Republicans respect her.

We live in a world that is far removed from the Queen's; where celebrities queue up to share their innermost secrets with millions of strangers, and where crying in public is a sign that you care. The public reaction to Diana's death epitomised the new age. Months later, counsellors were still treating people unable to come to terms with their grief. Diana had shared *her* innermost secrets with them and that was part of her magic and her appeal. The public identified with her suffering and fed from it, just as she was sustained by the love of millions of strangers. But hers was not the only way of communicating.

There are many thousands of people who have been visited by the Queen after floods, famines or disasters, who will tell you that she is very far from cold and that the visit did wonders for their morale. But the perception in those touchy-feely days when Diana had such a hold on the world was that the rest of the Windsors were glacial, aloof and out of touch.

After Diana's death the Prince of Wales rightly foresaw a backlash against the Royal Family and he kept his head below the parapet for several weeks; indeed he was terrified of raising it. When he did, it was a visit to Manchester that culminated at a Salvation Army drop-in centre in one of the most notorious estates in the city. No one knew what to expect. His office had written a speech, which he discarded, and acting on instinct, as he often did, he walked into a hall full of cameras and delivered the most touching, brave, tear-jerking tribute to the courage of his sons and to the public, who had shown such kindness in what had been an unbelievably difficult time. He won the respect and sympathy of millions.

'I think they are handling a very difficult time with enormous courage and the greatest possible dignity,' he said. 'I also want to say how particularly moved and enormously comforted my children and I were, and indeed still are, by the public's response to Diana's death. It has been really quite remarkable and indeed in many ways overwhelming. I think, as many of you will know from experiences of family loss in your own lives, it is inevitably difficult to cope with grief at any time. But you may realise, it is even harder when the whole world is watching at the same time. But obviously the public support, and the warmth of that support, has helped us enormously. I can't tell you how enormously grateful and touched both the boys and myself are.'

The possibility that he wasn't the bad, uncaring father that Diana had suggested started to dawn and slowly the tide of public opinion began to turn in his favour, but not without a little help.

The public knew a great deal about Mrs Parker Bowles. The Princes knew surprisingly little.

Their father had never introduced them, aware that they wouldn't welcome it, any more than they had welcomed meeting their mother's paramours. In the summer of 1997, however, two months before Diana's death, he broached the subject. He sat them down together and tried to explain a bit about the situation, but the boys were very quiet and William was not at all receptive. He told Tiggy afterwards that William didn't want to know about it, and he sensibly left it.

He had also been planning to introduce Camilla to the wider world in September that year. As patron of the National Osteoporosis Society (a disease from which her mother died a most painful death), she was hosting a fundraising party, which the Prince was planning to attend. The gradual coming out was being masterminded by Alan Kilkenny, a public relations guru, who had been behind the phenomenally successful Wishing Well Appeal for Great Ormond Street Hospital. When the Princess died all plans had to be abolished. Camilla, who was as vilified as Charles at that time, retreated to her Wiltshire home.

The monarchy had survived by a hair's breadth. The Queen had redeemed herself with her eleventh-hour television tribute—and a long and blameless track record; Charles's fate was still precarious, and as heir to the throne this was a problem. More of a problem was his determination, at all costs, to hang on to Camilla. Through no fault of her own, she had been the cause of monumental upset. The clear solution was to let her go, but Charles wouldn't. She had saved him from the brink of despair, she had given him faith in himself, she was a support he couldn't move forward without; he loved her, and he made it clear that she was 'non-negotiable'.

At dinner one night with Camilla's divorce lawyer, Hilary Browne-Wilkinson, not long after the Dimbleby debacle, Charles heard the name Mark Bolland for the first time. He was the Canadian-born, comprehensive-school educated, bright, powerful thirty-year-old head of the Press Complaints Commission. Hilary suggested a meeting. She thought he could be useful in helping to improve the Prince's image. In a manoeuvre of thinly veiled subterfuge, he arrived in July 1996 as assistant to Sandy Henney, who was then Deputy Press Secretary, and swiftly rose to Assistant Private Secretary, during which process Richard Aylard, who shouldered the blame for having allowed Jonathan Dimbleby into the inner sanctum, was eased out of the top job.

Bolland became the Prince's golden boy. He dispensed with Kilkenny and took on the task he had been hired to do, that of raising the Prince's stock and making Mrs Parker Bowles acceptable to the British public. It was a challenging task from the beginning but after Diana's death it was well nigh impossible. But he achieved it, and it was entirely thanks to him that Camilla is now the Prince's wife and widely accepted as the Duchess of Cornwall. But that acceptance came at a high price.

# UNEASY RELATIONSHIP

Diana's brother, Earl Spencer, did not hold back when he heard the news of her death. Speaking from his home in South Africa, he said, 'I always believed the press would kill her in the end, but not even I could imagine that they would take such a direct hand in her death as seems to be the case.' At that time it was thought the paparazzi were entirely responsible for the accident, and he said that the editors and proprietors of every newspaper that had paid money for intrusive pictures of his sister had 'blood on their hands'.

Wherever the blame would finally be seen to lie, the industry took the Earl's message to heart. After heated debate about whether a privacy law was called for, the outcome was self-regulation and a strict new code of conduct binding on every editor and publisher in Britain was drawn up by the Press Complaints Commission. Published in November 1997, it was designed to prevent all the excesses of the previous ten years. Every aspect of intrusion that the Prince and Princess had suffered was covered, and the two boys were guaranteed privacy. For example:

Privacy
   i)  Everyone is entitled to respect for his or her private and family life, home, health and correspondence. A publication will be expected to justify intrusions into any individual's private life without consent.
   ii) The use of long lens photography to take pictures of people in private places without their consent is unacceptable. Note—private places are public or private property where there is a reasonable expectation of privacy.

Children
   i)  Young people should be free to complete their time at school without unnecessary intrusion.
   ii) Journalists must not interview or photograph children under the age of sixteen on subjects involving the welfare of the child or of any other child, in the absence of or without the consent of a parent or other adult who is responsible for the children.
   iii)Pupils must not be approached or photographed while at school without the permission of the school authorities.

iv) Where material about the private life of a child is published, there must be justification for publication other than the fame, notoriety or position of his or her parents or guardian.

Listening devices
Journalists must not obtain or publish material obtained by using clandestine listening devices or by intercepting private telephone conversations.

In the light of evidence given to the Leveson Inquiry, which began sitting in November 2011 in the wake of the News International phone-hacking scandal, the 1997 Code of Conduct looks laughable—and perhaps it always was.

For a time it kept William and Harry out of the newspapers, even if it didn't stop the paparazzi taking the photos. Sandy Henney has a photo of William that captures a wonderful moment; he has shot all the ducks at a funfair and is choosing what he'd like from the prizes hanging from the roof. 'They were being watched even though it was "leave the children alone",' she says. 'I had one fearful row with a particularly beastly editor in Fleet Street when he thought I was being ridiculously protective of the boys. I said, "I've got my responsibilities." He said, "I've got a load of photographs in my safe taken by paps done at Eton." They were still at it but because they didn't get published we weren't aware of it.'

But it was always going to be a balancing act. As the PCC made clear, 'that while their rights to privacy are the same as other children, Prince William and Prince Harry are different from them because of their proximity to the throne. As a result of this, the Palace has always recognised that rigid application of the Code with regard to the young Princes—and an insistence on absolute privacy—would be unsustainable. There is legitimate public interest in news and information about the way in which the Princes are growing up, and that includes the progress of their education. In such circumstances, a complete blackout on news would be contrary to the general public interest, and would undermine the authority of the Code.'

There is a common view today that William hates the press, and given his experiences it would be surprising if he didn't. But while he did hate the newspapers for many years, both before and after his mother's death, it's no longer so straightforward. He knows enough about the institution of monarchy to realise that if it is to have a future, it needs to be seen to be relevant—which means being visible. He still hates the paparazzi, but he reads everything and remembers who writes what about him (unlike his father who gave up reading anything but *The Times* years ago because they made him so cross). William will engage with the media in *his* way. He is extremely wary but utterly determined to remain in control. Control in all things is very important to William.

Sandy tells the story of the first anniversary. 'The year after Diana died, they were going to have a service at Crathie Church and William was adamant that if the press were going to be there—and you couldn't stop them being in the road—he didn't want to go, and I can understand that. The Prince of Wales asked me whether I would come and talk to them both. I said, "Okay, but I'm not going to say you've got to go. I'll give the pros and cons to them but they make up their own minds." We went for a walk round Loch Nigg and I said, "Okay, guys, why don't you want to go?" "Well, you know, the press are going to be there and we don't want to be gawped at." This was a year after their mum died and bloody right guys, but then you say, "Well, don't you think it would be a bit funny if everyone else turns up for a remembrance service for your mum and you don't?" "Well, yeah," says William, "but I still don't want to go." "Okay, but this is how it's going to be played out in the newspapers, but it's up to you to decide. I'm not telling you either way." And it was Harry who said, "I think we should go. We need to be there and we need to support Papa and to support everyone else. I think I'm going to go, William," and William then said, "Yeah you're right." I left them and said to the Prince, "I've talked to them and they may well go but, if so, it's their choice but no one will ever say they were forced into doing it." '

They weren't forced, but William did make one condition. He would go, he said, if Sandy would issue an announcement calling for an end to the mourning. He agreed a text with her and she read it out on his behalf during the photo call on the first day of the Michaelmas Half on 2 September, when Harry joined him as a pupil at Eton.

'They have asked me to say that they believe their mother would want people now to move on—because she would have known that constant reminders of her death can create nothing but pain to those she left behind. They therefore hope very much that their mother and her memory will now finally be allowed to rest in peace.'

That June, William turned sixteen and the *Mail on Sunday* published a special supplement about him. It was friendly and intended as a celebration, but it was speculative. Among many thousands of words, it claimed that palace aides vetted William's friends before they were invited to tea, which was nonsense. William was incensed and immediately instructed the press office to make a formal complaint on his behalf to the Press Complaints Commission. The claim, they said, was 'inaccurate and grossly intrusive'. The complaint was upheld.

His sixteenth birthday was an obvious landmark to be celebrated, and since the media had played ball with the palace, it was time for payback. 'You're *getting* at the moment,' explained Sandy, 'but we've got to *give* them something.' William took a lot of persuading. Eventually he agreed that she should come up with a list of questions to give to Peter Archer, a reporter who worked for the Press Association, which distributes news to every other media outlet. So one safe interview and some photographs. 'It was a bit anodyne,' she says, 'but it filled their pages.'

Colleen Harris, who joined the press office as Sandy's deputy, two months earlier—the first black member of the Household—was part of the persuasion process. 'I remember sitting with him, talking about the media plans for his sixteenth birthday, and I remember thinking, I wouldn't put up with this from my own children, I would just tell them, this is what you are doing. Why am I having to negotiate with a fifteen-year-old in this way?' She laughs at the memory, 'But you did; that's William. You had to discuss it and justify why you were doing certain things and explain what was in it for him and what was in it for them, and then he would come to a decision.

'He very much wanted to live his own life. Most children at that age don't want all the flummery and fuss; they just want to do what they want to do and I think it was the same for him. He couldn't quite understand why he had to put up with all this nonsense at that stage of his life—why he had to do so much at such a young age and I would argue he wasn't doing a lot of it, "You're only doing a little," but to him it felt like a lot.

'Our job at that point was to protect them, that was Sandy's strategy, she said let's just keep them out of the media, give them private time. It was only for landmark things and the skiing trips or when there was an incident or accident or something at school, then we would have to organise the media. It was always challenging because they never wanted to do things—and it was quite hard for us; we wanted to promote these fantastic kids and let the world see them and see how wonderfully they were growing up, and they didn't want to.'

After those early skiing holidays in Lech with their mother, Klosters became their regular haunt. Charles knew the runs like the back of his hand and had loved the place since he first went there in the 1970s. It had been the backdrop to some colourful and delightful photographs in the past, and the deal that evolved between the press office and the press was that the family would do one photo call at the beginning of the holiday and then be left alone.

When Colleen arrived with them all for her first skiing trip, there was no snow on the mountains so she postponed the photo call. But some of the media couldn't stay long enough for the weather to change and so all the Princes agreed to do an interim shot outside the hotel. Colleen made it clear that once there was some snow they would do the usual photo call for everyone else. 'They didn't hear that bit,' she says, laughing, so when, after heavy snowfall that night she announced the next morning that they were going to do a lovely photo call up in the mountains, some Princes were more cooperative than others.

'I asked the Prince of Wales and he said, "Yes, absolutely fine, go ahead. You talk to William." So I had to go and chat to William. Harry was there as well—they were watching something on the telly. It was hysterical, a programme called *Bansai* which they would shout every so often; Harry kept bursting into laughter; the Prince of Wales was sitting in the corner reading, looking up at me. So I said, "We've got to do this photo call." William said, "No, we've done a photo call." "No, that was only for some of the media, the ones that had to leave. Now we need to do another one, otherwise you're going to have all the paparazzi following you around for the rest of the week. So let's just go and do a nice big one up the mountain." "No, I'm not doing it."

'Now, I've got 150 media; it's my first trip, Sandy's sick so I can't ring her, and I'm sitting there with this belligerent young man. This carried on backwards and forwards for a bit and in the end, I just lost it, the Mummy in me came out and I said, "Look, you're doing it, otherwise you're all going to be in trouble and it will be a rotten week for everybody. It won't hurt you, it'll be good for you, dah, dah, dah, dah" and went mad, and he just sat there.

'Then Harry said, "Yeah, let's do it, William. Get out the way, Colleen, I'm watching something," and that was it. So Harry got the deal signed for me. That was the photo shoot where the public first heard William speak. I asked an ITN guy to ask him a question. He said 'How's it going?' and William responded. It was a great photo call. They laughed, they chatted, they did it brilliantly—the best one they'd ever done. It was a turning point and the media went crazy because they'd never heard him speak on camera before. It was a kind of two fingers up to me I think, it was like, "Yeah, I can do it if I want to, when the mood takes me. I can deliver." '

## THE MEETING WITH MRS P. B.

When his initial attempt to introduce William and Harry to Camilla met with reluctance, the Prince of Wales didn't push it. She was never at Highgrove when the boys were at home, nor at York House, where they now lived when in London, and although he was longing to bring her properly into his life, he felt that William and Harry's feelings were paramount.

As a preliminary move he invited her children, Tom, his godson, and Laura, to stay with them when they were up at Birkhall in Scotland during the Easter holidays in 1998; another guest in the house was the Poet Laureate, Ted Hughes. The meeting could not have been more successful, and thereafter the children met up from time to time, both in the country and in London, but still the Prince didn't push it. The initiative, he felt, had to come from the boys.

At much the same time, William and Harry began plotting a surprise party for their father's fiftieth birthday in November. It started out as a party for the Prince's godchildren and their parents. As Tom was his godson, William therefore wanted to invite Camilla, but first he wanted to meet her in more private circumstances.

William had heard a lot of terrible things about Camilla from his mother, and about his father too—she spared him little—but he was beginning to realise that not everything he'd heard was entirely true. The party was an opportunity to say the things that had perhaps gone unsaid in the past, and a meeting with Camilla was an important part of that. He told his father he would like to meet her, and in June telephoned to say he was coming to London. Camilla happened to be staying for a couple of nights. When she heard, she said she must leave immediately, but the Prince said, 'No, stay. This is ridiculous.' He then rang William to tell him that Mrs Parker Bowles would be in the house, would that be a problem? To which, William replied, 'No.'

The meeting took place on the afternoon of 13 June 1998. William said he would arrive at 7.00 p.m. but, typically, turned up at York House, at St James's Palace, at about 3.30 p.m. and went straight up to his flat at the top of the house. The Prince went to find Camilla who was with her PA, Amanda McManus, and said, 'He's here, let's just get on with it. I'm going to take you to meet him now.' So he took her up to William's flat, introduced them and left them alone to talk for about half an hour. At the end of the encounter, Camilla came out saying, 'I need a drink.' But it had been remarkably easy—William was friendly and Camilla was sympathetic and sensitive and understood the need to let things go at his pace. They met again for lunch a few days later and had tea a couple of times and, although it was some time before she spent a night at Highgrove when he was there, she did occasionally stay over when they were all in London and they would sometimes have breakfast together.

Nearly a month after the meeting at York House, Sandy Henney had a call from Rebekah Wade, then deputy editor of the *Sun* (and subsequently a prominent figure in the News International phone-hacking scandal). Wade was a good friend of Mark Bolland, whom William and Harry referred to as 'Blackadder', after the sitcom character, Lord Blackadder, played by Rowan Atkinson. Piers Morgan, editor of the *Daily Mirror*, was another friend and all three indulged in some mutual back-scratching. Wade said she'd heard there had been a meeting between Prince William and Mrs Parker Bowles. 'I said, "Rebekah, I'm not going to deny it but the shit's going to hit the proverbial fan when the young man finds out about this because he will think that someone's been spying on him and anything we've done in terms of trying to persuade him that the media have a place etc. . . . it ain't going to work. I'm really pissed off with this." So she said, "What do you want me to do?" I said, "Can I have twenty-four hours? I want to talk to William." "You've got it," she said, "and you can write the story." '

'A couple of hours before the *Sun* went to press, Piers Morgan rang me and said, "I hear the *Sun*'s got an exclusive William story." On a point of honour, my idea of dealing with the press was never to give one newspaper's story to another. I said, "Have they?" The call had come through to Mark, to whom Morgan spoke every other day, but Mark said it was a press inquiry and put him through to me. "Okay. What are you asking me? It's an exclusive story." "I want to know." "I wouldn't betray another paper, just like I wouldn't betray you." "Well, I'm not getting off the line until you tell me what's going on." "You can stay there till hell freezes over, I'm not going to bloody tell you." It caused real problems between Piers Morgan and me. He kept coming back with bits of the story and finally said, "There was a meeting and I suspect it was Camilla." I said, "Unless you can tell me the whole story I'm not going to deal with this." I think I signed my death warrant with that conversation. But it was a clever wheeze. You give a story to one journalist and then you give it to another. It's as old as the hills but there's some poor sod in the middle. I remember the time when Piers said I was over-protective about the boys and he did a really nasty piece about me. When he finally put the knife in at the end I should have seen it coming.' But that was not for a while.

So Sandy told William what had happened. 'I knew he wouldn't like it, because he would see it as intrusion, as I did—and he didn't trust the Prince's office at the best of times. I didn't like it, and I thought it was a cynical way of using William—if William's okay with Camilla then the public should be okay with her too. But I had to deal with this young man, so I said, "We can't win this battle but we can lose it slightly more gracefully. The story's going to go in but we have the opportunity to put it from our point of view." At the end of the day, I said to William, "This is what we're going to say, are you happy?" "Well,

I'm not happy," he said, "but I understand." And I thought, how grown up. He could have gone into a real teenage-boy sulk but no—he said, "I understand" and accepted it.'

When the story appeared, an internal inquiry was immediately launched and ten days later, Camilla's PA, Amanda McManus, fell on her sword. Her husband was a *Times* newspaper executive (a paper owned by News International, which also owns the *Sun*); she had gone home that night and told him what had happened. He mentioned it to 'a trusted third party, unconnected with journalism or News International', who had passed it on to the *Sun*. There was much regret on all sides at her departure, but it was not long before Amanda was quietly reinstated, and there are those who remain sceptical and believe she took the fall for someone else in the office.

'Mark had incredible contacts,' says Sandy, 'and balls to do some of the things he did. Whether or not you agreed with some of his methods, he got results. He was incredible fun to work with . . . but Christ, he had an incisive brain, no wonder the kids called him Blackadder; but scary sometimes. My view of him was that he was working primarily for Mrs Parker Bowles and then the Prince. He wanted to make Mrs Parker Bowles acceptable; but you can't treat the institution of monarchy as individuals, you need to treat it as a whole. They weathered the storm and the damage is behind them now but at the time, the public became almost indifferent to the institution and some of the stuff was very damaging.'

Colleen agrees. 'Everyone paints this negative picture of Mark and he was a spin master, but if you look at what he inherited and where the Prince was, in terms of reputation, image etc., he had to turn it around and he did turn that. Some of our decisions in the Press Office may have caused some emotional upheaval. It wasn't easy some of the time but I don't think the Prince of Wales could have married Camilla without that groundwork. There's payback each time. And sometimes he got that a bit out of kilter. He was very focused on the Prince of Wales and Camilla.'

As she says, 'Without Mark, the Prince would have been unhappy and the boys would have been unhappy as a consequence, and it would have been damaging to the monarchy as a whole, so he did help. You could call it one of the greatest love stories ever or one of the greatest tragedies.'

Sandy Henney doesn't believe that first meeting between William and Camilla healed all the wounds but it was a start, and William clearly didn't come away thinking Camilla was as poisonous as he had been led to believe. She was nevertheless the 'other woman' whom his mother had blamed and he may have felt that by fraternising with the enemy he was betraying Diana. But he could see that Camilla made his father very happy and when his father was happy, everyone was happy.

Harry was less complicated about it than his brother. As someone who knows him well says, 'Harry was just Harry.' He just got on with life. He had no qualms about meeting Camilla, and so after consulting both boys, Charles invited Camilla to bring Tom and Laura over to Highgrove for tea one Sunday. It was the beginning of a process.

The surprise party was held on the night of 31 July, four months before his actual birthday, which fell during the school term. They had chosen a date before the summer migration to Balmoral. The Prince was incredibly touched that his sons should have gone to such trouble on his behalf, but sadly, the surprise was ruined. The *Sunday Mirror* got wind of what was planned, inadvertently from one of the guests, and ran a story the Sunday before the party. It did nothing to improve anyone's relationship with the press, but the party was a huge success nonetheless.

Tiggy and the Prince's former valet, Michael Fawcett, helped translate their plans into action but it was William and Harry who steered the event. They recruited the actors Stephen Fry, Emma Thompson and Rowan Atkinson—all friends of the Prince through the work they've done for the Prince's Trust—to help them write and put together a revue. It was along the lines of *Blackadder*, in which they'd appeared themselves, in front of several hundred of the Prince's family and friends. The guests ate Highgrove lamb and organic vegetables and partied until 4 a.m.

The Prince was moved to tears by his children's thoughtfulness, but what touched him most was their seating plan. They had placed Camilla in the front row of the audience between him and William's godfather, King Constantine. Camilla was thrilled that they had asked her to be there. They couldn't have given their father a more welcome or perfect birthday present, and he stood up at the end of the evening and thanked them both profusely. According to those who were there, he thanked everyone who had a hand in the evening, with the notable exception of Tiggy. She was obviously not in his good books.

Tiggy shouldered huge responsibility and took very good care of the boys; she was everything they needed to keep them happy and amused. She lifted the Prince's spirits too, which, in the days before Camilla came out of the shadows, were often very low. As Colleen says, 'She had a really important role to play. She was more like a big sister. They used to tease each other and muck about a lot. She could have been stricter on occasion. But they liked her and needed her, she was good support for them. The general opinion within the Household was that the boys were short on discipline at the time and there was nobody saying "No"—apart from the press office.'

Charles was enormously fond of Tiggy but at times she exasperated him, not least because she had an unerring ability to find her way into trouble. He was furious when a photograph appeared in the newspapers of her, with a cigarette between her lips, driving the car, while Harry was shooting at rabbits through the open window. And when a photograph of Harry abseiling down a dam wall wearing no safety gear appeared in the *News of the World*, he became apoplectic. And as Sandy says, 'Tiggy and Mark [Dyer] got the bollocking of a lifetime and were told this must never happen again.'

Sandy had taken a call from Clive Goodman, the *News of the World* royal editor (who went to prison in 2007 for intercepting the Princes' mobile phone messages, and was arrested again in 2011 on charges of corruption for bribing police officers). It was common for newspapers to ask for a comment. 'It was a classic Saturday morning call. He said, "I've got this set of photographs, they're quite horrific. It's Harry going down the side of a dam on a safety line, abseiling." "Clive," I said, "come on, mate, it's Saturday morning, how do I know what these photos are showing?" He said, "I'll bike them to you." An hour or so later, I see them. No crash helmet, no safety line and I'm thinking, Oh my God. First of all, get hold of Tiggy. "Tiggy," "Yes, Granny," which was their nickname for me, "what have I done wrong now?"

"I don't know yet but I want to know the circumstances behind this," and she said, "Mmmm yes, we were there." So I said, "Where was bloody Mark Dyer? He's supposed to be in there acting like the big brother and sorting all this stuff out," and she said, "He was asleep on a rock somewhere." That's a fat lot of good.'

A passer-by had taken the photo at the Grwyne-Fawr dam in Monmouthshire, and although it showed only Harry, both boys had abseiled down the 160-foot dam wall without any safety equipment—and no doubt had the thrill of their lives.

Sandy was in a dilemma; the photos were in breach of the privacy rules but they did show the people responsible for the Princes' safety failing to protect them. In the interests of being open and honest with the press, she let the *News of the World* publish. The photograph ran on the front page with the headline 'MADNESS! The boy dangling 100 ft up with no helmet or safety line is PRINCE HARRY.' 'Could I have stopped it?' she says. 'I doubt it. Yes, all right, the photographs were taken in an intrusive way but they showed someone being put in danger who shouldn't have been, so I said, "I'm not going to complain to the PCC if you run it." It was a judgment call but for us to have suppressed that would have been more damaging to the monarchy than by admitting it was a stupid thing to do and taking it on the chin.'

Maintaining a good relationship with the media was vital—for every story that made it into the newspapers, many more were suppressed; and much of the time it was good old-fashioned horse-trading.

'We'd say, "Okay, you've got that but let's go with this, if you don't say anything about that."' 'There was a lot of negotiation like that going on,' says Colleen Harris. 'There were many times when we managed to protect William and Harry and keep them out of the media when they were up to mischievous things. Nothing terrible, nothing criminal but things they wouldn't have wanted the media to write about.' That was partly down to good relationships with the press, but partly because she and Sandy discussed things with the boys ahead of time. 'What could happen if you did this, and what might happen if you did that? They might not have always agreed but we worked through scenarios. William learned quite a lot from that about how to control and play the media.'

They were trying to prepare both boys for when the Code, which protected them to the age of eighteen, no longer applied. Sandy would always say, 'Don't ever do anything that you don't want to see in a newspaper at some stage.' But she admits that life is much tougher for William than it ever was for his father at the same age.

'Regardless of what the Prince of Wales might

think of the problems he had as a teenager, the media were still respectful. I don't think anyone has gone through what William's been through, which makes me admire him all the more. I'm not deriding it, but the cherry brandy incident was about as bad as it got [Charles, in his first year at Gordonstoun, accidentally found himself in a bar for the first time in his life, having become separated from his school group on a sailing trip, and in his terror and confusion, he ordered the only drink he'd heard of, which was a cherry brandy. A journalist happened to be standing at the bar at the time and the story of the Prince's underage drinking not only made headline news, but earned him severe and disproportionate punishment from the school].

'Look at what William's had to put up with; we had stories into the office weekend after weekend about him being seen in a nightclub, and if it wasn't him taking drugs, it was the people he was with. Once or twice I'd have to ask William himself about a [press] inquiry—and I always got an honest answer—but several times I'd find out which protection officer was on duty and I'd ask whether William had been at this place at that time. I'd never say, "Where was he?" because that's invading his privacy. Most of the time they'd reply, "No." The stories were complete crap. And then we'd find out that some kid in East London was a bit short of money and was making them up.'

# PARTNERS IN CRIME

One morning in her office in St James's Palace, Sandy Henney had a telephone call from the gardener at Highgrove. She was in the thick of organising an overseas tour, with a hundred and one other things kicking off. ' "Yes David." "I've got a problem." "Christ, I need another one. What is it?" He said, "The moorhen's dead." I thought, do I give a stuff about the moorhen? I said, "Right, well David, what do you want me to do about it?" "I want you to tell the boss." I said, "You're down at Highgrove [where the boss was], you go and tell him." He said, "But the Prince of Wales is very fond of this bird." So I said, "You want me, who's in London, to ring the boss to tell him the moorhen's dead because you won't do it?" "Yes, that's what I want." "Well, what's so special about this moorhen?" "It's because it's been shot," and I thought Oh and laughed. *Now* I know why he wants me to tell him, so I said, "Okay, but before I do I want you to tell me the full story." "Well, it's been shot." "Yes, but by whom?" "I don't know." "Come on David, there's a reason here." He was just like a policeman; he said, "The boys were seen walking in the vicinity of the pond." "Right, so you're telling me one of the boys has shot the bird?" "Well, I didn't see it." "No, but that's what your understanding is," and he said, "Yeah."

222

'So I rang the boss. "Bernie, can you put me through to the boss please?" "Yes, what's it about?" "Don't ask, Bernie." "Your Royal Highness." "Good afternoon, Sandy." "I'm so sorry to trouble you, Sir, but I've got some sad news." "Oh, what's that?" "The moorhen's dead," and he said, "Oh my God, I loved that bird." I said, "That's just what David said." One of the things he used to do to relax when he came home from a day out, was to go out and feed the chickens and walk down by that wonderful pool, and it relaxed him.

'Then he said, "Those bloody boys!" I hadn't said a word. I said, "I can't let you say that because I don't know that." And he said, "Where were they?" I said, "Well, they were seen in the vicinity of the pond." "Right," he said, "that's it. I want you to talk to them. I want you to find out which one of them did it, I want to know what happened, and I want an apology."

'So I thought, Right, they're at school—my friend Andrew Gailey. "Hello Sandy," he said. "Got a good one for you this time . . ." It's not funny, the bird's dead, but by this time I'm starting to giggle. "Would you mind getting the boys into your office, please, because the Prince is really hacked off about this. Could you tell the boys Granny [their nickname for Sandy] will give them twenty-four hours for one of them to cough to the boss. Twenty-four hours and that's it."

Some hours later, I'm driving home and Andrew rings and he's giggling before he starts. He says, "I got them into the office and I said, 'William. Harry. I've had Sandy on the phone and your father's very upset because someone has shot the moorhen.'" They're looking at each other and saying, "Shot the moorhen? Shot the moorhen?" Then William turns to Andrew and says, "Which moorhen is that, Dr Gailey?" And Harry says, "The one you told me not to shoot!"

'I said, "Tell Harry he's got twenty-four hours," and bless his heart he rang his dad and said, "I'm so sorry Papa, it was me, I shouldn't have done it." Those boys are so close to each other—the loyalty between them and the mischievousness and sense of honesty, not wishing to tell a lie. Andrew and I were wetting ourselves laughing. The Prince was delighted that Harry had coughed.'

It's interesting, however, that their father didn't simply pick up the phone to his two sons and say, 'What's the story?'

William and Harry were ever partners in crime. In Klosters one year, a year when their equally mischievous cousin Zara Phillips was with them, Sandy was sitting in the bar of the hotel, warming up after a freezing day but a very successful photo call. She had kicked her shoes off when she suddenly became aware of frantic waving at the window of the hotel and there, standing outside in the snow, were Tiggy and Harry. 'I thought, Oh my God, what's happened? So I ran out. I was just wearing a jumper and it was freezing bloody cold outside and I got outside the door and that little sod Wales—I mean the big one—was pelting me with snowballs. There's me thinking, Oh my God, something's happened to him, he's fallen over and broken his neck or something . . . Tiggy and Harry, and one of the policemen, who was also in on this joke, were roaring with laughter, and I'm chasing William up the road, saying, "Person of doubtful parentage, you wait till I get hold of you," and he ran around this car and he's throwing snowballs like nobody's business because he was prepared to include me in some of the fun. That was the nature of the kid, he loved mucking about and having fun.'

On another occasion, they were up at Birkhall, where the Queen Mother had a collection of eleven grandfather clocks in the dining room—which are still there today, along with the tartan walls and carpets. Sandy was having supper with them and at 10 o'clock practically jumped out of her skin when all the clocks suddenly started chiming. All three Princes could barely contain their mirth. After supper, they asked her to stay and play a game of cards the boys had made up. 'The idea was you were kneeling on the floor and had to get these cards down as quickly as you could and of course they thought it was just hysterical and William was pushing me out of the way and I went flying at one stage—everyone roaring with laughter, trying to get back into the game to put my cards down. Is William competitive? Not half. But fun and willing to include people in his life.

'I know he was young and should have been full of life but there was something else about him that meant you couldn't help but smile when he came into a room because he was always full of fun. It was not like when the Prince walked in and you thought, Oh God, where's it coming from today, good mood, bad mood or whatever? William or Harry used to walk in, "Oh hello, how are you?" '

In the summer of 2000, that easy relationship between Sandy and the boys came to a sad end. William's eighteenth birthday, a major milestone, was looming and Sandy was looking at the perennial problem of how to organise a photo call that he would happily agree to. She came up with a formula that worked brilliantly. It produced some of the best photographs of William ever taken, gave the media a collective snapshot of his life at Eton (which he was on the verge of leaving), and was effectively a big thank you to the media for having allowed him to spend his five years at the school in peace.

Rather than ask William to perform in front of dozens of cameras, which she knew would be counter-productive, she arranged for only two:

photographer Ian Jones from the *Daily Telegraph*, who had taken William's confirmation photographs, and television cameraman Eugene Campbell from ITN. She thought William would relax with them, as they were both young, sympathetic and good ambassadors for their profession. She guessed rightly that they would take some excellent shots—over which William would have the right of veto—which would then be 'pooled'. This is an arrangement the Palace and the media frequently practise; if space or circumstances don't allow for more than a few members of the press to be with the Royal Family during a visit or an event, the few that can be accommodated distribute their photographs or reports free of charge to every other newspaper and television channel. Ian and Eugene worked over a five-month period, dipping in and out of William's Eton life, building up a good rapport with him, which resulted in an intimate and hugely insightful view of the second in line to the throne as he turned eighteen.

'It was almost seen as a two-way learning street,' recalls Ian Jones. 'We were there to learn about his school life, but the Palace also saw it as a way for William to learn about the media and how press photographers and TV cameras work and how you put a piece of film together. He got very interested in the composition and the artistic side of it, also the technology and how shots would be edited together. It was an education for him in an area of the media that would be a very important part of his future life. It all went off very, very well and achieved exactly what it set out to do.

'It was lovely; he was very engaging. Once he saw how it worked and what we were looking for, at our next meeting he'd say, "I've had thoughts about this, or what do you think about that?" He'd been putting his mind to it and planning ideas for the project. The very first time he was a little bit cautious but when he realised there was a reason to it and what we were doing was worthwhile he was thoroughly involved and really up for it. The cookery was his idea and one of the best bits; he was making a rice dish with chicken stock and it was very good fun.'

To level out the playing field, the deal was that there would be no exclusives, no preferential treatment, and the photographs would be embargoed so that they all appeared on the same day. The dailies would have ten of them on the Friday for their Saturday editions and the Sundays would have an extra four a day later. Sandy discussed this entire deal at every stage with Stephen Lamport, the Prince's Private Secretary, with Mark Bolland, his Deputy, and with Les Hinton and Guy Black at the PCC. Everyone gave it their blessing.

Ian was a freelance under contract to the

*Daily Telegraph*; his editor was Charles Moore, and when he saw the prints, which had been electronically stored on the office system, he liked them so much he wanted to maximise the impact by running them in the glossy Saturday magazine which goes to print earlier than the main body of the paper. He therefore wanted them before the agreed date. Sandy Henney cleared this with Lamport and Bolland and the photographs were released. Shortly afterwards this was leaked to the *Daily Mail* and *The Times* and Lamport agreed to let them have a set of photos early for their magazines too. Charles Moore was indignant and refused to let the photographs go. The *Telegraph* had provided the photographer and the technology; it was not unreasonable, he felt, for the *Telegraph* to have this slight advantage over its competitors.

At this point Piers Morgan, editor of the *Daily Mirror*, got wind of the story. He turned on Sandy, and with scores to settle, wound up the rest of Fleet Street and it all turned very ugly. Sandy had made one crucial mistake. She had relied on a gentleman's agreement; she had nothing in writing.

That evening Ian arrived home from work and switched on the evening news to discover he was the lead story. Jenny Bond, the BBC's royal reporter, was standing in front of St James's Palace talking about the row, saying, 'The photographer stands to make millions of pounds out of these pictures.'

As a freelance, he did hold the copyright, but says, 'That would never have been the case. I was giving them free of charge to every media outlet in the world. Over time I suppose I might have made a couple of hundred, but considering the hours and hours and hours of work I did on that, all in my own time . . . it was such an honour, such a privilege and I really thought I was doing something special, not just for William but for the media, which is a profession I love.'

The issue of copyright took centre stage. 'It was made to sound as if I had conned them out of the copyright, but every freelance owns his copyright. ITN kept the copyright of the film, Mario Testino keeps the copyright of the pictures he takes, everyone who does portraits for the Royal Family keeps the copyright. I was asked to surrender it and I thought the only honourable course of action was to say, "It's yours." '

The final outcome was not catastrophic. The photographs were released to every newspaper at the same time, they all honoured the embargo and the next day, the media were on to another story. As Andrew Neil, then editor of the *Sunday Times* said, 'It was a storm in a Fleet Street teacup.'

Except at St James's Palace. Sandy offered Stephen Lamport her resignation as a matter of formality, never for a moment believing it would be accepted. She had consulted them at every stage, she had everyone's agreement at every stage; her mistake had been to trust men she thought were honourable. If it was a cock-up, it was a collective cock-up. But she was wrong; her resignation was accepted and by three o'clock that afternoon she had cleared her desk and was out on the street and out of a job. The Prince of Wales, for whom she'd tirelessly worked long and unreasonable hours, for seven years, never even said goodbye, but Prince William immediately telephoned.

'He tried to ring me three times but I was so upset—I really was gutted—and I remember saying, "I can't talk to him because I would be upset and I don't want to let myself down." Then he rang for the third time and I thought, Yeah, I can talk to him now. There was no "Poor me, all this horrible publicity and it's ruined my exams." It was "How are you? I am so sorry." There was no thought for himself, it was all about how I was. Total loyalty. I didn't hear a word from the Prince of Wales, and there's William, not quite eighteen and right in the middle of his A levels—the total opposite.

'That spoke volumes to me about the sort of man he was going to be: totally loyal to people, and that's why people won't let him down, they'd rather see something happen to themselves. They won't let him down because he will never let them down. Other things were said during that conversation but my last words to him were, "Trust your own judgment, William, it's sound. There are people you will come across that your instincts will tell you not to trust, there are people you will come across, you will never like, but if they can do a service for you, then let them do it, but you know how far you can trust them."

'Because he got it. He thought it was his fault; why he thought that, God alone knows; I don't know what had been said to him. I said, "It's got nothing to do with you. I accept I've done something silly, not dotting i's and crossing t's, I put my hands up to it but it's nothing to do with you. You just carry on with your A levels, it's fine." I didn't tell him what happened, it was a convoluted story and anyway it didn't matter. I was going and that was it—out, gone, clear your desk, away there's no looking back—someone else was going to look after him now. The saddest thing was the boys, knowing I would never see them again. I know they're Princes but they were a huge part of my life; I loved them to bits.'

Ian Jones heard nothing from William, but the next time he saw him was in Klosters for the traditional Easter photo call. When it was all over and he wired his shots back to London, Ian did some skiing and at lunch time, when everyone was going back up the mountain, boarded a cable car, only to find the Royal party had followed him in. He kept his head down but William noticed him among the crowd and shuffled over in his skis to say hello. Ian, as William knows, is a lifelong supporter of Bolton Wanderers, and Aston Villa had just beaten Bolton in the semi-final play-off at Wembley. 'We were robbed at Wembley,' he said with a big grin on his face.

# BLOODY PIRATES

During William's final year at Eton, before the photo fiasco, a body of wise men and one woman sat down to discuss his future. Among them were the Prince of Wales, Eric Anderson (Charles's English teacher at Gordonstoun who was about to return to Eton as Provost), the Right Reverend Richard Chartres (the Bishop of London), Major General Arthur Denaro (Commandant of Sandhurst, the Royal Military Academy) and Dr Andrew Gailey. William had got wind of the meeting and telephoned Sandy. ' "I want you to go," he said. "Okay, what do you want me to do?" "Well, I want you to tell them that I want a say in it." "Okay, William, I'll go." And I remember going and feeling slightly intimidated and the discussion was going round the table and I said, "Excuse me, has anyone asked William what he'd like to do? Don't you think we should?" and the discussion went on from there. Even at that age he was saying, I know people want to talk about me, but I will make my decisions and I thought, Good lad.'

He had done well at Eton by any standards, and, like most of his friends, he wanted to take a year off before starting university. There was a burgeoning market for companies offering tailor-made gap years and volunteering programmes that appealed to the parents of public school children. What most of the boys wanted to do was spend the year travelling and chilling on the beaches of Goa. Whatever dreams William might have had, he was never going to be allowed to spend his year doing anything that might have been construed by the press as a holiday.

Andrew Gailey had been an inspired choice of house master; a man with great humanity and humour, who everyone agrees was crucial in supporting and steering William and Harry through some nightmarish times. William thinks the world of him and he remains a friend, confidant and mentor, and guards his secrets faithfully. Eton can turn out some rather arrogant and self-important men; it also turns out some of the best, who appreciate that they have enjoyed great privilege and recognise that with privilege comes responsibility. Both Princes fall into the latter category, and possess the self-assurance that Eton, at its best, provides, along with the humility that recognises no one man is better than another simply by accident of birth, privilege or education.

William had loved his time at Eton and enjoyed everything the school had to offer, especially sport. At the end of it, he came away with three A Levels: an A grade in Geography, B in History of Art and C in Biology—plenty to get him into St Andrews, his first choice of university, where he planned to read History of Art.

He heard the news of his results in an email from his father, who is much more at home with pen and ink than a computer, but he wanted to be the first to congratulate him and tell him he had a firm place at St Andrews for the following year. He was in the jungle in Belize, in Central America, when the email arrived, doing survival exercises with the Welsh Guards (of which his father is Colonel-in-Chief). It was the first leg of his gap year. Belize, once a British colony known as British Honduras, gained full independence in 1981 but the British Army kept a presence in the country to protect it from invasion by its neighbour Guatemala, and still has a training base there. Mark Dyer had served in the Welsh Guards and done a tour of Belize so he knew it well, and William wanted something challenging. It was wild, hot, tropical and treacherous; he slept in a hammock, trekked through hostile, snake-infested jungle and lived off what he caught in the wild.

The year had been a compromise; his father had insisted it was to be constructive and must broaden his horizons, but William wanted some fun as well and had done his own research and had his own ideas. He had spoken to all sorts of people about what to do and where to go. Mark Dyer had been very influential and between them they came up with a plan. 'We'd put Mark Dyer in to act as the male version of Tiggy, to be a big brother,' says Sandy, and when Mark told her which part of the world William wanted to go to, she said, "Are you mad?" He said, "But he wants to go diving," and I said, "Yes, but there are bloody pirates in that part of the world." "Oh yeah, didn't think of that. Right, that one's off the list." '

Instead he went diving off the coast of Belize, which has the world's second largest barrier reef, and then off the tiny island of Rodrigues, to the east of Mauritius in the Indian Ocean, to join a project run by the Royal Geographical Society. It has a particularly interesting coral reef that is self-seeding and has species of coral and damselfish found nowhere else in the world. It was a magical escape into a watery world and a great opportunity to dive.

The bulk of William's year was divided between an eleven-week expedition to Chile with Raleigh International, followed by a brief spell working as a farm labourer and then on to three and a half months in Africa, which he fell in love with.

Raleigh had been his father's idea. Charles had been in at the beginning of the organisation, under the name Operation Raleigh, in 1984, along with the explorer Colonel John Blashford-Snell. It was a larger, more ambitious version of a venture called Operation Drake, both of which took young people from a mixture of countries and backgrounds, put them on a magnificent 1,900-ton schooner that they had to learn to sail, and gave them the chance to explore the world, do some good, face challenges and discover their potential. Since then, they had done away with the ship and changed the name but the vision remained the same.

William's involvement began with a call from Mark Dyer to Raleigh's then chief executive, Jamie Robertson-Macleod. He was ringing, he said, on behalf of Prince William, who wanted to hear more about the organisation and asked whether he might go down to Eton and make a presentation. He had been told by Mark to make it sound tough, and when he arrived at Manor House and was met by Andrew Gailey, Mark and the Prince, he'd pulled no punches. This was no holiday, he said. It was a rich mix of people and the mix was very important to Raleigh, demonstrating that everyone possessed inherent capabilities and deserved opportunities. 'William looked concerned about how tough I had made it sound,' says Jamie. 'But Chile is the toughest; it's remote and has changeable conditions. In their summer you can get whipping wind and cold conditions that could lead to hypothermia in short order.'

After the presentation he was sworn to secrecy. 'If it gets out,' he was told, 'William won't go.' But William did go, and shortly afterwards Malcolm Sutherland, who worked as an expedition leader for Raleigh, was asked to go to St James's Palace to meet him to discuss the finer details. Sutherland had spent seven years in the Parachute Regiment, and since leaving the Army had worked for Raleigh in Namibia, China and Mongolia.

'When I met William,' says Malcolm, 'he was in jeans and T-shirt—scruffy—he'd just been dragged out of bed and had driven up from Highgrove to St James's Palace for the briefing and chat, and he was sitting there with his cup of tea and his Sunblest white bread toast. You'd expect it to be better than that, but that's what it was, and it was actually very refreshing. You thought, Great, normal boy. It was in a little sitting room upstairs, tiny, all very casual, with computer games in the corner. It was quite surreal.

'He was apprehensive I think, keen to find out what life was going to be like, what the living conditions would be like, how rough was it going to be.' The answer was that it would be very rough. They might be living in tents or they might be camped out on a kitchen floor in a community project with twelve or fourteen bodies on mats and sleeping bags. It was going to be basic, one loo for everyone. 'I felt that giving him a taste of what to expect and the things to think about before he came and equipment that would make life easier was important. Also talking about the people that came on expeditions, there was a real mix, a diversity of people. There's a preconception that most people that come are middle class, and there are a lot, but there's also a lot of people who come through the Youth At Risk programme, and that is one of the most fulfilling elements of it. It's quite an interesting dynamic: you take these people and mix them with everyone else, who are a pretty diverse mix anyway, both in nationalities and types of people. Put them in this close environment and tell them to work together, to talk about things and work through problems. It could be very hard at times and often the projects were hard but they were also very rewarding; but the challenge could often be just to make it happen within the group itself.'

William flew out to Santiago, the capital of Chile, separately from the rest of the venturers. He was very apprehensive. This was the first time he had spent any significant time away from his family and the comforts of home and he was stepping into completely unknown territory. He knew none of the people in the group, with the exception of Malcolm, and would be with a mix of backgrounds and nationalities he had no experience of. It was not surprising he kept his head held down and appeared shy and rather quiet to begin with. Mark travelled with him and stayed for the first few days, and he had two PPOs, which was reassuring, but they kept a distance; he knew he had to crack this on his own.

Before any venturer arrives at their destination they need to raise about £3,000 to pay for their trip. William had raised five times that amount by playing in a polo match, for which his friends and others had sponsored him. It was one of those occasions when being second in line to the throne isn't such a handicap.

From Santiago the venturers flew to Coihaique in Patagonia, in the south of the country, two and a half hours away, where Raleigh had set up a permanent base and where they spent the next four days being trained for the challenges ahead. All they knew was that there would be an environmental project, a community project and an adventure that would be chosen for them, and that they would be split into different groups of eleven for each. The induction involved basic first aid—although a medic travelled with every group—and radio communications, so they could send twice-daily reports back to base, where there was twenty-four-hour back-up. They were also given an understanding of the local culture and some cooking lessons. Supplies were provided but it was up to the venturers to turn them into something edible, which at times was the biggest challenge of all.

William's first three weeks were the most difficult of the entire trip, both physically and psychologically. His group was sea-kayaking over very long distances in two-man kayaks carrying all their food and water, each day taking it in turns to be team leader and taking on the various other duties. At night they camped on the shoreline. 'The sea kayaking was probably the biggest shock to his system,' says Malcolm. 'He'd just arrived and was thrown straight into it and it was physically hard, the conditions were tough—it was the worst weather we had on the whole expedition and sometimes it was pretty precarious, they were on small rocks on the sea shore. Sometimes it was impossible to put tents up and they would use big tarpaulins and get in there like sardines because that was the best way of doing it.'

Sleeping cheek by jowl under a tarpaulin with strangers is not fun for anyone, particularly someone as private as William, but worse was to come. The weather turned extremely nasty; a massive belt of low pressure came in over the southern tip of Chile and brought driving rain and icy winds. The party was stranded on a beach for five nights while the storm raged over their heads and threatened to blow away their tents. They were soaked to the skin, and bitterly cold, with no way of getting dry or warm. 'It was pretty grim,' says Malcolm, with all the understatement of an ex-Para. 'There's no doubt about it, everyone found it tough.'

Not surprisingly, one of the party lost the plot. He was an English boy from a Youth at Risk programme, with a typical profile: serious family problems, a history of drugs and no experience of life outside the deprived squalor of the inner city where he was born. Cold and frightened, as they probably all were, in a wild and hostile coastline on the other side of the world, he lashed out, shouting and swearing aggressively. It was a shocking and intimidating display.

No one knew how to handle the situation, but to Malcolm's surprise, the one who defused it was William. 'It was great to see him realising that something had to be done and instead of going into his shell, as lots of people did, he energised the group, tried to keep things going, had a joke. Every project group relies on people like that and I would not have predicted that he would be the man to deal with people like that in those situations, definitely not, so it was incredible. You would expect someone like William to take a step back and not get involved and let someone else deal with it. But he connected with that boy and was the only person that could. He told him to sort himself out but in such a way that they became very good friends afterwards. William became the only person the guy would want to talk to if there were issues—he acted as a sort of go-between. He didn't have to do that, and I don't think I could have done it at that age; to be able to go to an eighteen- or nineteen-year-old with a shaved head, who'd had a hell of a tough upbringing and a drug issue and who was really, really angry.

'It was very impressive and it surprised a lot of people as well, but he got so much respect from that—he got so much respect anyway, because people liked him. I can't imagine anyone not liking William. He was just fantastic.'

The next three weeks were spent in a small coastal village called Tortel, with no more than a few hundred people. 'We never told anyone where he was going; the whole aim was to ensure his life on expedition was just like anyone else's, yet everyone knew who he was—even in the smallest Chilean communities. He must have been the most famous young boy in the world. People would gawp but they were pretty respectful. Tortel was built on a very steep slope that made movement around the village very difficult. They relied on wooden walkways and part of the work the venturers were brought in to do was to construct more walkways. As with every Raleigh project, the need is identified by local government, which brings in experts from the UK to work alongside local experts. The venturers provide the labour. But it wasn't all hard graft. Their other task in

Tortel was to help out in the primary school, where William was in his element.

'Again, I would never have predicted it, but the way he interacted with the kids was amazing. He was completely and utterly at one with himself and happy to be with them and to make a fool of himself and look silly; there was no pretence, it made him flower, it was his true self popping out. That was the one time his smile was non-stop, he was buzzing, he was natural, he was jumping around as if nobody was watching him. Most people are not quite as animated as he was. He was teaching a bit of English, playing games, drawing animals on a blackboard and writing the English name next to them; his drawings weren't too great and everyone was laughing at that. It's not everyone's natural environment but he was just great. Also, there was a local radio station in the village and he was the DJ for a moment and he loved it, choosing records, doing the chit-chat. Those were the times when he really got connected with the community.'

It was in Tortel that he agreed to do a dreaded photo call. The media had agreed to stay away while he was in Chile, in return for decent access and good photo opportunities at some stage during the eleven weeks. Colleen Harris, who after Sandy Henney's departure became Press Secretary, kept the numbers to the bare minimum, which she knew would work best; one television cameraman, one stills photographer and a reporter from the Press Association who conducted the interview. Mark Dyer travelled out with them. It turned out to be a public relations triumph. Compelling photographs of William filled the newspapers for two days and the film footage ran on the TV news. He was praised for his 'humility' and 'willingness to muck in with fellow volunteers' and for his 'caring touch', as he was seen on all fours cleaning the communal loo, and making porridge that he declared was the worst porridge he had ever tasted in his life. 'Here you are actually making a difference to other people's lives,' he said. It went down a storm.

The press kept to their side of the bargain, with one exception. *OK!* magazine had employed a local man from the mountains who was able to find the group, but the first anyone knew about it was when a photograph taken with a long lens appeared in the magazine. *OK!* was swiftly jumped on by the PCC.

The final three-week project took them away from the coast, working with the Chilean government's National Forestry Corporation (CONAF) and experts from the Natural History Museum in London on a study of the Huemul deer to try to prevent its extinction. It was once so common in Chile that in the late eighteenth century it was added to the national coat of arms, but loss of habitat and the introduction of red and fallow deer to the country in 1800, as well as hunters killing them for food, had brought about a serious decline in numbers. The study focused on the animals' behaviour and natural habitat and involved identifying, tagging and tracking a small number of deer to establish where they went and what they ate.

'William loved that whole element of living out of a tent in the middle of nowhere, tracking, monitoring and working with these deer,' recalls Malcolm. 'I think he could relate to it, he'd been involved in deer management up in Balmoral and could see the whole purpose. In the UK there are far too many deer but in Chile a management plan was needed to ensure that not too many were being shot by locals. So it was about educating locals as well as protecting the animals.' It was a theme William met again on the next leg of his gap year, in Africa, and one which fascinated him.

At the end of the eleven weeks there was a giant party back at base before everyone climbed onto their different planes and returned to their vastly differing lives. They had eaten porridge for breakfast, dry biscuits for lunch with a shared tin of sardines, if they were lucky, and supper was dehydrated more times than it was fresh. 'For certain projects we had Army rations but most of the time it wasn't as nice as that,' says Malcolm. And for eleven weeks there had been not a drop of alcohol. But at the party . . .

'He had a lot of steam to get rid of. You don't need that many beers to feel the effect, and he got on the plane with a very sore head. It was a massive blow-out, lots of energy, lots of relief, dancing and people swinging from the rafters— and he was one of them.

'At the end he said, "This has been a very long time." I'm sure he was homesick. That's fair enough, lots of people are, and it's a long time to be living on top of other people; he didn't get any space. Okay, you can go and sit on a rock or down a track, but you don't have space and I think that for him was quite difficult. But the great thing about the whole expedition was it was probably the last time he could go for a long period away from the public eye; I wonder if he knew that then.

'He grew a lot. He arrived quiet and shy, head down, and by the end he had made friends— people loved being around him—and he was swinging from the rafters, head high and very comfortable with everyone. I think it gave him great confidence.'

Jamie Robertson-Macleod now has a framed letter in his study from William saying how much he enjoyed the trip and thanking him for playing down the situation, which he said had been very helpful. There was just one plea. 'Next time, dryer, warmer and 20 miles of beach in each direction and no mountains!'

# THE SPORT OF KINGS

William's social life in the country largely revolved around horses and the Beaufort Polo Club. It's a small, friendly club no more than a stone's throw from Highgrove, started nineteen years ago by Simon and Claire Tomlinson. Claire is one of the best polo players in the country with a string of accolades to her name; she was the highest-rated woman player in the world, and among a host of other things, she coached the England team that she once captained. William and the Tomlinsons' youngest child Mark became very good friends when they were small and they were in and out of each other's houses, although more often at the Tomlinsons'. William always knew he was welcome there any time and if his parents were away or busy that was where he went. Mark has two elder siblings, Luke and Emma. It was a house full of dogs and wellies and not a butler in sight.

'He was just like the other boys and enjoyed doing things,' says Claire. 'If I was the only adult I had to kick them all into touch a bit, but I didn't treat him any differently from the others, because I thought that was the fairest thing for him.' They used to play together and ride their ponies and bicycles, and as they grew older they upgraded to horses and motorbikes and pubs and parties, and would often go off across the fields shooting rabbits. They went on summer holidays and skiing trips and Claire taught them both to play polo. She also taught Harry a little later.

'At the back of your mind there's always anxiety for their safety but as with your own children you wouldn't want them to see it. What boy isn't devil-may-care? Any boy who's got any sporting instinct will be like that. I don't think it's good to restrict them too much. They almost have to learn by their own mistakes. If you're always saying be careful, it's not very fair. You get on and enjoy life and he's enjoyed the things he's done and I'm sure would like to spend more time at them but can't any more. He's very competitive but if you're going to play a sport you might as well be competitive. And he's analytical about his own performance; he doesn't like playing badly.'

All the children of local horsey and hunting families are members of the pony club—it's a rite of passage for them (along with bossy pony club mothers). The five-year-olds start learning to ride and how to look after their ponies, and as they progress they learn jumping, cross-country, dressage and polo. It's good fun, hard work and makes for very capable, practical children, and for those who don't go to the local day schools, it's a great place to make friends in the area. During the school holidays there is a programme of training sessions and rallies, competitions and gymkhanas, camps of varying lengths in the summer and Christmas parties. And the most exciting days for most pony club children is when they are allowed to join the grown-ups and go foxhunting. Even though hunting with dogs was banned in 2005, the Beaufort, like most hunts, still goes out several times a week and still holds special Children's Meets.

William had already done a bit of riding when they first met but Claire took him up a level. 'We did a lot of riding and jumping and having fun. He loved jumping. He has no fear, he'd get stuck into anything, but equally he wasn't completely crazy.' When he was a little older, she lent him horses to hunt with. 'It's nice to have the right sort of horse to get going on. He was growing out of his pony and needed something a bit bigger.'

Prince Charles was passionate about hunting and polo and encouraged the boys from an early age in both sports, although hunting was always going to be controversial. He loved it because of the adrenalin rush and the fact that in the process of trying to stay on your horse, it's very difficult to worry about anything else. But he also loved it because he saw it as a natural part of the management of nature, and as a great leveller. As a fellow member of the Beaufort says, 'There's very little protocol on the hunting field, particularly when you're covered in mud and being hauled out of a ditch!' The killing of the fox is almost incidental.

William's particular enthusiasm regarding hunting was the hounds. Ian Farquhar, Master of the Beaufort, has pedigree records in bound volumes for the Beaufort hounds going back fifty-four generations or more. He is fascinating and passionate on the subject of breeding and bloodlines, knows the name and quirks of every dog in the pack and loves them like children. He once said, 'Hunting people support their hounds as others may support their football teams.' Having known William for most of his life, it would be surprising if some of it hadn't rubbed off. The best part of hunting for William was riding at the front of the field, alongside Ian, and watching the hounds work. Like his father, he was sad to have to stop. For although their friends might have carried on while the ban remains in place, they know they can't.

But he still has polo, the oldest ball game in the world, said to have first been played in 600 BC. The Royal Family's passion for it doesn't go back quite so far, but it is certainly in the blood. William doesn't get enough practice these days to play as well as he might, but he loves it, and he and Harry use it, as their father did for so many years, as a means of raising serious sums of money for charity. To be a decent polo player you must be an excellent horseman, have good hand–eye co-ordination and be a team player. According to Claire, 'He's not an advanced standard of horseman today [he is a one handicap; his friend Mark, now a professional, is a seven] because he hasn't done it enough, but he's a very sympathetic horseman. So many people who ride treat their horses like machines, but he has never done that—he treats a horse like a living being which has limits, and he will get the best out of it. He has great empathy with his horses.'

As a teenager, the polo club was the place where William and his friends hung out after matches and games. They would go into the bar where at weekends a rock band called Nobodys Business often used to play. It was made up of two locals, Steve Hoare and Frank McQueen. They were loud and gutsy and rapidly became everyone's favourites. They also played at two of the pubs polo club people drank in—the Rattlebone Inn, in the neighbouring village of Sherston, and the Vine Tree at Norton. Steve remembers the excitement the first time the heir to the throne stood six feet away from him, dancing to his music—and watching his friends form a protective barrier on the dance floor as some young girls attempted to move in on him. At the end of the evening, he and Frank were introduced to William and a group of them sat around on hay bales chatting.

William started wearing the band's black T-shirt. Once, he told Steve, he'd been wearing it over the weekend and 'Granny had asked what the logo was.' Their music always raised the roof and they regularly ended the gig with the Status Quo number 'Rockin' All Over the World'. William and a couple of his mates started rocking alongside them one night, belting out the words without a care in the world, and thereafter it became his cue to sing. Afterwards, the landlord of the Rattlebone, Dave Baker, often had an after-hours lock-in, with only friends and regulars. They would all sit around drinking and chatting until the small hours. Increasingly, Harry joined the party, and sometimes their cousins, Peter and Zara Phillips, who lived not many miles away at Gatcombe Park.

Steve and Frank were soon playing at all the local eighteenth and twenty-first birthday parties, and became chummy with the whole crowd. Sometimes William and Harry would act as their roadies, helping them carry their equipment and guitars from the back of the car to set up. Harry used to impersonate their strong Wiltshire accents—at a smart dinner, he once mischievously flung a bread roll at Frank, getting it back double-quick. As Steve said, 'It's not every day you get a bread roll hurled in your direction by a member of the Royal Family followed by a handshake and a hug.'

For a bit of a laugh, they all put together a Nobodys Business polo team with William, Mark

Tomlinson, Christian Blake-Dyke and Bruce Urquhart, and they successfully played their way through to the final of the Henderson Rosebowl in the summer of 2001. That same year the band played at the Beaufort Hunt Ball, a very grand event. They were not the main attraction—that was a twelve-piece band brought in from London, while Nobodys Business was put into a small side marquee. The minute they started playing, their faithful polo club fans were in there, and very soon the tent was bursting at the seams, as William and Harry, and Mark and Luke Tomlinson sang along at the tops of their voices to all the songs, leaving the smart London band playing to themselves and a small handful of ball goers.

## OUT OF AFRICA

About half a mile from the Beaufort Polo Club, the Tomlinsons had a further nine hundred acres at a farm called Hill Court, on the outskirts of Shipton Moyne (home to the Cat and Custard Pot, another favourite watering hole). It was organically farmed and supported two large dairy herds, beef cattle, cereals and nearly two hundred polo ponies. This was where William worked as a farm-hand for four exhausting weeks at the beginning of 2001. On the grounds that he will one day inherit the Duchy of Cornwall with all its tenant farms, his father (who, like his father before him, has long been a champion of the countryside) wanted him to get an understanding of the rural economy and how those hands-on farmers live. It was something he was keen to do. He always loved spending time at the Home Farm, and David Wilson remembers him as a small child sitting for hours with the animals. But rather than go to a Duchy farm, where he'd be the boss's son, he chose instead to work for his friend's parents.

It was hard work, getting up at 4 a.m. each day to bring the cows in from the fields and do the milking and the washing down of the milking sheds afterwards and all the other mucky, back-breaking chores that fall to the latest recruit. The only consolation was that he was paid, unlike for everything else he did in his gap year; he got the princely sum of £3.20 an hour. He loved it, particularly the feeling that he was 'just another guy on the farm'.

Next came Africa, the final and in many ways best part of the gap year. Africa has a way of getting into people's blood and it had already started to seep into his. He had been there once before and was smitten, as so many people are. It's the sheer size of the continent, the miles of nothingness, the friendly, laughing people, the adventure and the incomparable thrill of seeing wildlife in its natural untouched habitat.

He and Harry were taken to Kenya by old

family friends, the van Cutsems, shortly after their mother's death. Hugh van Cutsem had been at Cambridge with Prince Charles and he and his wife, Emilie, had been close friends of his ever since. Their four sons, Edward, Hugh, Nicholas and William, were almost like brothers to William and Harry—all but William, older than them—and although there was a brief rift in the relationship between Charles and Hugh and Emilie because of Camilla, the children remained firm friends. Emilie had been particularly good at scooping up the boys after Diana died and they had spent many happy days at their beautiful home in Norfolk. When William went to university, he gave them his black Labrador, Widgeon, to look after.

Their guide in Kenya was Geoffrey Kent, founder of the luxury travel company Abercrombie and Kent, a polo player, adventurer and a friend of the Prince of Wales. He had grown up on a farm in the Aberdare Highlands of Kenya and been educated in Nairobi. He knew the country like the back of his hand and his company specialised in up-market safaris to the most breathtaking parts of the continent.

He took them to Lewa, a game reserve on the northern foothills of Mount Kenya, which is as breathtaking as anywhere in Africa. The skies are big, the earth is red and scorched, the smells and the sounds are like nowhere else in the world and at night the stars are so bright and so close you feel you could reach up and stir them with your hand. And the place is bristling with wildlife.

Lewa was owned by the Craig family, whom Geoffrey knew well; he introduced them to his royal party. Ian Craig, like Geoffrey, was second generation; his father had gone out to Kenya from England in the early 1920s to farm cattle and owned about 35,000 acres of land, where game roamed freely. Poaching had always been a problem in Africa; elephants were killed for their tusks and rhinos for their horns, but in the late 1980s it became an epidemic. In ten years the estimated number of black rhino had dropped from 20,000 to fewer than 300. But they had a champion in a remarkable conservationist and philanthropist called Anna Merz. She persuaded Ian's father to give over part of his ranch to a rhino sanctuary.

Together they worked to track and capture every remaining wild rhino in northern Kenya and relocate them to the sanctuary for breeding and safekeeping. Over the next ten years it grew until the Craigs decided to give over the whole property to the rhinos and enclosed it with high, electrified fencing. Since then, the government and neighbouring landowners have added to it, bringing the total acreage to 61,000. It was renamed the Lewa Wildlife Conservancy and has become a flagship not only for Kenya but for the whole of Africa, and a catalyst for conservation. A number of endangered species have sanctuary there, including the Grevy's zebra, sitatunga and oryx antelope.

The van Cutsem party stayed in a magnificent tented camp—a far cry from the sort of tents William had occupied in Chile. This was the height of luxury: the tents were raised up on little stone decks, with proper beds and bathrooms and stunning views over the bush, which began just feet away. And for escaping the heat, there was a swimming pool. It was bliss. They went on early morning game drives, in open jeeps, wrapped in blankets against the cold, bouncing across the rough tracks in the grass, everyone's eyes peeled for the twitching of a tail in the half light, or the flapping of an ear that might reveal a herd of elephants emerging from the bush, or a cheetah quietly slinking through the trees. This is one of the best times of day to spot animals, before the sun comes up, and with it the heat, when they find themselves a shady spot to rest in after a night's hunting. Another good time is late afternoon. And because the animals don't see jeeps as a threat, provided no one makes a noise or a sudden movement, it's possible to get very close. William loved it.

But more exciting still was when Charlie Wheeler, one of Ian Craig's colleagues on Lewa, a fellow conservationist and another second-generation Kenyan, took them walking through the bush for a day's expedition on foot, with camels. Armed with a rifle, he took the lead— everyone who leaves the safety of the camp, whether on four wheels or foot or horse, goes with an armed ranger just in case they meet an angry buffalo or get between a rhino and her baby. On this occasion they had two armed PPOs as well, although their training was more to deal with would-be kidnappers and assassins than hungry hyenas or malevolent bull elephants. Everything needed for the perfect lunch was carried on the camels, and when they stopped at noon in the middle of nowhere, a makeshift camp was conjured up in the bush and lunch was served as it might have been in a five-star hotel, with a troop of Africans to prepare and serve it. On their way back, the sun suddenly set; and in Africa there is no twilight. They went from sunshine to moon-light and unexpectedly walked into a herd of elephants. It's the sort of experience that either thrills or terrifies. Harry, aged twelve, was hanging on to Charlie's shirt but William was exhilarated. They rendezvoused with some vehicles and returned safely to camp, but the day and the holiday as a whole made a big impression on William and inspired a determination to go back.

When plotting his gap year he contacted Ian Craig and asked whether there was any work he might usefully do on Lewa. He planned to go first to Botswana, which Mark Dyer knew well, but then wanted to return to the place he had so fallen in love with, but he made it absolutely clear he did not want a joy ride. Ian assured him he would be usefully employed and welcomed him with open arms.

Charlie Mayhew is the founder and Chief Executive of Tusk Trust, a charity set up in 1990, dedicated to halting the destruction of Africa's wildlife. Five years later he hooked up with Lewa, where the guiding philosophy so perfectly matched his own, and he became good friends with Ian Craig and his family. Their concern was not only the wildlife; it was also for the local communities and the need to educate them so that they could appreciate and manage the assets they had and profit from the tourism they brought. William heard about Tusk during this visit, and it was one of the first charities of which he agreed to become patron.

Charlie happened to be at Lewa the day William and Mark, shrouded in secrecy, arrived in March 2001. He was there with Ronnie Wood, the Rolling Stones guitarist and painter, plus a photographer and a journalist from the *Daily Mail*. Ronnie was a patron of Tusk and had painted a series of wildlife pictures at Lewa to raise money for the charity. The publication wanted to see Ronnie in situ and so Charlie had taken them all. Ronnie stayed with

Ian and his wife, Jane, while the journalists were accommodated in a lodge.

'Before I got there,' says Charlie, 'Ian sent me an email or phoned and said, "You are leaving on such and such a date and you will be gone by 11 o'clock won't you?" This was so unlike Ian to be so precise, very unKenyan. I said, "Yes, okay, we'll be gone." I was taking Ronnie up north for more interviews. When we arrived, Ian apologised and said, "You might have thought me a bit odd, but we've got William coming and the fact you've got a *Daily Mail* journalist in tow put everyone into a spin." And as William flew in, we flew out and the poor journalist never realised that he had the biggest scoop under his nose.'

William and Mark stayed with the Craig family for a couple of months while he worked on the Conservancy and they became very close. It has long been asserted that the Craigs' daughter, Jecca, was an early girlfriend, but friend is much closer to the mark. The Craigs were another normal, easy-going family by which William was happy to be embraced on his trips to Africa. Jecca was like a sister to him and their son Batian like another brother. In Kenya he could disappear; very few people knew who he was, and those that did, didn't care.

'You can see exactly why William has become so close to Ian Craig,' Charlie said. 'I wouldn't say he's a father figure but they have a very close relationship. He's very down to earth and has a lovely family, a wife and two children. They've all become close friends and what's interesting about William and his friends is how closely guarded they are and protective over that relationship and the privacy, and one can't help but admire it.'

'William was much more relaxed when he came back the second time,' says Charlie Wheeler. 'On that first trip his mother had just died and he was very quiet and reserved. This time he was a normal boy, and was treated like all the kids.' Charlie has two sons of his own of much the same age and his late wife, Carole, like most Kenyans, black and white, was completely unfazed by the royal tag. It meant nothing to them, which is at the heart of why Africa is so special to both William and Harry. It's the anonymity that they both crave. To her, William was just another boy, who should pull his weight, and she made no distinction between any of them.

While William was there, a big bull elephant had to be captured and transferred to another national park. He was causing huge damage on Lewa, breaking trees and being generally destructive because of the limited space. It was a major event in the local community and dozens of people were involved and lots of photographs were taken because the Craigs always liked to record these transfers. William was part of the operation and remarked that for the first time in his life, the cameras were not focused on him.

That was a major part of the magic of Africa for William. It was somewhere he could go where no one knew who he was, and those that did, didn't care. He was just another guy, and according to Charlie, 'He was in paradise. Lewa's a very dynamic place. There's always something exciting going on. It's thrilling for an adult, let alone a kid; and there's an element of danger. Yet it's not just fun for fun's sake, it's doing something worthwhile.'

A couple of monuments remain to mark William's two months in Kenya in the spring of 2001. First, he built the bird hide at Lewa. The initial attempt sank into the swamp, much to the amusement of the Kenyans; his second attempt survives to this day. He also built a flying fox, otherwise known as a foofy slide, across a deep, death-defying gully at Lake Rutundu in Mount Kenya National Park, a two-hour drive south of Lewa. It is one of the remotest places on the planet, accessed through several miles of single track—and at times trackless—forest and scrub; the sort of place where if you slipped off the path (easily done) or ran out of fuel, you might not be found for months. But when you finally reach the lake and the two-hut lodge above it, you realise it was worth the journey. It is one of the most breathtaking places—and because of the high altitude, literally breathtaking.

It was also the place where William took Kate Middleton—and his mother's diamond and sapphire ring—in 2010 and proposed marriage to her. He took her there no doubt to show off his amazing piece of handiwork with the flying fox. Or perhaps the place where he actually presented the ring (we shall never know exactly) was at Lake Alice, another ten thousand feet higher and an even more heavenly place and well worth the climb. What history does not relate is whether Kate risked life and limb and crossed the ravine in William's flying fox, which has a large safety sign beside it (widely disregarded) saying that it is for luggage only, or whether she took the safe option, and walked down to the bottom of the ravine and up the other side.

# THE OLD GREY TOWN

William arrived at the old university town of St Andrews in September 2001 and was almost immediately embroiled in an upsetting and ugly row that was not of his making. Colleen Harris had extended the deal with the media; in what was called The St Andrews Agreement, William would make himself available for a photo call when he arrived, and thereafter for an informal chat once a term. In return, he would be allowed to continue his education undisturbed by the media.

Unsurprisingly, he was nervous about starting

university. None of his friends had chosen St Andrews and home and family were a very long way away. It was a great choice, in which Andrew Gailey had played a significant role, it having been one of his alma maters. Other strong advocates had been James and Julia Ogilvy. James Ogilvy is the son of Princess Alexandra (a cousin of the Queen) and Angus Ogilvy, and he and Julia, who was a trusted friend of Diana's, met as students at St Andrews and subsequently married. They have since bought a house there and work nearby and, like many former students, have huge affection for the town. All three of them had obviously been agitating in favour of the place and the year before William started, they brought him for a quiet and unofficial look around. William liked what he saw.

St Andrews is familiar to most people from watching the Open Golf Championships on television. It's a picturesque coastal town, small enough to be a community, with a good reputation for the subjects he wanted to study. It is Scotland's oldest university, founded in 1413, and the third oldest in the English-speaking world. It is also now one of the best, but neither its age nor its credentials make up for the fact that it is a long way from anywhere and there are no trains or planes within easy reach. Beautiful and ancient though it is, it is a one-horse town with a limited amount to do—and the reason, no doubt, why it has the highest rate of student marriages of all universities in the UK (my own, as well as the Ogilvys' and Prince William's being among them).

A year before his arrival, only two people at the university knew that William had chosen St Andrews. They were Colin Vincent, who was acting principal at that time and William's academic adviser, and David Corner, a medieval historian, who as secretary and registrar at the university looked after his non-academic welfare. They both knew that William would be filling in the name of only one university on his UCAS application form. But the press, for some reason, thought he had applied for Edinburgh, which proved very convenient for St Andrews in allowing his application and everything else that followed to proceed quietly.

Like every other student, his place was dependent on achieving the required A level grades—which he did—and once those were through Brian Lang, the future principal, and David went to Eton to see Andrew Gailey and others to discuss security and how best to handle William's arrival and the relationship in general.

What none of them expected in the sleepy town of St Andrews was a terrorist attack. Within weeks of the announcement that he'd be starting in September 2001 (coincidentally the year of the 9/11 terrorist attacks in the United States), the university received a series of parcels that purported to contain the deadly virus anthrax. They came, it transpired, from a Scottish liberation group in protest over a Scottish university admitting an English Prince.

They turned out to be hoaxes but each one had to be taken seriously. 'I had one secretary,' recalls David Corner, 'who said, "If I get another one and have to take my clothes off in the department again, I'm going to charge for it."' The procedure was that anyone who might have been contaminated was put into quarantine until they had clearance from Porton Down, the germ warfare laboratories in England, where the substance had to be sent. Feeling sorry for the press office team quarantined in the police station, David popped in to see how they were, taking the principal, Brian Lang, and the boss of the company brought in to handle the tabloids. 'We walked in and the desk officer said, "Och, they're fine," and brought them out to meet us, which deemed us contaminated, so the boss of Beattie Media, the principal and I were locked up for three hours in the police station!'

On the Friday before William's arrival for his first term, David was asked to join him and his father for the evening, at the Palace of Holyroodhouse in Edinburgh. 'I think already some degree of nerves had set in; and I think he [William] thought it was going to be terribly formal, and it was quite the opposite.' David could not be less formal himself.

He is a cheerful, Moses-like figure with wild white hair and beard; rumour has it he owns a tie but it's seldom seen. He had already been to St James's Palace to talk reassuringly to the Prince of Wales about what William could expect at St Andrews. Like all Scottish universities—but different from most universities in the UK—students do a four-year honours degree, but rather than studying one subject in ever-greater depth as the years pass, they start with three different subjects in the first year and narrow them down.

'They had decided that this was not going to be a weekend about William going to St Andrews; it was William and his father visiting Scotland, so they did things like going to a housing estate in Glasgow, going to a dance studio in Edinburgh and eventually they turned up at St Andrews with Dad carrying the suitcase and putting him in his hall of residence.'

Most of the town had turned out to see them arrive, and quite a number of the world's media too. 'I think he was really nervous when he arrived,' says Colleen. 'All the press were there and it suddenly hit him, and he was very unsteady for a little while after that. He'd had a fantastic gap year, really enjoyed himself, and there he was stuck. He didn't know anybody, just one or two guys from Eton who he didn't know that well, and he was very much alone.'

Niall Scott, the university press officer, had

been briefed by Colleen Harris that if he spotted anyone in the town with anything larger than an instamatic, he was to get them removed. It was not only William's privacy that mattered but also the privacy of his fellow students. 'William was very sensitive to that,' says Niall. 'He knew the unsettling effect his presence could have and was keen that it should all be quietened down.'

Scarcely had the last media truck disappeared than Niall saw a camera crew blithely setting up to film outside his office window. 'It was a red rag to a bull,' he said. 'I walked out and asked them what they were doing. I was told, "We're Ardent, here's our card. We're making an A–Z of Royalty for an entertainment channel in the States and we're waiting to film William coming out of his lecture."' Ardent, they explained, was owned by Prince Edward, William's uncle. 'We had a full and frank exchange of views on the pavement,' says Niall, 'and I said, "You shouldn't be here, a deal's a deal, I don't care who you are, everyone else has left."

'It was the start of a very interesting week. We then discovered that Ardent had taken a group of our students, bought them dinner and then asked them to pretend that a year had passed and they were looking back at William's first year, and this was to be presented as fact. All a bit underhand.'

Colleen had stayed on for a couple of days and she too spotted the Ardent crew. 'They kept saying they had permission to be there and I said, "Well, I'm the person who would give you permission and I haven't, so you can't be here." "No," they said, "we've got permission from Prince Edward." They wouldn't go, so I rang Mark [Bolland]. It became a massive story. Edward rang and said he was sorry about the confusion, they were going to go, it was a misunderstanding.'

The *Daily Mail* claimed the Prince of Wales was 'incandescent' with rage: so angry that he had refused to take telephone calls from his youngest brother. The story escalated into a major attack on Prince Edward and his competence as a film-maker and ran in most of the newspapers for several days. Then Prince Philip was said to have weighed into the argument. He thought William was being 'overprotected' by his father and had 'overreacted' to the film crew. In a very rare reaction from Buckingham Palace, Prince Philip issued a strongly worded public statement saying he thought nothing of the sort; the views attributed to him were 'totally without foundation'.

'Who knows how the conversation went between them all at Sandringham that Christmas,' says Colleen. 'William and Harry would not have been happy about their uncle being made to look a fool.'

# A NORMAL STUDENT

Knowing his father was engaged in a major family row would have been upsetting for any student trying to settle quietly into a new university in a new part of the country, surrounded by strangers. How much more devastating then to have it splashed all over the newspapers.

The first few weeks and months were tough but he gradually found his feet and began to make friends. Inevitably, perhaps, he gravitated to the familiar and the safe—the only two old Etonians in his hall of residence, Alasdair Coutts-Wood and Fergus Boyd. He had known them vaguely at Eton and Andrew Gailey had done a little engineering to ensure that there were at least a couple of familiar faces in hall with whom he thought William might become friends.

William was cautious about letting people into his confidence, perhaps rightly. At Ludgrove and Eton he had been protected by the system and he was among children who came from solid middle- and upper-class backgrounds—not known for their anarchic or Republican sympathies. At university there were no safety nets and he was amongst a student population of nearly seven thousand very diverse people from every background under the sun and almost as many countries. There was no presumption that they would be sympathetic to him and no reason to suppose they might be supporters of the monarchy. Many of them, some of the lecturers included, were not. Equally, there were people who threw themselves at him, particularly star-struck American girls, whom he steered clear of. As his father discovered at the same age, those that came forward usually wanted to be friends for all the wrong reasons, while the more genuine people didn't want to be seen to be sucking up. There was also the very real fear of photographs or stories and snippets being sold to the media. He knew he could trust the sort of people he mixed with at school and at home. Sticking with them was a safer bet.

There was no shortage of people to choose from. The university struggles to shake off its public-school image and the student profile is mixed nationally—about one third are Scottish, one third European, including English, and one third from further overseas, mostly America—but in William's year there were dozens of boys from Eton. 'They can appear to be terribly posh,' says David. 'Most of them go home for the weekends, but put them all in a minibus together with the others for a week on a field trip and they all get on famously. St Andrews is an incredibly inclusive place.'

William did mix with the state school students in academic and sporting settings; 'It was almost a thing that William was determined to do,' says David. 'His very close friends were all from public schools. Interestingly though, he started playing very early for the university water polo team. Water polo is not a particularly public school sport, it is one of the roughest games you can play—it can be brutal—and he was playing in the Scottish league and the Celtic Nations Tournament, so he was going to places like Motherwell [a relatively depressed former steel town south-east of Glasgow], which is an utterly no-nonsense place. In his bathing cap they didn't know who he was.'

The hall of residence he chose was called St Salvator's Hall, commonly known as Sally's, which is one of the smallest and most central, where Kate Middleton also happened to be living that first year, which is how they came to meet. Most early friendships are formed with the people you live with at university, quite simply because you bump into each other all the time, in the corridors and bathrooms, over breakfast and the coffee machine, and clutching armfuls of dirty socks in the laundry room. William had missed Freshers' Week, when there are parties and discos and time for the new intake to work out the geography of the town and make a few friends before the work starts in earnest. In his absence, the public school element in Sally's had already sought each other out and Kate—with her

Marlborough College credentials, her fashionable clothes and her well-kempt mane of dark brown hair—was one of them.

They met with friends, and then found themselves attending the same lectures, walking to and from Sally's, bumping into each other at the sports centre, in bars and around the town—it's not a big place, there are just three main streets—and people with anything in common tend to gravitate to one another.

Sally's was purpose-built in the 1930s—out of the ubiquitous grey stone that is so characteristic of the town—with spacious gardens at the back. William had made it very clear that he didn't want anything fancy, so he had a standard room to himself but shared a bathroom. He also shared laundry and kitchen facilities, although most meals during the week were provided. At weekends they had to fend for themselves in the evenings but there were plenty of bars, pubs and restaurants serving food, or there was the chippy. The only difference between him and every other student in Sally's was that his PPOs had a room nearby.

'Some of the protection people came the year before William arrived and said, "We need to see the rooms,"' says David. 'So, because I'm not supposed to be telling anybody anything I had to say to the manager of St Salvator's, "Look, when is the present student who occupies that room likely to be out?" "She's never in between 9 and 11 in the morning," she says, so I took these burly policemen, about eleven of them, up to this room. It was empty, the manager unlocked it, we all stood in the room, they all chatted away. There was then a wonderful pitter-patter along the corridor of a naked student except for a bath towel coming back to her room to get dressed. She handled the police a lot better than the police handled her!

'The protection people were a scream. They dressed like seventies middle-class students—in cords and jackets. They stood out a mile trying to blend in and look like students.'

The university wanted no guns on campus. 'I don't know what they actually did,' says David. 'But everyone in the town used to refer casually to a certain vehicle which regularly toured the streets neighbouring the campus as "the gun van."'

David and William met every three or four weeks. 'Our meetings were not really businesslike because he was incredibly jovial, it was very knockabout and that was the level at which he wanted it—and not, perhaps, the level he expected from a university. I think he had this notion he was in a different hierarchy and it went up to people like me and it would be as formal as some of his other hierarchies were, and he enjoyed the fact that it wasn't like that. The fact that someone would say, "Ah come off it." So we got on extremely well, but it was not beyond the superficial in terms of personal things.'

David was much amused by a conversation with the Queen during her Golden Jubilee at Buckingham Palace. He was sent as a representative of one of the six ancient universities, 'to swear allegiance and say we were loyal citizens', he says, 'and I remember the Queen asking me, "How's William?" as if I saw him every day, as if St Andrews was one quad. I said, "As far as I know, he's absolutely fine."'

# HORSE-TRADING

At the beginning of William's second term he was upset by an even bigger family row hitting the news. The *News of the World* (with Rebekah Wade now at the helm) ran an exclusive story under the headline, 'HARRY'S DRUG SHAME'. Harry, then sixteen, had confessed he'd been smoking cannabis and drinking under-age and after-hours in the Rattlebone. According to the story, Harry's behaviour had come to light in November 2001 and his father had taken him for a short sharp shock to Featherstone Lodge, a drug rehabilitation centre in south London, to spend a day talking to recovering drug addicts.

It was another of Mark Bolland's attempts to repair the Prince of Wales's reputation. What could have been a wholly negative story had a

276

positive spin: Charles had masterfully handled the scenario that every parent dreads and can identify with. He was not a bad father, as the Prime Minister, Tony Blair, was one of the first to proclaim: 'The way Prince Charles and the Royal Family have handled it is absolutely right and they have done it in a very responsible and, as you would expect, a very sensitive way for their child.' Peter Martin, chief executive of Addaction, Britain's largest drug and alcohol treatment agency, said 'The Prince of Wales has acted with deep sensitivity and very quickly, which is exactly what is needed.' To which the Department of Education added, 'Parents play a very important role, as demonstrated by Prince Charles, who has set an extremely good example.'

The *News of the World* claimed that Harry had been smoking the cannabis in the shed at the back of the Rattlebone and on one occasion, at the end of a lock-in, a very drunk Harry, when asked to leave, had called the French under-manager, 'a f***ing frog'. Steve Hoare, from Nobodys Business, was there that night and was so disgusted by 'the lies' he read in the papers over the whole incident that he has never bought a newspaper since. No one ever used the shed out at the back, the lock-ins happened in the back bar, there were never any drugs in the pub when William or Harry were around and if anyone had produced any, Skip and Casper, instructors from the polo club or their PPOs, who were always there, would have been on it like a flash. As for the incident with the Frenchman, François Ortet, known as 'French Frank', it was playful banter; they were friends, and the Frenchman was giving as good as he got.

According to locals, the *News of the World* had sent a couple of young reporters to live in the village for a month and infiltrate the Rattlebone. They had been introduced by a regular as relatives and they got to know the locals. It's rumoured that it was not motivated by altruism. The figure of £35,000 has been mentioned.

What none of the media who flocked to the sleepy village of Sherston looking for locals to spill the beans on Harry knew was that Mark's release of the story to the *News of the World* was a skilful piece of damage limitation. During the summer, the *News of the World* had published a photograph of a very spaced-out Harry in a nightclub in Spain. They had kept a watch on him ever since, spoken to associates and compiled damning evidence of far more serious behaviour than that described in their story in January 2002. Some of it had been going on in the basement of Highgrove, which the Prince had done up for the boys as a den. They called it Club H and had wild parties there with their friends, playing loud techno music until the early hours.

Rebekah Wade had rung her friend Bolland to

alert him to what they had, and he brokered a deal which saved the young Prince's bacon and left his father smelling of roses.

'Worried Charles chose to "terrify" Harry away from drugs by sending him to therapy sessions with hard-core heroin addicts,' announced the *News of the World*, but a 'family friend' declared reassuringly that, 'he has never done drugs since. William is such a steadying influence. The two of them have had detailed discussions and Harry has changed his ways. He now understands the very real perils of drug-taking and excessive drinking. He has a lot to be thankful for. If his brother and father did not care so much about him there might well have been a different end to this story.'

Little did the friend know that the wild child was merely limbering up.

What incensed Harry—and William too, in defence of his brother—was that the two incidents were not connected. Harry had been to visit the rehab centre in June or July of 2001, with Mark Dyer, where he did speak to recovering addicts, but it had nothing to do with his own behaviour. The *News of the World* did not have the cannabis story until August or September of that year.

'Harry really resented the way he was made to look bad so that his father could look good,' says a friend. 'He understood why it happened, and I don't think he blamed his father, but the idea that Harry had gone to a rehab centre a year before because Prince Charles had seen the way things were going is a blatant load of b*****ks. Prince Charles didn't have any idea what his son was up to. It was PR panic and spin and he really resents that he was made to take the rap for that.'

This same friend says, 'The idea of Harry being the wild one and William the good one is nonsense. They were both wild. Harry was just the one that got caught.' He doubts, however, that William ever took drugs. 'He's quite canny, quite square in that way, I'd bet a lot of money he never has. He would never have been bullied into doing it because everyone else was. He's quite an intelligent man; he would know absolutely if he was caught taking drugs it would be a catastrophe. He lets his hair down and puts down some serious drink on occasions, certainly he did as a student, and when he's away he definitely lets his hair down, he likes a good night out with his friends, but he's always quite careful to protect his image and not do anything that would really damage him. You get pissed, so what? Nobody cares; you take drugs, it tarnishes you for ever and if you're going to be King? No. But the idea of good Prince, bad Prince was always a load of rubbish.'

What was almost more upsetting about the *News of the World* story, however, was that the boy who unjustly took the blame for the whole scenario was Guy Pelly, a polo-playing friend of both brothers but principally William, and a student at

Cirencester Agricultural College. He was said to 'have encouraged Harry to experiment with the drug at a private party in Tetbury', and taken it into Highgrove so Harry could smoke it at parties there. A family friend said, 'Prince Harry fell in with a bad lot. Guy Pelly, who has a drink-drive conviction and is a student at Cirencester, was the worst influence. It was Pelly who introduced Harry to cannabis in June last year.'

William has always been worried for his friends that their association with him could force them into the limelight or cause them embarrassment in any way—he is almost obsessive about it—and this was as bad as it could get. Pelly was and is a good friend whose name and reputation were trashed by the media, and he was forced to give up his farm management course because of the row. He only ever spoke once about it. 'I have never dealt in drugs at Highgrove, at the Rattlebone Inn or anywhere else,' he said. 'I have never taken drugs with Prince Harry or supplied any drugs to him. I have never used drugs at Highgrove or the Rattlebone Inn. I would like this categoric statement to put an end to the matter.' That was wishful thinking—his reputation has never fully recovered from the incident—but it is a measure of the depth of loyalty and affection he, like all their close friends, feels towards both Princes that he was prepared to put up with the indignity and never attempt to clear his name further.

And it is a measure of just how loyal both Princes are to their friends that just five weeks later, despite the newspapers telling us that Charles had forbidden Harry to see Guy Pelly again, they very publicly stood shoulder to shoulder with him on the terraces at Twickenham for a high-profile international rugby match.

Eighteen months later, after Mark Bolland had gone from his job, he admitted that the sequence of events in the story was distorted to portray Charles in a positive light and attempt to draw a line under the scandal. 'Presenting the [rehab] centre as the great solution to the problem was something that I was embarrassed about,' he said in an interview with the *Guardian*. 'It was misleading.'

# LOSS AND LEARNING

Colleen has sympathy for both Princes and understands why they were so upset by the shenanigans, but she says that nothing at that time was ever as clear-cut as it looked. 'You have no idea what else was being covered up. Yes, it was terrible but it could have been a lot worse. What William and Harry are forgetting is there were many times when we managed to keep them out of the media when they were up to mischievous things.' The Rattlebone (not far from where I live in Wiltshire) was undoubtedly the scene of some high-octane partying by both William and Harry, as were several other pubs within a ten-mile radius, and it is a measure of the affection engendered by both boys that locals keep their memories to themselves.

But sometimes the family was in the news quite simply because of who they were. Just a month into his second semester, when the story of Harry's drug-taking was beginning to subside, Princess Margaret, the Queen's troubled sister, died. It was not entirely unexpected; she had suffered a series of strokes and been unwell for some years but, in such a close family, it was a major upset. She had been a neighbour at Kensington Palace and a presence at every family get-together. The entire family gathered for a private funeral at St George's Chapel, Windsor, including the Queen Mother. Despite her own failing health and a fall just a few days before when she had damaged her arm, she was determined to be there to lay her youngest daughter to rest. She was flown from Sandringham to Windsor by helicopter and carefully helped into a car for the last part of the journey. She was very frail and hidden behind a black veil, but as Margaret's coffin was taken away, she struggled to her feet. It was the last time William saw his great-grandmother.

Six weeks later, the BBC interrupted a programme in the early evening of 30 March 2002 to announce that she had died peacefully in her sleep at Royal Lodge, Windsor, with her daughter, the Queen, at her side. The family, and this time the nation too, were again in mourning. The Queen Mother was an iconic figure in her flowing pastel silks and feathery hats; the very epitome of royal decorum and style, and a woman whose guts and courage while bombs were falling over London during the Blitz had inspired the nation. William used to relish being seated next to her at lunch and was fascinated by her stories about the past. There was no hysteria as there had been over Diana's death, but in a gross error of judgement, the BBC instructed the newscaster not to wear a black tie. No one foresaw the public's reaction to her death. Diana's death had been unnatural and untimely; the Queen Mother's was a peaceful conclusion to a long, full and largely very happy life. She was a hundred and one, had two new hips, a full set of marbles and a wonderful sense of humour. Yet there was no shortage of mourners. Thousands of bouquets were left on the lawns at St George's Chapel and the queue for the lying-in-state in Westminster Hall stretched for three miles.

William was skiing in Klosters with his father and Harry, and, as usual, a gang of friends, when they heard the news. His father was said to have been 'completely devastated' and it was William's turn to be the comforter. On their return home Charles gave a very personal and moving tribute on television to 'the original life enhancer—at once indomitable, somehow timeless, able to span the generations. Wise, loving, with an utterly irresistible mischievousness of spirit.' She was 'quite simply the most magical grandmother you could possibly have, and I was utterly devoted to her.'

Plans for her funeral—Operation Tay Bridge—had been drawn up years before and were very straightforward. It was a full-blown State funeral with ceremonial regalia in Westminster Abbey, the most solemn State occasion since her husband King George VI's funeral fifty years before. Her grandsons, the Prince of Wales, Prince Andrew, the Earl of Wessex and Viscount Linley, together with Prince Philip, Princes William and Harry and Peter Phillips—and breaking tradition, the Princess Royal—all walked behind the coffin, carried (as Diana's had been) on a gun carriage, drawn by the King's Troop, the Royal Horse Artillery. The Prince of Wales was visibly distressed. William and Harry, for whom so much of the day must have brought back memories of their mother's funeral, looked sad but composed.

William was a master at keeping his feelings hidden. He had been doing it since he was a child and the only person in the world who knew the turmoil that bubbled beneath the surface was Harry; and vice versa. He and Harry, so different in so many ways, and like most siblings not especially close as small children, now clung to one another, their relationship cemented by mutual need. Only they had experienced the full nightmare of life within the Wales Household; only they had known what it was like to be at an all-boys school when the newspapers were full of their parents' infidelities; only they had known what it was like to grieve for their mother while millions of strangers took ownership of her death, and to try to move on from that while the media did its best to keep her in the news.

They'd seen less of each other since William had left Eton—and after Harry left school in June 2003 and went off on his gap year, their meetings were even more infrequent—but the bond between them never wavered.

'How did he cope with all the awful things that were going on in the media?' says David Corner. 'He had a collection of support networks. He liked and talked to Colleen a lot. There were others in St James's Palace at that time that he trusted and talked to. That was not part of his life with me, or any of us. I think he built that fence not because of non-trust but because there was an absolute split in his mind in terms of his social activities, his problems that were coming from London and being a student. It was maybe something he learnt at St Andrews. He almost wanted to walk out of the front door and be as normal a student as he could be.'

• • •

There were not many ways in which William was treated differently at St Andrews, but how his marks were kept was slightly special. Instead of going into the registry along with everyone else's, Colin Vincent and David Corner guarded them so there would be no chance of a leak. 'On hearing this, William's immediate question was, "How are they marked?" "Exactly the same as everybody else's." Everything was extraordinarily normal and when it was finished we thanked God that it had been so normal, right through from admission to graduation, it had worked extraordinarily well and the other students agreed, they didn't feel they had been impeded in any way.'

'We had lots of funny conversations,' David says. 'We used to meet in the street and chat. I remember one day standing talking to him in front of the tourist bus. There were a whole load of tourists on it and the guide was pointing out to them that if they looked over there on the left and bent their heads, they could see where Prince William lives. If they'd only looked down!'

Professor Peter Humfrey remembers welcoming William to the History of Art department in his first week. 'There would have been two hundred or so people in the lecture theatre. He sat close to the front where I suppose people couldn't turn round and stare at him and he had a baseball cap pulled right down over his eyes.'

'It was just so obvious,' says Dr John Walden, his Geography tutor, 'he was uncomfortable about being watched.'

The academic staff were afraid the other students might come into lectures with their cameras but none of them saw any evidence of it and no one seemed to leak stories—or if they did the newspapers didn't use them. The students had been told, 'We are not going to talk about you and you aren't going to talk about him, are you?' And it appeared to work. Professor Brendan Cassidy, his first tutor for History of Art, was astonished by how casual people were. When he announced to the class that William would be joining them, there wasn't a flicker of interest. 'Then when he did turn up, they turned round and, I was so surprised, I was expecting some kind of buzz, but there was nothing. In the class there were seven women and two men; that's perfectly normal in History of Art. William seemed very uncomfortable with the girls, and in the second or third week, the other man didn't turn up for the tutorial, so William was there with his seven women. His body language said it all, he tried to wrap himself up, but within a couple of months he was so much more relaxed.'

Kate was not among the women in William's tutor group, although who knows if he would have felt any more comfortable if she had been. He was definitely more relaxed with familiar faces, and hers was growing familiar. They were becoming friends within a group that lived at Sally's, and while they attended the same History of Art lectures, they had different tutors.

In that first semester, Brendan Cassidy gave the group a very simple exercise, to compare two pictures that hang in the National Gallery, one by Giovanni Bellini and the other by Andrea Mantegna, both Venetian Renaissance artists. 'I never twigged, of course, that William couldn't just walk into the National Gallery and see Giovanni Bellini. I asked if he'd seen the pictures, assuming he had, and he said, no, he'd never been in the National Gallery.

'I had heard previously from [Lady] Jane Roberts [curator of the Print Room] at the Royal Collection at Windsor that she had given him little tutorials there but, of course, that's completely different. If I'd been smart I should have given him an essay on something at Windsor and he could have borrowed something from Granny's collection. The essay was good.

'There's no question about whether he should have been here. There was grumbling among some folk that he only got in because of who he was but that's not true, he was perfectly capable of doing his subject from my experience. In the old masters he was very competent, he wasn't a star but he was certainly competent, and he could certainly hold his own and deserved to be there;

he wrote well enough. I got the feeling if he had been allowed to roam around a bit more, get to the National Gallery, his work could have been better than it was.'

'I never really understood why he did History of Art in the first place,' confesses Peter Humfrey. 'I imagine there had been some charismatic school master who put him on to it, but I could see that he wasn't deeply engaged with it and, of course, he didn't carry on with it after his second year.'

# FINDING HIS FEET

Much has been made of William arriving at St Andrews to read History of Art and switching to Geography. It's not as dramatic as it sounds, and according to Colin Vincent a significant number of people do the same thing. William gave History of Art as his degree choice on the UCAS entry form but he was always going to study Geography alongside it for the first two years; he also did Social Anthropology and Moral Philosophy and briefly a bit of Arabic Culture. All that happened is he decided to take Geography through to honours level instead of the other subject. Colin was the one who helped him reach that decision. 'We had discussions and he wrote down the pros and cons of the two subjects. It was all to do with what he was finding stimulating and interesting. I think he had surprised himself with his ability to cope with the quantitative, mathematical side of Geography. He had a view he couldn't do it. His father had been concerned that, like him, he didn't have a quantitative brain.'

While not unusual or surprising in itself, the switch did cause the odd wry smile around the academic community. The campus had been marginally rearranged before William's arrival. The Art History department, which had been fragmented in buildings all over the town, was brought under one roof in what had been the principal's house. It was a grand building on the Scores (the most prestigious address in the town) overlooking the sea, and was a hundred-yard walk for William in the mornings from his hall of residence. The incoming principal, Dr Brian Lang, who arrived at the same time as William, took a modest modern house in the town. 'He conveniently took the view that modern principals didn't need to live in a house with thirty-seven rooms and have man servants,' says Niall Scott, tongue firmly in cheek. 'That allowed us to put all of Art History in one place, which for academic as well as security reasons was better.'

John Walden was William's Geography tutor throughout the four years and in his final year, supervised two big pieces of independent work, a review essay and a ten-thousand word dissertation. 'The academic stuff was fine,' he says, 'he was a perfectly capable student, no different from any other students in the cohort.' What fascinated him about William was the security circus. You could walk around the town and not know it was happening but then you got a little peek and realised it was a big operation. 'I had to discuss all the details of field trips with his PPOs, how many in the class, where we were going and the timings. The PPOs kept a very low profile but wanted to know everything. In the first year the Geography department was near the Scores but the lectures were down on the North Haugh in the Purdie building [on the other side of town], so William had a little commute. They eventually got bored with him having to walk and somebody bought him a pushbike, and thereafter, one PPO would stand in the halls of residence, put him on his bike, send him off down the road, where there was a black car with darkened windows and another PPO waiting to see him arrive safely on the North Haugh, "Yes, he's arrived," they would radio. Some terrorist could have come along and shot the wheels off his bike—so in that sense it was very relaxed—but there were a lot of people one way or another working on the operation.'

Brendan says, 'He always had an eye out for the press and would hang about after class after all the other students had gone. The first time he asked me if I minded and he said it was in case anyone was waiting outside. I remember asking him if he was going to take part in Raisin Monday, the day when students go bonkers and drink copiously, dress up, have foam fights in the Quad and do silly things. He said no, because he was just too vulnerable, if he did anything silly and the press got hold of it . . .'

Raisin Monday is an age-old tradition at St Andrews. Older students have always taken first years (Bejants/Bejantines) under their wing and shown them the ropes. They are called Academic Parents and on Raisin Monday their 'children' express their gratitude by giving them a pound of raisins—deemed as something of a luxury in the days when each student went up to the university with a sack of oatmeal and a barrel of salt-herring to see them through the term. Nowadays, the raisins are more likely to be in liquid form, while in return, the Parents give their 'children' formal receipts for the gift; these can be written on anything from a ladder to a chicken— the more awkward or comical the better—which the 'children' have to carry around with them for the rest of the day.

'Otherwise,' says Brendan, 'I don't think his style was cramped too much. St Andrews was the best place he could have come to. It was small, no one made a fuss of him, people were protective.'

Peter says, 'My feeling in the first year was that he hadn't quite clicked that this was going to be the freest moment of his whole life.

'In Tesco's people treated him as a normal customer. I saw him in a queue for the checkout once and an elderly lady from the town start chatting to him. He dealt with it very well. He wasn't so friendly she was encouraged to come back for more but he was not off-putting. But he was always aware that someone from the *News of the World* could be lurking with a lens. When he walked about the town he pulled his baseball cap down low and wrapped an Aston Villa scarf round his face, and you didn't really notice him.'

The odd paparazzo, of course, lurked. Despite all the agreements, there were still a few hanging around, hoping for a shot of him with a girl or doing something compromising that could be deemed to be in the public interest. One that appeared in several of the tabloids was certainly not in the public interest and, on the face of it, was harmless. It was a shot of him in the street laden with Tesco plastic shopping bags full of groceries. William was incensed and rang Colleen in his father's office. ' "Why are these photographers following me?" he was saying. "They shouldn't be, you've got to stop it." He assumed we could keep the cordon around them and we couldn't, it wasn't sustainable. In the PCC code it said up to the age of eighteen, but post-eighteen it was only goodwill and it was much harder to control the media then. He kicked up a real stink about it and it was really quite hard. He couldn't understand why the media would want these pictures and why it would happen.'

She wonders whether the St James's Palace press office did both boys a bit of a disservice after their mother died—whether they went too far in their determination to protect them. 'If you look back at some of the PCC wording, although it applies to everyone, it was skewed to protect those boys.

'I think we got carried away with it, kept it going too long and the boys got used to it, anyone would. So when they got to eighteen and the rules fell away, they couldn't understand why we couldn't control things. I had a lot of problems.

'I can remember having a conversation with them both when they were expecting that they could go off and do something and I would just sort the media out and no one would hear about it and it would all be fine. I thought, actually what have we done? That's not real life, we can't do that any more.'

Sandy disagrees. 'Maybe we didn't get it right all the time but I firmly believe that we had to come down [on the media] hard and fast after Diana died. The boys needed to see we could protect them from intrusion, tittle-tattle. Being constantly in the papers for the slightest thing could have been embarrassing for those teenagers within their peer group. Seeing the privacy and respect now extended to the Duchess of

Cambridge, I think we set the scene back then and William and Harry were allowed to develop into the men they are today without having a paranoid fear or dislike of the media.'

For all that, not many intrusive photographs made it into the press during William's four years in Scotland. All his tutors agreed that being able to shop for groceries, have a pint in a pub, walk around the town and come and go like anyone else was a positive element for him at St Andrews.

'The independence was probably the most important part of what he got out of the university; that, and meeting Catherine, of course. Forget the degree; the degree was probably somewhere quite low down the list. So while he started off more uncomfortable than a lot of kids who come to university on their own for the first time, once he got through that, into his second year maybe, he relaxed and began to really enjoy it.'

The consensus seems to be that he was comfortable when he could make an easy getaway but wasn't keen on confined spaces, of which the university library was one. Peter Humfrey wasn't the only one who felt William didn't spend enough time in the library. His explanation: 'It's one thing to walk around the place but quite another to sit somewhere where you can be immediately surrounded by the curious.'

William did agree to go on a field trip to

Dundee. It was a first-year human geography trip to look at urban activity, and see how it is separated into different zones. 'It's an interesting place,' says John. 'It used to have a bad reputation but parts of it have improved dramatically in the last ten or twelve years, although it's still got some colourful spots. William was amongst a group of students that went to the colourful spots. They were huddled in a group discussing some low-quality housing, when someone in a flat three floors above threw open the window and, in the broadest of accents, told the group, including the future King, to go f*** themselves.'

William's maternal grandparents. The Queen and Duke of Edinburgh were guests at Johnnie Althorp's wedding to Frances Roche at Westminster Abbey in 1954.

Princess Elizabeth on the day of her engagement to Prince Philip in 1947. Five years later she became Queen—and Johnnie Althorp was one of her equerries.

The young Prince
Charles with his
parents and sister
Princess Anne.
A corgi was never
far from the
Queen's side.

Charles with his
grandfather, King
George VI, whose
death brought an
end to anything
approaching normal
family life.

Three generations: Charles, his beloved
great-uncle and 'Honorary Grandfather',
Earl Mountbatten, and Prince Philip,
Mountbatten's nephew.

A young Lady Diana
Spencer with her
guinea pig, Peanuts.

And even younger, in
her pram in the
garden at Park House.

Diana's father, the 8th Earl Spencer with the stepmother, Raine, who swept into their lives.

Charles, Diana and her two sisters Jane and Sarah at their brother, Charles Spencer's, 21st birthday party in 1982, the year William was born.

Charles and Diana with Harvey, after their engagement, when it all started to go wrong.

Diana delighted the crowds with her informality.

Charles and Diana's wedding, declared the Archbishop of Canterbury, was 'the stuff of which fairytales are made'.

The first ever kiss on the balcony and the crowds went wild.

Diana's dress was the best-kept secret of the wedding. The train was 25 feet long.

Despite the smiles, there were already problems in the relationship.

Not even two weeks in the Mediterranean sunshine on board the Royal yacht Britannia could lift Diana's spirits.

Prince William's first public appearance leaving the Lindo Wing of St Mary's Hospital, Paddington less than 24 hours after his birth.

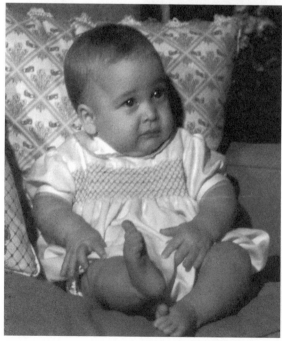

The first of many photo calls. At home in the comfort of Kensington Palace.

Stealing the show in Wellington, aged nine months, on his first tour of Australia and New Zealand in 1983.

Prince Harry making his first appearance in September 1984. For a brief period before his birth Charles and Diana were closer than ever but it soon fell apart.

William's playful antics at Prince Andrew's wedding did not amuse the Queen.

The family putting on a show of unity amongst the wild flowers at Highgrove.

William, aged four and a half, arriving for his first day at Wetherby School.

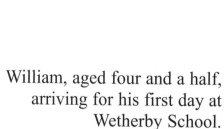

All dressed up for church at Windsor on
Easter Day with his cousins, already trained
to wave to the waiting crowds.

Another photo call for two
small boys to endure. On
holiday in Majorca with the
Spanish Royal Family.

Taken out of school for his first public
engagement aged nine. His father
thought he was too young.

Both boys have always had a warm and tactile
relationship with their father and all three of them
love their holidays in Scotland.

Diana strikes a lonely figure in front of the
Taj Mahal in February 1992, and knew
exactly what message it sent to the world.

The boys' first skiing holiday in 1991.

Diana ensured they did normal childish things—
and she enjoyed the thrill of the rides at Thorpe
Park just as much as they did.

Diana adored her boys but Olga Powell,
the nanny, was a more constant figure
in their early lives.

Another was Tiggy
Legge-Bourke of
whom Diana
reportedly became
jealous.

Ludgrove was a small family-run school where William was protected from the lurid headlines about his parents' marriage problems.

Eton was almost ten times bigger, and had no such mechanism. William often used to walk over the bridge to Windsor Castle to have tea with Granny and Grandpa.

William's confirmation in March 1997. The first time the Wales family had been together in four years—and it was to be the last. 'Granny Frances' wasn't invited.

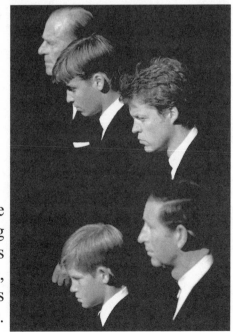

No one coerced the boys into walking behind their mother's cortège. The decision, brave as it was, was entirely theirs.

The outpouring of national grief for
Diana was unprecedented.

There were said
to be a million
bouquets outside
Kensington
Palace, 1.5 metres
deep in places.

The trip to Canada in 1998 with his father and brother, when William was mobbed by screaming teenagers. Mark Bolland, nicknamed Blackadder, in the blue shirt behind.

One of the set of 18th birthday photos that lost Sandy Henney her job.

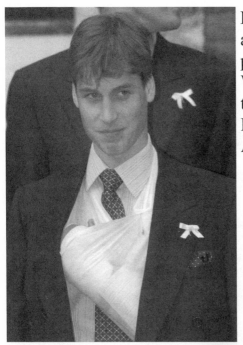

His arm in a sling after an injury on the rugby pitch, sixteen year old William is godfather at the christening of Prince Konstantine Alexios of Greece.

Arriving at the Guards Polo Club for the Eton Boys' Tea Party with James Meade. He is still one of a small band of loyal and trusted friends.

Another of the infamous 18th birthday pictures. Only the most popular and successful boys are elected to Pop.

Announcing his gap year plans and his place at St Andrews University. Despite the difference in style, father and son are very close.

Brothers, friends, confidants. They have
seen each other through difficult times.

William arrived in
Chile quiet and
shy. It was the
first time he had
been entirely out
of his comfort
zone. By the end
of eleven weeks
he was swinging
from the rafters.

A steadying hand for the Queen Mother on her 99th birthday, while his father looks on approvingly. William loved talking to his great-grandmother about the past. Charles was completely devoted to her and devastated when she died in April 2002 at the age of 101. It was then William's turn to be the comforter.

Walking behind the Queen Mother's coffin must have brought back painful memories.

The dress. Kate Middleton at a charity fashion show at the students' union in St Andrews in March 2002. William, sitting at the end of the catwalk, had a good view.

William and Kate had plenty of interests and activities in common. Skiing was just one of them.

The photo call that made the tabloids think he might not go into the Army after all but was destined to become a farmer.

They share a love of the countryside and one day William will inherit the Duchy of Cornwall—about 130,000 acres, mostly in the West Country and much of it farmland.

He took his studies seriously and came away with a respectable 2.1 in Geography.

He quickly became a member of the University water polo team.

A very proud grandmother in St Andrews on graduation day, June 2005.

Kate was much less nervous than William about graduation day. She got a 2.1 in History of Art.

The annual skiing trip was always one of the high spots of the year—once the dreaded photo call was over.

Charles and Camilla
leaving St George's
Chapel, Windsor in
April 2005. Man and
wife thirty years after
they first fell in love.

What mattered to
William was that
his father was
finally happy.

Sovereign's Parade with a difference. William's Passing Out ceremony from Sandhurst in December 2006.

The family together for Harry's Passing Out parade at Sandhurst in April 2006. Granny and Grandpa have been central figures for both Princes—each one dispensing their own brand of guidance, humour and affection.

Training with mountain rescue in Snowdonia. He was tempted by the service but helicopters won the day.

With his fellow graduates at RAF Cranwell in April 2008, having been presented with his wings by his father, the Air Chief Marshal.

Laying a wreath at the Cenotaph on Remembrance Day 2008. Like the rest of the family, he cares passionately about the welfare of members of the Armed Forces and their families.

Showing his grandmother how he spends the day when she visited RAF Valley in April 2011. They had been in weekly contact over his wedding plans.

Flying was very much in the blood.

Carole and Michael Middleton at their home in Bucklebury on the day of the engagement, November 16, 2011. William adores them and their home is an oasis of normality in his very abnormal world.

'Is that you, Ian?'

By giving Kate his
mother's sapphire and
diamond engagement
ring, William said he
hoped to include her in
all the fun and
excitement.

Always happy to have a go when it's for a good cause . . . training with five-to-eleven year olds in Newcastle; and taking part in a thousand-mile off-road motorbike ride in South Africa.

William specifically asked to go to New Zealand and Australia after a series of disasters in 2011 just a month before his wedding. The Queen wrote to congratulate him.

William and Kate's wedding day. 'What we want,' said William, 'is a day that is as enjoyable as possible for as many people as possible.'

He learned from the Queen to take the best of tradition and do it beautifully.

The task was to create a day that was
intimate for them and their families but
which would give the British people a
suitably royal and memorable celebration.

There was no disguising
the happiness of everyone
there that day—nor the
intimacy in the midst of
such formality.

'A quiet family wedding.'

William's greatest fear of the day was that he would
stall their going away car, his father's forty year old
Aston Martin—suitably modified by Prince Harry.

The bond between the brothers is as strong as ever and Harry has the sister he said he always wanted. Derby Day at Epsom in June 2011.

William has grown into the job and accepts the duties and responsibilities that come with who he is, and Kate had a long hard look at the life before choosing to join him in it. The Order of the Garter Service and meeting the Obamas on their state visit to Britain.

Canada Day in Ottawa at the start of their first overseas tour. It was a triumph and despite an exhausting schedule they appeared to be genuinely enjoying themselves.

And the welcome could not have been more enthusiastic.

Kate looked as
though she had been
born to walk on the
red carpet.

The most striking element of the tour was the body language between the two of them—the smiles, the laughter, the hugs, the reassuring hand. They clearly take huge delight in each other's company.

In eleven days they saw much of what Canada has to offer. One day they were canoeing with a tribal elder in the remote North West Territories.

The next they were in Calgary for the famous Stampede Parade.

After Canada came Los Angeles and a very different sort of red carpet. Arriving to promote British talent at a star-studded BAFTA gala dinner.

Barbra Streisand and her husband chat to William. Stars paid up to $16,000 for a table.

Visiting a community centre
in Birmingham after the
August riots in 2011, where
they met the families of
three men knocked down
and killed by a car.

Teasing each other over
their mince pie making
skills at a Centrepoint
hostel in Camberwell in
December 2011. Both are
keen cooks—and both
are competitive.

Church on Christmas
Day at Sandringham
and Kate's introduction
to the first of many
such royal traditions.

The future of the British monarchy and the look that
says this fairytale is the real thing.

# KATE

St Andrews in the sun is as beautiful and romantic a place as you could hope to find. The sea glistens, even the grey of the granite glistens, the sands stretch invitingly, and in the warmth of the summer, you wander around the cobbled streets and the ancient ruins of the Castle and the Cathedral and marvel at living in such an ancient and uplifting place. But in winter, when the temperature drops, the days are short, the sky is thunderous, the sea grey and angry, it can be as miserable as sin. William was not the first undergraduate to go through a period of wanting to leave the place.

David Corner began to realise at the end of the first term that he was worried. 'I would get halfway through a conversation about something boring and I would say, "How are you?" and he would say, "I'm okay" and you could tell he was not as okay as he had been two months before, and I would say, "Is there anything I can do?" and he would say, "David, that's awfully kind but no, I'm okay." And it was a stiff upper lip in a certain sense that was very difficult to break down. So what I did was, I said, "You've got my phone number. If ever you feel you want to ring it, you ring it—and I'd say that to any student, William, in this situation." I think we had one talk that pierced the surface but no more. One of his themes time and time and time again was, "How will this affect other students?" It was extraordinarily generous of him because he was under pressure, but that was the watchword for everything.'

The accepted wisdom is that William was homesick and felt cut off being so far away from his family. He himself has said he was not so much homesick as feeling daunted. David Corner thinks the real problem was one that afflicts a lot of students: self-doubt. 'I think he was enjoying some subjects more than others. Social anthropology is tough, very theoretical and William is quite a practical person. It was no coincidence he eventually got to geography, which is almost tangible. St Andrews has lots of very bright students. I remember my own experience of going to Oxford from a Birmingham school; you talk to your peers and they all seem to know more than you do, and it was that sort of reaction partly. Also perhaps loneliness.

'He was the sort of student who was never going to get into academic difficulty, a student who was conscientious. What I noticed as an outsider was this tremendous thing that I suspect most members of the family have, which is a notion of obedience, a notion that you do what you're told. That very obvious when they ever talked about the Queen, but it was also obvious about life in general. He's not the brightest student we've ever had but he was always a conscientious student and got it done. And when he couldn't get any peace, he used to go and sit in the top of the local police station and do his essays; there was a nest where Fife police met the protection squad and he used to go in there and do his work.

'I think it was because he was lonely that he became so close to the group that became housemates in his last three years and who were at his wedding. He needed them and they were a great lot, incredibly protective. I remember seeing them once in Anstruther [a fishing village along the coast]. He'd gone to get some fish and chips and I happened to be sitting outside in a car waiting for my wife, and I saw a local weaving his way up the road, pointing a finger and cursing and muttering. It was very interesting to see their group movement. They almost formed a shell around William and I thought how mature for kids of that age. He'd started doing things that were mostly male, water polo and rugby, sea swimming and scuba diving at Elie. I think he was on his way back from diving at Elie when I saw him having fish and chips. They ate it on the pavement out of paper.'

It was several months before he felt comfortable enough to engage with university life and there were many weekends when he disappeared to see friends at Edinburgh university, or visit Balmoral or Gloucestershire to hang out with his childhood friends. He thought long and hard about leaving St Andrews and had many conversations with his father who tried to dissuade him, also with his grandfather, who had no time for quitters. Another valuable voice was that of his old house master at Eton, Andrew Gailey, always understanding, calm and wise. You can be sure that in the end it was William's decision and his alone. He decided to stay and tough it out, which was undoubtedly a welcome decision for the university, the fortunes of which could have been seriously compromised had he left. It was certainly the right decision for William. There would have been unfortunate echoes of Prince Edward's decision at a similar age to quit the Royal Marines a third of the way through a gruelling year-long Commando course. Not many in the media saw it as the courageous decision it was—most of the press hung Edward out to dry.

One of the voices William listened to during that time was Kate Middleton's. She was also away from her comfort zone for the first time during that first year and was as daunted by some elements of this new life as he was.

Kate had been one of the least pushy of the girls he met in that first year. She had a quiet, confident presence and was friendly and laughed easily. She was the sort of person with whom it felt safe to open up a little, someone who had depth and empathy. They were both a long way from home and their backgrounds were very different, but by coincidence, they had both been Raleigh venturers to the same place in Chile the year before. Kate's expedition had followed immediately after William's, so they knew many of the same people and places and could compare notes, share stories and laugh about the discomforts together. They immediately had a bond. They were also, they discovered, both keen tennis players, swimmers and skiers and all-round sports enthusiasts. And they were both studying History of Art, so they went to lectures together and for coffees afterwards, and for drinks in the pubs and wine bars; they swam and surfed together and played tennis on the university courts. As time passed it developed into a close and mutually supportive friendship.

There had been no thunderbolt when they met. Asked for her first impression of William during their engagement interview, Kate said, 'I actually think I went bright red when I met you and sort of scuttled off, feeling very shy about meeting you.' As commonly happens, she started going out with a fourth-year student, Rupert Finch; and William's eye was also roving elsewhere. According to their fellow students, most girls' reaction to him at that time was, 'What a nice guy, and looking back he was cute, but girls didn't go, "Wow he's so good looking".' (Except perhaps for the Americans who fell at his feet.) Kate was said to have had a photograph of William on her wall at school but she knocked that myth on the head when asked about it in their engagement interview. 'There wasn't just one, there were about twenty,' said William. 'He wishes,' said Kate. 'No, I had the Levi's guy on my wall, not a picture of William, sorry.' To which William replied, 'It was me in Levi's, honestly.' The truth is, it was more than a year before they were anything other than very good friends, and making each other laugh was an important part of it.

Kate left little impression on the academic staff at St Andrews, who confess that when lecturing to a sea of faces, it's rare for one to stand out. 'She was another girl in a pashmina,' one said. 'I wouldn't have remembered her at all if I hadn't seen something in the newspaper in the second semester. When I read about her charismatic personality . . . well, maybe it's developed—but it wasn't that obvious then. Sometimes students passing through you know are headed for great things, but I didn't notice her in four years.' Those organising the Raleigh expedition have no strong memory of her either. They too, like university professors, are processing hundreds of young people every year and one more girl battling the elements, with unwashed hair and no make-up, in grubby jeans, is easy to miss. When Malcolm

Sutherland looks back at photographs of Kate in Chile, compared with how she looks now, he can't believe it's the same girl.

But part of her allure for William was that she didn't stand out. Today, with the designer frocks, the killer heels, the make-up and the perfectly tended hair, she looks as though she was made for the red carpet, but that wasn't how she looked when William fell in love with her. She looked like any number of attractive young girls, with a good figure and ready smile. She was natural and relaxed, pretty without ever looking as though she was trying too hard. Although her parents were extremely wealthy and she had been to a top school, she wasn't a 'Sloane Ranger' or a 'Ya', as so many of the girls he knew in Gloucestershire and London were—and like so many of the girls who hung around him at St Andrews too. Her parents were resoundingly middle class; she spoke without an exaggerated upper-class accent, and she was refreshingly shy, yet intelligent and strong.

Not so shy, however, that she wasn't prepared to stride down an improvised catwalk in the Students' Union wearing little more than a bra and pants—but it was for charity, and compared with what some of the other models had on she was modesty itself. It was an annual event called Just Walk, said to be 'Scotland's most prestigious fashion show'—and for the record did not happen at the 5-star St Andrew's Bay Hotel but at what is arguably the ugliest and tattiest building in the town. The event is entirely run by students to raise money for charity while supporting up-and-coming fashion designers, and William is said to have paid £200 for his ticket and seen Kate in an altogether new light, apparently remarking to his friend, 'Wow, Fergus, Kate's hot!' The flimsy dress, designed by Charlotte Todd, who was then a fashion student, was intended to be a skirt but someone decided it would look better worn as a dress. The photograph has become as iconic as the picture of Diana in her diaphanous skirt. As for the dress itself, it lay boxed in the bottom of Charlotte's mother's wardrobe for eight years and was sold at auction in 2011 for a staggering £78,000.

Yet William was never supposed to have been there that night, for what turned out to have been such a seminal moment in the history of the monarchy. Colleen had assured Niall Scott that he would not be going to the event, so Niall had allowed the media in to take photos of the catwalk show. 'Five minutes after I'd opened the Union doors to the press,' he says, 'William walked round the corner with his mates and into the hall and sat down at the table right at the end of the runway. The press thought they'd died and gone to heaven. I thought I might be destined for a slow death with no chance of heaven. I called Colleen, who was mildly displeased, but she is about the calmest woman I've ever met. That was when I learned that William, on occasion, would lead even his most trusted minders a merry dance.'

Kate's female contemporaries describe her as 'a sweet girl with no airs or graces, who was quiet and not outrageously flirty, but someone who always enjoyed attention from guys.' She struck those who shared lectures and tutorials with her as seeming rather vulnerable. She would sit quietly with one male friend (apart from those where she overlapped with William) and didn't hang around with the girls in her year. She didn't seem to like the ones that hung around William. They say she was diligent, in that she went to lectures and seemed to put in more work than most. 'I felt slightly sorry for her,' says one. 'I think she was more of a guy girl than a girly girl, but she was good fun and she laughed a lot. She was very chatty, very sporty, didn't normally wear make-up and always looked good.'

Having been educated at Marlborough College, a prestigious co-educational public school in Wiltshire, Kate was very comfortable in mixed company—unlike so many students who arrive at university from single-sex schools. She had done well at Marlborough and excelled at sport, egged on by her parents, Michael and Carole. They were fiercely ambitious for their eldest child. They were always there at the courtside or on the touchline or at the swimming baths to cheer their daughter on in matches and competitions.

Michael and Carole had both made their fortune in life through sheer hard work. One profile writer once said rather sniffily that Kate's lineage 'can't be traced much further back than the suburbanisation of Berkshire'. They were not members of the landed gentry, they had not been handed their fortune on a plate. They had come from modest origins and worked for every penny they owned. And after years of hard graft in the airline business—he as a member of ground staff, she, until she had children, as an air hostess—they had hit on a brilliant business plan. It grew out of Carole's experience as a stay-at-home mother with her young children. They created a company called Party Pieces in 1987, providing inspiration and supplies for parties for every age group, and shipping them out by mail order. Nearly twenty-five years later it is the UK's leading party company, and they have made enough money to have put their three children through public school and university and been able to pay a sizeable share of Kate's wedding costs.

They live in a comfortable five-bedroom detached house overlooking farmland in the village of Bucklebury in Berkshire, where they support all the local independent shops and are regulars at the local pub, the Bull Inn, in neighbouring Stanford Dingley. Michael, one of life's natural gentlemen, is loved by everyone in the village; Carole is a go-getter, a tough businesswoman who has been the force behind Party Pieces and the family's social ascent. Opinion about them is divided (there's nothing like fame on top of social climbing for dividing opinion), but it is universally agreed in the village that they are a happy family and have lovely, unassuming, friendly children.

# HOPE STREET

By the time William returned in September 2002 the 'wobble' was well and truly behind him and he was much more confident, as so many students are in their second year. The sun was shining and he had decided that he rather enjoyed life in the 'auld grey toun'. Most students move out of halls in their second year, and along with three friends, one of whom was Kate, he had rented a smart flat in Hope Street, which belonged to friends of friends. It was another central and attractive part of the town and a conventional move for wealthier students. His other flatmates were Fergus Boyd and Olivia Bleasdale, a friend of a friend formerly at Westonbirt (a girls' boarding school half a mile from Highgrove, many of whose pupils he'd met at local pubs and parties).

The four friends had decided it would be fun to share a house several months before, and the combination worked well. William and Kate were still nothing more than good mates when they moved in, but as the year progressed their relationship shifted a gear. As William said in their engagement interview, 'It just sort of blossomed from there really. We just saw more of each other, hung out a bit more and did stuff.'

Hope Street had innumerable student flats and there was no shortage of parties that went on noisily into the night. But not all the flats in Hope Street belonged to students and one was taken by a part-time lecturer called Dana. 'The poor girl was plagued with students partying three times a week,' says Brendan Cassidy. 'She was really suffering, on the verge of tears because she couldn't sleep. One night she got up and went and knocked on the door of one to ask them to keep the music down. The door was opened and who was in the hallway but William! It didn't make a blind bit of difference. I tried to get the people in College Gate [the university's administrative offices] to do something about it and I don't know whether it was because they couldn't do anything or whether they were aware that William was involved, but either way they did nothing.'

Anyone who invited William to a house party had a visit beforehand from his PPOs to give the flat or the building a quick security check and they would then get a call to say that William was on his way. Once he was there, he was no different from any other student. He dressed in jeans or chinos and shirt, with a collection of bracelets around his wrist, accumulated on his travels; he danced (he would say badly), he drank too much, he laughed and joked—memorably, on one occasion, over a rabbit vibrator that one of his hostesses had been given for her birthday. The only times in four years he dressed up were for ceilidhs and reeling balls, where he showed off his Scottish dancing enthusiasm but, despite being entitled to don a kilt, he firmly stuck to black tie. As he said in an interview at the end of his second year, he had only ever worn a kilt in private. 'It's a bit draughty,' he laughed. 'But I love Scottish dancing—it's great. I'm hopeless at it but I do enjoy it. I usually make a complete muck-up of the Dashing White Sergeant, I do throw my arms dangerously about and girls fly across the dance floor.'

Of course university wasn't just a round of parties. Some nights he and his housemates stayed in and cooked, taking it in turns. He revelled in the novelty of everyday life that most people take for granted. 'I do a lot of shopping—I enjoy the shopping, actually. I get very carried away. I cook quite regularly for them and they cook for me.'

Household chores were also shared between them. 'We all get on very well and start off having rotas, but, of course, it just broke down into complete chaos. Everyone helps out when they can. I try to help out when I can and they do the same for me, but usually you just fend for yourself.'

In my day as a student, apart from hotels, there was not much more than a dodgy Chinese and a fish-and-chip shop—and breakfast was a bacon roll at Pete's greasy spoon café on Market Street. The pubs served beers and spirits and maybe the odd salted peanut; wine was only served in restaurants and the word gastro had not attached itself to anything north of Hadrian's Wall. The town virtually closed down after 10 o'clock at night. By the time William was an undergraduate, the town had been revolutionised. There is still only one small, old-fashioned cinema, weirdly called The New Picture House, but in addition to the pubs, which have smartened up almost out of recognition, there are wine bars, like the pubs, all selling food, there are restaurants of every persuasion, Starbucks and Costa coffee bars, all manner of civilisation that had been absent in my day. As the university has grown in size and become more fashionable, and the student population more cosmopolitan and sophisticated, and in some cases wealthy, the town has grown to meet the market.

A favourite haunt of William and his friends was Ma Belles, a cosy bar and restaurant in the basement of the Golf Hotel in the Scores, one of the oldest and most traditional hotels in the town. Upstairs there are tartan carpets and cockaleekie soup, while downstairs an array of exotic cocktails are on offer, as well as coffee, afternoon teas and bar meals. Afternoon teas sell at £8.50, mojitos at £6.50 and champagne at £56 a bottle or £11 a glass. It is a cross between the bar in the American sitcom *Cheers*, and the Central Perk coffee house in *Friends*. It is big and spacious with bare, wooden floorboards and comfortable deep leather sofas, banquettes in the window seats, and giant television sets tuned to rolling sports channels. Whenever Aston Villa was playing, Ma Belles was where William was to be found glued to the TV, sitting at the bar on a high stool with a pint of cider by his side, loudly cheering the team on.

## COMING OF AGE

In the summer of 2003 William turned twenty-one and Mario Testino, the photographer who had taken such haunting pictures of his mother, was invited to take the official photographs. It was Colleen's idea and the natural choice.

'I think he was a little bit uncomfortable about that photo shoot but I pushed it a bit because I thought it would be lovely. It was about the similarity, and some of the pictures he caught were very like Diana, particularly the one of her in the black polo neck. It was not such a clever move but that was the power of Diana blinding us all, we weren't thinking straight. But he didn't say no. He could have really kicked off and he didn't. Again, that is him.'

He touched on the photographs in a characteristically self-deprecating way in an accompanying interview with Peter Archer from the Press Association. 'I chose Mario,' he said, 'because he's the only person who could make a moose look good!' It was the most revealing interview he had ever given and for someone who doesn't like to talk about himself, it was surprisingly expansive.

But in the midst of it was a heartfelt public defence of his father, who, he said, had been a 'huge influence' on him, and an appeal for his critics to give him a break.

His father had had a particularly nightmarish year with a series of shocking revelations and accusations directed at him and his Household. They began with the collapse of the notorious Burrell trial. Paul Burrell, the butler whom Diana referred to as her 'rock', had been accused of stealing several million pounds' worth of items belonging to the Princess of Wales's estate, most of which had been found squirrelled away at his home. What had not been found, however, was a mahogany box containing a tape Diana had recorded which her sister, Sarah, told police contained 'sensitive' material. Spurred on by the Spencers, who were Diana's executors, the Crown Prosecution Service prosecuted and the case came to court, only to stop a month later.

The Queen mentioned in passing to the Prince of Wales that Burrell had been to see her privately soon after Diana's death five years earlier, and told her that he was taking a number of papers from Kensington Palace for safekeeping. Burrell had started off in life as the Queen's footman and she had been fond of him, as had Charles and William and Harry, who used to play with his two sons when they were little. This connection was why she had agreed to see him. Charles mentioned it to Sir Michael Peat, his new Private Secretary, the police were alerted and the £1.5 million trial came to a shuddering halt. It was never quite explained why Burrell telling the Queen he had taken a few papers should have undermined a trial for theft of more than three hundred items found in his house and under his floorboards. Nevertheless, he walked away a free if rather broken man.

No fewer than four hundred media organisations approached him, offering vast sums for his story. He was persuaded to go with the *Mirror*. Piers Morgan, announcing the deal, said, 'He will protect the memory of Princess Diana and will honour his pledge to always protect the Queen. But I think there will be many others in the Royal

Family and close to the Royal Family who will be quaking in their boots tonight.' His story ran day after day and opened a very unpalatable can of worms. It seemed that taking home unwanted gifts that had been given to the Prince and/or Princess of Wales was seen as a perk of the job within the Household. More valuable gifts were either sold for charity or exchanged for something more useful. The Prince's valet, Michael Fawcett, handled these sales, and he became known as 'Fawcett the Fence'.

Worse was to come. A headline in the *Mail on Sunday* read, 'I WAS RAPED BY CHARLES'S SERVANT'. It was an unreliable story from an unreliable witness, George Smith, a former valet, and it was common knowledge that his allegations were on the tape in the missing mahogany box. But it prompted the Prince to set up an inquiry into the probity of his Household, which threw up plenty of room for improvement in creating systems but found no fundamental dishonesty.

'He's been given quite a hard time recently,' said William, 'and I just wish that people would give him a break. He does so many amazing things. I only wish people would see that more because he's had a very hard time and yet he's stuck it out and he's still very positive.'

William's father and grandmother were jointly organising a birthday party for him at Windsor Castle for three hundred family and friends—one of whom, camouflaged among a group from St Andrews, was Kate. He had chosen the theme 'Out of Africa' because he 'thought it would be quite fun to see the family out of black tie and get everyone to dress up.' A curious collection of costumes made their way into the Castle that Saturday night, including furry lions, legionaries, tribal chieftains, Tarzan and a banana. Someone who also made their way in, but not past security at the King Henry VIII Gate, was a thirty-six-year-old self-styled comedy terrorist, Aaron Barschak, dressed as Osama bin Laden. He made his way not only into the grounds, but into the very heart of the party and onto the stage where Prince William was making a speech. For a moment, everyone thought he was part of the entertainment, but when he grabbed the microphone it became clear he was an intruder, and he was very quickly seized by security and taken in handcuffs to the local police station. The following day, the Home Secretary ordered an inquiry.

On a more personal note in the birthday interview, William said, 'My guiding principles in life are to be honest, genuine, thoughtful and caring. I'm not an over-dominant person. I don't go around and expect everyone to listen to me the whole time; but I like to be in control of my life because I have so many people around me, I can get pulled in one direction and then the other. If I don't have any say in it, then I end up just losing complete control and I don't like the idea of that. I could actually lose my identity.

'A lot of people think I'm hugely stubborn about the whole thing, but you have to be slightly stubborn because everybody wants you for one reason or another. If you don't stick to your guns and stick to your decision, then you lose control.'

He insisted, however, that he did listen to advice. 'I do listen, of course I listen. I listen to what people have to say to me and I make my own judgements from there. I think it's very important that you make your own decision about what you are. Therefore you're responsible for your actions, so you don't blame other people.'

Asked whether he wanted to be King, he said, 'All these questions about do you want to be King? It's not a question of wanting to be, it's something I was born into and it's my duty. Wanting is not the right word. But those stories about me not wanting to be King [which had been circulating] are all wrong. It's a very important role and it's one that I don't take lightly. It's all about helping people and dedication and loyalty, which I hope I have—I know I have. Sometimes I do get anxious about it but I don't really worry a lot. I want to get through university and then maybe start thinking seriously about that in the future. I don't really ever talk about it publicly.

It's not something you talk about with whoever. I think about it a lot but they are my own personal thoughts. I'll take each step as it comes and deal with it as best I can.'

He also mentioned his love of speed and motorbikes. He had a Yamaha 600 trials bike that he rode on and off road, mostly around Highgrove. 'My father is concerned about the fact that I'm into motorbikes but he doesn't want to keep me all wrapped up in cotton wool,' he said. 'So you might as well live if you're going to live. It's just something I'm passionate about. I've always had a passion for motorbikes ever since I was very small. I used to do a lot of go-karting when I was younger and then after that I went on to quad bikes and eventually motorbikes. It does help being anonymous with my motorcycle helmet on because it does enable me to relax; but I just enjoy everything about motorbikes and the camaraderie that comes with it.'

Cars, on the other hand, he could take or leave—and drove a second-hand Volkswagen Golf. 'Everyone, I'm sure, hopes some day they'll get a new car but I'm very lucky with the car I've got at the moment. It's fast enough and it's very comfortable. I've got a good stereo in it. I'm sure my father would go absolutely bananas if he saw me driving, blaring music out of the windows.'

Not long afterwards, someone did go bananas when they saw him driving but it wasn't his father; it was the septuagenarian and rather grumpy 8th Earl Bathurst, owner of Cirencester Park where William had been playing polo.

The Earl was driving through the Park on his way home from the same polo match, when his Land Rover was overtaken on the grass verge by a Volkswagen Golf travelling at 40 to 50 mph. Roused to heights of fury by this flagrant breach of the estate's 20 mph speed limit, Bathurst gave chase, flashing his lights, sounding his horn and engaging in off-road manoeuvres to try to get the offender to stop. But it was the Earl himself who was forced to stop—by the security team protecting Prince William, as he sped home.

Although Clarence House issued an apology, the Earl remained unrepentant: 'There are rules in the polo club about driving on the estate, and people have to stick to them', he told an interviewer. 'I don't care who it is, royalty or not—speeding is not allowed on my estate. If I was to drive like that in Windsor Park, I'd end up in the Tower.' He did not recognise the Prince, he explained, observing that he 'thought he was some young yob in a beat-up car'.

For his last two years at St Andrews, William and Kate, now an item, and their two housemates moved out of town. For people with cars, there is no shortage of farmhouses and cottages to rent along the coastline or in the surrounding farmland, and many third- and fourth-year students prefer to be in the countryside. They rented a stone cottage about a mile to the west of the town, off the A91. It was part of a typical nineteenth-century farm courtyard with a combination of living quarters and storage units and a right of way straight through the middle of it. 'I got the impression,' says David Corner, 'that William just did these things and security picked up the problem afterwards, whether it was good or bad.' It lay more than half a mile up a pot-holed farm track off the main Guardbridge road, well hidden by trees. The 'yob's' beat-up car was essential kit for getting in and out, and although less convenient than Hope Street, for 9 a.m. lectures—and post 9 p.m. nightlife—it was infinitely more private. With open countryside to walk in without fear of being spotted, and open fires to come home to in the dark evenings, it was little short of idyllic and provided the perfect sanctuary for William and Kate to explore their relationship further.

It was not an easy start to the new academic year. Within weeks of William going back up to Scotland, Paul Burrell was making headlines again and effectively calling the Prince of Wales a murderer. In the intervening year he had written his memoirs, *A Royal Duty*, about his time in the Wales Household, which were serialised in the *Daily Mirror*. Piers Morgan was on a roll. Burrell quoted from letters written by the Princess. One suggested Charles was planning a fatal car crash so that he would be free to remarry, which, of course, played nicely into the conspiracy theorists' hands. The letter was undoubtedly in her handwriting but was actually thought to have been written several years before she died. In another more recent one, she had written, 'I have been battered, bruised and abused mentally by a system for fifteen years now . . . Thank you, Charles, for putting me through such hell and for giving me the opportunity to learn from the cruel things you have done to me.'

William read these accusations day after day with mounting fury, and by the end of the week he had had enough. He rang Harry, who was then on his gap year in Australia, and they agreed a joint statement that Colleen released on their behalf. Many were shocked by the vehemence of their words.

The statement said, 'We cannot believe that Paul, who was entrusted with so much, could abuse his position in such a cold and overt betrayal. It is not only deeply painful for the two of us but also for everyone else affected and it would mortify our mother if she were alive today and, if we might say so, we feel we are more able to speak for our mother than Paul. We ask Paul please to bring these revelations to an end.'

Burrell issued his own statement. He said: 'I

am saddened at the statement issued on behalf of Prince William and Prince Harry. Saddened because I know that this book is nothing more than a tribute to their mother. I am convinced that when the Princes, and everyone else, read this book in its entirety they will think differently. My only intention in writing this book was to defend the Princess and stand in her corner. I have been greatly encouraged by calls of support from some of the Princess's closest friends within the past 48 hours. I would also like to point out that, following the collapse of my trial at the Old Bailey last year, no one from the Royal Family contacted me or said sorry for the unnecessary ordeal myself, my wife and my sons were put through. Neither do I say sorry for writing this book of which I am extremely proud and I am convinced the Princess would be proud of too. I have told the truth where the British public should know the truth.'

Speaking on the BBC's *Real Story*, he said he would never have written the book if the boys had contacted him after the trial. 'I was saddened but slightly angry because I know those boys. I felt immediately that those boys were being manipulated and massaged by the system, by the palace, by the grey men in suits—whatever you want to call them. By those people who did exactly the same to their mother. The spin machine has gone forward again. Too many people busy spinning and William and Harry sent out as the emotional cannon.'

If he thought that William could have been manipulated by anyone, it had clearly been a very long time since he'd spent any time with him.

# FINAL YEARS OF FREEDOM

By William's final years at St Andrews he had long since given up the baseball cap. Head up, he walked tall and confidently through the town, popped in and out of shops, pubs and cafés with scarcely a second thought, and where he had once been a bit of a passenger in seminars and tutorials, he began to speak up. His tutors all noticed him growing before their very eyes and taking a genuine interest.

Having dropped History of Art, he was concentrating on more advanced physical geography, which he found much more exciting. 'The bits of the course that got him most motivated,' says John Walden, 'were those that had a social context. He did a course on HIV and AIDS and he got really interested in that because he could see in the outside world where that was an issue. He did a course with [Dr] Charles Warren [a colleague] on environmental management in Scotland—and they're a family with a country tradition—and he was really interested in that. The other piece of independent work was a review essay on some issue to do with big game hunting in Africa and the damage that that is doing to populations of big game.'

Charles Warren found William strikingly humble. 'I formed a very high opinion of him as a man with his feet on the ground, earthed and normal; always a pleasure to deal with and interact with. He had no sense of entitlement, was never pushy. He was an outstanding young man by any standards but the fact that he's had all that privilege and extraordinary life, yet he was most normal. Whoever the people were that had a hand in bringing him up they deserve a lot of credit.'

When it came to roll calls, for security reasons William's name never appeared on any lists. Charles remembers William and another boy turning up late one day in the second year, and without looking up he said, 'Names please.' William's companion sang out his name, while William kept his mouth firmly shut. 'The look on his face said, "You're not expecting me to say my name, are you?" He was embarrassed, he hated standing out.'

In June 2004, Charles took fifteen junior honours students, including William, on a field trip to the Jostedalen ice cap in western Norway, which is the biggest and most dramatic in mainland Europe. It is one of the most beautiful places on earth, particularly at that time of year, with spring in the valley floor but snow still on the mountains; it is also one of the most remote. Their base was at a self-catering campsite that belonged to a small hotel in the tiny settlement of Gjerde, and every day they walked up the valley to the field site on the eastern flank of the ice cap to measure, record and map where the glaciers have been in retreat to establish the evolution of the landscape.

William came alive in those surroundings. No one knew where he was. The British media knew he was out of the country but they had no idea he was in Norway; there was not a photographer within hundreds of miles and Charles says he had never seen him so relaxed. 'It was great to see; he was in an environment he loved—he loves wild places; we talked a lot about Patagonia, which he had also really loved. I had been a scientific leader on a number of Raleigh expeditions to Chile so I knew exactly the places he was talking about.' At night, over hearty stews provided by the hotel (where the staff were ensconced, while the students roughed it on bunks in wooden cabins, cooking breakfast and lunch for themselves), William let his hair down. 'He's a born raconteur,' says Charles. 'He told some highly entertaining anecdotes about the goings-on behind the scenes at royal dos—the imminent disasters and chaos. There is this image he painted of the swan effortlessly gliding past while lots of frantic paddling is going on underneath the surface of the water. He told them in such an amusing and entertaining way, we were all in stitches of laughter.'

Unhappily the idyll was cut short. Protocol insists that if a member of the British Royal Family is visiting another country, even in a private capacity, the government has to be informed. Word filtered down from Oslo to the local policeman, and somewhere along the line, someone leaked it to the Norwegian press. The party woke up on day three to find the peaceful little settlement of Gjerde had become a media city. There were television trucks with satellite dishes and radio cars and print journalists and photographers crawling all over the place.

'William's security people negotiated a deal that if he walked from the cabins down to the main street and they got their shot, they would all go away. Which they did, except for one independent guy who stuck with us, but finally William's PPOs lost him.

'What struck me most was the change that immediately came over William. On went the cap, pulled well down, the head went down. You could see him putting on his psychological armour. I found it profoundly sad; it was a tiny glimpse of what happens to him every day of life; the intense weight of the world on his shoulders.'

Two days before the end of the trip William had to leave. He had sad news. His grandmother,

Frances Shand Kydd, had died at her home near Oban on the Isle of Seil off the west coast of Scotland. She was just sixty-eight and had become a rather tragic figure. The last time she had appeared in public was at the Burrell trial as a witness for the prosecution, when under oath she had been forced to admit that she and Diana had been estranged for four months before her daughter's death. They had had no contact. Life had been very hard on her: she had endured an unhappy marriage, lost custody of her children when they needed her, her second husband, Peter Shand Kydd, had left her in 1986, her brother had committed suicide two years before and she had buried two children—the newborn son and Diana. It was not surprising that she should have turned to two of life's great comforters, religion and the bottle. When she returned to Scotland after Diana's funeral she was trapped indoors for eleven days by reporters; and after the Burrell trial, she found she had been burgled in her high-profile absence and had her jewellery stolen. She had been living as a recluse for many years in a two-roomed bungalow, doing relentless charity work, supported by the local community in Oban and by the Roman Catholic church. She once said, 'It takes very little to make you happy if you've had real sadness. It makes you take less for granted, and it's a very enriching experience, really.'

Her funeral at St Columba's Cathedral a week after her death was a large gathering of the Spencer clan. The Prince of Wales, her former son-in-law, was not there—according to the *Daily Mail*, because he had not been invited. The rift between the older generation had never healed and Earl Spencer's promise at Diana's funeral to be there for the Princes had turned out to be little more than rhetoric. He had pledged that their 'blood family' would do all they could to steer their lives 'so that their souls are not simply immersed by duty and tradition but can sing openly as you [Diana] planned.'

William, who had returned from Norway, and Harry, who had flown back from Africa, both looked immensely sad. They hadn't seen much of their grandmother in recent years but they had happy memories of times with her and holidays spent on Seil when they were younger. She and Diana had been alike in so many ways and she had been a reassuring link to their mother's memory.

# HARRY

Harry was never university material. He had covered himself in glory as a sportsman at Eton and had been Parade Commander in the Combined Cadet Force, but academically he struggled. When he left school at eighteen he had just one goal in life: to join the Army. But first came a gap year of his own, which he and Mark Dyer devised between them. They went to Australia, Africa and Argentina, and it was during the trip to Africa, to the tiny mountainous Kingdom of Lesotho, which has the third highest rate of HIV/AIDS in the world, that Harry discovered where his true talents and passions lay.

The people in this beautiful but impoverished country were slowly being wiped out. In 2000, King Letsie III had declared the pandemic a 'national disaster' and the country's 'number one enemy'. There were then an estimated four thousand orphans and vulnerable children in a country of just 1.8 million, most of whom were in denial about AIDS. Harry's itinerary was arranged by the King's brother, Prince Seeiso, but he spent some of his two months in the country working with AIDS orphans in the Mants'ase Children's Home in Mohale's Hoek. He was incredibly moved by the plight of the children. He played with them, he taught them English, he built rooms, put up fences, painted walls. All the children loved him but, in particular, one little four-year-old boy, who followed him like a shadow, wearing a pair of big blue wellington boots Harry had given him. In another home, a ten-month-old baby girl, raped by her mother's boyfriend and so badly damaged she had to have her womb removed, lay motionless in his arms; she couldn't even cry. Witch doctors tell men that they will be cleansed if they rape a child, the younger the better.

For all his hell-raising, Harry has a deeply compassionate side to him and the most remarkable affinity with young children. He found it impossible to walk away from these children when his time was up, step onto an aeroplane and get on with his life of plenty without doing something positive to help.

During his first week in the orphanage, a photo call had been arranged for the media and one of those who went out to Lesotho was Tom Bradby, ITN's royal correspondent. He had also done some filming of William during his gap year and was a familiar figure at royal events; he had come to know Mark Dyer very well, and both Mark and Colleen Harris identified him to William and Harry as the presentable face of journalism—someone they could trust. They did various bits of filming together and he got on well with them both. After the photo call, he persuaded Harry to let him make an exclusive documentary about Lesotho to highlight the country's plight. The result was an extraordinarily powerful and touching film called *The Forgotten Kingdom*, which was shown on ITV in Britain in 2004 and sold to America for a large amount of money. An appeal was launched off the back of the film and all the money raised was used to found Sentebale (which means 'Forget me not'),

Harry's charity, of which Prince Seeiso is co-patron.

Some of the shots in the film were taken by Harry himself with the video camera he used to record his gap year. Tom had looked through all the tapes to find suitable clips for the documentary, and finding a lot of it very funny, offered to edit them into a video as a present for Harry. The next time Tom saw William, William said he had seen the video and thought it was great, so Tom offered to do the same for him. Trusting Tom completely, as Harry had done, he handed over all of his own, very private, tapes, which Tom spent several days turning into a video. Having crossed the Rubicon, Tom was then trusted with all sorts of confidences and both Princes would ring and ask his advice from time to time.

Harry's oldest and possibly best friend, Henry van Straubenzee, whom he'd known since his first day at Ludgrove, had also planned to work with children in Africa on his gap year. He was heading for Uganda, where his elder brother Thomas, William's contemporary and close friend, had gone on his gap year two years before. But Henry never made it. He was tragically killed in a car crash just before Christmas 2002 at the age of eighteen.

Henry had spent the first few months of his gap

year between Harrow School and university working at their old prep school. He was going to Newcastle to read business studies, sponsored by the MoD, having won an army scholarship. After Newcastle, he would go to Sandhurst, and possibly his father's old regiment, the Royal Green Jackets (now the Rifles), continuing a family military tradition that hadn't been broken in over 150 years. His future was mapped out for him. More immediately, he was going home to Hertfordshire and after Christmas was flying to Uganda. The term was over and they were having a farewell Christmas party that had gone on way past midnight. In the early hours the sound system gave out, so he and a friend nipped down the school's long narrow drive to borrow a CD player. His friend was at the wheel and in the fog on the way back, doing no more than 27 mph, the car hit the only tree in the driveway. Both boys had been drinking, neither was wearing a seat belt and the car was old and had no airbag on the passenger side. Henry was killed instantly and his friend gravely injured.

He was the first friend of William and Harry's generation to die and both were intensely shocked and upset. They had lost their great-grandmother earlier in the year, also Princess Margaret, and while both deaths were immensely sad, they had had a good innings and neither of them had been well. Henry was young, handsome, healthy, mischievous and happy, with everything to live for. His death was as sudden and senseless as their mother's.

They knew the van Straubenzees intimately. The boys all stayed at each other's houses. The Princes had been on family seaside holidays with them. For years, Henry's parents, Alex and Claire, had taken a house on the cliff top at Polzeath in north Cornwall, as they still do, and every year they took a gang of boys, each of their three sons inviting their closest friends. William and Harry were always part of it—William as Thomas's friend and Harry as Henry's. They went surfing with boogie boards—William always going out further than anyone else ever dared—and shrimping in rock pools; they played French cricket on the flat sandy beach, and barbecued and partied into the night. Thomas and Henry had been to stay with William and Harry at home and on holiday more times than they could count. And if Diana was not there, Tiggy would look after them all. They'd been to Highgrove and, before Diana's death, to Kensington Palace, which they adored because Diana was always such fun. Thomas van Straubenzee is one of the very few friends the Princes have now who knew their mother. The brothers had been on the super-luxurious *Alexander*, the third biggest yacht in the world, which the late Greek shipping tycoon, John Latsis, used to lend the Prince of Wales. They had wonderful, wild *Boy's Own* holidays in the Mediterranean, jumping from the highest deck into the sea.

By coincidence, the Vans, as they are known, were friends of the Spencers. In 1979, Alex had shared a flat with Diana's sister Sarah—and Diana had been the charlady—one of several domestic jobs she did when she first came to London.

Alex and Claire heard the news about Henry at 4.30 in the morning. They were asleep in bed when the headmaster of Ludgrove telephoned to tell them the news every parent dreads: their son was dead. Numb with shock and grief, they quickly organised what they imagined would be a small family funeral for him on 23 December in their local parish church. To their amazement, and comfort, people kept ringing and asking whether they could come. In the end, 350 of Henry's and his brothers' friends squeezed into the little church, including William, Harry, Tiggy and two of the Princes' PPOs who had regularly been with them in Cornwall and knew Henry well.

The following month, Harrow School held a service of thanksgiving for him in the school chapel, to which a thousand people turned up, including William and Harry. The Vans say that both boys were hugely kind and supportive to the whole family, but particularly to Thomas and his younger brother Charlie, who was only fourteen when Henry died. With their own experience of loss still with them every day of their lives, they were able to understand better than most the pain their friends were going through. They are all still very close, still go to Cornwall and elsewhere together and are all determined to keep Henry's memory alive and make his death less senseless.

After the memorial service Harry went back to Eton, William to St Andrews and to Kate Middleton, who was instinctively empathetic. Where most of his male friends would hide in safe subjects like sport after a perfunctory acknowledgement when anything heavy was in the air, she was prepared to engage in conversations about feelings and delicately probe and allow him to unburden his soul a little. This was not the first time he'd had difficult emotions to cope with during his time at university, and it wasn't the first or the last time she would be there for him.

Their relationship was becoming the subject of gossip and speculation in St Andrews and there had been the odd photograph of them deep in conversation, but the first confirmation the wider world had about William's affection for Kate was when the *Sun* published a photograph of the two of them kissing on the ski slopes at Klosters during the Easter holidays in 2004, when they were in their third year. He went with his father and his father's friends, and, as usual, had taken a group of his own friends. He and his father posed for the customary photo call at the start of the holiday and the legitimate press put away their cameras, but not everyone did. Using the age-old excuse that any girl with a future King is of public interest because she may become Queen, the editor had published what was otherwise an intrusive and illegitimate photograph. William was furious and his father's office responded swiftly.

# NEW REGIME

There had been big changes in the Prince of Wales's office, including its location. Following the death of the Queen Mother, Clarence House, where she had lived, was refurbished at a cost of nearly £5 million to provide a new home for the Prince of Wales and his family. Since the divorce, they had lived at York House, across the courtyard, and the office had been in St James's Palace next door. They are all part of the same complex but Clarence House has the advantage of having state rooms and a large, private garden at the back, where the Prince can entertain. They moved in in 2003, by which time the Household was looking very different.

Stephen Lamport had left in the summer of 2002 to join the Royal Bank of Scotland. He had been Deputy and then Private Secretary for nine years. His replacement was Sir Michael Peat, who came from Buckingham Palace. As Keeper of the Privy Purse, he had been the architect of a major modernisation programme there and his appointment was seen as a way of repairing the relationship between the two Palaces—a relationship that, to quote one member of the Household, 'had been comprehensively bulldozed'. Mark Bolland, Deputy Private Secretary, widely thought to have been driving the bulldozer, left to set up his own public relations consultancy. He also began writing a gossipy column in the *News of the World* under the pseudonym Blackadder, in which he occasionally bit the hand that had once fed him. And Colleen Harris, the Prince's Press Secretary, left in the autumn of 2003, exhausted by the long hours and constant fire-fighting and wanting to see something of her teenage sons.

The man brought in to mastermind the relationship with the press was forty-year-old Paddy Harverson, a former *Financial Times* sports journalist, who had spent the previous three years at Manchester United, the world's biggest and most successful football club. There he had been dealing with giant egos, millionaires and mega-stars like David Beckham and Rio Ferdinand, and perpetually managing intense tabloid interest and scandal. He arrived in October 2003 with a brand-new broom, and no sense of awe towards his employer and his family. Michael Peat's remit was to get the Prince of Wales's private life out of the newspapers and his good works into them, and

Paddy's was to rebuild trust and bridges with Buckingham Palace. He is an imposing figure at six feet four inches tall, and brought his height's worth of integrity into the mire of cunning spin and favouritism that had blighted the previous regime.

He made it clear from the beginning that there was to be no spin, no favours and that the Palace was no longer going to lie down and take whatever the tabloids threw at it.

He had scarcely had time to make his first cup of coffee in the office when an action that Clarence House had taken against the *Mail on Sunday* before he arrived came to fruition. The newspaper had run a story that Prince William had speared and killed a dwarf antelope (called a dik-dik) during a holiday in Kenya. It spawned national outrage, despite a statement from Clarence House that the story was untrue. The *Mail on Sunday* claimed it had a good source and refused to back down, so the Palace issued a formal complaint to the PCC and the newspaper folded its tents. Speaking on BBC Radio 4's *Today* programme, Paddy said, 'Now, hopefully, they will understand that we do take things seriously and will hold them to account where we feel that they are wrong and have evidence to prove that they are wrong.'

Just a few months later he leaped to nineteen-year-old Harry's defence. When Carol Sarler, a

*Daily Express* columnist, wrote a vicious comment piece calling Harry a 'horrible young man' and 'national disgrace' who 'rarely lifted a finger unless it's to feel up a cheap tart in a nightclub', Paddy wrote a furious letter of complaint to the newspaper, which was printed in full. Harry was on his gap year, which she called 'a space between no work whatsoever at school and utter privilege at Sandhurst'; in Australia, he had spent it 'slumped in front of the television waiting to behave badly at the next available rugby match', while in Lesotho in Africa, where he currently was, he was spending 'eight lavish weeks . . . [during which] he has reluctantly agreed to spend a bit of the trip staring at poor people. His exploits have been making headlines for years: the drinking, the drugging, the yobbing, the waste of the costliest education in the land, the explicit disdain for the lower orders, the increasingly sexual public romps—we've seen it all, we've heard it all.'

Paddy took her points one by one. He wrote that, 'These comments make it entirely clear that Ms Sarler has little or no understanding of Harry as a person and how he has spent his current gap year.' It was a 'very unfair and unfounded attack' full of 'ill-informed and insensitive criticism'. The next week, her column was an out-and-out attack on Paddy Harverson.

Two months later when the *Sun* ran the

photograph of William and Kate kissing in the snow at Klosters, Paddy punished the newspaper. In an unprecedented move he banned Arthur Edwards, its veteran royal photographer, from future photo calls with both William and Harry. Arthur had been outside the Lindo Wing the day of William's birth, he'd been one of Diana's favourites, a real gentleman of the profession. The industry was as shocked as he was, but it sent out a powerful message.

During William's final year, with the first set of his exams looming, Harry was in the news again. During the Christmas vacation, the two of them had been to a fancy dress party in Wiltshire given by his great friend James Meade, son of Richard Meade, the Olympic show jumper. The theme had been 'colonial and native'. William had dressed as a lion and Harry, in a local fancy dress shop, had found a German desert costume with a Nazi armband. With all the awareness of the average twenty-year-old, he had thought nothing beyond its colonial connotation; meanwhile the adults around him, who perhaps ought to have been more conscious that a Nazi outfit was not such a good idea, did not think to point that out to him. Someone at the party took a photograph.

'HARRY THE NAZI' screamed the *Sun* headline. As luck would have it, the party was shortly before Holocaust Memorial Day, in which the Royal Family were taking a leading role. The newspapers milked it for all it was worth, drawing attention also to the cigarette and the drink in his hand. Some of his critics, tall on their soap-boxes, suggested that Harry wasn't fit to attend Sandhurst, where he was due to go later in the year.

Clarence House immediately put out a statement. 'Prince Harry has apologised for any offence or embarrassment he has caused. He realises it was a poor choice of costume.' But there were those, of course, who were not prepared to accept this apology.

William took the whole incident, removed as he was from Harry and home, very badly. 'The university has an amazingly over-the-top system for dealing with students who have got personal or medical issues that impact upon their work,' says John Walden, 'and the student can ask for special circumstances to be taken into account. William had obviously spent a lot of time talking to his brother and not revising for exams and so he came to me and said, "I'm having a bit of a crisis. What do I do about my exams?" He was really wound up about the way the press was treating his brother. It was obvious that he was very upset, so we had a conversation.'

In the end, William sat the first lot of his final exams that January with no special dispensation. Final exams are no longer as important as they used to be at St Andrews. An honours degree is now modular, a calculation of all the marks gained during the final two years at the university, so a proportion of the outcome had already been determined by module exams, class work, course work, essays, field trips and the dissertation.

He had thought long and hard about his dissertation, as do most students, and been to see Charles Warren the summer before about the subjects he was chewing over. He had thought he might do a study on the impact of deer management on wild land in the Highlands. It was never mentioned by name, but Balmoral would have been the obvious location for any such study.

He decided, instead, to write about conservation in the tropical seas, or more accurately indigenous fishing practices on the island of Rodrigues and the effect these practices have on coral reefs. 'It was one of these things where the locals take dynamite and blow the fish out of the water, which obviously doesn't do the coral reef any good,' says John Walden. 'I suspect he must have had some involvement with a conservation group that were working on this island and may have had some previous contact with them, because he went out and did two or three weeks' field work out there with this group, which essentially involved a lot of scuba diving on the corals.'

He was absolutely right. Rodrigues was the island in the Indian Ocean William had visited during his gap year with Mark Dyer where they had dived. This time he could indulge his passion for scuba diving in the interests of academe.

Looking back on it all, John Walden says, 'My real specialism is looking at long-term climate records. He was interested in climate change; everybody could be interested in that, but if I started to talk to him about the minutiae of how you interpret a pollen record, his eyes would be glazed over. I did nag him and say he should go off and support some major conservation works and become a figurehead for solving the climate change problem—your mum would have liked that, I said—but he wasn't having any of it, he was going to go off and do his military training.'

# GRADUATION

William had already given an inkling of his ambition to join the Armed Forces in the autumn of his final year. He had come down from St Andrews specially to be at the Cenotaph on 11 November 2004, believing that by his presence he could speak for young people.

'I just thought what with the Iraq War and troops being abroad and particularly the Black Watch going through a very tough time—I thought it was just the right time for me probably to make an entrance and be there for the youth and make a point that the young still haven't forgotten and still very much appreciate what's been done for everyone.

'The Army is obviously a lot more in the spotlight at the moment . . . The Remembrance Service really does bring it home when you're there and there's actually a war going on somewhere at the time and the guys are fighting their hearts out.'

Before he could think of joining them, there was his graduation ceremony on 23 June 2005, and yet another concern that he was going to be given special treatment.

'I took him and Kate over the graduation ceremony two days before,' says David Corner. 'It was a slightly interesting time because Kate was not formally recognised, and the parents were coming up. I didn't want Kate's graduation to be messed up. So I said to the two of them, "Come on, we'll go into the Younger Hall and I'll show you what's going to happen." William was ten times more nervous than Kate about it. All he could say was, "There's nothing special about this is there?" and I said, "No, the only thing that's special is that your grandparents will probably get a better seat than my grandparents would, but there's nothing different whatsoever."'

David had met Kate only a couple of times, and then because he'd worried she might be adversely affected by all the fuss that was going on. 'When she was with William at that stage, she seemed to be very much a practical guide to him. If I would say, "Look William, we'll do it this way," William would say, "Ooooohhh," and Kate would say, "That's right, do that," and it would be done in that way. It was an extraordinarily down-to-earth approach. Those stories in the media breaking over his head compound my notion that he was dealing with it at a distance with the people he trusted.'

Like all the academic staff at St Andrews, David noticed a 'tremendous growth in maturity' in William during the four years, as there is with most students. 'I saw a degree of greater relaxation. He had a tendency in earlier years if there was something to be discussed or agreed, a practical arrangement or whatever, to say, "Oh I'll think about it." He gradually became more decisive. And he was coming forward and saying things. I think he had always been forthright with the Palace, he told them what he wanted, but he wasn't with us. "I'll fit in with the university" was the general thing. But he had decided views; he became more his own person.

'He had an extraordinarily strong bond with his father. I probably didn't know about it at the beginning. Charles and I could not be more different and again we had a rather knockabout relationship. When we got to graduation, I was wearing academic dress; he introduced me to the Queen and said, "This is the first time David's ever dressed up to tell me what to do." Charles had had such a different university experience, he had virtually taken the Court to Cambridge—it hadn't been a normal student experience. He didn't quite get universities and William was the person who was going home and telling him what it was like. There was immense fondness between the two of them.

'It was one of the first times Camilla was meeting the Queen in her new married role, and I remember Camilla being more nervous than I was about what she should do when the Queen and Duke of Edinburgh arrived because there was a degree of protocol about the graduation that was very odd. We did not want it to be a formal visit because that would have messed it up for every other parent sitting there, but the only way to prevent it being a formal visit was for Charles to go to the door and say "Welcome, mother" and take her in. So Charles and Camilla had to arrive early, stand on the steps of the graduation hall with nonentities like myself and say, "Come in." Then it could be done like any other parent or grandparent going to graduation.'

William's university career had been a resounding success. He had enjoyed more freedom than he would ever have again, he had met his future wife and he had been awarded a respectable 2:1 degree. Before driving away for a family meal, William warmly greeted the crowds who had gathered around the Younger Hall to thank them and everyone in the community—including the local Fife police—who had helped to make his time at St Andrews so enjoyable, saying that he was 'sad to leave. I have been able to lead as normal a student life as I could have hoped for and I'm very grateful to everyone, particularly the locals, who have helped make this happen.'

And while William Wales, MA Hons, set off to the other side of the world to meet the British and Irish Lions on their tour of New Zealand, the university heaved an enormous and collective sigh of relief that nothing disastrous had happened on their patch, and held a large party to celebrate. David Corner was not the only one who had had misgivings at the outset. 'I and others had worked incredibly hard for fifteen years to get St Andrews fourth in the UK research tables, from thirty-seventh to fourth, and we were now very good at science, not just medieval history, and I didn't want the image to come back of posh people in red gowns walking along the pier. But he did us no harm in that respect at all.'

# HIS FATHER'S WITNESS

More than thirty years after he first fell in love with her, the Prince of Wales finally married Camilla Parker Bowles on 9 April 2005 in the Guildhall at Windsor. The Queen had taken a long time to come round to giving her consent. The relationship had, after all, practically brought the monarchy to its knees, and while she had no personal animosity towards Camilla, had the earth mysteriously swallowed her up, she would have been delighted. Life would have been very much easier for everyone. But Charles, normally duty personified, had insisted that Camilla was 'non-negotiable'. He loved her and he needed her and as everyone who has known him any length of time will say, he is a different man now that he is married to her—happy, relaxed, utterly transformed.

But it was never going to be a straightforward affair. As one of his Household says, 'Their marriage was a matter of huge constitutional and political importance and you had to court the approval of the Queen, Number Ten, the Archbishop of Canterbury and arguably a few others besides.' Top of the list of the 'others besides' were William and Harry; and concern for their feelings was one of the principal reasons why, even after the Queen was on side, the Prince had taken so long to make

Camilla his wife. Mark Bolland had worked so tirelessly (if dangerously) during his six years with the Prince of Wales to make their marriage acceptable to the British public, that large sections of them were baying for him to make an honest woman of Camilla after all these years.

The boys had been unashamedly used as part of the process. William's first meeting with Camilla in 1998, which was leaked to the press, did her popularity no harm whatsoever. The meeting was known to have been amicable, and Harry's meeting with her some months later was known to have gone equally well. They had both been on sparkling form at Charles's fiftieth birthday party at Highgrove, and it was known they had invited Camilla.

The next move was for Charles and Camilla to be seen in public together. For years they had engaged in tedious subterfuge to foil the paparazzi, never travelling in the same car (unless Camilla was hidden under a blanket), never arriving through the same door and never being together unless they were certain the location was safe. So in January 1999, when Camilla's sister Annabel Elliot was having a fiftieth birthday party at the Ritz Hotel in London, Mark masterminded a plan to thwart the paparazzi and test public opinion.

The media were briefed that the couple might be leaving the party that evening together, and during the course of the day the pavement outside the Ritz filled several lines deep with photographers and film crews jostling for position. As predicted, they emerged shortly before midnight through the revolving doors and, without stopping, walked the few steps to their waiting car, Charles holding a guiding hand behind Camilla. It was the picture they had been avoiding for thirteen years, but terrified though they had both been, it brought an end to all the pretence. They were able to behave like a couple thereafter and because all the media had that first shot, the value of it fell through the floor. And to their great relief, the majority of the British public scarcely turned a hair.

Ian Jones was there that night. 'It was a pivotal moment because from then on they could do things together. When that happened the biggest and most noticeable factor was the closeness of Charles and Camilla as a unit and how happy they were and how good they were together.'

What was needed next was for William to be seen in public with Camilla, and this was another clever piece of engineering. The occasion was a party to mark the tenth anniversary of the PCC (run by Mark's partner, Guy Black) at Somerset House in February 2001. It was billed as William's first official engagement, during which he wanted to express his thanks to the media for having allowed him to enjoy his time at Eton unmolested, and appeal to them to allow him the same privacy during his time at St Andrews. The unstated aim was to have Charles, William and Camilla—who arrived and left separately—together in the same room, with every editor in Fleet Street there to witness it.

As one of those involved says, 'Part of the thinking was that in order for the public to approve of Camilla she had to be seen with the boys or it wouldn't work. I think the relationship between them all is warm now but if I'm honest, it wasn't then. I think they found it hard when they were little. I remember Harry being uncomfortable and saying something awkward. It was difficult for them; it was a natural thing. You want your mum, you don't want her, and she had her own family. To be fair to Camilla, she never tried to be mummy but she was the "other woman" and she was there and taking daddy's time. It wasn't all happy families for quite a long time, but William was happy to see his father happy.'

Camilla was sensitive; as a mother herself she entirely understood the need to go at their pace. After that first meeting she started to stay over at York House when William and Harry were in London, but whenever they were at Highgrove, the house in which Diana had at one time lived, she would drive home to her house in Laycock after dinner. Neither she nor the Prince wanted to foist a stepmother on the boys before they had fully grown up and were ready to accept her into their lives.

Their next public get-together included Harry, the Queen, the Duke of Edinburgh and twenty-five of the younger members of the Royal Family—and there were rather more than a bunch of Fleet Street editors to witness it. It was the Party at the Palace, in June 2002, the biggest and most revolutionary of all the Queen's Golden Jubilee events. For the first time, the gardens at Buckingham Palace were opened up to ordinary members of the public, twelve thousand of them who won their tickets in a ballot, for a star-studded evening of rock and pop. A million people watched on giant screens in the Mall and Green Park, and a further two hundred million watched it on television worldwide. It began with Brian May of the band Queen standing on the roof belting out the National Anthem at goodness knows how many decibels, and ended with a spectacular pyrotechnic display and a tribute from Prince Charles to his mother, which to deafening cheers began, 'Your Majesty . . . Mummy . . .'

The Prince's popularity rating was riding high. At the time of Diana's death it had plunged to 20 per cent; by 2002, largely because William and Harry had turned out so well, he was credited with being a good parent, and it was up to 75 per cent. They could have married. There would always have been some people unable to stomach it, but most of the public would have been supportive—

as they were when they finally did marry three years later.

The reticence was over William and Harry, whose allegiance was inevitably torn. They had loved their mother and known that she had been tormented by the woman she saw as her rival. William had watched the *Panorama* programme and, whatever his feelings about it, Camilla had been the villain in that. Equally, they could see that their father was lonely and that this woman lit up his life; that he was good fun to be with when she was around, and sank easily into gloom and despondency when she was not. And both of them were old enough to know that nothing was as black and white as it had seemed when they were children.

Colleen still feels for them. She believes they have had a tough time although there have been some exceptional and supportive characters along the way who have all played a part in helping them through those tough times. In particular, she sites Sandy Henney, who played a slightly maternal role for a while (as she herself did); Tiggy, who was always there for them; Mark Dyer, who, if a bit hair-brained at times, was a true friend to them and being slightly older provided a useful steer. Edward van Cutsem was also valuable; and Andrew Gailey played a very important part. Then there was the Prince of Wales; and not least of all the Queen and Duke of

Edinburgh, who she has no doubt have privately given William a lot of support and a lot of counsel.

'But at the end of the day there's no substitute for mum and it's been very, very hard and then to have another woman thrust into it, and all in the public eye. It's great that they have turned out the way they have but they've had a lot of love around them and a lot of support from the staff as well. And their mum did love them and that has stood them in very good stead.'

By the time it came to the wedding, both boys had put their own feelings to one side and were simply delighted for their father. They released a joint statement saying, 'We are both very happy for our father and Camilla, and we wish them all the luck in the future.' The news of their engagement, however, leaked and Robert Jobson, then writing for the *London Evening Standard*, had the story that earned him the Scoop of the Year award. 'We were planning it,' says a member of the Household. 'The circle of knowledge was having to widen each week almost, as we made more plans. We had a target date for announcing it. I said to Michael [Peat], "There's no way this is going to hold, we'll have a large glass of champagne if we can hold it, but we won't, so I will devise a media plan for every single day between now and then, so if it leaks on that day, we're ready to go." And bless him, Robert Jobson broke it on the one day [in February

2005] that was the best day of the whole three weeks. The Thursday—the Prince was going to visit Goldsmiths in the City, and there was a charity ball that night at Windsor Castle; they were both going to be dressed up in their finest. It was a complete coincidence. Perfect for us. Imagine if it had been a day when they weren't going to be out and about or seen together.'

After a multitude of obstacles along the way, including postponement for a day because the original date clashed with the funeral of Pope John Paul II in Rome, and arguments about whether it was right or wrong for the country, good or bad for the boys, what kind of service it should be, whether Camilla should be called HRH The Duchess of Cornwall or something more low key, and what the Princess of Wales would have thought, the marriage finally happened. The unknown quantity was whether the public would turn out. I happened to be there that day. I had been asked to commentate by various television companies and when I arrived in Windsor at 5.30 in the morning, there was just one brave family who had camped outside the Guildhall all night. I couldn't help thinking about the hundreds who had camped for days along the route to St Paul's twenty-four years before. By 10.00 there was still only a smattering and it looked as though the overriding emotion of the day was going to be overwhelming indifference. But half an hour later the street was suddenly filled to bursting. People of every age chatted excitedly to strangers, hemmed in behind police barriers, all but a few of them delighted that Charles would finally take the plunge and wed the woman he had loved for over thirty years.

Camilla was so nervous, she had to be dragged out of her bed that day, and she looked endearingly frightened, but it was clear that the crowd loved her. The civil ceremony was conducted by Clair Williams, the Royal Borough of Windsor's Superintendent Registrar, to which only a small group of family and close friends—twenty-eight in all—were invited. William and Tom Parker Bowles, being their elder children, were their witnesses, and William carried the wedding ring for his father. The only notable absentee from the register office was the Queen, who has never attended a register office wedding in her life—and that was perhaps why. She certainly didn't seem anything other than delighted during the religious service in St George's Chapel and the reception that followed. It was a Service of Prayer and Dedication conducted by the Archbishop of Canterbury, Dr Rowan Williams, and the Dean of Westminster, David Conner, that was a much more public affair—with newspaper photographers, television cameras and 800 of their closest friends.

Ian Jones was among them, and after years of

studying the Windsors at close quarters through powerful lenses, he has noticed every nuance. 'One of the best, best moments was when they came out of the Chapel. Having photographed him for quite a few years around the world on tours alone, he always seemed to be lacking someone by his side. He was passionate about what he was doing but he had no one to share it with, no one to appreciate what he was doing and you could see the loneliness. It was so different when she was there with him and able to support him. When you think of all the grief she went through to get to that stage . . . It was transparent that William was happy for them—and Harry, but more so William. Harry is "Yeah fine, get on with it, let's have a beer", but the caring side of William came out and from that first moment you could see on that wedding day that what mattered to him was the happiness of his father and how good Camilla was for him. You could see the genuine happiness of them all together. There's a lovely moment when the newly-weds are leaving by car and William and Harry are there seeing them off. There's real engagement and real confidence between Camilla and the boys.'

Different in style, temperament and every aspect of their lives, there is no doubting the huge affection both Princes feel towards their father.

# IN HIS MOTHER'S FOOTSTEPS

In January 2005, five months before William graduated from St Andrews, Jamie Lowther-Pinkerton was appointed part-time Private Secretary to both Princes. Harry was just coming to the end of an extended gap year and was due to start Sandhurst in the autumn. William, after his graduation in June, had six months to fill before he too began the gruelling forty-four week officer training course. Both were young adults, and charities were circling, hoping to interest one or other of them in their causes and to become patrons. With full-time education at an end, there would be royal duties to prepare for and organise. There was also a need for some strategic planning about their future—and more immediately, a plan to devise for William's next six months.

Mark Dyer had been fantastic in showing them the world, particularly Africa, which he knew so well. He had been a good, loyal friend, and remains one, but he was not the one to take them on to this next stage in their lives. He had worked unpaid (as so many people who work for the Prince of Wales do) on a part-time basis for eight years, but he had a business to run—a chain of gastro pubs in London—and wanted to get on with his life.

The only other person working specifically for

William and Harry was Helen Asprey, a member of the jewellery family, who had worked as a PA in the Lord Chamberlain's office and then the Duke of Edinburgh's. Although young, she is described by someone who knows her well as, 'Very old school, very formal, very Buckingham Palace,' but also very good fun. Their father had brought her in when the boys were teenagers as someone less intimidating than anyone from his office, who could begin to guide them into the world they would soon have to inhabit. She set up a private office for them, initially with just her, but later a secretary to help answer correspondence. She handled their diaries and personal lives, organised house parties, shooting weekends and birthday parties. She managed big events for them and their polo matches, fixed dentists' and doctors' appointments, did their shopping, booked flights and holidays, handled personal invitations, liaised with the police about their plans and helped in their relationships with family friends and other foreign royal families. And in the early days, when both William and Harry turned eighteen, she also went to their first official engagements with them. She no longer has anything to do with the public side of their lives— purely the private and personal—but she is still with them, a trusted and much-loved member of the team that has gradually grown around her.

Jamie Lowther-Pinkerton was perfect for the job

of taking William and Harry on to the next stage in their lives, and already knew the Prince of Wales, having been one of the Queen Mother's favourite equerries. He is a former SAS man, then in his mid-forties, who came with all the right credentials. He had been a professional (and colleagues say 'completely brilliant') soldier for twenty years—perfect for two young men about to go into the military. He had served in the first Iraq War and in the Balkans, and at the time of his appointment was working as a part-time consultant to an international security firm and co-running a company that advised gap-year students and others on how to stay alive and avoid trouble when travelling abroad. He is an old Etonian, married with three young children (one of whom was a pageboy at William's wedding) and he won an MBE in the early 1990s, busting drug cartels for the government in Colombia. His experience of working at Clarence House was a bonus. At the age of twenty-three he had done a stint with the Queen Mother and there is no doubt his stories about their great-grandmother will have endeared him to William and Harry, who were both very involved in his selection, along with Prince Charles, Sir Michael Peat and Mark Dyer, who was already a friend of Jamie's.

Jamie had been 'dozing in a frozen trench with fellow Irish Guards somewhere between West and East Germany' when he got a call telling him he had been chosen for the job at Clarence House. Within forty-eight hours he was sitting down to lunch with the Queen Mother, nervously discussing how best to judge distance when flicking peas into a crystal chandelier with a fork.

Some time later, after a boisterous stag party, he invited all his friends—already well oiled—back to his equerry's room (with free bar) at Clarence House. It was the night before the Trooping the Colour ceremony and the Queen Mother was in residence. As he has often told the story, 'The next morning, with the Private Secretary eyeing me darkly and my room strewn with empty bottles and glasses, I crawled into my uniform just in time to attend Queen Elizabeth the Queen Mother as she mounted the carriage to take her to Horse Guards. "Did you have a party here last night, Jamie?" I stared at my boots and mumbled, "Ma'am, I'm terribly sorry. I hope we didn't disturb you," knowing full well they had. "I'm so glad to see the place being properly used," Her Majesty sparked, hopping into the carriage.'

First item on the agenda for William was an eleven-day trip to New Zealand at the invitation of Sir Clive Woodward to support the British and Irish Lions rugby team on what turned out to be their fateful 2005 tour. Sir Clive, former England coach, had been appointed coach for this tour after he had heroically led the England team to victory in the Rugby World Cup in 2003. The tour was a huge event: he took fifty-one players and forty-four back-room staff—the biggest party ever; thirty-thousand fans travelled from the UK, but Woodward sadly failed to work his magic on the Lions. His captain, Brian O'Driscoll, was lost to injury in the first few minutes of the first test match and they comprehensively lost the series 3–0 to the All Blacks. As a genuine rugby fan, William shared their pain—he had taken part in a training session with the team and had lunch with them, and was as disappointed as anyone.

But he thoroughly enjoyed the trip, nevertheless. It was the beginning of a love affair with the Antipodes, which he had only previously visited as a baby with his parents. In between the rugby and some sightseeing, he did his first solo engagements, and planted his first tree in the immaculate garden of Government House, where his father and grandparents had all planted trees before him. He represented the Queen in ceremonies in Wellington and Auckland to commemorate the sixtieth anniversary of the end of the Second World War, and caused a sensation—particularly among the young girls who crowded around the National War Memorial. During a walkabout, a nineteen-year-old called out, 'High five, William!' and to her astonishment, the twenty-three-year-old Prince raised his hand above his shoulder and glanced it off hers.

He had his close friend Thomas van Straubenzee

to keep him company, who was still a university student and struggled to find the smart clothes necessary for the official functions they had to attend. But for much of the time they just had fun. There were no official cars, no pomp; they were holiday-makers. They drove around in a minibus, exploring the country, just four of them—William, Thomas, Jamie Lowther-Pinkerton and Patrick Harrison from the press office—they went out and about, ate in bars and popped into cafés and no New Zealander ever came up to William wanting to take a photograph. The most attention he had was a family sitting at the table next to theirs who said, 'Good to see you here. Thanks for coming.' The friendly, laid-back nature of New Zealanders was a joy and ensured his lasting affection for the country.

On his arrival in New Zealand, Sir Clive Woodward said of William, 'I'm delighted he's here. It's great for the sport, great for New Zealand and great for the Lions.' Having an heir to the throne who is a genuine fan does automatically give the sport a huge boost. Harry also loves the game and the two of them regularly go to matches, although now in their capacity as Royal Vice Patrons—William of the Welsh Rugby Union (fitting for someone who will one day be Prince of Wales) and Harry of the English Rugby Union. David Pickering, chairman of the WRU, said on the day it was announced, 'I am delighted that Prince William has agreed to become our Vice Royal Patron. Rugby truly is our national sport in Wales, and the Prince's passion for and commitment to the game is well known. I saw his tremendous ambassadorial qualities first-hand during the British and Irish Lions tour last summer and during his visit to Cardiff for the FA Cup Final in May. He has particular qualities when it comes to interacting with young people and I am sure he will prove inspirational in his new role within Welsh rugby. We're all thrilled.'

Back at home, among those charities hoping to catch his eye was Centrepoint, the charity for young homeless people. Diana had become patron of Centrepoint in 1992 and had taken both William and Harry on several occasions to visit and talk to the young people in their shelters. It was one of only six charities she kept on after she stunned the charitable world (and her husband) by announcing that she was stepping down from public life in December 1993. A fax that came into her office from the Welsh National Opera, one of nearly a hundred charities which had relied on her for their income, was typical of many others. 'Your Royal Highness, it is just so helpful to be able to use your name. We only ask you to do one engagement a year, which is a reception followed by an opera, but twenty per cent or so of all our fundraising is achieved that night. What are we going to do now?'

Centrepoint had been lucky, but when the Princess died, they decided not to replace her, hoping that at a later date one of her sons might be interested in taking on the role. Anthony Lawton was then chief executive and says that when he read William's remarks in the newspapers about homelessness, a light went on in his head. 'I've always just felt they [homeless people] are over-looked and they need help, basically,' William was reported as saying. 'I have done a bit privately and publicly over the last few years and that is one particular area I am passionate about. My mother introduced that sort of area to me a long time ago. It was a real eye-opener and I am very glad she did. It has been something I have held close to me for a long time.' Less known is the fact that Prince Charles had also been involved with Centrepoint and visited in the early days of the charity when he was refining ideas for the Prince's Trust.

But first there was a discussion internally. 'We sat around with the senior management team and said, "Do we want to try to get Wills?" We all paraded our republican sympathies for about twenty minutes and then said, "It's a no-brainer; of course we'd like to get Prince William involved." For several reasons. The first was it would make a difference to lots of young people and young adults living with us. I didn't know how but I thought it would make those young people, who spend most of their lives feeling lousy, feel a little bit better, at least temporarily. The second was, it would be helpful for us making contacts and raising funds, and for our general legitimacy. If I wrote to twenty chairs of the boards of the FTSE 100 companies and said, "How would you like to come to a breakfast when we might brief you about the situation of young people and explore how you might be able to help?" On a good day I might get two who said they were interested and one who might come, and I intuited that if I said, "Our patron would be around for breakfast," I'd get nineteen who'd say "Yes" and come. And the third reason, Centrepoint's always been about trying to influence public policy and not just about helping individuals, and this might be an opportunity in some way to influence the thoughts of the future King. So we set about trying to enthuse him.'

Knowing that Jamie was putting together a programme of work experience for William during the months before Sandhurst, Anthony Lawton quickly approached him via contacts he had and found he was pushing against an open door; William had always wanted to be connected with Centrepoint. He suggested building into William's programme some time in the charitable sector and invited him to spend a few days working as a volunteer for them.

Centrepoint does more than put a roof over

homeless young people's heads, although it has been doing that to a rapidly growing number since 1969. Today, the charity describes the process of people who come through their system as being on a journey. Each young person is supported while they work towards overcoming the causes of their homelessness, which could be family, mental health, criminal activity, substance abuse or any number of reasons, and then building themselves a future in which they can live interdependent and successful lives. But a vital ingredient is that each one of those sixteen- to twenty-five-year-olds has to want to help him- or herself; otherwise they are out. I think of it as a deal.

From its origins in the basement of a church in Soho, there is now a network of houses, providing 800 beds, from emergency shelter to longer-stay housing. William visited three different sorts of homes. The first was in Dean Street in Soho, which was in the first category.

'I remember it was a Monday morning, seven o'clock, William and Jamie turned up at Dean Street, plus one of his security details. I gave William a condensed one-hour induction and training programme to get him up to speed and then he was thrown in the deep end. He took the history of one or two people as they arrived—we couldn't control who turned up. Most of the young people recognised him and were astonished to find him there; the ones who didn't were maybe refugees. He talked to them about their situation, helped with the cooking, served breakfast and quietly befriended them. While the whole philosophy of Centrepoint is about trying to make people stand on their own two feet, volunteers do sometimes act as their advocates with people in the local housing department or benefits office if they are having problems. William got on the phone and made a call for someone almost his first morning. We had a regular volunteer called William at the time and I have this fantasy that, come the Wednesday when it was announced that Prince William was going to become our patron, one or two rather obstructionist people in the local government housing office would have been thinking, Oooh, was it *that* William?

'We tried to get him involved in a little bit of everything and to understand the journey a certain sort of young person, who came in maybe off the street, would work through. If everything went really well they might eventually move out of Camberwell into their own little bedsit or flat and live on their own but with support from Centrepoint.

'There was a young man we set up to have a conversation with William, just the two of them, about how he was, how he ended up. He had been in the Army, but had either left before they could kick him out or was kicked out for drug use. This young man had two or three children by the age of nineteen, and was a serious cocaine user but he'd got himself sorted. It sticks in my mind not just because William will have learned a great deal from that conversation but because it was clear immediately that he was a good listener. Interestingly, a bit later this young man decided he wanted to get back into the Army and chose the Household Cavalry because of William's association with it.'

In drawing up the programme for Jamie's approval before the day, Anthony had put a question mark about whether a car would take William between Dean Street and a second shelter in Berwick Street, a distance of less than half a mile but in a very crowded part of London.

'Jamie had said, "No, we'll walk," and I remember walking with them and the PPO saying, "No one recognises him until he's past," and no one did—but all the way there was a 4x4 twenty yards behind. The PPO was an important person in William's life at that time because they spent so much time together. He had two teenagers himself and told me some funny story about William nipping out to a nightclub—a version of climbing down a drainpipe—and getting him back in was almost as tricky as getting him out. He totally understood his role was protection but there was a fatherly aspect to his role too.

'William was the same age as my son, and

over time as we got to know each other, him as patron, me as CEO, the relationship became quite banterish and he used to tease me, in exactly the same way as my son did.'

On the third day they took William to the Camberwell Foyer, where, amongst other life skills, the young people learn how to cook. 'I remember it tickled me. William took part in a cookery workshop where they were being taught to make lasagne. When we sat down to eat it, a young, sassy British African Caribbean girl, good looking, flirtatious, sexy and quite stroppy, sat next to William. She was being quite flirtatious and I think he was quite liking it, and suddenly a hand went out behind him and she was getting a bit closer and my colleague was kicking her under the table and the more she kicked, the closer the girl got. Even though he was younger and it was early days of his operating in public, he handled it really well; he quite liked the banterish flirtation and he entirely knew what was going on.'

It was the same kitchen in which he and Kate made biscuits and mince pies just before Christmas last year on a more publicised visit to the Camberwell Foyer. Another sassy young girl, once homeless, who is now training to be a nursery nurse, fell into conversation with him about the wedding. William asked whether she'd thought his suit looked 'dapper'. 'Nooooo,' she replied, 'your swag was on point' meaning she approved. 'Swag?' he said, looking puzzled, and brushing his shoulder rhythmically, whereupon she brushed her shoulder and the two of them made up an impromptu dance they called 'the Swag'—you dust your shoulders off twice—which they repeated for the cameras, while Kate and everyone else in the foyer, watched and laughed. 'He's fantastic,' said the girl, 'he's great, me and him are friends.' She said he had told her that when he and Kate have children, 'he's going to make them come here and I can discipline them.'

It hadn't taken long for William to decide he wanted to become patron of Centrepoint back in 2005. By the end of the second day of volunteering he had made his mind up, so it was hastily arranged for a formal announcement to be made on the third day. It remains one of the charities he is closest to and most passionate about and it's not unusual for him to pop into one of the shelters, informally and unofficially, to serve breakfast or sit around and chat to the young people over a cup of tea—and no one beyond the shelter ever hears about it. At Christmas he 'begs, borrows or steals' hampers full of treats to give to them.

The effect of that is enormous. Seyi Obakin, who took over from Anthony Lawton when he stepped down as CEO in January 2008 after his wife became very ill, is in no doubt about William's value. 'His mother was never just a figurehead patron either. She understood the effect she could have on the young people she met, and that has carried on through to William. His presence is unbelievably inspiring and motivating for young people. I couldn't exaggerate the influence.

'He has this incredible knack of putting people at their ease. In November 2008 we were gathered at HSBC Private Bank's offices in London for the launch of our 40th anniversary year and he agreed to make a speech. As he came in, I had the task of introducing him to the young people who were around. He made a beeline for them, as he always does. I'd say who they were and where they were from and they got chatting and it was a task to move him on to the next. We got to this young woman, Jasmine, who had been so excited all day that she was going to meet him and when I introduced him she just froze, completely froze, she couldn't get her words out and that set off her stammer. With many of us it would have been an awkward silence. He's tall, she was quite short; he bent down and whispered to her, "Don't worry about it, just imagine me naked." She burst out laughing and then the flood gates opened. She talked and talked and couldn't stop.'

# THE SQUARE MILE

In the summer of 2004, Charlie Mayhew, chief executive of Tusk, the conservation charity that supports the Conservancy at Lewa in Kenya, had a telephone call out of the blue from Robert ffrench Blake, William and Harry's polo manager. He asked whether Tusk would like to be one of three beneficiaries of a charity polo match they were playing at Coworth Park, near Ascot in Berkshire. 'It was great fun,' he says, 'William was still at university, only twenty-two, but I was amazed, shocked almost, by how mature he was. I had a very brief meeting with him because a lot of people were trying to get a bit of his time, but he was friendly and definitely interested; and we got a very nice donation. I think that match raised about £15,000 or £20,000 for us. So I wrote to William afterwards to say thank you, and being as pushy as I am, said, "I don't know whether or when you are considering taking on any patronages, but we would love to be considered." I got back, "Thanks but no thanks, but keep in touch."

'In 2005 we were again chosen to be beneficiary of the same day, one of just two charities that year—things were looking up. At that point William started to express interest in the annual marathon event we hold at Lewa. It is regarded as one of the ten toughest marathons in the world, situated at 5,500 feet on the foothills of Mount Kenya. He said he would love to do it, so I said come on out and do it. Next thing, I was invited to a meeting at Clarence House to discuss the logistics and reality of him taking part in this thing. Unfortunately the marathon that year coincided with the Rugby World Cup in New Zealand, which he was already committed to. So I was sitting there thinking, this could be my one and only time to be here at Clarence House and I still don't understand the protocol of patronages, so before I was booted out I rather cheekily said, "I don't know if you remember, but I wrote and asked and you kindly said keep in touch." The meeting was with Helen Asprey, but Jamie was sitting in, having just been appointed. "He's still at university," was the reply, "and not taking on anything at the moment, but don't worry, you're on the radar screen, keep in touch."

'About six months later I got a phone call from Jamie: were we still interested? William had chosen to take on a couple of charities and if we wanted him he'd be delighted to be our patron alongside Centrepoint. It was a huge honour, a real opportunity to put us on the map; and it has. There is a graph which I've shown William and he just pooh-poohs it. It shows our revenue which has just shot up. He very sweetly says, "You've just started talking more," but I'm talking just as much as I've always done. I think what it's done—and this is where patronage of someone like him really helps us, apart from raising the profile and awareness of the existence of charity—it also gives it credibility.'

Politics is one area in which William has not yet had much experience. Unlike his father, he doesn't have meetings with the Prime Minister or other ministers (other than in passing, although he did get to know David Cameron quite well during the World Cup 2018 bid) and he doesn't see state papers, but all of that will come when he takes up full-time royal duties in the future.

What he did have during his six months of work experience, in addition to his three days at Centrepoint, was a cursory introduction to the City of London and most of the major financial institutions, and a crash course in the financing of charities, which has stood him in good stead. It covered everything from estate management to wealth management. He also worked on a small, isolated Duchy farm, and, at the other end of the scale, he worked at Chatsworth, in Derbyshire, the stately home of the Devonshire family, which the Dowager Duchess turned into a thriving business. In the City he spent three weeks at HSBC, the world's second biggest bank, working at grass-roots level, mostly in the charity department where he shadowed a small team and prepared slides for weekly meetings with the directors. He spent a day with the Lord Mayor, and a day each at Lloyds of London, the Stock Exchange, the Bank of England, Farrer and Co. (the Royal Family's firm of solicitors), Billingsgate Market to learn about the Worshipful Company of Fishmongers and the regulation of the fish trade, and a couple of days volunteering in the Children's Unit at the Royal Marsden Hospital, pushing trolleys round the wards and manning the hospital radio station. He also spent a few days with the Football Association.

He knew nothing about the financial world but has retained everything he learned and still refers back to it if he is ever talking about the banking industry, but the biggest lesson for William was the realisation that if you're charismatic you can talk about the most complex matters and keep people engaged. But if you're not . . . there were times when he and his companion had to pinch themselves to avoid nodding off.

Another hugely influential part of the programme was time spent with the emergency services. Knowing he was going into the Army in January, Jamie had organised a spell with the RAF at Valley in Angelsey, where William joined the search and rescue teams in Snowdonia. Two days spent with the helicopter force there were enough to hook him. He was also impressed by the individuals who walked up Snowdonia—members of the mountain rescue teams—but it was the helicopters that did it for him, and that's why three years later he went for search and rescue and probably why he chose to join the team at Valley.

The programme ended with five days with Bertie Ross, chief executive of the Duchy of Cornwall. It was a swift introduction to the estate that currently finances his father's lifestyle—as well as his own—and which, when his father accedes to the throne, will be his.

William had agreed to be president designate of the Football Association in September 2005, with the plan that he would take over from his uncle, Prince Andrew, the Duke of York, in May the following year.

Sir Trevor Booking, player turned pundit, turned FA executive responsible for youth development, was running a flagship scheme for five- to eleven-year-olds, which seemed the perfect fit. The idea was to develop physical literacy in children who increasingly, because they have no sports lessons in school and no access to open spaces out of school, are growing up unable to enjoy basic physical literacy such as running, throwing and catching. There is also an obesity issue.

'We took William out to one or two venues and to be honest we were then locked in because he loved seeing the youngsters work, he joins in, then he starts to take some of the sessions and deliberately makes mistakes and the youngsters laugh.

'They honestly don't realise who he is, they know he's something important because mum and dad tell them he is, but once they start talking he could be anyone, which is what I think he likes.'

# SOLDIERING

In 2011 the BBC made an observational documentary about the Royal Military Academy Sandhurst, filmed over the course of a year. It was an eye-opener to anyone who still thinks that officers are the rather dim second sons of the aristocracy who have it easy while the foot soldiers do all the work. In his welcoming address to recruits, the Commandant said, 'The basic aim is to develop leadership, and using Field Marshal Montgomery's definition, that leadership "is the capacity and the will to rally men and women to a common purpose and the character which inspires confidence. That leadership must be based on a moral authority and it must be based on the truth."'

If William didn't get that exact address, he will have had something close to it when he began his officer training at Camberley in Surrey in January 2006, just days after returning from a skiing holiday with Kate in Klosters. In October he passed the Regular Commissions Board, the four days of selection tests and tasks to assess mental, physical and emotional aptitude—the first hurdle at which most of the applicants fail. Sandhurst has been training leaders of the British Army—and some foreigners too—for two hundred years, and it is no holiday camp. The sophistication and precision of modern warfare has seen to that. It is forty-four weeks of getting up at dawn, polishing boots, ironing uniform, intensive drill sessions and punishing physical exercise. It is tough, brutal, relentless, intolerant of mistakes, failure or weakness; and there are no concessions for Princes. It is not for the faint-hearted or the sensitive; it's not for people who might have qualms about killing the enemy, or who don't like being shouted at, sworn at and told what to do, and when and how to do it without question.

'They need to know what it's like to be tired and to be hungry to lead their soldiers in demanding situations around the world,' said Commandant Major-General Ritchie, when William arrived. The Prince, he insisted, would have no special privileges. 'He will be up early tomorrow morning and will then get stuck into military training. The fitness regime and tactic will begin in earnest. Everyone is judged on merit. There are no exceptions made.' The flipside to it all, however, is that when they have breaks and time off they party with a vengeance—but not, according to the rules, within a three-mile radius of the place.

William was delivered to the academy by his father, but once inside the building he was no different from any of the other 270 recruits who arrived that day. Everyone came with a bag of belongings and their own ironing board, and they were all in it together. The belongings had to be arranged in a set pattern in their rooms— toothbrush and toothpaste with exact spaces in between. Every morning, beds had to be made uniformly and flawlessly, boots polished like mirrors, uniforms ironed to perfection, and everything ready for inspection at 5.30 a.m. Mistakes, creases, rumples were met with a terrifying barrage of abuse, and press-ups by way of punishment followed, often for the whole group.

This was one place where William got his wish to be treated like everyone else, and where, behind the heavily fortified gates, he had no fear of any kind of media intrusion. It is an environment in which strong bonds are forged, second only to the bond forged in combat, where the enemy is not simply exhaustion and the Colour Sergeant yelling at you, but very real. Those that come through the forty-four weeks—and a high percentage don't—know that effective teamwork is essential to survival, both at Sandhurst and in places like Afghanistan. Active service is what these young people are training for. Many choose which regiment they want to join at the end of it, according to which will give them the best chance of front-line service.

Like every recruit, Officer Cadet Wales was confined to barracks for the first five weeks with no visitors, no alcohol, and not even his trademark floppy fair hair; like everyone, his head was shaved. For those weeks, Kate became a fond but distant memory. The infamous first five weeks are renowned for being one of the toughest experiences most people will ever go through. Many of them are begging to leave after the second day and 15 per cent drop out by the end of the five weeks. William, like Harry before him, found it very tough going, but he was better prepared than most, knowing what Harry, now beginning his third term, had gone through. Harry had found it physically very tough going at the start, but had done predictably well. Being a little older, at twenty-three, William was that bit stronger, which gave him a slight advantage.

'I don't think William liked living in a ditch quite as much as Harry,' says someone who knows them both well. 'Harry would roll out his sleeping bag and sleep in the rain. William can do that but very sensibly prefers not to. So choosing to join an armoured regiment [such as the Household Cavalry at the end of it], where you're in a tank, was easier for William than it was for Harry.' They nevertheless both chose the Household Cavalry, made up of the Life Guards and the Blues and

Royals, who are the personal bodyguards of the Monarch.

For a while it was touch and go, however. Halfway through the training, the various regiments visit and over two days attempt to lure cadets their way. William was very tempted by the Irish Guards. 'The Household Cavalry had a very tough SAS commander who sent William off on a twenty-four-hour, night navigation exercise with a paratrooper. The Irish Guards got them all absolutely howling drunk and then gave them five thousand rounds of tracer ammunition and told them to try to shoot sheep on a range in Yorkshire. [Sheep-lovers: not serious.] So he went whoomph across to the Irish Guards but then sense got the better of him and, like Harry, he went for the Household Cavalry. It was lovely for him to join Harry; that was a huge factor.'

Their commanding officer was Lieutenant Colonel Edward Smyth-Osbourne, a Life Guards officer and former member of the SAS; a man unfazed by anyone and an important figure in both their lives. Early in 2007 there was an announcement that Harry would deploy to Iraq commanding a troop of four Scimitar light tanks. He was thrilled, as only soldiers who are trained for combat can be, but after three months of intensive training and preparation with his men, the decision was reversed. The Chief of General Staff, General Sir Richard Dannatt, said it was the result of 'specific' threats from insurgents. 'These threats expose not only him but also those around him to a degree of risk that I now deem unacceptable.'

Harry had to watch his men go off to war without him. He contemplated leaving the Army. 'It was a case of, I very much feel like if I'm going to cause this much chaos to a lot of people then maybe I should bow out and not just for my own sake, for everyone else's sake.' Always the Prince with the wild child image, he made a good effort at drowning his sorrows. 'The man who picked Harry up out of the gutter and said, "Don't worry, I'll get you to Afghanistan," and did it, was Ed Smyth-Osbourne. His contribution was phenomenal and they absolutely adore him, they worship him and always will,' says a member of their Household. 'When Harry did go to Afghanistan, he said, "He's going right up to the front because that's the safest place for him." A lot of lesser men would have wrapped him in cotton wool and wouldn't have allowed him to do that. He's a great guy and they were very lucky to have him.'

William was commissioned as an Army officer in December 2006, in a ceremony known as Passing Out, in which he and his fellow newly commissioned officers marched past the Queen and the Duke of Edinburgh in the historic Sovereign's Parade at the Old College. They stood to attention for the National Anthem, then the Queen inspected those on parade, chatting to some as she walked through the lines. She stopped in front of her grandson, demonstrably a proud grandmother, and exchanged a word and a big grin, before continuing down the line. Back in Sovereign mode, she told them all that a 'great deal' was expected of them. 'You must be courageous, yet selfless, leaders yet carers, confident yet considerate and you must be all these things in some of the most challenging environments around the world.'

His father was there watching proudly along-side Camilla, but also in the party were Kate Middleton and her parents, Michael and Carole. It was the first time Kate had been William's guest at a high-profile public event with senior members of the Royal Family and it was immediately seen as an indication that an engagement was on the way. Kate and her family might have been forgiven for thinking much the same. She had become a regular sight at Highgrove and at all the pubs and parties around Gloucestershire, as well as at Clarence House and the London clubs William and Harry frequented. She'd been enthusiastically embraced by the Prince of Wales and Camilla; she had been to family birthday parties, and to Cheltenham Races with them, and for several years she'd been part of the annual skiing trip.

And William was no stranger to the Middletons by then. Kate had taken him home on many occasions and in April that year they had all been on holiday together to Mustique, the Middletons' favourite island in the Caribbean. He and Kate had been to friends' weddings together, including Laura Parker Bowles's, and in the summer they'd been to Ibiza.

William and the Middletons took to one another from the start, and it was already a relaxed and warm relationship. It was unsurprising he wanted them there that day—they had heard so much about the gruelling training. William delighted in the closeness of Kate's family, the relaxed atmosphere in the house and the humdrum nature of their daily lives. Everything that so many of us take for granted was precious to him; so different to everything he had grown up with. They were uncomplicated and normal, and that very normality created a kind of security that he relished. With them, he could do everyday things and feel like any normal person; he could disappear into their happy, safe, anonymous world.

As Kate said of the close-knit nature of her family at their engagement interview, 'It's very important to me, and I hope we will be able to have a happy family ourselves because they've been great over the years—helping me with difficult times. We see a lot of each other and they are very, very dear to me.'

Michael's family were middle-class professionals but Carole's family on her mother's side were from a coal-mining region in the north of England. She came from a line of strong women who were determined to improve their family's lot in life. The media was not slow to see Kate's attachment to the second in line to the throne as the ultimate in social climbing. Carole Middleton was said to have looked like the cat that got the cream on the day the engagement was announced, but such snide and snobbish comments spoke more about the commentators than about the Middletons. And credit William with a little awareness: if he had thought there was even the slightest element of Kate or her family liking him for his Royal status, he would have been long gone.

He also talked about them in the engagement interview: 'Kate's got a very, very close family. I get on really well with them and I'm very lucky that they've been so supportive. Mike and Carole have been really loving and caring and really fun and have been really welcoming towards me so I've felt really a part of the family and I hope that Kate's felt the same with my family.'

Their fondness of William—like that of everyone I have spoken to—is and was because of *what* he was, not *who* he was. In his early twenties when they first met he wore his HRH so lightly that within moments of meeting him people forgot that he was anything special. When someone remarked that Kate was very lucky to be going out with Prince William, she didn't hesitate before replying, 'He is very lucky to be going out with me.'

# BREAK-UP

In April 2007, just four months after including the Middletons in such a high-profile and public event, which seemed to confirm that one day the two families would be joined, the *Sun* shocked the world with the news that the relationship was over. The golden couple were said to have gone their separate ways—which was a blow to the manufacturers of wedding memorabilia who had slightly jumped the gun. It was by 'amicable agreement', and no one else was thought to be involved. Clarence House, as always, refused to comment on a private matter.

William was by this time a fully-fledged member of the Blues and Royals, which are based at Combermere Barracks in Windsor, but no sooner had he joined them than he was sent off for four months of specialist tank training at Bovington Camp in Dorset. Kate was working part-time as an accessories buyer for the fashion chain Jigsaw, owned by family friends.

The break was initiated by William, who could be forgiven for feeling some of the pressure his father had felt nearly thirty years earlier. On Kate's twenty-fifth birthday in January, the scenes outside her house in London had taken everyone back to the bad old days of Diana's harassment before her engagement to Charles. The media seemed to have made up their collective minds about who William would marry, even if he hadn't yet. And no one makes up William's mind for him.

He was perhaps feeling a bit claustrophobic. They had been together since the age of twenty and Kate had always wanted rather more commitment than he was prepared to give. His friends had not been universally enamoured, resentful perhaps of the time he spent with her where once they had had him to themselves. Some of them thought she was a bit too sensible and serious, disapproving of some of their wilder antics. It's the complaint of single young men up and down the country when one of their number gets a steady girlfriend who stops them drinking quite so much or staying out all night.

He was mindful that he hadn't had any other serious relationship before he met Kate. Perhaps he felt there was something he was missing. He became laddish at Sandhurst, in such a physical environment. Now he was miles away in Dorset and Kate was in London. They scarcely saw each other, and there were days off when he chose to go clubbing with his friends in London without seeing her. Unsurprisingly, there had been arguments.

The break-up was brief—and it was clearly a very unhappy time for Kate, who fortunately had the support and closeness of her family to fall back on. It only lasted a few weeks but what brought William running back, according to someone who knows him well, was jealousy. Kate was unhappy but she was not sitting at home moping; she was putting a brave face on it, also a sexy dress, and hitting the town. He was doing the same (minus the dress) but what was sauce for the goose was definitely not sauce for the gander. He is quite old-fashioned in his outlook and he couldn't bear the thought of her with another man.

When asked about the break-up during their engagement interview, William said, 'We were both very young, at university, we were both finding ourselves as such and being different characters and stuff, it was very much trying to find our own way and we were growing up, it was a bit of space and a bit of things like that and it worked out for the better.'

Kate was more articulate on the subject. 'I think at the time I wasn't very happy about it, but actually it made me a stronger person. You find out things about yourself that maybe you hadn't realised, I think you can get quite consumed by a relationship when you are younger and I really valued that time for me as well, although I didn't think it at the time.'

They agreed that after such a long period, their relationship was based on friendship as well as love.

'I think if you do go out with someone for quite a long time,' said Kate, 'you do get to know each other very, very well, you go through the good times, you go through the bad times. Both personally and within a relationship as well. I think if you can come out of that stronger and learn things about yourself, it certainly helps, . . . it's been a good how many years?'

The answer, by the time they were giving that interview in November 2010, was eight years in all. Although the rift was healed in a matter of weeks, and their relationship appeared to be rock-steady thereafter, it was another three and a half years before William asked Kate to marry him.

# PHONE HACKING

William's ambition in the Army, like Harry's, was to be deployed to the front line. To his frustration, while he was at Bovington playing with tanks, the rest of his squadron, who were already trained up for immediate deployment, left for Afghanistan without him. Winning one of the two top prizes on the course was no consolation. In reality he could never have gone into battle with his squadron at that particular moment. Harry was about to deploy to Iraq, and it would have been unacceptable to have both the second and third in line to the throne in a war zone at the same time. As it turned out, Harry didn't go to Iraq after all, but he did get to Afghanistan in December 2007.

Harry was there for ten weeks of a fourteen-week tour, serving as a battlefield air controller in Helmand Province—based only 500 yards from Taliban enemy bunkers—responsible for providing cover for troops on the front line, for scrutinising hours of surveillance footage beamed from aircraft flying over enemy positions to a laptop terminal, known as 'Taliban TV', for setting co-ordinates for bomb drops and preventing deaths by friendly fire. In all the hours he spent each day talking on the radio to pilots, he was known only by his call sign Widow Six Seven. His base came under mortar and machine-gun attack five times every day and he was personally involved in a firefight with the Taliban, fighting alongside Gurkha troops.

On Christmas Day, while the rest of the Royal Family was gathered at Sandringham, he was sharing a goat curry with his colleagues. The Ministry of Defence and Clarence House had done a deal with the UK and US media, which had agreed to a news blackout until Harry was safely back on British soil. In return, he agreed to give an interview every four weeks 'in theatre' (which would not be used until he was home) and another when he arrived home. No one at the MoD expected his cover to last more than a couple of days. The British media were getting tips about him every day from soldiers, but they were not using them. It was an Australian magazine that first broke the news he was in Afghanistan. Plans were quickly put in place to bring him home but, on consideration, everyone involved decided to sit tight and keep their nerve. Miraculously, the story wasn't picked up for two weeks, but then a US blogger, with a big following, ran it on his gossipy website, the Drudge Report. Once the news was on the internet there was no containing it and Harry was pulled out and flown home the same day. It was a sad moment but tinged with pride for those who had managed to keep him there under wraps for as long as ten weeks.

His commanding officer in Helmand, Brigadier Andrew Mackay, was full of praise for Harry. 'He has shared the same risks, endured the same austerity and undergone the same moments of fears and euphoria that are part of conducting operations in this most complex of environments. A Forward Air Controller provides essential cover to those soldiers deployed on the ground. He controls the airspace, the aircraft that enter it and the release of any ordnance. It requires an individual of cool nerve, mental agility and an ability to make critical decisions in the heat of battle . . . He has acquitted himself with distinction.'

William had been consulted at every point in Harry's deployment. He had wanted his brother to get out to the front line, no less than he wanted to go there himself, and was as much a part of the decision-making process as Harry.

Both Princes had always made it very clear that they wanted to see active service. I first met William over a pint of cider one evening in a pub in Gloucestershire. He was twenty-one and had just finished his third year at St Andrews. The meeting was off-the-record but it was clear he was thinking of joining the Army. His only hesitation was the fear that he might be prevented from going to the front line because of who he was. As he articulated it, on-the-record, a little later, 'The last thing I want to do is be mollycoddled or wrapped up in cotton wool, because if I was to join the Army I'd want to go where my men went and I'd want to do what they did. I would not want to be kept back for being precious or whatever, that's the last thing I'd want. It's the most humiliating thing and it would be something I'd find very awkward to live with, being told I couldn't go out there when these guys have got to go out there and do a bad job.'

I had a call from Paddy Harverson, who had not long been in his job, earlier that evening. I was writing a book about the monarchy and had met and spoken to him several times about the Prince of Wales. I'd rung him earlier to ask if he could help with some background information about William. Knowing I lived nearby, he asked me to join him in the Hare and Hounds at Westonbirt, less than a mile from Highgrove. 'I hope Prince William is going to join us in the pub,' he told me. He was, and is, firmly of the belief that it is good for the Princes to meet the press informally. His theory is that it's harder to be critical about someone you have looked in the eye. He has recently been organising private lunches with media groups to build relationships and under-standing between the two sides. On foreign tours he also organises parties for the accredited media that follow. The Queen and Prince Philip used to do the same, but the Prince of Wales was so hurt by the media during the break-up of his marriage that he stopped the parties. Paddy admits that not everyone buys into his theory but thinks William does and says he's very good at being polite to someone 'he knows writes cock and bull about him'.

When I arrived, the saloon bar was filled with journalists and photographers—about fifteen in all—some familiar to me, some not. They had all come down to Gloucestershire in preparation for an informal photo call the following morning—the latest in the St Andrews Agreement. For a change, Paddy had decided to do it on the Home Farm, feeding pigs, driving a tractor—little thinking that it would lead one of the tabloids to announce that, according to 'senior courtiers', William was planning to turn his back on the Army after university to pursue a career in farming. Paddy was there in jeans, as was his deputy, Patrick Harrison, and as I chatted to my media colleagues I realised that none of them knew who was about to walk through the door. Paddy had simply invited them to join him for a drink.

At about 9.25 the door opened and in walked William with Mark Dyer. He was wearing jeans and a sweatshirt and, apart from the familiar face, could have been any tall, slim, tousle-headed twenty-one-year-old. Paddy immediately sprang up to greet him and introduced him to the people standing around, even the most hardened of whom were looking flushed—and I don't think it was the beer. Having shaken each and every hand and looked us all in the eye as he did so, he said he would like a pint of cider and sat down on a bench with his back against the wall. Those who could find chairs sat in a circle around him; others stood and, for nearly an hour, we all chatted. Seldom had I seen such a self-possessed and skilful operator—nor such a group of seasoned hacks (myself included) leaning forward so intently to catch and savour every word. Questions he didn't want to answer he simply bounced back or laughed knowingly at, as if to say he wasn't going to fall into that trap, but it was done with such charm that there was no offence. He asked the *News of the World* royal correspondent, Clive Goodman, whether he came here often, did he know the area? 'Oh, yes,' said Clive, 'I've been here quite a lot but I can't say I've ever been invited.'

Clive Goodman was one of three men arrested two years later and imprisoned for four months for intercepting the mobile phone messages of Clarence House staff. He had taken over from Mark Bolland in March 2005 and it was stories in that Blackadder column, under his own by-line, which first aroused suspicion.

William and Harry had been convinced for years—at least five years before Clive Goodman was arrested—that someone had been leaking stories to the tabloids. It created a corrosive mistrust within the Household as well as outside. Everyone was looking suspiciously at everyone else; it was an uneasy time. The Princes suspected their friends. It was the only possible explanation for the constant trickle of stories; some of them trivial, some more substantial, but all of them private. 'They were paranoid for years and years about various of their friends selling stories,' says a friend. 'They used to get really wound up about it. There were various friends they doubted—of both of theirs—and they talked to each other about, "Did you tell him? Is he trustworthy?" These were not William's best friends, like James Meade or Thomas van Straubenzee or any of his inner "Masonic circle", but people maybe one step removed.

'As a result, trust is William's big thing. He is very slow to trust people and I should think the single biggest driver of his relationship with Kate is trust.'

'A few things happened at once,' says one of the team, all of whose phones were being hacked. They had all been trying to work out how titbits were getting into the *News of the World* when a short piece appeared in November 2005 about Tom Bradby, who was by this time ITN's political editor. He had offered to edit William's gap year videos, as he had Harry's, and the two of them had been finding a time when they were both free to meet up.

'If ITN do a stocktake on their portable editing suites this week,' said the piece in Clive Goodman's 'Blackadder' column, 'they might notice they're one down. That's because their pin-up political editor Tom Bradby has lent it to close pal Prince William so he can edit together all his gap year videos and DVDs into one very posh home movie.'

Tom and William had had a phone conversation on the Saturday—the very day before the piece appeared—and agreed to meet on the Monday; Tom would come to Clarence House with some equipment.

When he arrived on the Monday, he and William just looked at each other and said, 'How the hell did the *News of the World* get that?' William then said that he'd been equally puzzled by a story about a knee injury he'd had that had appeared in the same column the previous week.

'William pulled a tendon in his knee after last week's kids' kickabout with Premiership club Charlton Athletic', wrote Goodman. 'Now medics have put him on the sick list. He has seen Prince Charles's personal doc and is now having physiotherapy at Cirencester hospital, near his country home Highgrove.'

William had been thinking the surgeon must have spoken to the *News of the World* or his secretary, but he knew, and Tom agreed, it was unthinkable. Then they started going through all the alternatives. Tom knew from his years as a royal correspondent that during Diana's lifetime tabloid reporters had listened to one another's voicemail messages to get stories. If they were doing it then, why not now? Slowly it dawned. After they had spoken on the Saturday, William had phoned Helen and left a message on her voicemail asking her to leave Tom's name with security at the gate. After he had seen the doctor, he had left a message on Helen's voicemail asking her to fix physiotherapy in Circencester . . .

'The other one' says one of the Household, 'was William leaving a jokey message on Harry's voicemail pretending to be Chelsy [Harry's girlfriend] and giving him a bollocking in a South African accent—there'd been a story about him visiting a lap-dancing club. This story ran in the *News of the World*. How did they know William had left a message on Harry's voicemail?

'At the same time three of us noticed in conversation that all of our voicemail was playing up. We were discovering messages that had been listened to but not by us. They were being saved as having been listened to, as in "You have four new messages and six saved messages", and I would always listen to a message then delete it and I think the others did too. Initially we thought it was a fault with the phones but we had different phones and one was on a different network, so we thought how does that work? I remember sitting in Helen's room and it dawned on us that there might be more to this, that the *News of the World* stories and the funny voicemail situation might be connected, so we called in Royalty Protection, who are always the first port of call.'

Because of the security implications, in that their messages were often about the Princes' flights and movements, the police brought in the anti-terrorism squad, who very quickly confirmed that their messages were being hacked and discovered who was doing it. Although, as one of them says, 'It wasn't rocket science.

'We decided very quickly to prosecute—William and Harry were very angry and very keen to get something done about it. We told the police, and off we went. There was quite a long period when we carried on as normal while they gathered the evidence, knowing that they were listening to our voicemails. It was evil stuff. I never believed it was just us—as it all subsequently unravelled.' In that unravelling, in November 2011, it transpired that while the *News of the World* was being investigated for hacking into William's voicemail, it had hired a private investigator, ex-police detective Derek Webb, to follow him. It was no surprise; both boys had known for years that they were being followed.

Diana had talked about telephone tapping, the Squidgy and Camillagate tapes had been the result of some sort of interception; from an early age William and Harry had lived with the fear of leaks and betrayals. William particularly was wary of people, questioning motives, wondering whether they could be trusted. Their reaction to the hacking was anger, not disbelief. The *News of the World* had been prying into their lives for as long as they could remember, and to discover that they had found some new way was not entirely surprising.

'The phone-hacking thing was a complete

liberation to them,' says a friend, 'because all those stories just stopped; they don't appear any more. If you look five years before the hacking arrests and five years after, it's like night and day in terms of what appears and what doesn't. It's unbelievable. Every week there would be something in the news: an argument William was supposed to have had with his commanding officer at Sandhurst . . . masses and masses of stuff, some of it trivial, some a bit damaging when presented the wrong way. With those arrests, they realised that their friends weren't talking and don't talk and that has helped them relax about things.'

## GOING SOLO

For the next eighteen months after his graduation from Sandhurst, William was a part of regimental life but he had signed up for a short-term commission and it became clear that, because of the way the squadrons within the regiment were rotating, he was not going to get out to Afghanistan within that time. Rather than doing more of the same, he decided to spend the remaining eighteen months experiencing life in the other services. One day in the future he would be Commander-in-Chief of all three, the highest rank he could hold, and he wanted to know more about how they worked at the other end of the scale. It would make him unique among monarchs but also among high-ranking servicemen, and put him in a position to contradict anybody from the Chief of Defence Staff down, none of whom would have had his breadth of experience.

So at the beginning of January 2008, as Flying Officer William Wales, he arrived at RAF Cranwell in Lincolnshire, where he was stationed with 1 Squadron of 1 Elementary Flying Training School. It was the start of four months of specially tailored, intensive training with the Royal Air Force, where he spent just enough time with each aspect of the service—from logistics to flying—to soak up the ethos and traditions of the RAF as well as its military role. Flying was where his passion lay. It was very much in the blood. His father had started his military career in the RAF, and already had a private pilot's licence when he'd arrived at Cranwell in 1971 to train as a jet pilot. Charles loved flying, as did his father, but both men were ultimately persuaded to follow the family tradition and join the Navy. Charles finally got his wish to join the Fleet Air Arm and did a helicopter conversion course to become a pilot on the commando carrier HMS *Hermes*. He described those as 'the happiest and most rewarding' days of his naval career, but he was perpetually frustrated by restrictions forced on him because of fears for his safety. He would wonder why an aircraft deemed too dangerous for him to fly was safe enough for his friends. The Duke of Edinburgh took up flying when he gave up his naval career. He gained his RAF wings in 1953, then his helicopter wings, then his private pilot's licence, and when he finally gave up flying in 1997 at the age of seventy-six, he had flown 5,986 hours in fifty-nine types of aircraft. And Prince Andrew had been a naval pilot in the Falklands War.

So it was not surprising that after eight days, and just eight and a half hours' flying time, William made his first solo flight in a Grob 115E light aircraft, known as a Tutor. 'God knows how somebody trusted me with an aircraft and my own life,' he said afterwards. 'It was an amazing feeling, I couldn't believe it. I was doing a few circuits going round and round, then Roger my instructor basically turned round and said, "Right, I'm going to jump out now," and I said, "What, where are you going?" He said, "You're going on your own," and I said, "There's no way I'm going to do that," but he said I was ready for it and jumped out. The next thing I knew I was taxiing down the runway and I was sitting there saying, "Oh my God, this is a bit odd, there's no one in here." Going solo is one of those things—if you had a list of the top fifty things to do before you die, it would be in there.'

From the Grob he graduated to the faster Tucano T1 based at RAF Linton-on-Ouse in North

Yorkshire, and from there he moved to RAF Shawbury in Shropshire and helicopters, starting with the Squirrel.

After the four months, he had flown most of the aircraft in the service including a Typhoon jet fighter and, as one of his Household describes it, 'had had the most amazing panoply of experiences'. He even made it to the front line. He was on a thirty-hour mission to Afghanistan to repatriate the body of Robert Pearson, a twenty-two-year-old trooper killed in action. He wasn't qualified to fly the massive four-engine C-17 Globemaster military transport plane, but did take the controls of it under supervision during the flight. During the three hours on the ground at Kandahar, he met fellow servicemen, and surprised them all. Only a handful of people knew he was on his way, because of a news blackout, but his visit was a huge morale boost. The news only broke when he was safely back on British soil when he said how 'deeply honoured' he felt being part of the crew that brought the body home. After they landed at RAF Lyneham, he asked for a private meeting with the parents of the dead soldier. He had gone to Afghanistan as a regular serving officer, but he was always a member of the Royal Family first and has a real understanding of the impact that a sympathetic word could have on people in times of distress.

Very serious efforts were made to get William to

the front in more than a token way, but they were thwarted by the fear that his being there would put in danger the lives of those around him. Jamie Lowther-Pinkerton and the Prince himself still harbour the hope that one day it will be achieved.

In April 2007, at the end of his bespoke course, he was one of twenty-five students presented with their RAF pilot wings by the Prince of Wales, in his capacity as Air Chief Marshal. The Duchess of Cornwall was in the audience, as was Kate Middleton and Diana's sister, Lady Sarah McCorquodale, the only member of the Spencer family with whom he has much contact. His training in the RAF had been accelerated but he had forty or fifty flying hours at the end of his time—as many as most people who get their wings conventionally are able to achieve over three to four years. He felt as though he had slightly cheated, but he came away a competent if not an operational flier with a real understanding of the Air Force and its capabilities, which was the original intention.

It was in the clocking-up of that flying time that William landed himself in trouble. In the last week before his graduation he was based at Odiham in Hampshire, learning to fly Chinooks—tandem-rotor heavy-lift helicopters. Two incidents happened within a couple of days of each other, the second making the headlines before the first. 'Prince William flies multi-million-pound RAF

Chinook helicopter to cousin's Isle of Wight stag do . . . and picks up Harry on the way,' announced the *Daily Mail*. 'Most young men,' it went on, 'are happy to jump in a taxi to get to a stag do. But not Prince William. The second in line to the throne used a £10 million RAF helicopter to fly to a drunken weekend in the Isle of Wight. He even stopped off in London to pick up his brother Prince Harry on the way.

'The 80-minute journey—it is understood it costs more than £5,000 to keep a Chinook in the air for an hour—saved William seven hours of driving through rush hour traffic and waiting for a ferry, meaning he and Harry arrived by 4 p.m., ready for the start of the three-day stag party for their cousin Peter Phillips.

'The Ministry of Defence claimed the sortie had always been planned as part of William's training and included important elements of a pilot's skills.'

This was not strictly true, and after a series of other 'joyrides' came to light and a variety of MPs had fulminated loudly and the anti-monarchy group Republic had asked to know the costs involved, the RAF admitted the flights had been 'naive' and a 'collective error of judgment'. The Isle of Wight trip cost the taxpayer £9,000.

The truth was the Chinook had flown up to Cranwell from Odiham on the day of William's graduation to put on a display for the passing-out students. William knew the pilot who said, 'Where do you want to go? We're going back to Odiham, we'll give you a lift.' William said he had to get to the Isle of Wight, whereupon the pilot said, 'That's no problem, we've got to do our three hours today to get our hours up, we'll drop you.' William turned to one of his team for reassurance, 'Do you think that's okay?' 'Yeah,' he said, 'go on,' thinking no more about it. On the way, which was perhaps the mistake, they diverted across London to pick up Harry from Woolwich Army Barracks. They touched down in a field on the Isle of Wight, William and Harry hopped out, and the helicopter flew back to Odiham. There was nothing unusual in what happened; RAF pilots do their hours and get in their landings wherever they can. Had anyone else jumped out of the Chinook, there would have been no story.

But it wasn't anyone else and the proverbial rapidly hit the fan. The moment it did, William put his hands up. As that same member of his team is quick to point out, 'He has a very good instinct for what is right and wrong', and will always do what is morally right. Those who have worked for his father say that Charles is not always so good at admitting ownership of plans or decisions that backfire. William immediately said it was his fault, that he had asked the crew to take him to the Isle of Wight. It didn't stop them being dropped on from a dizzy height, but if he had not come forward, their plight might have been considerably worse. As one of them put it, 'If it wasn't for him we'd be hanging from a gibbet.'

The second incident caused equal outrage and was equally legitimate. William had taken a Chinook the week before while he was training at Odiham, and 'bounced' into a field belonging to the Middletons behind their house in Bucklebury. The RAF have been doing this for seventy years. Trainees, needing to practise their take-offs and landings, choose a field belonging to somebody they know so they don't have to pay a landing fee. No one had got in or out of the Chinook; he was simply practising, and his planned route and descent had been cleared and authorised before he left the base. Somehow there was a crossed line between the RAF and the MoD and when the press (tipped off, no doubt, by someone in the village on the make) started making enquiries, the MoD said they knew nothing about it. The *Daily Mail* lost no time in declaring 'RAF fury over Prince William's £30,000 helicopter stunt in Kate Middleton's backyard.'

Righteously indignant on William's behalf, his team at Clarence House wanted to object but William refused to let them. 'No,' he said, 'what will happen is that it will bounce down the line and some poor pilot in the crew planning room who misunderstood the question will get it in the neck at Odiham and I'm not prepared to do that. We can ride this. Let's do the right thing, which is for us to take the hit.' He wasn't going to have that guy, whoever he was, swinging from a yardarm.

At the next meeting of the Princes' Charities Forum, which is a periodic gathering of the chief executives of all their charities, Harry lost no time in taking the mickey out of his brother. While William chaired the meeting, Harry made continual references to helicopters, which had everyone in fits of laughter. Each time William simply put his head down in an embarrassed way while struggling for a suitable riposte.

# LIFE ON THE OCEAN WAVE

With his wings successfully won, and the flying bug well and truly established, William moved on from the RAF to the Royal Navy, in which his father, grandfather, great-grandfather George VI and great-great-grandfather George V had all served. After the first four weeks of basic training and learning about every aspect of the service, which included taking part in war games exercises on board a nuclear submarine and a minesweeper, he was sent on an operational attachment to the West Indies. He joined HMS *Iron Duke*, a frigate under the command of Commander Mark Newland, one of several ships deployed to the Caribbean during the hurricane season in case they are needed for humanitarian purposes. The rest of the time they work with the US Coast Guard on counter-narcotics patrols, stopping and boarding suspicious-looking boats. Typically the traffickers they intercept are from South America bound for Europe and North Africa and use speedboats packed with petrol and drugs, known as 'go fasts'.

Commander Newland had been told to expose the Prince to every aspect of front-line operations on the ship and, as luck would have it, within four days of his arrival, they seized a massive cocaine haul from a 50-foot speedboat 300 miles north-east of Barbados. It was the culmination of a three-day operation in rough seas and stormy weather. William was part of the frigate's helicopter crew that first spotted the boat, suspiciously far out to sea for such a small craft, and after a high-speed chase, ordered it to stop. He hovered overhead while US coastguards boarded the speedboat and arrested five men. They found forty-five bales of cocaine—with a total weight of 900 kg and a street value of £40 million—bound for Europe.

Newland was full of praise for William after the raid. 'He is someone who contributes at every level,' he said. 'He is a very professional military officer, and very astute. He acts as I would expect a young officer of his experience and maturity to act in this type of operation.'

It was the beginning of another of several important relationships for Prince William. 'They were absolutely outstanding with William,' says a member of the Household of his time on *Iron Duke*, 'and the commander of that frigate is a real genius, a charismatic sort of guy who William absolutely adored.' He was treated as just another naval officer on board, who had to sleep four to a cabin, get up early, be on watch through the nights and pull his weight. A fellow crew member from *Iron Duke* was one of the twenty-four Armed Forces personnel chosen to line the path outside Westminster Abbey after William and Kate's wedding. Leading Physical Trainer Gavin Rees, who was with William throughout those five weeks, said, 'My abiding memory of Prince William was that he was always late for circuit training, so I always had to give him extra press-ups! Looking back on it now it's amazing to think that I took the future King for circuit training.'

After the excitement of the narcotics haul they went on to engage in a hurricane disaster rescue exercise on the volcanic island of Montserrat. William was involved in the planning and was a member of the forward command team who were the first Navy personnel to come ashore after an imaginary category 5 storm hit the island. He had to help senior officers and local leaders direct the emergency operations and, according to Mark Newland, Sub-Lieutenant William Wales was a natural leader; commanding small teams of people came as 'second nature' to him.

Had such a storm hit for real it would have flattened almost all the buildings on the island and threatened the lives of hundreds of people. Just two months later, Hurricane Ike did precisely that on the Turks and Caicos Islands, and the *Iron Duke* was involved in a genuine relief operation. But by this time William was back on dry land.

After almost two years of service life near the bottom of the pile, carrying out strategies devised in Whitehall, William's next assignment took him on a stratospheric leap into the heart of that decision-making process. He spent a week at the Ministry of Defence on attachment to the Secretary of State, Des Browne, shadowing the staff of the Chief of Defence Staff, Air Chief Marshal Sir Jock Stirrup. William sat in on meetings with the military representative from NATO, visiting four-star generals and the like, and did not resist the temptation to join in their discussions. In meeting after meeting he was the only one around the table who had experience of all three services, and had been primed by people such as Mark Newland, Commander of *Iron Duke*, and Ed Smyth-Osbourne from the Blues and Royals to ask difficult questions.

One of the meetings he sat in on was a discussion about the aircraft carrier programme. This was, and still is, a political and financial hot potato—the decision, which came out of the new Labour government's Strategic Defence Review in 1997, to build two new 'supercarriers', HMS *Queen Elizabeth* and HMS *Prince of Wales*. At 280 metres long, displacing 65,000 metric tons and capable of deploying forty aircraft including helicopters, they are by far the biggest warships ever to be constructed for the Royal Navy and are expected to enter service in 2016 and 2018. The original cost was estimated at £3.65 billion, although almost double that figure is now the cost of completing just one of the ships (they survived the latest Strategic Defence Review cuts on the grounds that the contracts the last government signed made them more expensive to cancel than to complete).

When William sat in on this meeting in September 2008, the contracts to build them had just been signed and a rather splendid Air Commodore had brought along a model of one of the carriers. As he was pointing out the guns on the decks, where the aircraft would take off and land and explaining that a number of technical specifications in the original plans had been stripped out because of cost, William listened quietly and then asked very politely, 'Sir, can I just ask one very quick question? Is the plan for these ships to be degaussed?' Degaussing is a process used on every naval ship since 1917 to demagnetise the hull. It is basically a band of copper that stops magnetic mines going off underneath the ship. It was indeed one of the things they had decided to remove.

The Air Commodore went bright red and said, 'Yes, we don't need it.' William said, 'But surely, if you're not degaussed then you won't be able to go on the continental shelf—because, obviously, magnetic mines have to sit in shallow water so they can pick up the magnetic field—and that will restrict the range of your strike aircraft by 150 nautical miles from both directions, won't it? And give you time over target of five minutes instead of three hours or whatever it is?' He was voicing the concerns he had picked up from the men and women at the sharp end, whose lives were potentially being put in danger by the men in brass. The Air Commodore very quickly moved on.

No further illustration was needed about the value of those commissions. He now knows how soldiers, sailors and airmen tick, each one differently from the next. He has made friends in all the services of men and women of his own age with whom he is still in regular contact, and if they stay in the services when William is Commander-in-Chief, his old chums will be the ones calling the shots in the corridors of power.

# DRAWING A LINE

William is unlikely to forget the date of his Passing Out Parade from Sandhurst in December 2006, not just because it saw his father, grandparents and future in-laws in public together for the first time. It took place the day after the official three-year investigation into the death of his mother concluded. The verdict was that Diana had died in 'a tragic accident'. That was the finding of Lord Stevens, former Commissioner of the Metropolitan Police. 'There was no conspiracy to murder any of the occupants of that car,' he said. The evidence suggested that Diana was not engaged or about to get engaged and scientific tests showed she was not pregnant. The £3.69 million inquiry had interviewed some four hundred people, including Prince Charles, the Duke of Edinburgh and the heads of MI5 and MI6.

'We have spoken to many of her family and closest friends and none of them have indicated to us that she was either about to or wished to get engaged,' he said. 'Prince William has confirmed to me that his mother had not given him the slightest indication about such plans for the future.'

Clarence House put out a statement saying that Princes William and Harry hoped that the 'conclusive findings' of the report would end speculation surrounding their mother's death.

But it was not to be. Mohamed Al Fayed, who had lost his son Dodi in the accident, remained noisily convinced there had been a cover-up. It was his allegations that had led the coroner, at the opening of the inquest in 2004, to order an inquiry in the first place. In October 2007 the inquest continued at the Royal Courts of Justice, led by Lord Justice Scott Baker.

As Sir Max Hastings, writing in the *Guardian*, said, halfway through the proceedings, 'The inquest into the death of Princess Diana is providing a circus for the prurient, a dirty-raincoat show for the world, of a kind that makes many of us reach for a waxed bag.

'Day after day for almost three months, a procession of charlatans, spivs, fantasists, retired policemen, royal hangers-on and servants who make [Shakespeare's] Iago seem a model of loyalty has occupied the witness box at the law courts in the Strand. They have itemised the Princess's alleged lovers, her supposed opinions of the royal family (and vice versa), her contraceptive practices and her menstrual cycle.

'The business of an inquest is to examine the cause of a death. In the case of the Princess, we might assume that this would focus exclusively upon what did, or did not, happen in a Paris tunnel more than a decade ago. It should not have been difficult to conclude such an inquiry in a matter of days. Every police officer, French and British, who has examined the case since 1997 has reported that the Princess's death was the result of a tragic accident.'

In April 2008, the jury released an official statement that Diana and Dodi were unlawfully killed by the 'grossly negligent driving of the following vehicles and of the Mercedes', adding that additional factors were 'the impairment of the judgment of the driver of the Mercedes through alcohol' and 'the death of the deceased was caused or contributed to by the fact that the deceased was not wearing a seat-belt, the fact that the Mercedes struck the pillar in the Alma Tunnel, rather than colliding with something else'.

It had been a very difficult time for William and Harry but it was something they knew had to happen if their mother's memory was ever to be laid to rest in peace. 'The great guy there was Lord Justice Scott Baker. He was a genius,' says a member of the Prince's Household, who spent many hours at the inquest. 'He was completely even-handed, he didn't stand any nonsense, he was tough, considerate, straight as a die, analytical. There were a lot of pressures coming in from left and right and he was just very cool. We owe quite a lot to him.

'It would be presumptuous to suggest it was cathartic for the Princes. It was probably cathartic for the country, but she wasn't the country's mum; she was their mum.'

The year before, as the tenth anniversary of her death approached, they had come up with a plan to celebrate and commemorate her. They wanted to stage a spectacular concert of music and dance with all the artists she loved most, to be held on what would have been her forty-sixth birthday, followed by a memorial service, again with the music she loved, on the date of her death. This was the first time either brother, apart from choosing which regiment they wanted to join on leaving Sandhurst, had been so demonstrative about anything. They thought of the idea, they knew what they wanted and they were adamant about how they wanted to do it. The Household remembers it being a very exciting time, the first time there was a real buzz, and some memorable meetings where they chose the music. 'I know zero about pop music so they were taking the mickey furiously and at the time, they knew absolutely zero about classical music, so I was feeding a bit in there. Having said that, they knew a lot of their mother's favourites and probably all of those pieces in the memorial service were ones which they had remembered she loved.'

But first was the pop, and in the run-up to the concert the Princes agreed to do two interviews, one with American television, NBC's *Today* programme, and the other with Fearne Cotton for the BBC. For the first time, they spoke publicly about their mother and their loss.

'We were left in no doubt that we were the most important thing in her life,' said William, 'and then after that there was everyone else, there were all her charities and everything like that and, to me, that's a really good philosophy—she just loved caring for people and she loved helping.

'We were so lucky to have her as our mother and there's not a day that goes past when we don't think about her and miss her influence, because she was a massive example to both of us.

'It's one of those things that is very sad but you learn to deal with it and there are plenty of other people out there who have got the same or worse problems than we've had.'

Harry added, 'She was a happy, fun, bubbly person who cared for so many people. She's very much missed by not only us, but by a lot of people and I think that's all that needs to be said, really.'

The six-hour extravaganza took seven months and the help and expertise of a cast of many to organise, with both Princes overseeing every detail, but the result was worth every minute of preparation. When William and Harry went out onto the stage at the new £798 million Wembley Stadium on 1 July 2007, dressed casually in jeans, jackets and open-necked shirts, Harry simply said, 'Hello, Wembley!' The place erupted and the applause was deafening as 63,000 people got to their feet to clap and cheer. 'This evening is about all that our mother loved in life—her music, her dance, her charities and her family and friends.' And Harry, mindful of those he had hoped to be serving alongside in Iraq, added a word of encouragement: 'I wish I was there with you. I'm sorry I can't be. To you and everyone on operations we'd both like to say, "stay safe".'

Twenty-two thousand five hundred tickets had been made available in December and sold out within seventeen minutes. It was broadcast in 140 countries to an audience of around 500 million people, and raised a total of £1 million for the Diana Memorial Fund and her five main charities, including Centrepoint and Sentebale, which William had said were 'both charities that continue on from our mother's legacy'.

Nothing like it had ever been staged before. There was music of every sort, there were dancers from the English National Ballet, there were songs from Andrew Lloyd Webber musicals, a comedy sketch (and an agonisingly prolonged improvisation when the next act failed to appear) from Ricky Gervais, there were speakers including Sienna Miller and Dennis Hopper, Kiefer Sutherland, Jamie Oliver and David Beckham introducing acts and artists, and pre-recorded video tributes from Nelson Mandela, Bill Clinton and Tony Blair.

Sir Elton John, who had performed a specially

adapted version of 'Candle in the Wind' at Diana's funeral, opened the concert with 'Your Song', and was followed by Duran Duran, her favourite band, and stars like James Morrison, Lily Allen, Status Quo, Sir Tom Jones, Rod Stewart, P. Diddy and Take That, while iconic black and white images of Diana, taken by Mario Testino, looked down on them from a giant screen at the back of the stage.

After Sir Elton's closing song, William and Harry returned to the stage for the final word. William thanked everyone for coming and praised the artists for an 'incredible evening. Thank you to all of you who have come here tonight to celebrate our mother's life. For us this has been the most perfect way to remember her, and this is how she would want to be remembered.'

At the VIP party afterwards, Simon Cowell, from *The X Factor* and *Britain's Got Talent*, praised both Princes. 'You've put on one heck of a show,' he told them. 'In years to come, if you ever get tired of running the country, you can come and work for me producing TV shows.'

Perhaps to avoid unnecessary awkwardness with their father, the Princes banned all senior members of the Royal Family from the concert and the Royal box was filled with their cousins and friends, including Harry's on-off girlfriend, Chelsy Davy, and Kate Middleton and her brother James. After their very public split earlier in the year, her presence at the concert, albeit two rows behind William, was seen as proof that their relationship was back on course.

'There is no doubt that they love their father,' says a friend, 'but from everything I've seen he is a complex man and difficult to be the son of sometimes, and his reactions to things aren't always as elevated as we might want them to be. Anything to do with their mother is really tricky. Any event, like the memorial interview they gave, their sensitivity about being seen to say anything about their mother is very noticeable. "Talk about our mother? Oh God, we don't talk enough about our dad." They are very careful of Charles's sensitivities and dance around them a lot. Like at the service. He was very sensitive about where he sat and what it said.'

After their exclusion from Wembley, the senior members of the Royal Family were invited to the memorial service at the Guards' Chapel in St James's, and despite it being in the middle of their holiday at Balmoral, they all came. This was more intimate, designed, as much as anything, to bring together the two sides of the family, which had been so divided by Diana's death. And the seating was an important part of that.

'It became hugely complicated and William got very fed up even just thinking about it and finally said to his office, "Right, that's it. I'm off. You sort it out." They were left trying to deal with Charles via Michael Peat, which was not easy, and at the end of the day it was Harry who sorted it out. He just said, "F*** that," picked up the phone and said, "I want to speak to my father, put him through." And he just said, "Right, Dad, you're sitting here, someone else is sitting there, and the reason we've done it is blah and blah. All right? Are you happy?" "Oh yes," said Charles, "I suppose so." Problem solved.

'William gets quite buttoned up inside and angry about things and often it's his brother who makes it happen. He's the sort of "Can do, f*** that, let's just sort it out" kind of guy. William's quite complicated and Harry's not at all complicated. He's one of the most straightforward people I've ever met. Everyone adores him.'

William sat on one side of the altar next to the Queen and with his father and senior members of the Royal Family, and Harry sat on the other side of the altar with the Spencers—Diana's brother Charles, sisters Sarah and Jane and all their spouses and children.

One person conspicuously absent from the front pews was Camilla. The Princes had invited her and she had accepted, but just days before the event Rosa Monckton, one of Diana's closest friends, and the mother of one of her godchildren, wrote an inflammatory article in the press in which she said Camilla should stay away. 'I know such occasions should be an occasion for forgiveness, but I can't help feeling Camilla's attendance is deeply inappropriate,' she wrote. Diana would be 'astonished' at the presence of the 'third person' in the marriage. It had the desired effect and Camilla stayed away. She had intended to go to support Princes William and Harry, she said in a statement, but decided that her attendance 'could divert attention from the purpose of the occasion which is to focus on the life and service of Diana.'

There were screens and loudspeakers relaying the service to the crowds that lined Birdcage Walk outside, but inside it was for family, Diana's godchildren, bridesmaids and pages from her wedding, friends, a few celebrities, representatives from her charities and people who had known her or been involved with her in some personal way. The brothers chose the Guards' Chapel because it was more intimate than most other churches in London—it holds no more than 450 people—and being Guards' officers they were entitled to use it. The music was central to the day—as it had been central to her life—and it was sublime. They had the Chapel's own choir as well as the choirs from Eton and the Chapel Royal all singing together and the orchestra from the Royal Academy of Music, of which Diana had been President. They played Elgar, Mozart, Bach and Handel among others, and the first anthem was from 'The Vespers' by Rachmaninov, which Diana used to play to the boys on car journeys.

And the choirs sang all Diana's favourite hymns including 'I Vow To Thee My Country', which she had chosen for her wedding. William and Kate also chose it for theirs.

William read from St Paul's Letter to the Ephesians; Diana's sister, Sarah, read J. G. Hoyland's poem 'The Bridge Is Love'; and Harry, unable to find anything already written that said what he wanted to say, wrote his own words.

'William and I can separate life into two parts,' he said. 'There were those years when we were blessed with the physical presence beside us of both our mother and father.

'And then there are the ten years since our mother's death. When she was alive we completely took for granted her unrivalled love of life, laughter, fun and folly. She was our guardian, friend and protector. She never once allowed her unfaltering love for us to go unspoken or undemonstrated.

'She will always be remembered for her amazing public work. But behind the media glare, to us, just two loving children, she was quite simply the best mother in the world. We would say that, wouldn't we? But we miss her.

'She kissed us last thing at night. Her beaming smile greeted us from school. She laughed hysterically and uncontrollably when sharing something silly she might have said or done that day. She encouraged us when we were nervous or unsure.

'She—like our father—was determined to provide us with a stable and secure childhood.

'To lose a parent so suddenly at such a young age—as others have experienced—is indescribably shocking and sad. It was an event which changed our lives forever, as it must have done for everyone who lost someone that night. [A reference to Camilla Fayed who was sitting in the congregation, whose brother Dodi died in the car with Diana.]

'But what is far more important to us now, and into the future, is that we remember our mother as she would have wished to be remembered, as she was—fun-loving, generous, down-to-earth, entirely genuine.

'We both think of her every day. We speak about her and laugh together at all the memories. Put simply, she made us, and so many other people, happy. May this be the way that she is remembered.'

It was left to their father's friend, Richard Chartres, Bishop of London, to give the eulogy in which he articulated the message that they hoped both events—the concert and the memorial service—would finally achieve closure. 'It's easy,' he said, 'to lose the real person in the image, to insist that all is darkness or all is light. Still, ten years after her tragic death, there are regular reports of "fury" at this or that incident, and the Princess's memory is used for scoring points. Let it end here. Let this service mark the point at which we let her rest in peace and dwell on her memory with thanksgiving and compassion.'

# FOOTBALL ASSOCIATION

The concert for Diana was not the first time William had been centre stage at the new Wembley Stadium. As President of the FA he had opened it two months earlier, on the day of the 2007 FA Cup Final, when Chelsea beat Manchester United 1–0. Simon Johnson, then director of corporate affairs, was the point of liaison between Clarence House and the FA and had put in a bid for William to attend the match, present the trophy and declare the stadium open. He agreed but Simon sensed some reticence, which turned out to be nerves; William had scarcely spoken in public before.

They had met the year before when William came to a board meeting as the new President, and Simon subsequently helped smooth the way for the Princes to use the stadium as the venue for the concert for Diana, getting them the best possible terms, which William was clearly aware of when they next met at the Cup Final in May. That in itself had taken months of planning and preparation and included the official opening, a fly-past by the Red Arrows display team, and a parade on the pitch of former winners at the old Wembley Stadium.

Dozens of VIPs there that day were keen to meet Prince William—and there were many he was just as keen to meet, including some of the giants of football. Simon had arranged for these meetings to take place in private, in a small room off the Royal suite, known as the Royal anteroom, and it was agreed with security that he would escort them in one by one. William had just met Sir Geoff Hurst, Sir Henry Cooper and a collection of football dignitaries, when there was a knock on the door and one of the security guards said, 'Bob Geldof's here.' He was on the list of people that William said he wanted to meet, so Simon said he should show him in. 'Well, he's got one of his friends with him,' came the reply, 'and he wants to come as well.' 'Who's that?' asked Simon. 'It's Sir Mick Jagger [of the Rolling Stones].' Thinking he should check whether the Prince was happy, he put his head round the door and said, 'Excuse me, Sir, but Mick Jagger would also like to come and meet you.' 'Bring him in, bring him in!' said William, excitedly. 'What are you doing in July?' he asked during the conversation. 'Do you want to come and play at the concert?' 'I'd love to, mate,' said Jagger, 'but we're in Brazil.'

William was very nervous about his speech. All

he had to do was say, 'As President of the Football Association, it is my honour to declare Wembley Stadium open,' but he had to do it in front of nearly 90,000 people who were football fans and not famed for being quiet and listening to prepared speeches. While they were waiting in the tunnel before going out onto the pitch, he was agitating about whether his speech was on the lectern and whether the lectern would be set at the right height. The trophy was to go out first and be placed on a plinth, then William would go out and make his speech, then the teams would go out and William would be introduced to them. The trophy is usually carried by someone from the military, and on this occasion it was Lance Corporal Johnson Beharry, the Grenada-born soldier who received serious head injuries in Iraq and in 2005 was awarded the Victoria Cross, the highest military decoration for bravery. 'As Johnson came into the tunnel area where we were waiting,' recalls Simon, 'he went to salute Prince William, and William told him not to; it should be the other way round—he, as a serving military man, has to salute a VC holder. In his view, the military hierarchy trumped any other hierarchy, but Beharry's instinct was to salute his future monarch.

'William loves football and can talk knowledge-ably about it. He knows who everybody is and enjoys meeting players, former players and managers. He always likes to meet the England manager, always has a good conversation and across his time as President he's spent a lot of time with the England players.'

He first met the squad at the 2006 FIFA World Cup in Germany in his new capacity as President, when David Beckham was captain. 'He's a proper fan,' says one of his Household, 'he likes the big games, England's his big thing and I think he was excited, like any football fan, to meet some of the players. Funnily enough, when he met them, they were more excited to meet *him*. They were like a bunch of kids. They're so used to being the stars of the show; when someone came along with more star power they were tongue-tied.

'There was a lovely moment when he went to the training camp for the 2006 World Cup to see them train and several of the England players were queuing up for an autograph but were too nervous to ask him. These are players who normally dispense autographs to very nervous fans and there they were wondering whether they could ask him to sign a shirt. Having come from that world, to see footballers behave like fans was quite funny, but he's very good with that, very relaxed and good at putting them at their ease and trying not to make them feel nervous. The whole football thing works. He also takes it very seriously, he believes the FA is an important institution for football and the nation because it's the national sport and he follows its ups and downs and plays quite an active role as President, probably more so than previous ones, mostly behind the scenes.'

Simon Johnson endorses that. 'From 2007 we saw a lot of him. He came to see the England v. Croatia match at Wembley when we failed to quality for the 2008 European Championships, but he also came and did a grass roots training event in Newcastle with Sir Trevor Brooking's five- to eleven-year-olds, just after England had lost to Russia. Jamie was very good at arranging for him to send good luck or congratulations messages to the team and I think they really appreciated that he was taking an interest. He recognises his role is to sit there in the centre seat in the Royal box and present the trophy and the medals, but he wants to be seen to be making a difference to the grass roots game. He enjoys that stuff and it's really important to him. He doesn't just want to do the glory stuff, as Jamie calls it, he wants to use his presidency to make a real difference.'

In January 2009, Simon was appointed Chief Operating Officer of England 2018 Limited, the company putting together England's bid to host the World Cup, at which point he should have relinquished his role as liaison with the Palace, but they had built up a good rapport and Jamie asked him to continue. Thus in May 2009, just days before the UEFA Champions League Final in Rome between Manchester United and Barcelona, it was Simon who put through a desperate call to Clarence House. England's bid company had got word that the King of Spain would be at the match, and since Spain was one of the other bidders for the 2018 World Cup, it was important not to let them steal a march on England. 'We got an anguished phone call on the Thursday before the Final, that was on the following Wednesday, from UEFA, the organisers,' says Simon. 'They said, "What are you doing, you English? The Prime Minister of Italy's coming, the King of Spain is coming and you're not sending anyone, not even a government minister." My job as COO of the World Cup bid was to manage this sort of thing and I was told get someone from the government or try to get someone from the Royal Family. Those people don't just appear and I said to everyone, "I'm not a bloody magician but I'll do what I can."

'I phoned Jamie for some advice, "Here's the scenario, I'm in a bit of a bind. How do I go about approaching somebody from within the Royal Family? I know Prince William can't do it." At the end Jamie said, "You said William can't come. Does that mean you don't want Prince William?" "No, Jamie, I'm assuming that he isn't available." "Where are you going to be for the next hour?" "In traffic driving down to Dorset." "I'll call you back." He called back and said, "If I was to tell you Prince William was available would you like him to go?" "I would swim the Channel if he were able to go." "Well, it so happens he would quite like to go to the game and he's free and if it would be useful for him to be there, we'll see what we can do." "It would definitely be useful." "Okay," said Jamie, "but we need some help getting him there and you're going to have to come with us because he doesn't know anyone, doesn't know the protocol and he's beginning to rely on you to take him through that." So we organised every-thing, the Embassy in Rome was detailed with preparing the protocol and he was going to fly in, watch the game, and fly back again because he had to be on duty the next morning in Anglesey.

'Jamie warned me I should expect some questioning from him as to why this wasn't in his diary in the first place and why he wasn't notified of the possibility of it. So I said, "Do I just have to take this on the chin, Jamie?" and he said, "I'm afraid you're going to have to." So I was really nervous about this and, of course, William was politeness personified and we had a good chat and then he said, "I was very surprised that I was asked at such short notice." So I said, "Sir, I take full responsibility for that. Early on I think we knew that this wasn't a period that was available in your diary and we factored it out of our plans." And he said, "Well, that's not good planning and I

482

hope that in future you will at least give us early warning of potential events so that we can be aware of them and if circumstances change, we know how we can react to those changes." And I thought, that's the best way I've been bollocked in my life, and it was very, very effective because he was absolutely right; even though I knew that he wasn't going to be there I ought to have notified the Household that there was a possibility of a set of circumstances arising. He said to me, "You've got to plan everything in advance, you've got to forward plan." Then he said, "But don't worry, I'm coming", and it was fine.

'At that moment, I thought, that is leadership, real leadership because, firstly, he's turned up and done something, he's weighed up whether he should or not but he's let it be known that if we're going to manage a relationship in the future, where he's our President and we might need him, then we need to work in a particular way. During that conversation—all the way to Rome and to the stadium and back—we also had a long, long discussion about discipline in football. What could he do, as President, to help to put across a message that players are role models; that what they do on the pitch is seen on TV and has an impact upon young people who copy and emulate their heroes? "What can we do, what can I do as President to bring people together to try and make things happen?"

'We had a long and interesting brainstorm about how he could have an effective role. He said, "I can't chair meetings, it's not my business, but if I can get involved in something in the right way at the right point and start something off then perhaps it can have an impact; use my presidency to make a difference." It was clear to me he saw that he could be the catalyst for change and this was an area he cared very deeply about.' He never got the initiative they envisaged off the ground but the FA was running a programme at grass-roots level called Respect and Fair Play—respect the game, respect the referee, etc.—and he became involved in that and presented the first awards at the 2010 FA Cup Final at Wembley.

'Unfashionable as the word may sound,' William said, 'sportsmanship underpins everything good and worthwhile about our national game. What is so important about these Respect and Fair Play Awards is that they acknowledge and reward those who play fair and encourage fair play—true sportsmen and women. Everything about why I wanted to become President of the Football Association is encapsulated by what the winners this afternoon represent. Whilst I remain President of the FA, promoting sportsmanship, and stamping out the deplorable scenes that have blighted our game in the past, will be my goal.'

# GETTING IT RIGHT

Notwithstanding his determination to get William out to Afghanistan, Jamie Lowther-Pinkerton had thought that William's last attachment would be the finale to his military service and was working on a post-military five-year plan. But William took everyone by surprise when he came into the office one day and announced that he was not yet ready to leave the Forces.

His eighteen months in the Household Cavalry had felt like a proper job, which indeed it was—if frustrating for not being operational—but for the nine months since then he had been on the road, doing different kinds of work each week. Fascinating though it was and at times challenging, it left him feeling as though he was viewing life through a kaleidoscope. He was longing to get stuck into something and to do a proper job again—and what he wanted to do above all else, he said, was search and rescue.

'Absolutely brilliant,' says one of the team, knocked out that William had come up with such a perfect solution to the problem they had all been wrestling with. He was being prevented from doing what he really wanted to do, which was to serve on the front line, because he would be endangering not just himself but those around him. With search and rescue, flying in all weathers and visibilities, day and night, manoeuvring in treacherous conditions and into difficult locations, he would be endangering himself but he would be getting other people *out* of danger. 'We were agonising about how he could fulfil this bit in here,' says that same spokesman, thumping his chest, 'with his deployment and military career, without going down the route of Afghanistan, which at that time was pretty difficult, and he came up with this. It's the complete flip side of the coin because it's operational and highly dangerous; before [the wars in] Afghanistan and Iraq, search and rescue were among the most decorated people in the forces, and they continue to be. As the pilot, everybody relies on you for their safety. It's absolutely perfect and he hit on the idea himself. I just sat down and I thought, Bloody hell, on the button. Really good.'

The Chief of Air Staff, Sir Glenn Torpy, was delighted when he heard that Prince William was wondering whether there might be a chance of him transferring into the Royal Air Force to train as a search and rescue pilot. His immediate response was, 'Yup, no problem, it will happen and it will happen properly.'

During that year when he'd jumped from one service to another, it had been agreed by the MoD and the Queen that William would be commissioned in each one, which makes him the only person who has a non-ceremonial commission in the Royal Navy, the Royal Air Force and the Army. To his delight, it also makes him the only person who can mix his dress, which he frequently threatens to do.

His training began back at RAF Cranwell and Barkston Heath, on light fixed-wing aircraft. From there he moved to the prestigious Defence Helicopter Flying School at RAF Shawbury— Britain's own Top Gun—on the Welsh borders. This is where all the services' helicopter pilots do their basic training. 'It is really the top two or three per cent of the UK that we are looking at employing,' says the school's Commandant. 'Five per cent of the intake don't make it to graduation.'

Prince Harry also happened to be at Shawbury, having volunteered for the Army Air Corps to be an Army pilot. He was desperate to get back to the front line and knew that his best chance would be in a helicopter, and made no secret that his dream was to fly £37-million Apache attack helicopters. They are designed to hunt and destroy tanks and to operate in all weathers, day and night. Their pilots have to be the best of the best, but Harry admitted he struggled with the academic side of the course and feared he didn't have the brain capacity to be allowed to fly Apaches. He thought a future flying the utilitarian Lynx (carrying troops and gathering intelligence) was more realistic.

For about six months the brothers overlapped

and shared a tiny cottage off the base—living together properly for the first time since childhood. 'The first time and the *last* time, I can assure you of that,' said Harry in a joint interview to the media, in June 2009, which was peppered with jokey banter. Both were studying hard and putting in a lot of flying hours but they clearly had good fun together, as was apparent when they answered questions from journalists. William claimed he did all the cooking and clearing up after his messy brother (who also snored a lot) and said, tongue-in-cheek, that living together had been 'an emotional experience. Harry does do the washing up,' William added, 'but then he leaves it in the sink and then it comes back in the morning and I have to wash it up.' 'Oh the lies, the lies,' said Harry. He said William definitely had more brains than he did but pointed out that William was losing his hair. 'That's pretty rich coming from a ginger.' William said he'd been helping his brother quite a bit. 'It's the RAF way,' he joked, 'you have to help the Army out.'

William was three months ahead of Harry at Shawbury and just having gone through the same module, he was very helpful to his younger brother when they were doing their prep in the evenings. There was a lot of prep. The first four to five weeks were spent on the ground taking exams, which had never been Harry's forte, as he was the first to admit. But between the flying and cooking and tutoring, William also tried to keep abreast of his charities. Charlie Mayhew, CEO of Tusk, was pleasantly surprised to receive a call from Jamie. 'He said William wondered whether I'd like to go up there for an evening to brief him on what Tusk's doing. We had a really good evening in his cottage; there was no one else around, just me and him. It was a sweet little cottage, you could hardly swing a cat in there. He was working so it wasn't a late night; he showed me some of the technical books he was studying and they looked horrific. But it was a good example of him wanting to spend quality time with one of his charities and understand the issues, and how we were dealing with the economic downturn; what we were doing, where we were going, what our strategy was. It was fantastic because one wonders, as he gets older and takes on a more public role, how much time will he be able to give to his charities, whether he wants to or not.'

A couple of years before, when William was based at Bovington Camp in Dorset, he had a similar briefing at Tusk's office in the small town of Gillingham nearby, where he met the team. They have since taken over what used to be a hairdresser's in the High Street, but at that time they were tucked away in a converted abattoir. He arrived with Jamie Lowther-Pinkerton late one afternoon and Charlie offered to give them both supper at his house afterwards, 'which sent my wife into a bit of a spin,' he says. 'Caroline said, "Oh my God, what am I going to cook?" and I said, "Don't worry, I'll find out from Jamie what the form is." He said, "He'd love something really normal; shepherd's pie would be great," so that's what he got.

'It was very relaxed. Our chairman and his wife came too so there were about eight or ten of us. It's not every day you have royalty to supper and our house is a bit of a tip most of the time, with four young children and a dog. We'd been trying to clean it for days beforehand and our eldest daughter, who's quite perceptive, said, "What's going on? You've been cleaning everything." It was spring so I said, "You've heard of spring cleaning." We'd had the carpets cleaned and the upholstery cleaned and the funny thing was the smell; carpets are bad but upholstery is even worse and I came back from work about two days before they were due and the whole house was smelling of chemicals. "Oh my God, this is awful," and I opened all the windows. My brother-in-law said, "Well they probably all think that other people's houses smell like that." I worked my butt off in the garden too. Yes, I probably did tell him—he's the sort of person you can have a good laugh with about things like that.'

'We had drinks outside in the garden, it was a lovely evening and my son got very confused as to which one was Prince William, because there was Jamie and the protection team. Jamie has children of the same age and was chatting to him, and my son got very excited thinking it was Prince William and said to him, "Can I show you my den?" And they trotted off down the garden. But William was good with the children too, and with the dog. At one point he was sitting in the dog basket.

'Just as we were about to sit down for dinner, Caroline said to the kids, "Off to bed, we don't want to see you again and just remember there are police outside, armed, so behave yourselves." She said to William, "I don't know if that's going to work. I bet those little faces are going to be poking their heads round the corner in no time." We sat down and there was a pitter-patter of feet coming down the stairs and at that very moment two protection officers came in through the front door to have their supper in the kitchen and met the children coming down the stairs. They were two quite heavy-looking chaps. The children saw them and shot back and we never saw them again for the rest of the night.'

After six months of domestic bliss, the brothers went their separate ways. Harry left Shawbury in October 2009 to complete his training with the Army Air Corps at Middle Wallop in Hampshire, graduating the following April. William stayed on at Shawbury until January 2010, when he graduated, according to the MoD, 'with flying colours'. His father once again presented him with his certificate and Kate was again in the audience to applaud his triumph. The final nine months of his training as a search and rescue pilot were followed almost immediately with a transfer to RAF Valley on the island of Anglesey. But while the military was his day job—and a very full-time job—it was not his only job. The next day he flew to New Zealand to represent the Queen at the opening of the new Supreme Court in Wellington and deliver his first major speech as a senior member of the Royal Family.

# A HOUSEHOLD
# OF THEIR OWN

The day Prince Harry arrived back from Afghanistan, in March 2008, the media were waiting at RAF Brize Norton in Oxfordshire for the promised interview. The man tasked with overseeing it was Miguel Head, Chief Press Officer at the MoD. As such, he had liaised with Clarence House to organise the media blackout before Harry's deployment.

It was a Saturday morning and, to his surprise, Prince Charles and Prince William appeared at the airfield to welcome Harry home. It was very sweet.

Harry spoke movingly about who the real heroes

were, dismissing suggestions that he was one of them. On his incoming flight there were two such heroes, both men comatose for the entire trip, one with an arm and a leg missing, the other having taken shrapnel in the neck. Miguel had never met Harry before so he didn't know his comfort levels, but twenty minutes into the interview, when Harry was asked what was next for him and he started to answer, William, who was sitting to one side during the press conference, turned to Miguel and ran his finger across his throat, to say it was time to end the interview.

Aware that he was supposed to be the one supervising the interview—and there was still a good ten minutes to run—but loath to ignore the heir to the throne, Miguel got to his feet and stood in front of the camera and said, 'Thank you, the interview's over.' Everyone was very surprised, not least William and Harry. They went off to Clarence House and sent a message later saying how impressed they'd been that they had asked a press officer to end an interview and he'd actually done it.

A few months later, Miguel received a call from Clarence House, which culminated in an interview with the Princes. They had decided they wanted their own spokesperson and had talked to their father, who had agreed. He doesn't think they remembered him from that day but Paddy and Patrick [Harrison, number two in the press office] did and they tapped him on the shoulder. Their principal focus was inevitably on Charles and Camilla and, because of William and Harry's historically rocky relationship with the media, they wanted someone whose focus would be on them alone.

As one of them says, 'Harry had gone through a period when he'd been spotted falling in and out of nightclubs a lot and one of the things that both of them got fed up with was that, compared to most other lads of his age, he was almost monk-like. What was happening again and again was, he would go out on a Friday night and admittedly he would have a big night and be up until six in the morning and, of course, he would be drunk—all those pictures speak for themselves—but those pictures taken that night would be repeated for about three weeks, often as different stories, so you were left with the impression, as a reader, that he was out every night. He wasn't at all and he got very fed up with it. They felt they needed someone to put the record straight on things like that and they wanted someone to help them take them through their career, help ensure that the coverage about them was balanced, nothing more than that. I remember them saying this in the interview. They said it didn't have to be positive, they just wanted it to be fair and balanced.'

Miguel joined the team as Assistant Press Secretary in September 2008; four years later, he says the only instruction he has ever had from them is, 'Please, please, always, always tell the truth.'

He was absolutely astounded that someone not much younger than him should say, 'What is the right thing to do here? Let's do it.' Not right as in what's the clever thing, what's going to get us a good headline; right in the moral sense. There have been a couple of occasions when William has taken the hit for something and won the admiration of everyone in his office. His instincts have always been absolutely spot on.

'The first example was when he borrowed the Chinook for that stag party. He could have defended that. There isn't a single pilot who hasn't landed in a wife or girlfriend's field, and it had been cleared at the very highest level. But he thinks it's terribly unfair when other people take the rap for him and will send me to do the very opposite of what everyone else in public life will do—because that's the straightforward and honest thing to do. He is an incredibly moral guy, I barely know one who's more moral than him. His motto to us is, "Do the right thing": don't ever take a short cut just to get to the right place.

'He knows he's playing a long game; he's in this job for the rest of his life and doesn't need to get short-term bonus points. He's got enough confidence in his own integrity and character that by doing the right thing he will earn the respect he wants. He takes after his grandmother in that respect, who has played her cards very close to her chest, and she's never put a foot wrong, never taken a short cut either. She's never done anything to court public opinion, nothing populist, always played things incredibly straight, and he sees her life and marriage as a model. He's taken a leaf out of her book.'

In January 2009, just a few months after Miguel had settled in, it was announced that the Queen had 'graciously agreed to the creation of a joint Household for Prince William and Prince Harry'. It was to be funded, as before, by the Prince of Wales and have offices in St James's Palace, but remain close to their father's Household in Clarence House (the two buildings are in the same complex), and although they had Miguel as their own dedicated Press Secretary, they still came under the umbrella of their father's press office and continued to share other back-room offices like personnel, IT and finance.

The Prince of Wales funds his sons one hundred per cent in their royal lives and takes a keen interest in how they spend his money. They have to seek his approval for all their initiatives—the two private secretaries are in constant touch, and according to a friend, 'their father gives them stick about every penny. There are constant arguments about money.' [A member of the

Household points out that it is the private secretaries who slug it out and says the arguments are never fractious.] He was in no rush to set them up on their own. It was his view that the process should evolve, slowly and naturally, and he allowed their office to grow up within his Household until it reached the stage where their team were doing most things autonomously. At that point the Queen—in whose gift the creation of a Royal Household is—agreed they should have their own.

With it came the announcement that, 'Sir David Manning, the former British Ambassador to the United States of America, has been appointed by the Queen to a part-time, advisory role with the Princes and the Household.'

Jamie Lowther-Pinkerton had a call from the Queen's Private Secretary, Sir Christopher Geidt, asking him over for a chat. The gist of it was that out of the blue the Queen had said she felt that William, moving into the next phase of his life, would benefit from the guidance of the sort of wise old man she'd had as a young Princess. Hers had been Lieutenant-General Sir Frederick Browning, known as 'Boy' Browning, who had given her advice on how to survive in the realm that she would one day inherit. For William, she had identified Sir David, then in his late fifties, whom the Queen had met on her last State visit to America in 2007. He was just back from

Washington and was invited to see the Queen—who personally gave him the job.

As he says, 'The idea was to have the old grey-haired guy who had a bit of experience of government and international relations as William moves on to the national and international stage.'

The small team were at first taken aback; things seemed to be going rather well. Was this some form of criticism, were they failing to give the Princes the right advice? They were assured this was not the case. They were also nervous, as the Princes were too, about the idea of a British Ambassador coming into their little Household of three. They were afraid things would change.

Now, as one of them says, 'We don't know how we survived before David came into our office. He knows everybody, he's politically very astute, he has been there and done everything and been through some of the most controversial political decisions of the twentieth century, Iraq and all the rest of it. His advice is incredibly wise and he knows how to advise, and the questions to ask. He's a phenomenal guy, very understated as well and very modest. He's there as a sounding board.

'Things were hotting up and the Princes were beginning to step onto the national stage and do foreign trips, and it hasn't changed things. It's just added a whole new skill to the support we can give them.'

Having been at the Foreign Office for thirty-six

years and knowing the ins and outs of international politics as well as the machinations of Whitehall, David was particularly valuable in Zurich in December 2010, when William was part of England's bid for the 2018 World Cup. He found himself in the company of presidents, including Bill Clinton, and the great and the good from around the world, most of whom David had met many times. He could give William the lowdown on personalities based on first-hand knowledge, he could tell him who he could be open with, who to be wary of, alert him to bones of contention between countries, and the subjects it would be diplomatic to mention and those to avoid.

He had also been a very reassuring presence in New Zealand at the beginning of 2010, where William, carrying out his first solo official foreign tour, was under an intense spotlight. It was followed by an unofficial visit to Australia, parts of which had been ravaged by bush fires the year before. The trip was only five days in all, but there are very strong Republican movements in the two countries and political tensions with the indigenous populations of both.

In Wellington, he was given an enthusiastic welcome outside the Supreme Court by Maoris delighted that the grandson of the 'Great White Heron' had come among them. The welcome included a fearsome *haka* dance, the gift of a

Maori cloak or *korowai* made of flax and kiwi feathers, and a *hongi* (a traditional pressing of noses) with four Maori dignitaries. With the cloak over his suit, he began his speech with a concern for the people of Haiti, struck by an earthquake just days before, who were 'in all our thoughts and prayers'. Of New Zealand, he said, 'The overwhelming impression I have is of a nation that believes passionately in itself, in the value of democracy, in each other and other peoples, and in the rule of law.' It was, he said, a 'young, entrepreneurial and forward-looking nation. After all,' he joked, 'you've even managed to catapult my family into the digital ether. The Queen started tweeting a few months ago and now, thanks to New Zealand, I am being Bebo-d and Facebooked for the first time—rapidly catching up with my grandmother.'

Afterwards, he spent a good half-hour chatting easily to the hundreds of supporters waiting outside to greet him. Some of them were chanting 'We love Prince William', but they were nearly drowned out by a noisy crowd of Republicans and even noisier civil servants protesting about their pay.

In the afternoon, he took a boat trip to the wildlife reserve on Kapiti Island where he cradled a little-spotted kiwi, abandoned by its mother. As he held the struggling bird, he joked with photographers, 'My date with a kiwi!' When one of them replied, 'You look like you are plucking it', the Prince shot back with the comment, 'That's how rumours start.'

His charm and humour worked its magic in Australia no less than it did in New Zealand. In Sydney, the Aborigines who live in a dismal slum area called the Block in Redfern came out in their thousands to welcome him. Like his mother before him, William hugged babies in hospital wards and spontaneously put his arms around elderly Aboriginal ladies. Putting this visit at the top of the tour was a shrewd piece of programming; the children loved him, and time and again women were heard to say, 'He has his mother's heart.'

He also showed he could use a weapon, when he had a go in a live ammunition firing exercise with the 3rd Battalion Royal Australian Regiment at their barracks outside Sydney. He was using an F-88 AuSteyr rifle, which he had never fired before, but he proved himself a formidable shot.

A last-minute addition to the schedule was a visit to a hostel for the homeless, arranged after Kevin Rudd (the Australian Prime Minister) discovered William's interest in working with disadvantaged young people. Four of them did a three-minute rap song and dance for William, which ended in a discussion about his taste in music. 'Mine is very varied. Bit of rock, bit of Linkin Park [a nu-metal band] and Kanye West [the rock artist].' 'That's my man,' whooped Austin Anyimba, aged sixteen, clearly impressed with the Royal taste in music. After loud laughter all round, the Prince added: 'I have said something right then. Quite rappy. I can't do beat box. I normally get the piss taken out of me for my choice of music.'

No day would be complete in Australia without a 'barbie', and William's was hosted by Kristina Keneally, the first woman Premier of New South Wales, who called him 'a friend of Australia'. In thanking her he said he had received 'the most warm welcome ever—not just from the weather.'

Arriving in Melbourne on his final day, he went straight to visit the area near the city where more than two thousand homes had been destroyed in terrifying bush fires in February 2009. Firestorms, fuelled by winds of up to 100 mph, tore through the state of Victoria killing 175 people. Three schools and more than a hundred businesses were destroyed and more than 11,000 farm animals were killed or injured. William listened gravely to the stories of survivors, looked at photographs taken on the day and heard about the reconstruction and recovery programme that was underway. The Premier of Victoria told him that the energy of the fire on 'Black Saturday' 'was the equivalent of forty atomic bombs'. Temperatures were as high as 45°C (133°F).

By the time William, Jamie, David, Miguel and

the PPOs were back on their scheduled flight home, the newspapers were singing his praises. The pro-Republican Melbourne *Age* newspaper ran the headline 'All-round Good Egg William Snares Many with his Charm Offensive', observing that the Prince 'may have done more to set back the Republican cause than anything since the 1999 referendum'—which the Republicans narrowly lost. The *Australian* newspaper declared he had 'won the hearts of Australians' with his relaxed, unpretentious and endearing manner. Paul Colgan, writing in the *Sydney Daily Telegraph*, said, 'William is a powerful weapon for the Royals in Australia. You'd be happy to have a beer with him. He has a sense of humour, applies himself to his work, loves sport and enjoys a night on the turps with his brother and his mates.'

As Sir David Manning says, 'There is emotional intelligence in both of the Princes. They react to people they're with and their ability to connect is very striking. The first time I saw this was in New Zealand when we went to open the Supreme Court. It was the first time William had represented the Queen and it was obvious he had a gift of getting on with and connecting to people. It's all about moving people because of who you are, not what you are. He has that quality.'

Those who accompany the Princes say they have the same surety of touch during the hospital visits they make, both privately and officially, and suggest it might be, in part, as a result of having lost their mother. When Harry was visiting Selly Oak, the critical military hospital in Birmingham where casualties from Afghanistan used to be sent (they now go to the Queen Elizabeth Hospital in the same NHS Trust), there were two soldiers who had been unconscious for five days, and their families were sitting around their beds. These boys were in a very bad way but it seemed probable that they would pull through. The staff had put diaries at the ends of their beds, in which the nurses, families and visitors were encouraged to write entries during their time in intensive care. These diaries were introduced in 2008 and have been shown to be helpful when the patient comes round. They are usually disorientated and think they're still on the battlefield under attack. According to the critical care manager, soldiers read the diaries over and over again and it helps to put their experience into perspective. Harry wrote, 'For God's sake, mate. Came to see you and what were you doing? You were kipping.' The families were delighted.

# THE DAY JOB

When Jamie Lowther-Pinkerton began working for the two Princes, he took William up to his home in Suffolk, determined to have a serious conversation about William's role as a member of the Royal Family and his understanding of what that meant in an existential sense. William, then twenty-two and about to go to Sandhurst, listened as he always does and made intelligent comments, but Jamie quickly realised that it was the wrong time and the wrong place for this discussion. What mattered before they worried about any of that was for William and Harry to get their hearts and minds in the right place—and Jamie's job was to let that happen.

They needed to be allowed to reach their full potential during their military careers so that they would go into their thirties and take up Royal duties full time, able to look anyone and everyone in the eye. That has been a strong mantra for him and the rest of the Household over the last few years. They believe it's an important part of their job to make sure that William and Harry hit their own personal goals. From that springs self-confidence and self-belief and means that twenty years down the line, they will be able to say, 'I've been there; I did it.' As one of them says, 'William does it flying out to the middle of the Atlantic in a force 9, rescuing people. Harry does it on the front line in Afghanistan, and they can then look at anyone at the end of it and say, "Yes fine, I'm on these tramlines now and I know what I've got to do and it's not necessarily everything that I want to do but I know my duty. But, I knew the day when I was a brave young thing . . ." It's incredibly important for that reason alone that they get it right in here [he says, passionately thumping his chest].' For William, it was becoming a search and rescue pilot.

The island of Anglesey is off the north-west coast of Wales, separated from the mainland by the Menai Strait, twenty miles from the Snowdonia National Park and one of the most beautiful parts of the United Kingdom. At the end of January 2010, soon after his triumphant tour of Australia and New Zealand, William began his advanced helicopter training there, at RAF Valley. It's the busiest station in the RAF, well integrated into the local community and, according to the Station Commander, Group Captain Adrian Hill, 'a watersports paradise' with clubs for most of William's favourite activities: water-skiing, windsurfing, surfing, sailing, canoeing, angling and sub-aqua. As well as being an operational base—home to C Flight of 22 Search and Rescue Squadron—it's also a major training centre for fast jet crew and search and rescue pilots and crew. During his year at Shawbury, he had easily qualified for this next step.

Training began on a Griffin, in which he learned 'general-handling flying, underslung-load carrying, night-vision goggle training, procedural instrument flying, formation flying, low-flying navigation and an introduction to tactical employment, including operations from confined areas, plus elements of mountain flying and maritime rescue winching'. With all that under his belt he moved to Royal Naval Air Station Culdrose in Cornwall, where the RAF do Sea King conversion training because the Sea Kings—the distinctive big yellow helicopters—are basically Navy helicopters but the RAF use them for search and rescue.

Having mastered the basics, William then went back to Valley to train with the operational search and rescue unit, refining techniques and taking part in genuine rescues, but only as an observer. In September, after nineteen months of training, having completed seventy hours of live flying and fifty hours of training in a simulator, practising rescue missions over the Irish Sea, the Atlantic and in the mountains of Snowdonia, he graduated as a fully qualified RAF search and rescue pilot. It was a very informal ceremony; he and his fellow trainees—four pilots and four rear crew—were handed their certificates and squadron badges. The course, he admitted, had been challenging 'but I have enjoyed it immensely,' he said. 'I absolutely love flying, so it will be an honour to serve operationally with the search and rescue force, helping to provide such a vital emergency service.' The RAF was keen to emphasise that he had no special treatment because of who he is. 'There can be no place for people who are not up to scratch,' said Wing Commander Peter Lloyd. 'You are exposed to your weaknesses and therefore have to adapt to them. The crews have to work with you as a team—there is nowhere to hide in the crew of a helicopter.'

The next week he began a three-year tour as a member of 22 Squadron based at Valley, which involves an automatic six-month attachment in the Falkland Islands. (When the attachment came up in February 2012, by an unfortunate quirk of timing, thirty years after the war, the Argentinians saw it as an act of aggression. The Foreign Office was bullish about it; William was there in a humanitarian role, in theory to rescue downed Typhoon fighter pilots, but in practice he was more likely to be rescuing sick Argentinian fishermen from trawlers than to be doing anything remotely confrontational.)

When his three years come to an end in 2013, he has indicated that, if circumstances allow, he might like to stay in search and rescue for a second tour of duty. His second choice of base had been RAF Lossiemouth in Moray in the north of

Scotland, and, although nothing has been decided, there's a possibility he might move there. Beyond 2016, there will be no military search and rescue service for him to be a part of. In November 2011, just a day after William was involved in the dramatic rescue of two sailors off the coast of Wales, the Government announced that the mountains and coastlines would be patrolled by civilian contractors instead.

At Valley he works on a shift system. He is part of a team of four, doing eight twenty-four-hour watches a month, and when on duty they live on the base next to their helicopters. During the daytime they can be in the air in fifteen minutes, at night-time it's forty-five minutes, and when the scramble bell goes they have no idea what lies ahead of them or where they are headed. It could be anywhere in the UK or beyond, it could be miles out into the Atlantic, it could be to rescue a stricken tanker or a capsized yacht, a walker who is lost or has fallen and broken a limb in the mountains, a heart-attack victim, a fire on an oil rig, or a community that has been cut off by floods and needs evacuating. As William has said, it's the 'fourth emergency service'.

'It doesn't sound very many shifts,' says one of the team, 'but it's very stressful because it's foul weather and you have to work out in double quick time how you're going to get there, how you're going to make your fuel last, how long you can stay over the target area, how many people you can carry, how many you have to rescue, what you strip out, etc. They tend to group them in three watches, so three lots of three, or two of three, and that will be twenty-four hours on, twenty-four hours off, so it lasts for a short week, then a gap for three or four days to have a rest, concentrate on your other work, do your helicopter training—training flights continue where you practise with the mountain rescue teams—and then you go back on watch for three days.'

When the Queen and Duke of Edinburgh came to visit RAF Valley in April 2011, William gave them a personal tour of a Sea King—and his grandmother nearly had her hat blown off in the 50 mph wind. The media followed and he spoke about the job: 'It's definitely advanced flying and it's rewarding, so put the two together and it's a fantastic job. It's rewarding because every day you come into work you don't quite know what's going to happen, it's quite exciting in that sense, it's unpredictable. But at the same time it's great that you get to go out and actually save someone's life, hopefully, or at least make a difference to somebody; when you know that they are in trouble, you do everything you can to get there.' The team, he said, was a 'big family in the sky' and he felt 'very privileged to be flying with some of the best pilots, I think, in the world. The guys do a fantastic job and they are very happy to do it.

It's a job but it's emotional, it's physical and it's very demanding.' At times it could get 'hairy—especially with someone like me at the controls,' he quipped. But more seriously, what was hairy, he said, was 'flying at night in 40-knot winds over Snowdonia with the cloud at 200 feet searching for someone with a broken leg.'

William has been involved in dozens of rescue missions during his time at Valley—search and rescue teams are called out five to six times a day. But perhaps the most dramatic and dangerous was in November 2011 when the *Swanland*, a cargo ship with a Russian crew of eight, started to break up and sink in the Irish Sea. It was about twenty miles off the coast, carrying 3,000 tons of limestone, when it was hit by a massive wave in a force 8 storm. The ship's back was broken by the wave and it was taking on water when the captain put out a Mayday call at 2 a.m. on a Sunday morning. The crew scrambled from base shortly afterwards, as did crews from elsewhere, including the Irish Republic and several lifeboats and an Irish naval vessel. Two other cargo ships also went to the rescue. The Valley team was the first to reach the scene, by which time all that was left of the ship was a scattering of debris and an inflatable life raft with two sailors clinging to it. Sadly six men lost their lives that night, but William played a vital role in saving the lives of two of the crew members. While their Sea King struggled in the strong winds to hover overhead, with 40-foot waves beneath them, William and his team plucked the two men from the icy water, winched them to safety and took them back to Valley.

It's not hard to see why William has been so happy living on Anglesey. 'He's loving it, wallowing in it,' says one of the Household. The job gives him immense satisfaction. And it is another small and protective community that allows him to live a normal life, as St Andrews did. He and Kate can go for long walks across the fields—and now they have a little black cocker spaniel to take with them (the offspring of the Middletons' dog). They can do all the normal things the rest of us take for granted. They can wander into shops, browse in galleries, drink in pubs, eat in restaurants, pick up groceries in the supermarket, go to see a film and, for the most part, no one turns a hair. It is six to seven hours from London and outstandingly beautiful. He has been renting a very modest cottage off the base, hidden away in the countryside, which is completely private. He lived there on his own initially, doing all his own shopping and cooking and, apart from a cleaner coming in to tidy up, was looking after himself. Friends came to stay and Kate was a frequent visitor and, since their marriage, it has been their principal home.

# KEEPING THE MEMORY ALIVE

It must have been about five years ago. William and his old friend Thomas van Straubenzee were chatting. His parents, Alex and Claire, were thinking about setting up a charity in the name of their late son Henry. William immediately asked whether he could be its patron. Harry, who happened to be within earshot, asked if he could be patron too since Henry was his friend. So it was that in January 2009, the Henry van Straubenzee Memorial Fund was launched with William and Harry as joint patrons—possibly the only charity that has ever had two Royal patrons.

Since Henry's death, his family had been wanting to find some way of ensuring that their much-loved middle son was not forgotten. The collection at the thanksgiving service at Harrow had raised an astonishing £6,000, which they decided should go to the school in Uganda, Bupadhengo Primary, where Henry was due to have worked with Asia Africa Venture (AV). Through AV, whose motto is 'Transforming Lives through Education', they got in touch with the boy who had taken Henry's place that year, Peter Gate, and he made sure that every penny of the money went directly to the headmaster to be spent on the school. It was enough to build a classroom block for sixty children. But that was not an end to it.

Money kept arriving. Friends kept ringing and saying to Henry's mother, 'Mrs Van, what are we raising money for?' The young wanted to do something in his memory—the first thing was a canoe race from Devizes to London, then there were polo matches, university balls and marathons, 600-mile bike rides and concerts. More and more money arrived for Henry.

At first Alex and Claire thought of putting it into a scholarship in Henry's name at Harrow, but felt that wasn't quite personal enough. They went out to Uganda, where a little money, in western terms, goes a very long way. Peter Gate, inspired by his gap-year experience, had set up the Ugandan Rural Schools Initiative, under the umbrella of AV, and in the end they decided to join forces. The Henry van Straubenzee Fund raises money for projects and schools identified by Peter's Initiative which goes directly to the schools. They are currently helping over 18,000 children in twenty-five schools in Uganda, and the difference they are making is abundantly clear.

The launch was at the Troubadour, a bohemian café and basement club in Earl's Court Road, where Jimi Hendrix, Joni Mitchell, Bob Dylan and Paul Simon all played in the 1960s. Reading his speech nervously from cards, William said he was 'delighted' to be involved and that it was one of the 'easiest decisions' he had ever made. 'Having lost someone so close in similar circumstances, Harry and I understand how important it is to keep their memory alive. There's no finer way than that Alex and Claire have chosen. This is the first charity of which we have both become patron and it couldn't have been a better one, as Henry was such a very close friend of ours and because we believe so strongly in the need to alleviate poverty and assist development in African countries.'

Harry, also reading falteringly from cards, said, 'As some of you know, Henry was one of my greatest friends and his death was truly shocking. Henry would be so proud of his family for what they are doing in his name. Everything that's going on in Uganda and the way they are carrying his memory on is remarkable.'

Their confidence has developed in leaps and bounds since then, and at the charity's annual Christmas carol service in London last December, which is always a sell-out, Harry delivered a touching and very funny tribute to Henry. And having Pippa Middleton, Kate's younger sister, hand round the mince pies and collection box afterwards did no harm at all to the funds.

Harry finished his helicopter training and was awarded his wings at the Army Air Corps Base in Middle Wallop in May 2010, and despite his earlier worries about insufficient brain power, was accepted to fly Apaches. The man in charge of training him was deeply sceptical at the outset and, according to someone who knows him, 'quite cross that he had been landed with Harry on his watch. He thought there was no way he was going to fly an Apache. He loves Harry now. He's deeply impressed by him. There's no side to Harry; he doesn't expect any special treatment and the guys all love him. He really struggled with the academic stuff but put his head down and forced his way through it and now he's one of the best Apache pilots of the lot.'

As someone who knows the Princes very well says, 'Harry can't pass an exam in his life but my God he can fly a helicopter. He flies an Apache better than anybody else on his course. You don't get to be an Apache pilot unless you're in the top ten per cent and if you're heading the course, you're a really exceptional flyer. He's a romantic. He'll be the sort of soldier who'll start to read poetry when he's thirty-five, that sort of guy. He's a fantastic wit, he's hysterical.

'William's a steady bloke, unemotional and unflappable. That's why he's doing search and rescue; he doesn't get massively excited about stuff. His way of approaching life is considered. Harry's an adventurer, you just have to look at the helicopters they fly, they sum them up. William's flying a huge mountain of a helicopter that would go through storms and be battered left and right and just keep going. Whereas, Harry is, turn off the computer and fly the thing at 150 knots over the treetops. It's an Apache, that's what it's all about and it's completely instinctive.'

William became patron of another charity close to his heart in 2009. The Child Bereavement Charity (CBC) of which Julia Samuel, one of his mother's good friends, was founder patron and trustee. She used to live very near Ludgrove and has four children, two of whom are exactly the same age as William and Harry. Diana would often take both boys to stay with them on exeats from school, where they would muck in with the rest of the family, or they'd do fun things in London, all go to the movies together or to a concert at Wembley. When she launched the charity in 1994 (strictly speaking, as co-patron), Diana had taken a step back from public life but she came as a friend. She helped Julia with her speech, took her off to find a suit to wear, sent her flowers, and although she was never a patron, she remained interested and supportive. There was a year during which Julia heard nothing from Diana (cut off, like so many of her friends), which she never really understood, but the friendship resumed as suddenly as it had ceased.

CBC's work is twofold: providing support and education. They support families which have lost a child, and children who have been bereaved either by the death of a parent or a sibling. And they train professionals—doctors, teachers, midwives, health visitors, coroners, police—

anyone who comes into contact with families in which a child has died or been bereaved. As Julia explains (which is interesting in terms of William and Harry's experience), 'The belief is that the way in which you are supported following the death has a big impact on your ability to manage it and to prevent it derailing you and your whole family.' A lot of research has been done, she says, which shows that loss, or a death that has never been dealt with, is a big contributor to depression, psychosis and many other mental health problems.

After Diana's death, Julia, who is a psycho-therapist and bereavement counsellor herself, attempted to see William and Harry—as several of Diana's old friends did—but all invitations were politely and graciously rebuffed by Helen Asprey, and so she gave up.

Ten years later she had a phone call. They were planning their mother's memorial service and asked whether Julia would write a piece about Diana for the programme. After the service she wrote asking whether William would consider becoming patron of CBC and was told he was too busy with his military life, but when she wrote again a year later the answer was yes.

His patronage was announced at the launch of the charity's Mother's Day Campaign in March 2009, and for the first time since Diana's death, William spoke publicly about her.

'My mother, Diana, was present at your launch fifteen years ago and, today, I am incredibly proud to be able to continue her support of such an extraordinary charity by becoming your Royal Patron. What my mother recognised then—and what I understand now—is that losing a close family member is one of the hardest experiences that anyone can ever endure. Never being able to say the word "Mummy" again in your life sounds like a small thing. However, for many, including me, it is now really just a word—hollow and evoking only memories. I can therefore whole-heartedly relate to the Mother's Day Campaign as I too have felt—and still feel—the emptiness on such a day as Mother's Day.'

His decision to talk about his mother in such a personal way guaranteed fantastic media coverage, which achieved exactly what the charity is about: raising awareness so people know where to go for help, and with his involvement there have been many more hits on the website and many more families have come to seek support.

He can also raise money in a way that few people can. He has said he will do one event a year for CBC, which is no more nor less than he does for all his other charities, but that one event can make a huge amount of money. In November 2011 (on the eve of his engagement), he hosted a dinner at Windsor Castle for the charity's high hitters. William made a short speech in which he thanked his grandmother for allowing them to be at Windsor Castle—and for trusting him with the keys for a night. Once again, he clearly spoke from his own experience. 'Bereavement is rightly seen as a time of intense private grief. But this is often misinterpreted as meaning a time of solitude, a time to let the bereaved sort themselves out on their own. I know that this is very far from the reality of what's needed. The wonderful staff of the Child Bereavement Charity also understands this instinctively. A little non-intrusive help and understanding can make all the difference to people, young and old, going through what is one of the most traumatic times in life.'

That night they raised £280,000 in donations; one person gave £100,000. No previous dinner has ever come close.

# DOSSING DOWN

On the morning of 16 December 2009, the residents at Centrepoint's hostel in Soho's Greek Street came down to breakfast to find Prince William in the kitchen, apron on, cooking their breakfast alongside the chef. While they were comfortably and safely asleep in their beds upstairs, he had been sleeping under a cardboard box close to the Embankment in sub-zero temperatures.

The idea came to him in very different surroundings. During a dinner for Centrepoint he'd hosted for donors and celebrities at St James's Palace nine months earlier, one of them mentioned that he had taken part in a Sleep Out in Leadenhall Market. Fifty donors had spent the night in sleeping bags to raise money. It was a fun event, attracted publicity and was a good fundraiser. 'You wouldn't dare do that, would you?' said Seyi Obakin, Chief Executive of Centrepoint. 'Of course I would,' said William. 'Then I'm going to take you up on it,' said Seyi.

Later in the year William said, 'If I'm going to do Sleep Out, I don't want to do a fun Sleep Out event, I want to do it properly and get a feel for what a young person really experiences when they have to sleep rough.' 'It quickly became clear,' says Seyi, 'that our fundraising, comfortable-as-it-can-be sort of Sleep Out wouldn't work. So on the night of 15 December—I remember it very well because I decided to do it with him, having instigated this thing—four of us set off at about midnight: myself, Prince William, Jamie and one police protection officer. It was not what I had intended when I asked him to do it—and if the truth be told, if I'd thought he'd say yes in which case I'd have to do it as well, I wouldn't have suggested it! We did what anyone who had to sleep out would have to do—we looked around, found a little place where there might be a bit of shelter, in our case a set of wheelie bins, put down our cardboard, covered ourselves as best we could, and hunkered down for the night—pretending to sleep. I said it was a pity we didn't have a camera to take a photo of this, but Jamie had a mobile phone so we used that to take a grainy picture.

'We each had a sleeping bag but it was an unbelievably cold night out there; the temperature dropped to minus 4 degrees, but it felt colder; it was bone-chillingly cold. At about 3 a.m., a road-sweeper came by which got us all to pop our heads out of our sleeping bags and get our legs out of the way pretty quickly. We got up at about 5.45, and walked from Blackfriars to Greek Street, where we took turns to have a shower. It's about a 45-minute walk and none of the people we passed blinked. You wouldn't expect Prince William to be walking down the road at that time in the morning in a beany hat, tattered jeans, looking dishevelled like a rough sleeper. A lot of people have said to me, "I don't believe you, there must have been security next door." Actually, the anonymity was security itself. No one expected him to be there.

'The 16th was our exact 40th anniversary day and we'd said we'd like him to cut a cake. So he said, "If I'm going to cut a cake, why not make breakfast?" The young people just sat down as they would normally and there was Prince

William making and serving them their food. Of course they wouldn't leave then, so they had their breakfast and stayed and he finished cooking and went and sat along with them and chatted.' Among those he chatted to that morning was a nineteen-year-old called Tres B. He had fled the war in Congo and landed up at Centrepoint. William asked him what he was doing. Tres B said he was learning to play the guitar. After he'd expressed an interest in music, Centrepoint had bought him a guitar, thinking it might also help improve his English. 'William said, "Play something for me,"' recalls Seyi. '"Oh no, I can't." "Go on." So Tres B went and brought the guitar from his room and played and it was really good.

'William has a remarkable knack that is magic. He somehow remembers strands of conversation that he has with different young people, so that if he meets Tres B tomorrow, he'll ask him about his guitar. Can you imagine what that does for Tres B? I've never briefed him to remind him. And he did meet Tres B again and remembered.'

At the beginning of 2010, William became patron of 100 Women in Hedgefunds' Philanthropic Initiatives. For the next three years they committed to raising money for three of his charities: Centrepoint, Child Bereavement Charity and SkillForce—and their Gala dinner that first year raised nearly £500,000 for Centrepoint.

Amongst the speakers, who included William, was a young woman called Shozna. At the age of nineteen, she had had a severe stroke, and for various reasons became homeless and came to live at Centrepoint. Although she was not very confident, her mentor felt that, if she could do it, speaking at the Gala dinner could be the making of her. Seyi takes up the story. 'We said, "Don't worry about performing, you just have to say who you are, how you came to be at Centrepoint and what work your mentor has done for you. Finish." She said she would do it but as the day approached, Shozna said, "Oh God." I said, "If you are uncomfortable, please don't do it." "But I said I would." "Then how can we make it easier?" We agreed she would write what she wanted to say on cards that I would hold in front of her so she could read from the card. When it was Shozna's turn to speak, I started holding the cards, then after a short while she didn't need them.

'On his way out, Prince William said, "I can't go without having a word with Shozna." So he came along and said, "What a fantastic speech you gave. Well done. Can I give you a hug before I go?" "Oh yes!" And he did. She is very small and he bent down and gave her a hug and when they separated she was full of tears. "I got a hug from a Prince!" She is thriving. Her mentor was right. It was like it flicked a switch for her. I'm not saying it was the hug, but the whole experience culminating in his behaviour that night. It was entirely his initiative to seek her out. That's what he does; that's why he's so good for us.'

# HELPING HEROES

Almost without exception, every charity that secures a Royal patron enjoys huge benefit, but William and Harry have found a new way of spreading their stardust. The first to experience it was Help for Heroes, the phenomenally successful charity started by cartoonist and former Royal Green Jacket Bryn Parry and his wife Emma. With a son in the Army, they knew what it was like for families to have their loved ones on the front line and they had seen friends of his come home wounded with their lives changed forever. But it was a visit to a critical ward at Selly Oak hospital in Birmingham that inspired them to found a charity to help those soldiers. 'That was shocking and moving and the defining moment,' says Bryn. 'It changed everything.'

On 1 October 2007, Help for Heroes was born, and the injured that Bryn and Emma had seen lying in their beds at Selly Oak that day are now immortalised on the home page of the website: 'It's about the "blokes", our men and women of the Armed Forces. It's about Derek, a rugby player who has lost both his legs; it's about Carl, whose jaw is wired up so he has been drinking through a straw. It's about Richard, who was handed a mobile phone as he lay on the stretcher so he could say goodbye to his wife. It's about Ben, it's about Steven and Andy and Mark, it's about them all. They are just blokes but they are our blokes; they are our heroes. We want to help our heroes.'

General Sir Richard Dannatt, Chief of General Staff (now Lord Dannatt), suggested raising money for a swimming pool at Headley Court, the military rehabilitation centre near Leatherhead in Surrey. The charity's simple message, 'It's not about the rights and wrongs of war, we just want to support those who serve our country and are injured in doing so', caught the public imagination. The media gave it a massive boost, particularly the *Sun*, which launched a campaign on 29 October called HELP OUR HEROES, encouraging readers to wear the distinctive tricoloured wristband.

A few days earlier, Bryn had spoken to Jamie Lowther-Pinkerton on the phone and asked whether he could send some wristbands to Clarence House for the Princes; he had a friend who had served with Jamie, which no doubt eased the way. He sent a few over, and on 30 October William was pictured wearing one. Shortly afterwards, Harry was photographed wearing one too, and the bands became a familiar sight. A multitude of celebrities were soon seen wearing them and Help for Heroes took off. Within six months the *Sun* had helped raise over £4 million.

The Princes were happy to give their tacit patronage but when Bryn wrote asking whether, as serving officers, they would become patrons, he was told they preferred not to be patron of any service charity. It was by no means the end of the road, however. After many conversations with Jamie about where Bryn wanted to go with the charity, he was invited to Clarence House to the Princes' Charities Forum, where all the service charities sat around the table. 'We were completely new to charity when we started and I got a lot of very sensible advice from Jamie and Geoffrey Matthews, their project manager [former McKinsey consultant and one-time managing director of the National Gallery's commercial arm]. I've been able to use them as a sounding board. "This is what we're doing," I'd say. "Oh that's interesting, have you talked to so and so?"

'William and Harry wearing our wristband gave us fantastic credibility and their support is hugely appreciated,' says Bryn. 'We were honoured when they chose H4H to be one of the beneficiaries of the James Bond film *Quantum of Solace* premiere.'

Both Princes were wary about their invitation from the producers of the Bond film—neither of them wanting to be seen as celebrities. They only agreed to go if they could do it their way. They asked for the proceeds to be split between Help for Heroes and the Royal British Legion, and insisted that both sides of the red carpet in Leicester Square should be lined with veterans from Headley Court. It was a cold night but they spent an hour outside chatting to the wounded and their families on their way into the film—and avoided the glitzy, star-studded champagne party after the show.

The support for their wounded comrades didn't stop there. In May 2008, they were the inspiration behind a fundraising extravaganza raising almost £1 million, which was split between the Help for Heroes rehabilitation complex project and SSAFA (the Soldiers, Sailors, Airmen and Families Association). With the help of the team at Clarence House, particularly Geoffrey, who harnessed some big-hitting sponsors and bene-factors, they put together a magnificent military pageant called City Salute in Paternoster Square in the shadow of St Paul's Cathedral. As darkness fell, the glorious Wren building was lit up by a state-of-the-art light show and provided a dramatic backdrop to an extraordinary evening. Hosted by Jeremy Clarkson, it began with the roar of three Eurofighter Typhoon jets flying overhead, followed by a display of Chinook helicopters. 'It's a bit of a lumbering tank,' said Clarkson, unable to resist the joke. 'Not exactly hard to miss. You can't even land one on the Isle of Wight without the newspapers finding out.'

The evening was a massive celebration of all three services, attended by celebrities, soldiers—many of them wounded—and thousands of ordinary Londoners and visitors. One of the wounded was Ben McBean, one of the two comatose soldiers who had been on Harry's flight home from Afghanistan, whom he had described as the real 'heroes'. McBean had lost his right leg and left arm. Harry was particularly interested in his progress and visited him at Headley Court. Such was the twenty-one-year-old Marine's determination that a year later he miraculously conquered the London marathon with his prosthetic limbs, finishing in six hours and twenty minutes.

'Clarence House were very helpful because they commissioned an artist's impression of what the swimming pool would look like,' says Bryn. 'At City Salute people could see what was going to happen and no one was left in any doubt of the Princes' view about the need for a swimming pool'.

And on 4 June, 2010 William was there to open it.

William wore a suit that day, aware that in uniform he would outrank most of the patients, which might be awkward for them. Colonel Jerry Tuck, Commanding Officer at Headley Court, was very impressed by William's sensitivity in talking to the men. 'It was an action-packed programme and during it he spoke to maybe two hundred people. You get no sense from him that he's talking to people because he has to; there were times where I tried to move him along a bit and maybe bypass a couple of people, and he would not allow anyone to be bypassed. So we got further and further behind on the programme. When you're talking to him you feel you matter to him. The break in is, "How's it going?" or "What's happened since I last saw you?" [he and Harry visited in 2007 and again in 2008] and "Where are you going? What does the future hold for you?" A genuine desire to know what was going on without unnecessarily picking at the scab and making the patient contemplate the fact that in reality they are going to be leaving the service.'

As William said in his speech that day, he and his brother had not known what to expect when they first came to Headley Court. 'We expected to find a place of suffering with, perhaps, a pervading atmosphere of desolation. Nothing could be further from the truth. Here reigns courage, humour, compassion and, above all, hope for the future. "How can this be?" Well, part of it—it seems to me—is down to the extraordinary spirit and indomitable nature of the British soldier, sailor and airman. However, it is also about individual courage, the refusal to give up—even in those darkest moments that each and every one of you must have gone through. But if courage is the foundation stone of recovery, the unconditional love and support of friends and family, and the unstinting dedication and selfless care of the staff here, and at Selly Oak, are the tools by which this stone is levered into place. And that unconditional love is exemplified by that of Help for Heroes for this place, Headley Court. This great day—the opening of this state-of-the-art complex behind me—has been brought about by this unique charity and the millions who support it.

'Very occasionally—perhaps once or twice in a generation—something or someone pops up to change the entire landscape. Help for Heroes, under the magnificent and brilliantly quirky leadership of the mad cartoonist, Bryn, and his equally inspirational wife, Emma, is one such phenomenon. What it has achieved here at Headley Court is, in truth, but the tip of the iceberg. Help for Heroes has galvanised the entire British people. Always supportive of its men and women in uniform, this country has been elevated by Help for Heroes to a state of realisation and proactive support for our military that has made me personally, very, very proud to be British, and a member of our Armed Forces.'

By the time the swimming pool was up and running, the charity had built up such momentum and such staggering funds (£53 million, and that figure has been going up every day since) that Bryn and Emma realised they were in for the longer term. 'The overwhelming support of the wounded and the desire of the public to help made it clear we had to go on,' he says. 'The road to recovery is a very long and hard path, these are young men and women today but they will grow old. We at H4H want to ensure that when the current level of public support has passed, as it inevitably will, they are not forgotten; they deserve the best and we are doing our best to get it.'

Colonel Jerry Tuck has a good idea of how their lives will be. Showing me around the centre, he said, 'You don't get a flavour for Headley Court until you see the prosthetics department, because it is that which delivers the feel-good headlines. It's a strength and a weakness of this place. As a strength, we can demonstrate to the nation that we are doing the best we possibly can for our patients; the weakness is that that might be interpreted by the nation as Happy Ever After, and for our complex trauma survivors, we don't do Happy Ever After. We do maximum functional capacity that your injuries will allow you to do but if you are a triple amputee, at the end of every day before you go to bed, you take off your very expensive componentry and you see, surgically, what is left of three previously fully functional limbs. I don't believe that's happy ever after. I don't know what's going to happen in ten, twenty or twenty-five years, thirty years, forty years. What are the mental health implications down range? I'm not necessarily talking about post-traumatic stress disorder but I am talking about reactive depression. It's going to be very difficult if you are depressed because of the way your body looks, because your body's going to look like that until the day you die.'

## CREATING SYNERGY

Every six months, all the charities of which William and Harry are patrons, and a few of which they are not, gather at St James's Palace for the regular meeting of the Princes' Charities Forum. It is, according to everyone I have spoken to who attends it, a brilliant concept, which today has nearly thirty disparate organisations working in harmony. 'They have been very clever in creating this,' says Charlie Mayhew of Tusk Trust. 'I heard the other day it's so successful that some of the other Royal Households are rather jealous of what it has achieved.'

Its genesis, however, was more through luck than judgement. The Princes had taken on their first few charities and were about to enter the Forces. Jamie came up with the idea of getting them all together around a table so they could work out who wanted which Prince and when and which charities could be accommodated. 'It was a diary thing really,' says one of them, a means of demonstrating in a transparent way to each charity that one was not getting more of the Princes' time than another. In the early days when there were just a handful of charities, the meetings were more frequent, less formal and had no fancy name, but the magical effect of bringing these disparate charities together was apparent from the start, and nowadays, the Forum has almost taken on a life of its own.

'It's all about seeing where we can work together,' says Charlie. 'The first time we met, the only other charities were Centrepoint and Sentebale, and there didn't seem to be any synergy between us, but we quickly did see there were opportunities to share ideas and thoughts and one of the results of that was some Centrepoint young people came out to work on a Tusk project.'

'I don't think anyone envisaged at the beginning going beyond that initial remit,' says one of the Household. 'But what happened was that these charities got into a room and found that they could help each other out with all sorts of things that had nothing to do with the Princes.'

Today the Princes have well over twenty charities between them and most of them are as different in their remits as you could hope to find, and yet the Royal Marsden Hospital, expert fundraisers, have given advice to the English Schools Swimming Association on fundraising—nothing to do with Prince William, just a friendly exchange of information. Mountain Rescue (England and Wales) took some young people from Centrepoint on a fell walk to give them a taste of adventure. They've done it twice and the first time William wasn't there—and wasn't even invited. A couple of Centrepoint young people cycled over a thousand miles through Botswana and Namibia in aid of Tusk. It was the first leg of a 5,000-mile cycling expedition, called the Cycle of Life; and as Charlie remarked at the time, charities concerned with the homeless and conservation were, 'by normal standards, strange bedfellows'.

'The Princes' Forum extends our reach into areas that we would never have been in otherwise,' says Julia Samuel from the Child Bereavement Charity, which is now working with the Armed Forces, WellChild and Centrepoint, providing training and resources to each. 'The Forum means we don't compete because we all feel so pleased with ourselves to be sitting round the table. There's a real generosity of spirit; we are all very lucky and want to help each other and learn from each other.'

'Once the Princes realised what was happening, they encouraged it,' says one of the team. 'They realised it's a model that can work, although the other factor is it's a model that can only work up to a certain size.'

William and Harry's trip to southern Africa in June 2010, their first official overseas tour together, was the ethos of the Princes' Charities Forum writ large. They were there for six days, visited three countries, gave a huge boost to four of their charities, which, because of the Forum, they both knew and cared about, watched England play Algeria in the FIFA World Cup in Cape Town and lent support to the 2018 bid. They began in Botswana with Tusk, which was celebrating its twentieth anniversary year—which William had launched at a reception in London—but this was the first time in the five years he had been patron that he had been to Africa for them.

They began at an environmental education centre in the Mokolodi Nature Reserve, twenty minutes outside the capital Gaborone. It is one of Tusk's flagship projects in southern Africa, teaching 12,000 children a year, in short residential courses, about conservation and the wildlife that sustains the country through tourism. As Charlie points out, 'Many of them are growing up in a part of the country where there's no contact with that world, no connection with the environment and yet they are the future leaders of the country.'

Also there that day were four young people from

Centrepoint, who, but for the Princes' Forum, might never have set foot in Africa. They were working for six weeks on a Tusk project at a disused quarry near Francistown in the north. It was being turned into a nature reserve to mirror Mokolodi, and would not only protect wildlife but bring tourism to the local community. They were working twelve-hour days building a snake enclosure. Nineteen-year-old Iesha had never been out of the UK before and had no passport. It arrived the day they left, and 'took ten years off my life', says Pat Randall, one of two support workers with the group. They all shared a house, and he said it was like the TV show *Big Brother* at times, with terrible rows between the inmates. 'But the effect on the guys was incredible to see. They were really shy and anxious at the start, with arguments between everyone, and people wanting to come home because they missed their friends and didn't like the conditions they were living in; it was very hard work. By the end, none of them wanted to come home; they were all so proud of what they'd achieved and the friends they'd made in the local community and between themselves. It is really going to help them through their lives; they've all gone on to do good things. Two have gone to university, one is doing a course in dental nursing and the other is at college.'

Pat, who is the same age as William, was amazed by how quickly and easily the Prince broke down the barriers between them all. 'Within thirty seconds he had Iesha in stitches of laughter.' 'He was really cool,' she said. 'I asked him for his fleece, and he said, "As a souvenir or to keep you warm?" I said, "Both," and he said, "You can have a picture instead." And Harry was really cool too and really funny. He said, "Back off, Iesha." I thought they'd be stuck up but they were really friendly, and the best part was they remembered our names and used them. I kept jumping because I was scared of flies and William kept saying, "Don't worry, Iesha, they're only leaves falling." '

Once the press had left, the entire party, which included politicians, tucked into a buffet lunch in the open air beside a lake. After filling his plate with food, William chose to sit next to Iesha on the young people's table. 'There was never a lull. He was asking us about our lives and about the project and was joking and laughing and making everyone smile.'

After a private meeting with the President, Ian Khama, a pro-active conservationist, the Princes flew (separately, as they usually do for safety reasons) to Maun, where William went to the sports stadium for another bit of synergy in action, while Harry flew on to Lesotho ahead of him. It was a scheme called Coaching for Conservation, backed by Tusk, which cunningly combines football with lessons about wildlife for primary school children. Before leaving for Lesotho,

William looked at a potentially ground-breaking project that could solve the age-old problem of farmers having their livestock taken by predators. 'It's an initiative we're supporting', explains Charlie, 'to break down the make-up of scent—its DNA—so that it could be mimicked. It's called the Bio Boundary Project and the idea is to produce virtual fencing, so the predators think they're on someone else's territory and back off. Early results are very encouraging and it could have a fantastic impact. William was absolutely fascinated by this and spent a lot of time in the lab with the scientists trying to understand it. On the flight from Maun to Lesotho, he said, "Please keep me in touch with that one, I really want to know how it's going."'

In Botswana, William had been in charge. Lesotho was Harry's patch, and Sentebale his charity. This was the first time William had seen its work for himself, although he had raised money for it many times, including jointly taking part in a 1,000-mile motorbike adventure in the Eastern Cape of South Africa. It was an endurance test over the most inhospitable terrain in the country's poorest province—mountains, gorges, scrubland, dry river beds and coastline—and some rivers that were not so dry. 'It's not just a bimble across the countryside, that's for sure,' Harry said before they left. 'We're expecting to fall off many a time.' Of the river crossings,

William joked, 'We've got our armbands in our pack. We're ready to go.' One of the riders clearly failed to pack his and when he fell into the water up to his waist, Harry leaped in to rescue him, earning himself the 'spirit of the day' award. Between the eighty participants, they raised over £300,000 for Sentebale, Nelson Mandela's Children's Fund and UNICEF. Simon Smith, who organised the eight-day trip, and had kept their involvement in it secret for a year, said, 'They were both fantastic riders and didn't run from anything. They asked us to treat them as one of the group and that's what we did. They mucked in with chores and shared a beer and food round the BBQ. They were outstanding companions.'

Arriving in Lesotho, William could at last see what it had all been for, and, according to Charlie, who was there throughout the visits to both countries, there was a very definite shift between the brothers. 'It was extremely interesting to see how much regard Harry is held in within Lesotho, from government level to the little children, in the projects on the ground, in very remote mountain villages. They absolutely adore him there, there's no doubt about it. Harry's really good with little kids. And it was very interesting to see Harry take the lead because he was effectively then hosting us and showing William his work, and that was part of the idea: for William to show Harry his charity's work and

Harry show William his, and the two CEOs would tag along.'

Charlie was tagging along for more than just the ride. In the spirit of the Forum's ethos, he was invited along to see whether Tusk might be able to get involved in Lesotho. 'I hadn't been aware of the deforestation in the country,' he says, 'or the extreme poverty, so I had a really interesting couple of days there, looking at what Sentebale was doing and how we might potentially work with them. I'm sure that will evolve.

'Sometimes, through the Forum you get a sense that although Harry's not our patron, he is almost as interested in Tusk as William is and that he is happy to be an ambassador for Tusk if he gets the opportunity and it's appropriate. It's not an exclusive patronage. They both wore the logos. I rather nervously asked, "Do you think William would be prepared to wear branded clothing during the tour?" "Yes, no problem, he's there to promote the charity," was the reply. "Great, then can we have his size?" At which point Miguel said, "What about Harry? He's going to be there too." I hadn't presumed I could ask both. Harry was so enthusiastic about wearing it, he lived in our fleece, even in Lesotho. It was freezing cold because it was winter there, and at one point Kedge [Martin], who is Sentebale's CEO, said "Harry, no disrespect to Tusk, but we're on a Sentebale engagement now, would you mind taking the Tusk fleece off?" "Drat," said Harry. "Well you'd better get some Sentebale ones." '

At the end of the tour, Charlie did an online search for press cuttings that mentioned Tusk and found 391 articles in publications all over the world—and that didn't count the hundreds of photographs, two of which appeared everywhere: William and Harry laughing with an eight-foot rock python twined around their necks, and William attempting to blow a vuvuzela (the sound of the 2010 World Cup) for a child. In both photographs the Tusk logo was on their fleeces. 'It was a fantastic demonstration of the power of the Windsor brand,' says Charlie, 'a good example of how William and Harry can come together and make a big impact.'

# TWENTY EIGHTEEN

England's 0–0 draw against Algeria in Cape Town at the end of the Princes' week in Africa was, according to Simon Johnson, Chief Operating Officer of England's 2018 bid, 'One of the worst games of football any of us have ever seen. England played terribly and at the end of it were booed off—and we didn't know it at the time, but Wayne Rooney, on his way off, spoke into the lens of one of the TV cameras and insulted the people booing.' Simon was sitting with William and Harry throughout the match and, as usual, William wanted to go down to speak to the team afterwards. He had sent them a video before the game wishing them luck. 'The drill we'd arranged was I would phone the team's administrator to check if it was all right for William to come down,' said Simon. 'He said, "Oh, I don't know, it's a very bad dressing room down there." So I said to William, "Do you want to go?" "Only if it's okay with Fabio [Capello, England's manager]." "Well, I think they're having a bit of an inquest at the moment." "Well then, no, no, no, I don't want to go; I don't want to interfere, they've got another game to play." I'm not sure Harry was of the same view. He said, "Come on, we should go down." I thought people were being a little bit protective of the team and as President of the FA he was perfectly entitled to see them, so I phoned the administrator and said, "They're coming down, you've got five seconds to tell me if it's not okay."

'William and Harry went into the dressing room and spent about twenty minutes in there. The players had just come out of the shower. William and Harry already had a rapport with David Beckham and he introduced them to everybody. When they came out I asked William how he thought it had gone and he said, "They were fairly upset with how they played, but we tried to raise their spirits . . . I used some of my analogies from the military, they've got more to go, they're strong players; I did my best to gee them up." To which Prince Harry said, "Oh, they'll have really enjoyed being told how to play better by a posh soldier!"'

The final stop before flying home was Johannesburg, where, as President of the FA, William hosted a reception for FIFA to promote England's bid to host the 2018 World Cup. World Cup Bid had originally asked whether he would be President of the company and head up the entire bid process. William, according to one of his team, went straight to his grandmother for advice. He was well aware of what a highly sensitive subject it was, and that he would be involved in lobbying for the UK on the global stage, which would be new to him (as well as nerve-racking). He wanted to help and to represent the country but how could he do that and survive in such a political and back-biting environment? After much discussion he decided that he should not take any formal role in the process.

'They all felt it was important to keep him a step removed,' says Simon, 'and that was how we played everything. He came to the FA Cup Final in 2010 for us, where there were executive committee members, and he did the job as President of the FA, he came to the Algeria game, he hosted the reception with Harry, but as the campaign went on, I think the more he got to know, the more he became involved. He would ask for briefings beforehand, written and verbal, about who he was meeting, how the lie of the land was, how the politics were working, he was very interested in that.

'He didn't just want to turn up and say, "How do you do?" to so and so. He wanted to know the context of who we were meeting, why, what was important about that person, how we were sitting in the campaign, how was it going, would his meeting this person potentially make a difference? He wanted a proper evaluation of his role and I had to provide regular briefings of how we were doing. In the last six months of the campaign, we had two big flagship occasions. One was the visit by the FIFA inspectors who were coming to England to view our facilities and so on; the other was the final presentation in Zurich in December 2010.

'There was a discussion about whether William would participate in the inspection in August, and I spent a lot of time with Jamie going through the pros and cons. In the end it couldn't work from a diary perspective and I think we felt it was not using him to his best advantage; he was better used at the event we put on in South Africa. He agreed twice to record video messages for us to use in our materials and films.

'The debate about whether he should appear in the final presentation in Zurich was very, very interesting. We'd had it blocked off in his diary for two years and he said he was happy to come and do whatever lobbying we needed, meet whoever, but it was very clear, he couldn't ask anybody to vote for us. All he would do was meet, form a good relationship, create a warm feeling, tee it up for the others to go and do the real business. I think he felt as a member of the Royal Family it wouldn't have been appropriate and I agree with that. He was there to show that the country was united behind the bid. So he was always committed to do that. Everything was sorted: when he would arrive and leave, where he'd stay; everything was recced. The big question was, would he participate in the final presentation to the FIFA executive committee?

'We only had five places so we had to be very careful how we used them. We were always going to use David Beckham but there were lots of other people who could be used too. We were very clear we wanted William to be part of it. As well as selling the message of the bid, we felt what better way to show how wholeheartedly the country was behind it than to have the Prime Minister and the President of the FA, who just happened to be the future King?

'Earlier on, William had always said he didn't want to speak or be in the final presentation, but he had clearly weighed it up because he came back and said he would appear if we wanted him, but we would need to agree what he said and he would need to be speaking as President of the FA. That was quite a tough decision and for whatever reason he decided to do it. So he came in. We helped him to craft what he would say, Jamie and I, we rehearsed it with him, he inputted and moved things around and he gave his presentation. We choreographed how it would go and he was very, very good. He not only rehearsed privately, one on one, but he came to join the full rehearsal with the rest of the team, he really played his part. So there was the Prime Minister, David Cameron, Prince William, David Beckham and a young man called Eddie Afekafe, a twenty-six-year-old community worker from a troubled background who had used football to rebuild his life; also Andy Anson, the CEO of the bid.

'During the time he was in Zurich, he didn't go around giving inspirational speeches, but he came and he said to everybody, "How are you, and how are you doing, and how do you think it's going?" And just by taking that degree of interest and being involved with everybody, talking to David Beckham and the other presenters, he became team captain. He assumed that role naturally. He was the leader.'

The Household were all intensely proud of the Prince when they watched him in action in Zurich. 'He knew that would be a very difficult back-stabbing environment, one he'd never experienced before, but having staked his colours to the mast many years before, it was more than duty, it was about showing leadership on behalf of the country but not doing anything that you feel uncomfortable about. He never crossed the line. They had councils of war and the Prime Minister had his sleeves rolled up, and the Downing Street team was there, Boris Johnson [the Mayor of London] was there and the FA and all its legions; they were all in a big room where there was coffee and press officers running around. William came in and somebody pushed a chair out in the middle and he sat down and the whole room went quiet and somebody in the FA said something, and William thought about it in a really considered way and said, "This is the way I think we should do it." It was one of those straight, "What is the right thing to do?" moments. It was straightforward common sense and everyone metaphorically sighed and thought, "Yes, that is the way to do it." He wasn't being pushy; it was just great to see him apply what we know he's got coming out of every pore, come out in that environment.'

Simon takes up the story. 'On the first rehearsal, which was taped, he couldn't be there so I stood in as Prince William. I do very poor amateur impressions . . . We showed it to him so he could see the layout and I could see him looking at me as I did this rubbish impression of him. No

548

comment was made, but at the final rehearsal I did an impression of Sepp Blatter, the FIFA President, because he was going to introduce the whole thing and would introduce Prince William. When we got in the car afterwards, I said, "So, today I have been both Prince William and Sepp Blatter." And he said, "I'll tell you something. Your Sepp Blatter is a lot better than your Prince William!" '

Despite emotional and impassioned speeches from William, David Beckham and David Cameron, the hero of the hour was, arguably, Eddie Afekafe, who opened the pitch by saying, 'Football changed my life. I grew up in one of the roughest parts of Manchester. Most of the guys I grew up with were in gangs—some still are, some are in prison. What they didn't get, but I got, was an opportunity—and that was through football.' William, following him, picked up on his story. 'What Eddie represents is a credit to FIFA, because it's your game that transformed his life. As exceptional as Eddie is, in 2018 FIFA has the opportunity to create more opportunities for people like Eddie the whole world over. It is England's national game, a supremely powerful force for binding the country together. It's our passion. I love football, the English love football. That's why it would be such an honour to host the England 2018 World Cup.'

'He did his presentation extremely well,' says

Simon. 'Our entire presentation was very good. It didn't win in the end but it was good.

'The announcement was going to be made at some big conference centre. William travelled there with us and we'd agreed with him and the Household that if we had won Sepp Blatter was going to present the World Cup to somebody nominated by the delegation, and that should be the President, Prince William. He would then be invited to say a few words.

'As we went down, I came with him, [Bill] Clinton joined us, and the FIFA executive committee came out of their meeting to go into the announcement as well. Ahead was a bank of press. Our executive committee member, Geoff Thompson, came out, said to Andy Anson, my boss, "We haven't won, we got knocked out in the first round." Andy told me, I told Prince William. At this point, we've got Bill Clinton right by us, we're walking to a bank of media and I just slowed him down a moment and said, "We haven't won." He said, "How do you know?" I said, "I've just been told we got knocked out in the first round," and he composed himself and said, "Right, please make sure that the whole team retain their dignity." I replied, "Can I suggest that we get you out of the hall at the first convenient moment?" And then I said, "During the entire time that I've served you as President of the FA, I seem to have spent my time smuggling you out of buildings at the earliest possible opportunity. This will be the last time." And he laughed.

'We went in and he was very dignified. I was impressed because it was a shattering piece of news to have to assimilate in eight or ten seconds before walking past the press, who didn't know.

'At the end of it, I fought my way through to where he was sitting and he said, "I just want to go and commiserate with the Australian governor general." They were the bidder for 2022 and they'd lost as well, and then I said, "Let's go. Are you willing to give a media interview on the way out?" and he said, "Yes, that's fine."

'We'd arranged that if we'd won everyone would stay together but if we'd lost, FIFA had arranged an escape route, but there was a media pool [a small number of reporters and photographers given access, who pool their stories and photographs with their colleagues]. He gave a very dignified interview. Very disappointed for the team, worked very hard, the team did their best, I'm very proud of them, congratulations to Russia, etc. etc. And off he went. I saw him into the car. I shook his hand but knew my duties with him had come to an end because my contract was finishing with the FA. He shook hands and said, "Keep in touch. I'm really very disappointed for you, I feel very bad for you." I said, "Sir, I'm really sorry I got you involved in all of this. But I'd like to thank you." He said, "Please, I've enjoyed it, you guys have done brilliantly," and off he went.

'I understand he was very grumpy for the rest of the weekend about the result. He really wanted us to win; he'd been to every meeting we'd asked him to go to and I think a number of people had said to him they were going to vote for England and then didn't. I'm not sure any of us can understand what sort of a person would do that, particularly as he is such a commanding figure: he's pleasant, he's funny, he's a leader, he's tough, he knows his stuff and he's scrupulously honest. The role that he played with us, and a lot of what he did behind the scenes for us, was tremendous. He's been fantastic for football: he likes the game, likes football players, likes talking about it. He's been an inspiring person to spend time with.'

England's failure to get beyond the first vote was a crushing blow but in the previous few weeks, the whole voting system and the propriety of some FIFA members had been questioned by the British media. The *Sunday Times* ran an exposé of alleged bribery and corruption and the BBC's *Panorama* did likewise.

Asked by the media if he felt members had lied to the bid about their support, Andy Anson said, 'I do feel people let us down, I'd be lying if I said they didn't. People who promised us their vote obviously went the other way. I honestly felt that we had enough comfort, enough people, enough room to hope that things would go all right and we would go through the first round.'

Geoff Thompson said the same, 'I cannot believe what has happened . . . The votes that were promised clearly didn't materialise.'

Speaking at a dinner a few days later, David Cameron, who had spent three days pressing England's case in Zurich, said, 'According to FIFA we had the best technical bid and the strongest commercial bid and the country is passionate about football. But it turns out that is not enough.'

Cameron also revealed the lengths that Prince William had gone to, to convince FIFA members to vote for England. 'I met Prince William coming out of one of these meetings and said, "How did it go?" He said it had gone really, really well. I said, "Gosh, how did you do it, what did you offer him? An invitation to the wedding?" He said, "Prime Minister, I went so far I think I offered to marry him."'

# FOUNDATION FOR THE FUTURE

Nick Booth, who for ten years ran the NSPCC's high-profile Full Stop campaign against child abuse, was settling into a new life in America. He had gone there to be vice president of external affairs for Big Brothers Big Sisters, the world's largest mentoring organisation. As he says, he was applying for his green card and living in a Philadelphia suburb with his white picket fence and the yellow school bus picking up the kids every day, when he was approached by the Princes' office. Would he like to help them both set up a brand-new charitable foundation?

After three interviews, the last of which was with Prince William, he announced to the family that they were packing up and going home. There was a mixture of sadness at leaving friends in America and excitement at being back in the UK. They moved house, schools and job all at once, and he arrived at St James's Palace in October 2010. In the next twelve weeks he made eighteen transatlantic flights.

'The Foundation had been registered but this was building it from scratch and the chance to put something together from the beginning doesn't come along very often,' he says. 'And when that is the first Royal foundation of its type in living memory, and possibly ever in the way it's now operating, it's very exciting. Also the two Princes are remarkable in the sense of their commitment to do the right thing and to use their position to change things that they are passionate about, and the Foundation was a really interesting vehicle to do that with.'

The Princes and their team were doing some serious thinking about the future. Charity work is now one of the monarchy's main and most important functions. And as the historian Frank Prochaska wrote in *Royal Bounty: The Making of a Welfare Monarchy*, 'Barring cataclysm or self-destruction, the monarchy is only likely to be in real danger when the begging letters cease to arrive at Buckingham Palace.' As its constitutional importance declined, it forged a new role for itself as patron, promoter and fund-raiser for the underprivileged and deserving.

The tradition of a charitable monarchy goes back to George III at the end of the eighteenth century, but it was during the present Queen's reign that it became an integral part of her family's daily work. There are currently more than 160,000 registered charities and other charitable organisations in the UK, and about three thousand of them have a Royal patron or president. The Queen has over six hundred patronages; the Duke of Edinburgh, over seven hundred; the Prince of Wales, over six hundred; the Princess Royal nearly three hundred. The Duke of York and the Earl and Countess of Wessex have fewer but still significant numbers, as do the Queen's cousins, the Gloucesters and the Kents. William and Harry's generation of Royals have chosen to lead normal lives, and aside from Princesses Beatrice and Eugenie, the Duke of York's daughters, they have no Royal titles. As the older generation starts falling by the wayside, the number of Royal patrons left to go round will be drastically diminished. Essentially, there will only be William, Harry and their two wives, assuming Harry will also marry in the not too distant future. Even if they were to have four children each in double-quick time, there would still be a gap of twenty-five years or so while those children were growing up, with no more than four working members of the Family Firm in the interim. There are currently eighteen. The existing model of charitable patronage couldn't possibly work.

The whole issue of the future was raised, quite unintentionally, by a question from the Duke of Edinburgh's office three or four years ago. His ninetieth birthday was looming and there was an assumption—erroneous as it turned out—that he might want to slow down. Were any other members of the Family interested in taking on some of his patronages?

There were lengthy discussions about how the Royal landscape might look in twenty or thirty years' time, which led to two conclusions. One was that it wasn't necessary to become patron of a charity in order to help it—as their support for Help for Heroes had convincingly demonstrated. 'They wore the wristbands and it just kind of went whoosh. That wasn't down to them,' says one of the team, 'but they were a catalyst. So they recognise that backing a particular project can have massive strategic consequences.'

They wanted to find a means of bringing about change and making an impact on the issues they care about, but without getting locked into long-term commitments with particular charities and organisations—and thus spreading themselves too thinly between the many that want their patronage. Their ideal would be to remain at one remove and simply give a kick-start to specific projects. Once a project was up and running or had achieved its aims, they could wish it well and move on to other deserving causes. Harry did this very successfully with Walking for the Wounded, a charity that helps veterans reintegrate and retrain for civilian life. He became patron of one of their fundraising initiatives, the North Pole 2011 Expedition, and in April of that year he trained with the team in Norway and then for four days walked alongside four wounded soldiers, two of them amputees, on their record-breaking trek to the North Pole. The aim was to raise £2 million, and Harry's presence ensured that the cameras followed them; their feat was not only in the news but the subject of a two-part documentary.

Dipping in and out was William's preference anyway. He has always been more interested in the need or issue than in the charity per se. His support for injured servicemen and women is a good example. Both he and Harry care passionately about this, having had so many friends of their own come back from Iraq and Afghanistan with missing limbs and other injuries. They know that help is crucial, and although there are a whole range of charities endeavouring to help, rather than directly supporting one or two of them, and risk offending the others, they have nailed their colours to the issue itself and are backing whichever project launched by whichever charity they think is doing the most to meet this particular need. As one of the Household says, 'They've done it incredibly effectively without ever being patron of those organisations, and yet I don't think there's a single person out there who doesn't think the two of them have a real passion for the issue of wounded servicemen. But they haven't had to go down the traditional route to do that.'

The second conclusion they reached was that they needed some funds of their own to distribute from time to time. Initially it was a very human response—witnessing human tragedy and wanting to do something about it. The Queen and the Prince of Wales have their own funds which they occasionally dip into when they visit an earthquake zone or other catastrophe. However, because of the way their finances are set up, the two Princes have never been able to do this. They wanted to be able to put their hands in their pockets, as seed corn, *and* encourage others to give.

The Foundation was the solution to both conclusions. 'After all those years of royal patronage, for them to say, "Let's try something different, let's build a Foundation that finds really exciting projects, put some money, some leverage and awareness into them, but not necessarily stay with them for ever," is very interesting,' says Nick Booth.

Speaking of its creation, William said, 'We are incredibly excited about our new Foundation. We believe that it will provide a unique opportunity for us to use our privileged position to make a real difference in the future to many areas of charitable work. We feel passionately that, working closely together with those who contribute to our Foundation, we can help to make a long-lasting and tangible difference.'

'The Princes were the first people to put money into it,' Nick says, 'which is good philanthropy— "I'll give and I'd like others to support, and we're busy fundraising." ' The Foundation has no big endowment; it has to raise all the money it distributes, which in the first year was about £4 million. Within weeks of Nick arriving, three private donors paid all its administration and staff costs for the first three years. So every donation now goes straight into the projects being supported.

'Before I arrived they chose three areas of interest. We are not constrained by those, but currently those are: disadvantaged children and young people, veterans and military families, and sustainable development conservation. They may change over time but these are first baby steps. We are working out within those broad areas what our first priorities are going to be. Also what the DNA that runs across them is—and that's an interesting thought process because they feel quite disparate. I think they are linked by two things.

'One, because the Princes are passionate about them, and that's a perfectly valid reason to have three disparate areas. It's a personal foundation with two living principals, as opposed to an endowed historic institution.

'The second link is that in each of those areas you have a group of people who cannot fulfil their potential because of the circumstances they find themselves in. It may be because they are living in a disadvantaged community or haven't got the education or the parental support that they need. Or it may be because they've returned from Afghanistan and Iraq with their legs blown off, or because their husband has not come back and the family has a different life, no longer in the military community. Or because you have girls, children, young adults struggling to survive in challenging parts of the world without education, without water.

'So, in each of those areas, can we take a sensible approach with ourselves and with others? We are tiny but can we use our convening power and our leverage and our resources to either remove the blocks to those people fulfilling their potential or put in place accelerators that will help that process? What is it, in each of those areas, that will allow us to help those people really go on and be all they could be in their lives? For two young Princes, and now a young Duchess, that's a very compelling alignment of values and vision.'

Since their marriage, Kate—titled as the Duchess of Cambridge—is now an equal player in the Foundation, and the name may have to change, although as Nick says, 'The Foundation of Prince William and Prince Harry and the Duchess of Cambridge is not a snappy one.' The patronages that William and Harry already had, and the ones that Kate has taken on since her marriage, have not been affected by the Foundation. They could still take on new ones—and indeed William did in January 2012, when he became patron of the 50th Anniversary Year of St Giles Trust. It's a charity that works with prisoners and their families to break the cycle of reoffending. Prisoners, particularly young offenders, are some of the most excluded and disadvantaged people in society, and the majority are unable to realise their true potential.

The first project the Foundation put money into, in April 2011, was the Queen Elizabeth II Fields Challenge, which was the perfect fit and with a finite commitment. It was a Fields in Trust project to locate and protect for the future 2,012 green fields and open spaces as a lasting memorial to the Queen's Diamond Jubilee in 2012. The Foundation paid to protect the first ten. This was one of the charities that the Duke of Edinburgh first took on, in 1949, from his father-in-law, King George VI, and for which he has worked tirelessly ever since. It's had several name changes but its aim remains the same: to stop Britain's open spaces and playing fields being sold and concreted over by developers. Six thousand have been lost since 1992.

The idea appealed, not least as a personal tribute to his grandmother's sixty years on the throne, and William became patron of the Challenge in 2010, saying, 'Green spaces and playing fields are the beating heart of any community. Whether you live in a dense city or in the middle of the countryside, fields provide a safe place for team sports, for talent to be nurtured, for confidence to be built and for your children and teenagers to let off steam. For people of any age, fields provide spaces for sports days, fêtes and the kinds of events that hold communities together. Playing fields are not a luxury. They are a vital component of any healthy and happy community . . . As Fields in Trust is proud to say, please play on the grass!'

# A RING ON HER FINGER

There are plenty of St Andrews graduates who marry one another—more so, as I said earlier, than from any other British university—but there are no statistics for how many of them take eight years or more to get round to it.

The romance had grown slowly, out of friendship, laughter and trust—as was abundantly clear in the interview William and Kate gave ITN's Tom Bradby on the day of their engagement. They also have a multitude of common interests; and, as anyone who has seen them together will say, they are very much in love and a pleasure to watch together.

But the relationship had not been full-on throughout the eight years. Their break-up in 2007 was the most public evidence, but there were other times when things had cooled. William had very real worries about whether it was possible to love just one woman. His childhood experiences remain close to the surface, and he was, understandably, cautious about making a mistake or committing to a relationship he couldn't sustain for the rest of his life. His early years had been painful. He lost many people he was close to, starting with the sudden disappearance of his beloved nanny. He must have been afraid, albeit subconsciously, of allowing himself to become too attached to Kate, lest she turn out to be another woman who abandoned him.

Before the break-up in 2007, there might have been an element of taking Kate for granted. It is a cliché that you don't know what you've got until it's gone, but no less true for that. Thanks to their time at St Andrews, they knew each other inside out, in good times and in bad. He adored her family and they him; their house was an oasis of normality in his very abnormal world.

And if he *had* confided in Kate and shared his deepest, darkest thoughts and memories, and she had held them safely and helped to ease the buried grief that had never been fully expressed, and quieten some of the demons, he would have realised she was a very special human being and not to be cast lightly aside.

But if those few weeks apart were also some sort of test of loyalty and discretion, she passed with flying colours. She did not waver in her love for him; and she said nothing to anyone. (Celebrity publicist Max Clifford said she could have sold her story at that time for £5 million.) Throughout the years of their friendship and romance, and the ups and downs, she had been utterly discreet. She had proved herself trustworthy. She had been hounded and harassed and followed and photographed; she had put up with jokes about her middle-class origins, about 'doors to manual', she had been called 'Waity Katie' and criticised for not having a proper job. And never had she risen to the bait, confided in anyone outside her family, or put a foot wrong.

The Household was enraged by the 'Waity Katie' tag and is full of admiration for the way she coped. 'It was so sexist and offensive and ill-informed. We couldn't defend her—to do so would have been tantamount to an engagement announcement because we didn't represent her, but all the rubbish about her, all the criticism for sitting around doing nothing, when, in fact, she was working for the family business all along. Not giving her, or them, credit as two young modern adults for working it out themselves and deciding on their own timetable. Why on earth should they be pressurised into it by the media?'

They had been discussing marriage for at least a year before William proposed. 'We've talked about it lots,' he said in the interview. 'So it's always been something we've had a good chat about and . . . both of us have come to the decision pretty much together, I just chose when to do it and how to do it—and obviously being a real romantic I did it extremely well!' He also wanted to give Kate and her family time to have a good hard look at what life with him would mean, 'and to back out if she needed to before it all got too much.'

He finally proposed during a holiday in Kenya with friends, and had chosen Lake Rutundu in eastern Kenya, the remotest and most beautiful place imaginable, and despite their conversations in the past, he took Kate by surprise, not just with the proposal but with the ring.

'I had been carrying it around with me in my rucksack for about three weeks before that,' said William, 'and I literally would not let it go. Everywhere I went I was keeping hold of it because I knew this thing, if it disappeared, I would be in a lot of trouble, and because I'd planned it, it went fine. You hear a lot of horror stories about proposing and things going horribly wrong—it went really, really well and I was really pleased she said, "Yes."'

He had chosen his mother's ring because, 'I thought it was quite nice because obviously she's not going to be around to share any of the fun and excitement of it all—this was my way of keeping her sort of close to it all.'

Tom Bradby said how 'incredibly happy and relaxed' they both looked. 'We are. We are,' said William. 'We're like sort of ducks, very calm on the surface with little feet going under the water. But no, it's been really exciting because we've been talking about it for a long time, so for us, it's a real relief, and it's really nice to be able to tell everybody. Especially for the last two or three weeks it's been quite difficult not telling anyone, and keeping it to ourselves for reasons we had to. And it's really nice to finally be able to share it with everyone.'

The reason they delayed the announcement was that they came home from Africa to find Kate's much-loved and last remaining grandparent, Peter Middleton (aged ninety), was seriously ill. He had been a fighter pilot and instructor during the Second World War and had then gone on to fly civilian aircraft for British European Airways; by coincidence, he had been chosen as First Officer to fly with the Duke of Edinburgh on a two-month tour of South America in 1962. He sadly died and they waited until after his funeral to make the announcement.

The first person to hear the news was Kate's father, Mike. 'I was torn between asking Kate's dad first, and then the realisation that he might actually say "No" dawned upon me,' said William. 'So I thought if I ask Kate first then he can't really say no. So I did it that way round. And I managed to speak to Mike sort of soon after it happened.' He told his own father and grandmother a few days later, but the only element of surprise was that he'd finally got on and done it. Everyone in both families expressed the greatest delight. There did seem to be very genuine happiness all round.

There were no planning committees for an engagement, but the Household had been secretly preparing for some time—never certain when or if it would happen. A couple of people in the office had privately thought William might pop the question in Africa, but when there was nothing, they assumed it hadn't happened. So when William and Kate arrived that Tuesday morning, 16 November, and said, 'We've got engaged,' and started joking about their plans for a small family wedding, they were slightly caught on the back foot. Paddy Harverson was asleep in a hotel room in Washington DC when he got the call, at 4 a.m., from Patrick Harrison, his number two. Delighted, he jumped on the first plane and reached home to find the story all over the news. As one of them says, 'We had a brilliant plan but it's not such a great plan if your communications secretary is in the wrong country!'

The news first broke to the outside world on Twitter, the online social networking site. 'The Prince of Wales is delighted to announce the engagement of Prince William to Miss Catherine Middleton.' It was the first indication that Kate preferred to be called by her proper birth name, in preparation, perhaps, for the day when she becomes Queen. It is the name her parents have always called her and the name she was known by when she was at Marlborough. She first started using Kate at university, but it will be hard for the public and the headline writers to change—and to make it less confusing, I shall continue to use her abbreviated name.

By pure coincidence, Clarence House had just launched itself on Twitter, lagging behind the Queen who had been tweeting for some time, and who very swiftly tweeted back her congratulations. They put out a full-length press release on the website, which they also emailed to a long list of media recipients, but Twitter demands only 140 characters and is instantaneous, so it was first to break the news.

There had been conversations in the broadest terms about what William would ideally want in the event of an engagement. He indicated a preference for a single television interview, and the man he wanted to do it was Tom Bradby. Speaking on camera about their relationship would be a nerve-racking ordeal for them both, but less so with someone he knew, liked and trusted. Tom had become close personal friends with Jamie, who was able to quietly establish Tom's movements and availability, knowing that if some other news story was to take him abroad, they would have to go to Plan B, but it didn't come to that. What William wanted, at all costs, was to avoid the toe-curling embarrassment of an interview like the one his parents had given on their engagement, in which Prince Charles, when asked if he was 'in love' had famously replied, 'whatever love means'. He knew that the public had been waiting years to have a good look at Kate and would judge her on this first viewing. After the interview, when they were more relaxed, there would be a photo call.

The team knew the choice of Tom would not be

universally popular with the other networks and correspondents, and it was a slightly poisoned chalice for Tom himself. As a respected political editor he didn't want to be written off as 'a grim patsy asking really asinine questions', particularly with billions of people watching. He knew he had to touch on some difficult areas, while bearing in mind it was their engagement day and he shouldn't be rude and aggressive. 'It was slightly tricky,' says Tom, 'but we sat down for about half an hour in a separate room beforehand and had a laugh about it, and I said, "My main aim is not to f*** up your happy day," and William said, "That would be really helpful, Tom, thank you. Do try not to."

'Kate was very nervous—very, very nervous—understandably. She knew that everyone was curious, no one had ever heard her speak and they were probably going to make up their minds for the rest of their lives about what they thought of her in the next twenty minutes. First impressions are very important, and twenty minutes is quite a long time. But I think she was helped by being nervous, because when I got back into the edit suite and played it back, she looked less nervous on TV than in person, and it made her seem quite vulnerable. If she'd been too brassy it would have been unattractive. I think they both got it about right.'

The photo call afterwards was a scrum with

lights flashing furiously and every photographer wanting them to look directly into his or her lens. The paparazzi he hates with a vengeance, but William knows many of the legitimate photographers by name and immediately recognised Arthur Edwards' voice from behind the blinding lights. Arthur has been photographing William for the *Sun* since the day after he was born. 'Excuse me, Sir,' he said in his polite, inimitable Cockney accent. 'Could I just get the both of you to look down here?' 'Oh all right then, Arthur,' said William, which caused a bit of merriment in the ranks and gibes of 'You'll do it for Arthur!' Ian Jones, who took William's eighteenth birthday photos, was just in front of him. 'Excuse me, Will; sorry, Catherine. If you could both look into this camera, which is Arthur's, and then into mine . . .' William leaned forward and said, 'Is that you Ian?' 'Arthur got his shot,' says Ian, 'and I got a lovely one of them both arm in arm looking straight into my lens.'

Photographers hadn't always been so polite.

# ZERO TOLERANCE

Years ago, early on in his relationship with Kate, William promised Mike Middleton that he would protect his daughter from the media. He reiterated that promise when he asked him for her hand in marriage. Within days of the engagement William asked his office to let it be known that he was going to have a crackdown on any individual or media outlet that invaded their privacy—both before and after the wedding. In future there would be zero tolerance.

The promise was easier to give than to fulfil, but whenever she had problems, William's office provided the necessary legal advice and clout. For the first five or six months after leaving university, Kate was followed by photographers day and night. The Household was enormously impressed by how courageous, composed and sensible she has been—not just then but during all the years William has known her. 'Any situation in which a young woman on her own is followed by a man, or in some cases a number of men in vehicles, on motorbikes, in the middle of the night, chased through the streets in the driving rain, you'd bring the police in; you wouldn't allow it. No one should have to put up with that. She would start every conversation with, "I don't want to make a fuss but . . . there are twenty men camped outside my apartment and they're there all day and night." '

In October 2005, Harbottle and Lewis, the Prince of Wales's solicitors, complained to newspapers about harassment and appealed for the press to leave Kate and her family alone. Matters improved, but the odd paparazzo still followed her. Pictures appeared of her putting her rubbish bins out, of walking along the street, of shopping with her mother—all manner of mundane, everyday activities. In one she was sitting on a number 9 bus in Knightsbridge, staring out of the window, lost in thought. When challenged, the newspaper claimed the photographer had just happened to spot her. Kate said he had been following her all day. There were photographs of her at the wheel of her Audi, which a 'bystander' claimed was 'going quite quickly' along a country road near her home, and she was chatting on a mobile phone, which is illegal. She was, in fact, stationary, having pulled over to take the call, but the idea of the photo being taken by some random passer-by in Bucklebury, the Middleton's small Berkshire village, is laughable. Harbottle and Lewis wrote letters, but in January 2007 they issued another complaint when, on the morning of Kate's birthday, she came out of her London flat to find more than twenty photographers and five TV crews waiting. They swarmed around her, calling out to her, their lenses just feet from her face as she tried to get into her car to drive to work. It was a scene eerily reminiscent of the worst excesses of Diana's treatment in 1980. William issued a plea for the paparazzi to stop harassing her, and News International, publishers of the *Sun* and the *News of the World*, also the *Times* and the *Sunday Times*, agreed to stop using their photographs of her.

But News International wasn't the only market for snatched photos, and there were so many photographers surrounding William and Kate when they came out of a nightclub that same month that they had to call for a police escort. In March, Kate issued a formal complaint to the PCC about the *Mirror*, which published a photo of her walking to work holding a cup and her car keys. And in the week that the inquest into his mother's death was opened, the two of them were once again surrounded by photographers as they came out of a nightclub. This time their car was pursued by at least seven of them on motorbikes, scooters and in a car—in exactly the way that Diana's car had been pursued by the paparazzi in Paris on that fateful night in 1997. William found it utterly 'incomprehensible' and was so angry that he came within a whisker of taking legal action.

The PCC code of conduct ought to be sufficient. It states, 'It is unacceptable to photograph individuals in private places without their consent. Private places are public or private property where there is a reasonable expectation of privacy.' On harassment, it says, 'Journalists must not engage in intimidation, harassment or persistent pursuit. They must not persist in questioning, telephoning, pursuing or photographing individuals once asked to desist.' It was this breach of the harassment clause that Kate used against the *Mirror*. But the PCC code is voluntary and some would say toothless—and while that might change at the conclusion of the Leveson Inquiry, the market then would be the foreign media and the internet.

Protective of Kate (and of friends who suffer the same harassment because of their link to him), frustrated, and above all determined to be in control of his own life, William felt a heavier hand was needed. He has become an expert on privacy law, much of which is highly complex, and watches the latest legal rulings for the implications they might have on his own situation. He is advised by Gerrard Tyrrell, who is senior partner of Harbottle and Lewis, and one of the best media lawyers in the country, and has ongoing conversations about developments with him, and also with Paddy, Jamie and Miguel.

He is particularly interested in the implications of the landmark ruling from the European Court of Human Rights in 2004 in favour of Princess Caroline of Monaco's right to privacy. She and her children had been hounded by the German paparazzi for years. In France, where she lives, the media can only publish photos taken at official events, unless they get prior agreement from the subject. But that doesn't stop the paparazzi harassing her in France and selling the photos abroad, where in countries like the UK and Germany, any photo can be published provided it is in the 'public interest'. The ruling came down to the balance between the right to privacy, enshrined in the Human Rights Act 1998, and the right to freedom of expression, similarly enshrined; her right to privacy against the media's right to freedom of expression. The court said the balance should be in favour of privacy, as long as there was no overriding public interest justification. Going about your everyday life, even in public places, it decided, did not constitute justification.

It was the outcome of that test case, as much as anything, that encouraged William to issue the warning in the week after his engagement. He was not going to let Kate, or their relationship, suffer in the way his mother and father's had; history was not going to be allowed to repeat itself. It was made very clear to royal correspondents and editors that he would not hesitate from taking criminal or civil action, depending on the nature and severity of the intrusion. 'Prince William feels that he and his fiancée have a right to privacy when they are going about everyday, private activities—both before and after their marriage,' the press were told. 'He will not tolerate any form of pursuit [by cars or motorbikes] or harassment. They are not just disruptive but they are also very dangerous.' Nor would they any longer tolerate photographers using telephoto lenses from public land to capture photographs of them in private situations.

'He feels very strongly about what happened to his mother and father,' says one of the Household. 'I don't think it's anger in the sense of ranting and raging, it's more a cold-eyed assessment and understanding of it and desire to constantly draw the boundaries that protect their privacy and strengthen it.

'The key point is none of them has chosen this life; and their friends are friends because of them, not because they wish to have a public life, and so their privacy should be respected. What happened to his mother and his father informs and shapes that. He feels very passionately about it but it's not incoherent. He has a good understanding of how the media operates and he's always been aware of what the media wants and why they want it.'

The good humour on the evening of their engagement, and their friendliness to the accredited media that follow them in their public life—which I have seen for myself—makes that abundantly clear. There is mutual respect for people doing their job. But that is not the way the paparazzi operate.

Not long before the engagement, Kate was walking through an airport on her own when a couple of paparazzi spotted her. 'Bitch!' 'Whore!' 'Slag, look this way!' they shouted, hoping to provoke some kind of violent reaction. 'Ideally, they'd love her to slap them,' says one of the team. 'It would be a gift to them. Of course, the press never reports that side of pap activity so you never, ever see it, but that's how they operate at the rough end.'

# A QUIET FAMILY WEDDING

For a good two years before William and Kate bounced into their office and announced that they were engaged, his small team at Clarence House had been playing What If?, agonising over what kind of wedding it should be, if that moment were to come. The credit crunch was turning into full-blown recession, major banks and household names were going to the wall, thousands of people were losing their jobs and their homes. To suggest the kind of extravagant royal wedding his parents had had would have been insensitive and dangerously inflammatory. Should they be looking at some small venue like the Chapel Royal at St James's Palace? Keep the whole thing very low-key?

Come the day, William was in no doubt. 'What we want,' he said, 'is a personal day that's going to be special to us.' In an ideal world that would have been a normal wedding in a small country church, like St Mary's in Bucklebury, the kind of wedding that so many of their friends had had. But that wasn't possible. There was no shirking the fact that this was a royal occasion. He knew instinctively that it should not be cut-price, and not over the top, but a celebration, a day that was a pick-me-up for the whole country, a chance for people to enjoy themselves, a really beautiful display of royal pageantry that should look good, feel good and stand the test of time. 'We want a day,' said William, 'that is as enjoyable as possible, for as many people as possible.' Those, his exact words, became the mantra for the entire event. The task was to create a day that was intimate for them and their families, but which would give the British people a suitably royal and memorable celebration.

Both of them had very strong views about how the day should be; they drove it from start to finish, from the choice of Westminster Abbey to the twenty-foot trees lining the nave, which brought the country to London. And it *was* a very personal wedding, despite the forty television cameras, thirty journalists, scores of clergy and swathes of guests that neither of them knew. 'What made it an intimate day was nothing that we did,' says one of the team. 'It was the two of them, the smiles they gave one another, the comments—"You look beautiful, babe" and to Michael [Middleton], "Just a quiet family wedding . . ." It shows great presence. He knows the cameras are on him but has an ability to blot it out and just get on with it, and to crack that kind of joke to your father-in-law shows great confidence—which he has in spades.'

Without some timely advice from the Queen, the number of strangers might have been even higher. His office had been doing a little homework and at that first meeting, two days after the announcement, produced a list of guests the Lord Chamberlain recommended should be invited, according to protocol. It ran to 777 names—ambassadors, lord lieutenants, chancellors of universities, all sorts of people William neither knew nor cared about. 'Oh my God,' he said, 'I can't possibly do this'—there would be almost as many strangers as there would be friends and relations. So they tore up the list, and without any prompting from his team, William turned to his grandmother. Recounting the story to Robert Hardman, for his recent biography, *Our Queen*, William said, 'I rang her up the next day and said: "Do we need to be doing this?" And she said: "No. Start with your friends first and then go from there." She made the point that there are certain times when you have to strike the right balance [between personal and duty]. And it's advice like that, which is really key, when you know that she's seen and done it before.'

'He had no experience of big state weddings,' says one of the team, so his starting point was very different from his father, who did have a cathedral full of strangers. 'By the time Charles was married he had been invested in a coronation-like ceremony at Caernarfon Castle and was very used to big formal events with lots of pageantry, where you're an actor on the stage. William has not had that experience, so he approached his wedding day, genuinely, as, "I take thee, Catherine, to be my wife," and that was the most important thing about it.

'He had complete freedom to do what he wanted. It was very interesting. There's this assumption that the Queen is a real stickler for protocol and formality, but not at all. He's learned from her that you take the best of tradition and when you do it, you do it beautifully and well, but you start with what you want out of the event, because only then will it have any integrity, and feel like an event that the principals want to be at.'

In the run-up to the wedding, William saw his grandmother for about half an hour every week—it was timetabled into her schedule—and if they couldn't arrange a meeting, they spoke on the phone at length. They talked through every aspect of what he was planning for the day. His call would always be put straight through to her if she was free, and sometimes he would get her on her mobile phone (yes, at eighty-six she tweets and has a mobile). The conversations would be a mixture of gossip and general chit-chat, with William sometimes asking for advice, and being reminded, humorously, that the last time she gave him advice, he chose to ignore it.

She was the one person he could turn to when he

was being pressurised or pulled in different directions. She was of great help to him, both practically and emotionally, in guiding him through his big day and helping him achieve everything he wanted from it.

Early in the process, before they had even confirmed a date, the team sat down to discuss the media plan, knowing it would be in five or six months. They had an idea about how to play it; envisaging a steady flow of information throughout the period. William had a different and very strong view of his own. There had been a tremendous amount of media coverage in the week or so since the engagement; he wanted it to die down and for further information to be held back for as long as possible. The bulk of the details should be released no more than two or three weeks before the wedding, and he wanted to hold back a few secrets for the day itself. They take their hats off to him. 'I don't think there's a single person out there who looked at that media plan and didn't think, God, that was a really good strategy in terms of how you don't over-cook it, don't let people get bored. It was entirely his idea.'

There were obviously a few things that couldn't wait: the date, Friday, 29 April (which would be a bank holiday), and the place, Westminster Abbey. The Abbey would inevitably be filled with memories of his mother, and maybe that was why he chose it, but it is also a beautiful building and a big space with the illusion, in the chancel, of a much smaller church. In January a few more details were released, but the rest only started trickling out in the month before. It would be an 11 a.m. start, Kate would travel to the Abbey by car, not the traditional coach; the Dean of Westminster, the Very Reverend Dr John Hall, would conduct the service, the Archbishop of Canterbury, Dr Rowan Williams, would marry them, and the Bishop of London, Dr Richard Chartres, would give the address. They would make the journey back to Buckingham Palace in a carriage procession via Parliament Square, Whitehall, Horse Guards Arch, Horse Guards Parade and the Mall; the Queen would host a lunchtime reception for guests representing the couple's official and private lives; and in the evening the Prince of Wales would host a private dinner at the Palace for close friends and family, followed by dancing.

Another early announcement was that they were setting up a Royal wedding gift fund and asking anyone wanting to give them a present to make a donation instead to one of twenty-six little-known charities, which they chose together. It was the first time anything like this had been done and it raised over a million pounds.

There were three things the team agreed to keep secret until the day: the name of the designer Kate had chosen for her wedding dress—and they are astonished that the secret held; the vows, hymns and music—the very personal elements of the service; and the use of Prince Charles's Aston Martin—his twenty-first birthday present from the Queen—as their 'going away' car. Their reasoning was simply that with so much information going into the public arena in advance, they wanted everyone to experience some of the same surprises that arise at normal weddings.

There was early speculation that Richard Chartres might marry them, as he was a friend, but that was never a possibility. After the engagement, he did, however, quietly prepare Kate for confirmation into the Church of England. William accompanied her, and she was confirmed in March in a private and very small service at the Chapel Royal in St James's Palace. Only William and her family were present. As she explained, she chose not to do it at school when all her peers were being confirmed as if it were some sort of social rite of passage, but wanted to do it when it would really mean something.

Her husband, of course, will one day be Defender of the Faith, or, more probably, Defender of Faith, which is his father's preferred term, better suited to Britain's multi-faith society. William has a genuine faith, like his father, but he is a typical old-fashioned Anglican, who doesn't shout about it but quietly goes about his life following Christian ethics. He is not an extreme Anglican, as a number of his and Kate's friends are. They are members of Holy Trinity, Brompton (HTB), 'a vibrant Anglican church in the heart of London' is how it describes itself, 'with a vision to play our part in the re-evangelisation of the nations and the transformation of society.' It has particular appeal, some would say alarming appeal, to the young, particularly the moneyed, middle and upper classes in Britain, and HTB devised the Alpha course, which is on its way to taking over the world.

William has great respect for Richard Chartres, and over the years has spoken at length to him. He is a charismatic character who has great passion, presence and authority—also humanity and intellect; one can't help but be impressed by him. As one of the Household says, 'He is William's kind of bishop, the sort who rolls his sleeves up, and who believes in muscular Christianity, not intellectual, theological Christianity. His is much more William's end of the faith spectrum.'

When a massive earthquake hit the New Zealand city of Christchurch in February, two months before the wedding, William was working flat out, desperately trying to get his hours in because of the time he would be taking off for the wedding. He was flying day and night, and when he wasn't he was dealing with wedding arrange- ments. Yet, as shocking scenes of destruction filled our television screens, so soon after the horrifying images of floods and cyclones in Australia, his instinct was to show them they were not forgotten. There was heavy loss of life, homes and livelihoods in both countries and he wanted to stand alongside their shattered communities.

His Household knew his affection for the Antipodes, but also knew his workload, and didn't think in a million years that William would consider going. Then they received a phone call. 'The Royal Family has got to do something here,' William said. 'We've got to get down there and see them. Can you please ask who's going and if it's being debated, please put my hat in the ring? I really want to do this.' He pushed and pushed and wouldn't take no for an answer, and in the end he simply said, 'I'm off. I've got permission from my instructors to do this, let's go.'

His office normally clears any potential engagements with his search and rescue bosses, but he had done it himself, 'so you can't use that as an excuse,' he said. 'I've done it.'

In both countries people were so happy to see him, and grateful that he'd taken the trouble to come. Repeatedly people said his visit had boosted their morale. He looked in horror at the disaster zones, commiserated with the bereaved, chatted to survivors and congratulated the bravery of rescue workers. It was sombre stuff but he unfalteringly judged when the moment was right to leaven it with a little humour, and in some places he was treated like a rock star. 'Marry me, Prince William!' shouted a girl in the crowd in Australia. 'I'm sorry,' he said, 'you're too late!' Many people asked about Kate and congratulated him on his engagement, and when a New Zealander, no doubt speaking for thousands, said, 'We can't believe you've done this just before your wedding,' he said, 'Come on,' giving it the seriousness it deserved, 'a wedding is one thing but what's happened here in Christchurch is completely different.'

Speaking to a crowd of 30,000 people at a memorial service for the victims, he began with the Maori greeting, '*Tena koutou katoa*. Today I represent the Queen. I convey to you Her Majesty's message of deep sympathy and condolence. My grandmother once said that grief is the price we pay for love. Here, today, we love . . . and we grieve.'

He went on to say, 'I also bring a personal message. It arises from seeing this tragedy unfold from afar. It is a message about strength through kindness, about fortitude. For you who are so close to these events, and who have lost so much, it must be hard to grasp the degree of admiration—and indeed awe—with which you are regarded by the rest of the world. Courage and understated determination have always been the hallmark of New Zealanders and Cantabrians.

These things the world has long known. But to see them so starkly demonstrated over these terrible, painful months has been humbling. Put simply, you are an inspiration to all people.

'I count myself enormously privileged to be here to tell you that. This community, more than any other in the world at the moment, can appreciate the full horror of what is unfolding in Japan. Our thoughts and prayers are with them, too.

'In the last two days,' he concluded, 'I have heard tales of great tragedy—but also of extraordinary bravery and selfless courage. Throughout, one phrase unites them all. With the Queen's heartfelt good wishes, and those of the Prince of Wales and other members of my family, I say it to you now: *kia kaha*. Be strong.'

William was genuinely moved but also uplifted by everything he saw and heard in both countries. His speech in Christchurch, the most formal part of the visit, hit the perfect tone and was delivered with confidence and authority—also perfect timing. And although by the end of the five days he was emotionally drained, the trip had been a personal triumph.

If one had to pinpoint the moment when Prince William turned from an exceptional young man into a future King, that trip was it.

On his return to work, after a very long sleep, he told Robert Hardman that he had 'the most wonderful letter' from the Queen, 'saying "Congratulations and well done, you did well down there," which meant a lot to me. It's funny but when you get a letter from her or a bit of praise, it goes a long, long way, more so than anyone else saying, "Well done" to you. It's mainly because there's such gravitas behind those words. I say to people, "She's my grandmother to me first and then she's the Queen." Words that come from her, I take very personally and I really appreciate.'

Curiously, they are not words she has often addressed to her eldest son—praise is not common currency among the older members of the Royal Family—but perhaps the generation gap has made for an easier relationship. Or perhaps the Queen just has a soft spot for her rather special grandson.

# A RIGHT ROYAL CELEBRATION

The night before the wedding, the streets outside Clarence House and Buckingham Palace looked more like a festival site than busy London thoroughfares. People of all ages came in their thousands, and some with tents and sleeping bags had been there for a couple of days. They had tables and chairs, picnics, thermoses and bottles of champagne, some were in silly hats, some wrapped in Union Jacks, some waving paper flags, some from London, some from beyond, some from the other side of the world; all of them were in carnival mood and good voice. It was a giant jolly street party; everyone excited about what the morning would bring, everyone wanting to be a part of the big day, and to wish the couple luck.

At 8.30 p.m., to shrieks of surprise and delight, William and Harry appeared from Clarence House to say hello to them all. 'You're amazing,' said William. 'These crowds are amazing. Thank you so much.' For ten minutes he and his brother walked up and down chatting, joking, laughing and shaking hundreds of hands. William admitted he was a little nervous about the day ahead but said all he had to do was get his lines right. 'Will you be here tomorrow?' he asked one group. 'Oh good. Will you wave? I'll wave back.' It was an inspired gesture that set the tone for the following day to perfection. April 29th was a day that would be remembered and written about for decades to come, a dazzling Royal spectacle, but in essence it was about an ordinary young man, made extraordinary because he happened to have been born to be King. The press credited Paddy and Miguel with what it called a public relations masterstroke, but it had little to do with the Prince's professional PR team.

Miguel had been writing a press release about

the finer details of lace when William phoned him. He would normally have phoned Jamie, but he was with his son at the Goring Hotel (six-year-old Billy had been chosen as a page boy) around the corner, which the Middletons had taken over for the wedding. William said he wanted to go outside and see people who had been there for a couple of days now. He said he thought it would be a really nice thing to do. 'It was one of those moments when I thought, God, why didn't I think of that? It's a really obvious thing to do. "Of course," I said. "Have you told the police?" And he said he hadn't but they would be fine with it. He duly told them he would be going out in five minutes, and they ran around and made it happen. Those moments define him; it was completely his idea.'

The wedding was everything everyone could have dreamed of, and more. A masterpiece of vision and precision, a musical feast to tingle the spine, the very best of ancient and modern performed by two choirs, one orchestra and two fanfare teams—and William and Kate's favourite hymns, rousing numbers that everyone knew. It was a massive, joyful celebration that the whole country could feel a part of, and a skilful mixture of old and new. It was everything it set out to be. It was a day of huge enjoyment for millions of people. Traditional British pomp and ceremony at its very best, instantly shared with the nation on YouTube, Facebook, Twitter and Flicker. A spectacle to equal any of the grandest occasions of the last century, executed with heart-warming touches of informality. The most public event of the decade, beamed as it unfolded to billions of viewers throughout the world, and magically allowed to feel like an intimate and private gathering.

The public were very much a part of it—the diehards who had camped out in the Mall and around the Abbey were joined by hundreds of thousands of day-trippers and the streets and parks were full of them. But there was no mistaking the feeling that it was William and Kate's day, no mistaking the happiness that radiated from them both, and no doubting that this was anything other than a love match. It was an astonishing achievement, but somehow they managed to blot out the world. Their faces, and the jokes and asides, said it all; strip away the finery, and they could have been any couple, from any walk of life, madly in love and excited by the prospect of dedicating their lives to each other. Their happiness was infectious. Nineteen hundred people inside the Abbey were lit up by it; thousands outside, watching on giant screens as the couple smiled at each other, let out great cheers as they were pronounced man and wife, and, I'm prepared to bet, so did millions more watching on their televisions at home.

The doors to the Abbey opened at 8.15 a.m.

for the general congregation, and as the morning wore on, the guests became more royal and recognisable, the hats and the outfits more exotic. They provided plenty of fodder for the teams of running commentators broadcasting non-stop throughout the day. The last couple to arrive before the bride's party were the Queen and Duke of Edinburgh, whom the Prince of Wales kissed on both cheeks, before they all went to their seats. After William's discussion with the Queen, the guest list featured many more friends than strangers—including the postman, publican, butcher and village shopkeepers from Bucklebury, and the barman from Mustique where the Middletons, and William with them once or twice, holidayed. It broke down to more than a thousand friends. There were over fifty members of the Royal Family, and another forty foreign royals, more than two hundred members of government, Parliament and the diplomatic corps; eighty or so people from William's charities, sixty Governors-General and Realm Prime Ministers and thirty members of the defence services, and a sturdy collection of archbishops and other faith leaders. Among the more famous faces were David and a very pregnant Victoria Beckham, Rowan Atkinson, Sir Elton John and Joss Stone. Tara Palmer-Tomkinson was there and Harry's on-off girlfriend, Chelsy Davy, who was said to have helped him with his best man's speech.

Inevitably there were people who expected to be invited but weren't, and some for whom the invitation was a big surprise, like William's search and rescue team at Valley, and Charlie and Tiggy, landlords from the Vine Tree at Norton. But two rather more notable figures were missing from the list that went out to the press the week before the wedding: two former Labour prime ministers, Tony Blair and Gordon Brown—while it was known that Baroness Thatcher and Sir John Major, both Conservatives, had been invited. For several days the press analysed the possible reasons for the 'snub', while St James's Palace defended the decision; the wedding was not a State occasion, therefore there was no reason to invite former prime ministers, and that Thatcher and Major had been invited because they were Knights of the Garter and the other two were not.

'It was a cock-up from start to finish,' says one of William's team. One of the groups he cut out of the original list sent over by the Lord Chamberlain's office were former prime ministers. A group he kept in were Knights of the Garter. What no one noticed was that Thatcher and Major were among the Knights of the Garter. Thatcher's name vanished early on because it was known she couldn't attend, which left Major as the only former prime minister. 'No one spotted it until Roya Nikkhah from the *Sunday Telegraph* phoned one Saturday and said, "We've noticed

John Major's coming and none of the others. Why is that?" I remember my heart sank.' There was talk about the private office at Buckingham Palace getting in touch with their private offices with a last-minute invitation but Tony Blair then gave an interview saying he was very happy not to be invited and had never expected it. By that time, everyone in the Prince's office agreed it would be too humiliating and awkward to invite them. 'That was the only cock-up—and one thing had to go wrong.'

Harry, best man and keeper of the ring, looked immaculate in his Blues and Royals uniform (recently promoted to captain), and helped keep the mood light and informal in the midst of such formality. As Kate and her father and her posse of small attendants began their procession up the aisle to Hubert Parry's soaring anthem, 'I Was Glad', Harry took a peek over his shoulder, to the amusement of the congregation, then turned to his brother, presumably to reassure him she was on her way. The brothers had arrived forty-five minutes early so that they could chat to friends and relatives. It was all so different from their parents' stiffly formal wedding at St Paul's thirty years earlier.

Kate could scarcely keep the grin off her face. William was right: she did look beautiful, and her father was a pillar of strength by her side. As they stood alongside William and Harry, and William whispered to Mike, it was clear that he was already like a second son to him. She seemed oblivious to the illustrious figures in the congregation or the television cameras trained on her face. She had eyes for no one but William, and if she felt nervous in front of such a huge audience, she certainly didn't show it.

The dress—Sarah Burton at Alexander McQueen—was a triumph of close-fitting satin and lace, with a nine-foot train, and with it she wore a veil made of layers of ivory silk tulle with a trim of hand-embroidered flowers. It was held in place by a Cartier 'halo' tiara, loaned to her by the Queen. Her bouquet was full of symbolism: in the language of flowers, sweet William means gallantry; lily of the valley, return of happiness; hyacinth, constancy of love; and myrtle is the emblem of marriage and love. There was also ivy for fidelity, wedded love, friendship and affection. And no doubt for extra luck, one stem came from a myrtle planted at Osborne House on the Isle of Wight by Queen Victoria in 1845, and a single sprig was from the plant grown from the myrtle used in the Queen's wedding bouquet in 1947. No detail was too small.

Kate's sister, Pippa, was her Maid of Honour, also dressed in a figure-hugging Sarah Burton creation (and her bottom became an overnight sensation). It was her job to keep an eye on the four little bridesmaids: Lady Louise Windsor, 7, the Wessexes' daughter; the Hon. Margarita Armstrong-Jones, 8, the Linleys' daughter; Grace van Cutsem, 3, Hugh and Rose's daughter and William's goddaughter; Eliza Lopes, 3, the Duchess of Cornwall's granddaughter; and two page boys, Billy Lowther-Pinkerton and Tom Pettifer, Tiggy's son and William's godson. Both looked very smart in their little scarlet uniforms.

William was impeccably dressed in the same scarlet. It was the uniform of an Irish Guards Officer, with a blue Garter sash and star, RAF wings and Golden Jubilee medal. He had been uncertain about which uniform to wear, entitled as he is to wear all three services', but in February the Queen had appointed him to the honorary rank of Colonel of the 1st Battalion Irish Guards—his most senior military appointment. Where he wavered, she did not. 'I was given a categorical: "No, you'll wear this!"' he told Robert Hardman. 'So you don't always get what you want [from the Queen], put it that way. But I knew perfectly well that it was for the best. That "no" is a very good "no". So you just do as you're told!'

Richard Chartres wisely made no mention of fairytales in his address, although there were echoes of Diana in the choice of some of the music and hymns. He said that, 'In a sense every wedding is a royal wedding with the bride and groom as King and queen of creation, making a new life together so that life can flow through them into the future.' He ended by reading a prayer that he said William and Kate had composed together in preparation for the day.

'God our Father, we thank you for our families; for the love that we share and for the joy of our marriage. In the busyness of each day keep our eyes fixed on what is real and important in life and help us to be generous with our time and love and energy. Strengthened by our union help us to serve and comfort those who suffer. We ask this in the Spirit of Jesus Christ.'

They walked down the aisle together grinning at familiar faces, man and wife (albeit one who had chosen not to 'obey'), but also Their Royal Highnesses the Duke and Duchess of Cambridge— a gift from the Queen. She also gave him Scottish and Northern Irish titles—the Earl of Strathearn and Baron Carrickfergus—but Cambridge was the one he would be commonly called. But if the thousands of fans that greeted them in Canada a couple of months later are anything to go by, for most people they will always be simply Will and Kate.

# PARTY AT THE PALACE

What thousands of people had come to see was the kiss on the Buckingham Palace balcony, and it was duly delivered. Not once, but twice, which made the new Duchess giggle and the five hundred thousand or so well-wishers packed into the Mall below, and the thousands more watching it on the big screens in the parks, whoop and cheer with delight. Overhead, the sky was filled with aeroplanes as a Lancaster, Spitfire and Hurricane from the Battle of Britain Memorial Flight and RAF Tornados and Typhoons flew past in formation. For the newly-weds, the nerve-racking parts of the day were over. From now on, it was party time.

Inside the Palace their 650 lunch guests awaited them, happily nibbling canapés and admiring the Old Masters on the walls. This first reception was for a mixture of friends, including many of the parents of friends, family and people from William's official life. They were all bussed over from the Abbey, and William and Kate worked the rooms to make sure that they had a word with all those people not staying for the dinner in the evening. There were speeches; Prince William spoke charmingly about his beautiful bride and thanked his grandmother for her generosity in hosting the reception. Those who knew the Queen had seldom seen her so happy. One described her 'playful', another said she was 'literally skipping'. She had taken a very personal hand in it. Every detail was run past her, the precise canapé menus, the wines, the arrangement of the rooms. She walked through them all and checked that everything was in order, and had many meetings with the Master of the Household about it. She genuinely saw it as her party and she wanted her guests to have the best time possible.

The Prince of Wales humorously reminisced about the groom as a teenager, shut in his room playing his music at full blast for hours on end and refusing to come out. And he talked about the two-fingered response he used to get from him whenever he tried to give him advice about the clothes he wore, or when he told him to stop slouching. But for the guests, it could have been any father of the groom affectionately ribbing his son, and there was no doubting the affection.

When the speeches were over and the cakes cut and the champagne drunk, everyone was asked to go into the gardens at the back of the Palace to see the couple off. And there waiting for them, to everyone's surprise, was his father's dark blue Aston Martin DB6 Mk II, with a few adjustments courtesy of Harry. It was festooned with heart-shaped balloons and coloured streamers and rosettes, with an L plate on the front and a new number plate on the back—JU5T WED.

As far as the public knew, the day for them had finished with the kiss. So when the Aston Martin appeared, nosing its way slowly out of the Palace gates at 3.35 p.m., with William at the wheel and Kate beside him, those still milling around outside went mad. They'd watched the procession earlier with William and Kate in a 1902 State Landau, followed by all the King's horses and all the King's men, and the sight of them smiling and waving from an open-topped classic car—just like any other newly-weds—was sensational. But the new Duke and Duchess had their own surprise in store. As they crept slowly along the Mall to Clarence House, a yellow Sea King helicopter appeared and hovered noisily just a few feet over their heads—a tribute from the RAF to a fellow search and rescue pilot.

It had been William's idea to borrow the car and his father loved the idea. The person he had really wanted to surprise was Kate, but someone pointed out that she would need to be able to fit into it wearing her dress and only she knew how long the train was, so she was let in on the secret. But the car is very old and very tricky and William is not familiar with it. His greatest worry was that he would drive it out into the Mall in front of two billion people . . . and stall it. But it was not to be.

The evening party was for 300 of their closest friends and family. The Queen and the Duke of Edinburgh left the younger generations to it. The Queen had said to William, 'You don't really want me and Grandpa there in the evening, do you? So if you don't mind, we're going to allow you and your friends to have the run of the place.' She had invited William and Kate to spend their wedding night at the Palace, which for logistical reasons was sensible, and she personally selected the suite they should stay in and checked that all was in order for them. She chose the Belgian Suite that President Obama and his wife had stayed in, a stunning set of rooms which get the morning light.

As the guests arrived back at the Palace, having gone away for a few hours after the lunch and changed into black tie, they were bagpiped through a candlelit courtyard into pre-dinner drinks where vintage pink champagne and peach bellinis awaited. Kate had changed into another flowing white satin Sarah Burton creation, with a little angora bolero cardigan, and looked radiant. Dinner, at tables of ten in the ballroom, was a veritable feast devised by top chef and restaurateur Anton Mosimann. They began with seafood from Wales, went on to lamb from Highgrove and finished with a trio of mini-puddings—all of it accompanied by distinguished wines. After coffee and petit fours came the speeches and the high spot of the night.

Harry, acting as compère, completely stole the show, with impeccable comic timing and brilliant one-liners. He had everyone in tears of laughter as he hilariously recounted tales from their childhood of being beaten up by his older brother and shot by air rifles, and teased him rotten about everything from his romantic style to his receding hairline. But there were emotional moments too. William had said at his engagement that in giving

Kate his mother's ring, he hoped to include her in all the fun and excitement, and both boys made sure she was part of the evening celebrations, by each making moving tributes to her in the midst of all the mirth.

The father of the bride joked about the time William had almost blown the roof off the house when he landed his helicopter in the garden, and the awkward conversation they had had when he asked for his daughter's hand in marriage, but he also spoke warmly about William and about how well he fitted into the family. William returned the compliment and spoke movingly about Kate. The final speech was a double-act. Thomas van Straubenzee and James Meade took to the floor and delivered a series of quick gags about their friend, which again had the audience helpless with laughter.

Dancing followed until three o'clock in the morning. For two full hours the Brit Award–winning singer Ellie Goulding and her band played live, then DJs took over with a mixture of music, and the booming bass could be heard halfway down the Mall. The final number was 'She Loves You' by the Beatles, which had everyone on the dance floor singing their hearts out, after which they were shepherded out into the gardens once again, for William and Kate to make their second and final departure of the day. This time their going-away car was a bright yellow little Fiat 500—another surprise for their friends and family—which William had secretly borrowed from David Linley. But since they were spending the night at the Palace, the chauffeur didn't have far to go. While the guests drunkenly cheered and waved and wished them luck, including both sets of parents—everyone stayed to the very end— they stood up with their heads through the open roof laughing and waving, while they were driven around two corners and delivered to another door. 'It was simply magical,' said one guest. 'The best party ever imaginable.'

Harry, still in party mood, as they all were, then led all the young onto a waiting coach and over to the Goring Hotel where they carried on partying safely and privately until five. The brothers had discussed what might happen when they were kicked out of the Palace and realised that if everyone just spilled out into Mayfair and the usual nightclubs at three in the morning, those places would be crawling with inquisitive diary journalists. Better to keep everyone together, and so they organised an after-party at the Goring.

Nothing gave them greater satisfaction than successfully thwarting the press, and in the case of William's stag weekend, completely out-witting them. Harry and Guy Pelly organised it and, it was said, at first booked a weekend of watersports in Exmouth, Devon. News of that venue had supposedly been leaked, and so they went to Norfolk instead, almost certainly to the van Cutsems' estate. The *Sun* was the first newspaper to get it right. A group of about twelve of William's best friends drove down to north Devon on the Friday of the last weekend in March, and stayed at Hartland Abbey, a secluded twelfth-century former monastery surrounded by beautiful gardens and parkland that lead to the Atlantic coast. It is owned and lived in by his friend, George Stucley and his family, and although house and gardens are open to the public at times, they took over the whole place and enjoyed complete privacy.

Speculation was also rife about where they would spend their honeymoon, and the Prince's office were as tight-lipped about that as about the stag do. The bookmakers had Kenya as the favourite, with Scotland and Jordan—where Kate spent a couple of years as a child—as runners-up. Other suggestions were the Caribbean islands of Mustique, Bequia and Necker or Lizard Island off the coast of Queensland. As their helicopter took off from Buckingham Palace the morning after the wedding, it was assumed they were going to one of these locations; if not, then to somewhere equally exotic. But to everyone's surprise it was announced that very afternoon that after a Bank Holiday weekend in Britain, William was going back to work at Valley, Kate to their cottage and the housekeeping, and the honeymoon would happen at an unspecified date in the future.

The reason for the sudden change of plan was that the hotel where they had chosen to go was fully booked for the period immediately after the wedding. And they were not prepared to ask the hotel for special favours, which would undoubtedly have meant either moving people around or turning some other couple away. 'There's no way we're going to do that,' said William. 'It could be *their* honeymoon.' Clarence House gave no explanation for the change of plan. If they had given the real reason, it would have allowed the media, frantic to know where they were going, to narrow their search. As it was, when they flew off in a private jet nearly two weeks later, their destination took the bookies by surprise—but it didn't take the press long to figure out that they had flown to the Seychelles. What they didn't know was which of the many small islands they had hopped to from the mainland.

They had chosen North Island. It fitted everything they were looking for, and the Seychelles' government was very happy to help keep the media at bay. In the Seychelles it's against the law to take someone's photograph without their permission—and just to be sure, the local coastguards patrolled off-shore around the island for the ten days William and Kate stayed there.

The day before they left they personally thanked the individual coastguards.

They wanted to find somewhere that neither of them had been to before, and although they went to the Seychelles after their reconciliation in 2007, they'd stayed on a different island. They also wanted somewhere that was fun, exciting and different, and where they could do some serious diving—something they both loved. And perhaps most important of all, it had to be somewhere that was guaranteed to be totally private—and in this day and age, privacy doesn't come cheap. The rate at North Island is a fraction under £2,000 per person per night, and includes all meals and virtually all drinks, scuba diving and snorkelling; also windsurfing, sea kayaking, and just about everything else you could dream of, including mountain bikes and a buggy for getting around the island. The hotel owns all 462 acres of it, and has only eleven rooms, which are large and luxurious individual villas, each with a private plunge pool and butler service. There is no mobile phone signal, and nobody comes to the island unless they are a guest at the hotel.

They found the suitably eco-friendly North Island themselves—and paid for it themselves. The use of the private jet to take them there and back was a wedding gift from the Duke of Westminster, but the hotel was down to them—and they researched how they were spending their money very carefully. They trawled the internet and consulted *Time Out* guide books, and books about the best diving sites in the world, and gradually narrowed the search down to this one speck of an island in the Indian Ocean, which promised peace and privacy.

While they were there, the Queen was on her first-ever state visit to the Republic of Ireland, an historic exercise in reconciliation and friendship, and, between dives, William assiduously followed her progress online. 'She was so excited about it,' he said. 'This was like a big door opening up to her that had been locked for so long. We all wanted it to go smoothly because it was such a big deal. I was keeping a careful watch.' The visit was a triumph and the Queen was visibly delighted by the outcome. 'As far as she was concerned, in terms of the relationship between Britain and Ireland and the Troubles, it was time to move on from that. What's happened has happened and no one wants to cover it up. We must make sure all the right things are done and that the right people are said sorry to or vice versa.'

After ten days on their paradise island they left more than footprints behind. They had made a lasting impression. The Seychelles High Commissioner to Great Britain, Patrick Pillay, said of them, 'In a world of so much turmoil, they bring a welcome and much-needed breath of fresh air with their warmth and humility.'

# CROSSING CONTINENTS

When the twenty-year-old Diana Spencer married the Prince of Wales, he was already working as a full-time member of the Family Firm, so, immediately after their honeymoon, she was thrown into Royal duties alongside him—the first of which, fittingly for the new Princess, was a tour of the principality of Wales. William is still a full-time search and rescue pilot, fitting in occasional Royal duties around his work schedule, and after the honeymoon he was back on duty at RAF Valley. So Kate's introduction to official Royal life was to be gradual. But before his engagement, William had agreed to carry out an official tour of Canada in the summer of 2011, the country where he had caused such a sensation as a shy teenager the year after his mother's death. Kate's initiation, therefore, by accident rather than design, would be ten days alongside him in Canada.

They arrived in Ottawa on 30 June. At that point, they were the world's most famous and feted couple, and were treated to a rapturous reception. It was the eve of Canada Day, the most important day in the country's calendar, when everyone takes to the streets to celebrate with parties and fireworks. The Canadians, a warm and friendly people, who had doted on the Princess of Wales, were thrilled that William and Kate had chosen their country for their first foreign tour. It was also, poignantly, the eve of what would have been his mother's fiftieth birthday.

The Governor General, David Johnston, set the mood of the tour by saying, 'Welcome to Canada—the honeymoon capital of the Commonwealth'. The crowd of thousands cheered loudly. William responded with the first of many bilingual speeches, and won hearts, as he struggled with his French pronunciation, by saying, 'It will improve as we go on.'

I was one of fourteen hundred accredited international media who flocked to Canada to observe their progress around the country, and I was there in Ottawa that day. Having also been in Wales in 1981, to observe Diana work her magic on the Welsh people on that first tour with Prince Charles, it was interesting to compare the two—and I had a strong sense of déjà vu.

When Diana had stepped from their car thirty years ago, and stretched out her arms to clasp the dozens of hands reaching for hers, it was obvious that she had something special. She was just twenty-one, and had done nothing like this in her life—she had even been rather shy meeting strangers—but she had an instinctive ability to engage with the public that no amount of training could ever have bettered. At one engagement after another, as the rain soaked her beautiful outfits, she smiled, she laughed, she patted children's heads or rubbed their cold hands between her own. She bent down to chat to people in wheelchairs, and sat on hospital beds, holding patients' hands, always managing to find the perfect remark for everyone she met.

Strange as it might sound to today's readers, such familiarity was new to the Royal Family. Even the walkabout was still quite new. Until the Queen's visit to Australia and New Zealand in 1970, neither she nor her family wandered over to talk randomly to the crowds that lined the streets. Those crowds received a smile and a royal wave. Theirs was the formality of a bygone age and Diana's approach struck a chord with the people. The Welsh fell in love with her. The crowds groaned audibly, and embarrassingly, when they saw that Diana was not taking their side of the street, and that they were getting Charles instead. He ended up joking that he was just there to collect flowers for his wife, but it must have hurt.

There was none of that in Canada. William and Kate travelled extensively, visiting seven cities in five provinces, and people were thrilled to see them both. Everywhere they went there were chants of 'Will and Kate, Will and Kate'; people held up placards with big hearts on them and slogans like 'Canada loves Will and Kate' and 'Will and Kate, You Were Worth The Wait', and the young screamed when either one of them headed in their direction. People turned out in their thousands, many had come from hundreds of miles away and the wait was really long—five or six hours was not unusual, sometimes for nothing more than a fleeting glimpse of the pair—but no one seemed to mind. They all had mobile phones or cameras and they were just happy to have the picture that showed they were there.

Kate took to it like a duck to water. She might have been Diana's double, except that she clearly had the confidence of being older and more worldly wise. She had no training either, but she looked as though she had spent a lifetime schmoozing prime ministers and governor generals, and making small talk with strangers. Like Diana, she was full of smiles and easy laughter, she clasped hands, stretched into the crowd to greet the people at the back, bent down for children and wheelchairs, and never seemed to be lost for words or more than momentarily unsure of herself. When the father of a little two-year-old wished her luck starting her own family, she thanked him and said, yes, she hoped to. A throwaway remark was suddenly heavy with meaning when front and centre in the next day's newspapers.

The media contingent in Wales had been tiny by comparison with the numbers that followed William and Kate around Canada; camera technology was thirty years behind and there was no internet, YouTube or instant messaging. This time, not only was the world's media picking up every remark and watching every muscle, but every man, woman and child in the crowd could post their own report.

Kate seemed unfazed; and as the days went by, and she saw more of the country and met more of the people, she seemed to be positively enjoying herself. They both did; despite a gruelling schedule, they looked as though they were having fun together, which was not how Charles and Diana had looked in Wales, barely two months after their wedding. The body language just wasn't there with his parents. These two looked at each other all the time, chatted and whispered to each other, giggled every now and again, and were forever touching. William would give Kate's hand a reassuring squeeze or he would place a hand on her back, and always seemed to be looking out for her.

She, in turn, seemed to be taking her cues from him and was clearly learning as she went. She looked painfully thin—a more worrying reminder of Diana, and one which is worrying several of their friends—but she certainly understood what the job was all about. She did the formal, ceremonial bit, the frothy Canada Day celebrations, the barbecues and concerts, and was undaunted by cancer wards and potentially difficult conversations. She met young and old, war veterans with tales of conflict and small children who refused to surrender their bouquets. She got it right every time. And she was game for the outdoor activities. She rowed like fury in a dragon-boat race, determined, but failing, to beat her competitive husband, who, as he gave her a consolation hug declared, 'There's no chivalry in sport!' In everything they did there was a feeling of partnership.

One visit not on the itinerary was to the small town of Slave Lake in northern Alberta, which had been devastated by a massive wildfire three weeks earlier. All seven thousand inhabitants had been forced to flee their homes with nothing more than the clothes they stood in. They commiserated with townsfolk who had lost everything and spoke to the rescue workers, including the fire chief Jamie Coutts, whose team had finally put out the fire. Their visit had been a real morale boost, he said. 'I'm happy for the people of Slave Lake. They got to have a happy day today, lots of smiles, and we haven't had a lot of those. It's easy to forget they're real people,' he said reflecting on William and Kate. 'He's a search and rescue pilot, she sits at home and worries about him when he's on missions—and that's a lot like what we did out on the front lines and what our families had to go through.'

Kate won't worry any less about William's missions, but she does now have a better understanding of what he does on them. At Dalvay-by-the-Sea in Prince Edward Island, on a day of torrential rain, William took to a Sea King helicopter to learn an emergency landing technique developed by search and rescue services in Canada. It's called 'waterbirding' and involves making a controlled landing on water in the event of engine failure—something he could no doubt take back to RAF Valley with him. He had specifically asked for it to be fitted into their schedule and after sitting alongside the pilot a couple of times, he took the controls himself and gently lowered the aircraft onto the water so many times that Kate must have wondered if he'd ever stop.

On the same theme, the Canadian Coast Guard put on a search and rescue demonstration for them in the harbour at Summerside. From the helicopter deck of a coastguard ship, they watched men being rescued from a capsized boat and winched aboard a Sea King hovering deftly overhead. Even in the calm of the harbour on a summer's day, the skill was clear to see. It wasn't hard to imagine how dangerous the whole operation must be on a stormy night twenty miles out over a black and angry sea. Afterwards they met people who had been rescued and owed their lives to the service. Among them was a man William spent a moment or two longer with. He was a lobster fisherman whose boat, a year ago, had capsized several miles out in the early morning. Three of the crew had been saved but his sixty-two-year-old father-in-law had drowned. The dead man's widow and daughter were there with him and also spoke to William, who was visibly moved by their story.

It was a tour as emotionally varied as it was geographically; and while their welcome was tumultuous everywhere they went, not every Canadian was pleased to see them. There were noisy demonstrations by separatists in Quebec province, where more than 80 per cent of the population speak French. About three hundred protestors carried banners that read 'Royal Parasites! Go Home!' and other, less polite messages. They were angry about the cost of the tour—said to be over 1.5 million Canadian dollars. In 1964, protestors had turned their backs on the Queen during her visit and booed her; she has not been back to the province since. And just the year before William and Kate's visit, Charles and Camilla were held up by scuffles between protestors and the police in Montreal.

William's biggest worry was that Kate would encounter some ugly incident on this first trip, and so the media were told there would be no walkabouts in Quebec City, where he spoke at the City Hall and he reviewed the Royal 22nd Regiment (and their hairy goat mascot), known as the Van Doos. They are the biggest French-speaking unit in Her Majesty's Canadian Forces and recently returned from Afghanistan. He diplomatically delivered this speech entirely in French: 'Thank you Premier, and Mr Mayor for your warm welcome. It's an honour for me to be here with you in Quebec today. For me, as a soldier and an airman, it is a privilege to have inspected a great regiment like the Royal 22nd. Your reputation is as strong as it is legendary. This place has such beauty and history. You, the Québécois and Québécoise, have such vitality and vigour. It is simply a pleasure to be here. Thank you for your patience with my accent, and I hope that we will have the chance to get to know each other over the years to come. Until the next time.'

The plan was for them to walk back to the heavily armed motorcade and make a swift getaway to the next event, but the thousands of people crowded into the city square, who had been soaked earlier by a heavy shower of rain, were calling out to them so excitedly that to everyone's surprise (not least of all his team and the press corralled halfway up the street), William suddenly put an arm on Kate's shoulder and led her past the waiting cars towards the crowds. The Quebecers were ecstatic, and it was a well-judged move—entirely his own—even if it did make the security officers very jumpy indeed.

# TINSEL TOWN

For ten days in Canada, William and Kate had been cheered and applauded as the nation's future King and Queen, and they had as much of a buzz from the experience as their future subjects. In his final speech in Alberta, William said, 'A week ago in Ottawa I spoke of how much Catherine and I looked forward to getting to know Canada and Canadians. I can only say that the experience of this past seven days has exceeded all our expectations. We have been hugely struck by the diversity of this beautiful country: from Ottawa to Quebec; from Prince Edward Island to the Northwest Territories; and now the excitement of Calgary—and what about these fantastic white hats [stetsons given to them for the Stampede Parade] . . . Canada has far surpassed all that we were promised.' He meant it. They were exhausted, it had been hard work, but every time their energy had started to flag something different presented itself and they were revived.

It had been a triumph. Once again he had looked like a King in waiting, and he had been received as such; and Kate by his side completed the picture. In every situation, in formal suit or jeans and an open-necked shirt, he hit the right note and charmed the birds from the trees. His speeches, delivered with perfect timing, also hit the right note and delighted his audience.

As they took off into the sky above Calgary after ten full days and countless flights, they must have wished they were going home. (The exhausted press pack certainly did.) Instead they flew to Los Angeles for two days, which had a very different feel for them and which, in my view, throws up some important questions for the future. It was essentially a fundraising trip that was tacked on to the end of the Canadian tour at the last minute—and a very profitable one it was too. Hollywood celebrities, rich Californians, wealthy Brits living in Los Angeles, everyone wanted to meet the Duke and Duchess of Cambridge and were prepared to pay big bucks for the privilege. But is this what our Royal Family should be doing?

Shortly before they left for Canada they topped the bill at one of the most star-studded and ostentatious displays of wealth in London's social calendar. It was the £10,000-a-head gala dinner for Absolute Return for Kids (ARK), which was co-founded by Swiss-born financier Arpad Busson. The charity funds projects for disadvantaged children in the UK and around the world, and one year the auction alone at one of these dinners raised £14 million. Kate, in a beautiful gown designed by Jenny Packham costing nearly £4,000, looked stunning, and William, on sparkling form, was there to announce a joint venture between ARK and his Foundation. He began by saying he didn't know how he was going to explain the spectacle before him to his grandmother when he saw her in the morning.

'I am delighted that this evening marks the start of a new joint-partnership between Absolute Return for Kids—ARK—and The Foundation of Prince William and Prince Harry and The Duchess of Cambridge—F P W P H A T D C . . . This new joint-partnership is based on our shared vision and commitment to transform the lives of thousands of young people. I know that I am very fortunate. I have had a good education, a secure home and a loving and supportive family. So many young people, however, do not have these advantages and, as a result, can lack the confidence and knowledge to realise their full potential.

'I count myself fortunate for another reason too. Harry and I find ourselves in a position to be able to help. I really believe that individuals can make a serious difference—whether it's through wealth, through position, or some other advantage. It is so heartening to see that so many of you here tonight, through your commitment, share that belief. It is in this spirit that my brother, Catherine and I hope to use our philanthropy as a long-term catalyst for meaningful change.'

His sincerely felt words no doubt brought the partnership a massive injection of cash, but there was something discordant about the sight of such a carefully modest pair among such opulence—albeit raising money for a good cause—at a time when working people all over the country were struggling to make ends meet.

California was a similar exercise; they were using all their many advantages—and using them very effectively. In two days, they raised an enormous amount of money and there is no doubt that that money will be used to make a difference. And they did it charmingly and in the style that Hollywood respects. Kate's dresses were by top designers; she borrowed jewellery from the Queen. At one event they arrived by helicopter. It was along the coast at Santa Barbara: a lavish lunch for sixty followed by a match at the prestigious Santa Barbara Polo Club to raise money for the American Friends of the Foundation of Prince William and Prince Harry. It was the Club's centenary year and William said in his speech, 'My father, the Prince of Wales, and my brother, Harry, were as green as that grass out there when I told them I'd be here.' Guests paid on a sliding scale depending on how close they came to the couple—$2,500 to be inside the tent, $250 to be on the other side of the pitch—and those that played polo with him were rumoured to have paid up to $60,000. He was playing rather well that afternoon and scored four goals, winning the Tiffany Cup for his team, presented to him by his wife. In five hours, in the blistering Californian sunshine, he raised $1.6 million.

That evening they hosted a glittering, red-carpet, all-star, A-list BAFTA dinner, of which William is President, for three hundred at the opulent Belasco Theater in downtown Los Angeles. It was aimed at persuading American film-makers to use young British talent; and stars such as Tom Hanks, Nicole Kidman and Quentin Tarantino were queuing up to pay $16,000 a table. But the hottest ticket was to an exclusive brunch the following morning at the Beverly Hills home of billionaire Hollywood producer and owner of the New York Giants football team, Steve Tisch. Forty-five guests including some of the richest philanthropists in the country, plus a few stars, like Reese Witherspoon and Catherine Keener, enjoyed a personal introduction to the Duke and Duchess. It was to launch Tusk Trust's US Patrons' Circle. How much they paid was left to the guests but 45 minutes of royal time brought in donations and forward pledges of nearly $1 million.

The assault on California was a quick and easy way to part the mega-rich from their money to help the poor. It was done in the best possible faith and with good taste—and it was an excellent outcome for everyone concerned. It seems churlish to find fault. Yet, having watched him earn such admiration and respect from those hundreds of thousands of people of Canada, who look up to him as their future King, there was something distasteful about the sight of him—he who oozes integrity from every pore—and his intelligent young wife selling themselves so brazenly.

That said, the trip wasn't all pay-to-view, and my suspicion is he was happier during the two and a half hours spent with ex-servicemen than he was at any of the champagne-fuelled celebrity dos. It was an event Nick Booth at the Foundation had arranged, called 'Hiring Our Heroes', in partnership with the organisation ServiceNation: Mission Serve. It was essentially a giant job fair, held at the Sony Studios, as William said in his speech, 'to help those returning from active service to open a new chapter in their lives and find employment when they retire from the military. Catherine and I both have friends back in Britain who could benefit from a brilliant initiative like this. I am delighted, therefore, that our Foundation—and in that I include Harry, my low-flying Apache pilot of a kid brother—is a partner in today's event. We have much to learn from you.'

' "Hiring Our Heroes" was a good example of the convening power [of the Prince],' says Nick Booth. 'It was about moving the story forward for returning veterans. Physical rehabilitation has been done to a degree, but what next? It was a question that Prince Harry asked and it was a very good question.' A conversation over a cup of coffee with some former colleagues in America then led to the event at Sony where the Prince's name enabled them to bring together veterans in search of work with employers, government labour departments and chambers of commerce. Hundreds of servicemen and women were hired that day, and within a month forty cities said they would like to do hiring fairs across the US; there are now five a week and over a hundred have been completed. 'I spoke to the US head of the Chamber of Commerce last week,' says Nick, 'and they are swamped off their feet. It's a great example of catalytic philanthropy.'

The Foundation will go on raising and distributing money. In January 2012, it announced a three-year partnership with the newly launched Forces in Mind Trust set up to help veterans suffering, as many of them do, from poor mental health, family breakdowns and substance abuse. Speaking after the premiere of the film *War Horse* in London—the proceeds of which went to the Foundation for this partnership, and to which six hundred military personnel had been invited—William said, 'To support this vital process of transition, Catherine, my brother Harry and I are delighted that our Foundation will be working in partnership with the newly formed Forces in Mind

Trust. Together, our aim is to provide a cohesive approach to tackling the many problems that some ex-service personnel and their families experience when making the move back into civilian life. Whether through finding new opportunities in employment, in mentoring and training, or in support to families, it is our intention that no serviceman or woman—or their dependants—should fear a future out of uniform. Giving them this confidence, and the opportunity to develop their extraordinary skills and talent for the benefit of wider society, is the very least our country owes them.'

Members of the Household agree that they haven't always got the balance quite right but say, 'It's bloody difficult when you have got charities that can make millions and millions of pounds literally out of an afternoon, and it's not immediately understandable to them when we come back and tell them they can't because the Duke and Duchess don't do that. What it demonstrates starkly is the difference between realm and non-realm. In the realm it's all about meeting the people, future subjects, and there's none of that in America. There, they are nothing more than grade A celebrities and what do you do with them? You exploit them; you make money out of them, they make money out of you and everyone pats each other on the back.

'But if you think about it, most royal visits are

in support of Foreign Office objectives and what are they? They're about prosperity in the UK, about bringing in business—it's about money. But, no, we shouldn't be going the route to pay for access.'

# A NEW DECADE

William has striven for normality all his life; he has tried to brush aside his titles, to be plain William or Will, to hop on his Ducati 1198S for a game of five-a-side football with his mates in the park. He has enjoyed popping into the pub for a pint, shopping in the supermarket, stopping for a takeaway and seeing a good film at the cinema. All those things could have been brought to him at the touch of a button. He need never have made his bed or ironed a shirt or cooked himself an omelette. His house could have been full of staff and his bath run and his clothes laid out for him in the mornings by a valet. It's how his father has always lived and it's what William was brought up with. But he didn't want that. He chose to live the way his school friends lived. That has been a great part of his appeal and goes a long way to explain how someone born to his position and his circumstances has reached his thirty-first year with such sanity and so many endearing qualities.

But he was born to be King and as he goes into a new decade, as a married man, as the Duke of

Cambridge, with two official foreign tours under his belt and a third coming up shortly, there is a sense that those days of carefree normality may be waning. Next year he and Kate will move into Princess Margaret's apartments in Kensington Palace and will have a small number of staff to look after them. Their lives will be entering a new phase and supermarket shopping in central London will not be an option.

In the last two years, since his trip to Australia and New Zealand in 2010, the change in him has become very noticeable. He always knew what he wanted, but now he is far more sure of himself and instead of asking tentative questions or wanting advice, he says what he thinks and what he wants, and asks his team, in the politest possible way, to make it happen. He is also growing into his title. There is not a hint of entitlement but a definite shift from the boy who would like to have been able to forget he was an HRH, to the man who knows it can add value. 'It makes me do back-flips,' says one of his team, 'because it means he's really getting it—and Harry is pretty much on his heels, as usual. They've just evolved. They're now leaders in their own right, in a very cool way.'

Their advisors believe their role in life is to provide leadership. Not political leadership but moral and community leadership. 'You ask the man in the street, "What do you think of the leadership of this country?" and the really intelligent, instinctive, *Sun* reader, of which there are millions out there, full of common sense, will say, "What bloody leadership, mate?" And then you say, "What about the Queen?" And he'll say, "She's great." There's a disconnect because he immediately thinks you're talking about political leadership and it doesn't have to be political. Monarchy is about leadership; and these two are natural-born leaders. You can argue till the crack of dawn over whether leaders are born or made, but these guys have got it and that can't be wasted.'

It could be a very long time before William gets the top job. His father, who will accede to the throne before him (no matter what opinion polls might say the public wants), is still waiting. And as the Queen celebrates her Diamond Jubilee in the rudest of health at the age of eighty-six, Charles, now sixty-three, looks like having to wait a while himself.

There is no knowing quite what the monarchy will look like in the future; or how it will be funded. It is something that Buckingham Palace and the Treasury discuss and something that the Prince of Wales gives thought to and has views about. William and Harry are not yet interested in the grand strategic plan—'Who would when you're trying to fly a helicopter in a force 10?' says one of the Household, who now spends most of his time pondering the subject. 'That'll come. They don't want to work out the shape of the monarchy in twenty-five years' time and what their children's role in it will be and that sort of thing, which, let's face it, is finger in the wind sort of stuff. They're buzzing with ideas about soldiers and veterans and, "What about asking BAFTA to put on a show for the Centrepoint kids, and what about getting Wellchild kids to go up Helvellyn [a fell in the Lake District] with Mountain Rescue?" These are the sort of things they come up with every day and it's huge fun.'

The only detail that is certain about the future is that if they have children, the eldest child will inherit the throne regardless of sex. The Queen was keen to see the ancient law of primogeniture repealed; also the law prohibiting anyone marrying a Roman Catholic to accede.

Everyone who knows Jamie Lowther-Pinkerton, without exception, says what an incredible mentor he has been for William and Harry. He has helped them both through some difficult years, and understood the importance of giving them space and allowing them to achieve their personal goals. He is as pleased as punch with the finished product, but would say, 'They are such cool guys, it's very difficult to go wrong with them. Prince Harry has his moments but even with old Harry and his wild moments, the guy's instincts are absolutely one hundred per cent brilliant. He just gets it; a very light finger on the tiller. People used to say to me, "You really must find something for young Harry to do." Now they say, "God, you've got to find something where the country can really capitalise on Harry," which is so great.'

'I don't think you can underestimate Jamie's importance in all of this,' says Julia Samuel. 'He has great vision and William trusts him. He's a brilliant combination of being tough as old boots because of the SAS, so he doesn't get scared and quite likes danger and intensity, but he can think laterally. He plans; it's like doing a campaign, every step ahead, which is what you need to keep someone secure. And he has a real genuine love for them, and I think the boys feel that. He's put down very good foundation stones for their professional public role and taught them how to think about things.'

Having put those foundations in place, those who know him well say that Jamie may shortly hand over the reins to someone else. 'He believes that after seven or eight years even the best person runs out of ideas, and whoever works for William and Harry needs to be at the top of his game. We have the most brilliant team here who can deal with the operational and tactical level, but you've got to maintain the focus at the strategic level because otherwise this thing will lose its potency. These guys will be so busy that they'll need somebody behind them just to say, "Is that the right route actually? I know you want to go down it, but have you thought how that might influence the project in the Foundation you've got going at the moment? Or aren't there lots of other people doing that? Is that something where you can really add value?" If you look at the Queen's reign, she's been sixty years on the throne and she's had eight private secretaries, and there's been a normal, natural friendly evolution of all those. That's one every seven or eight years. I think there's a bit of a revolving door thing here; you go in, do your bit and you come out again and the worst thing you can do is hang on, the worst. The person who comes next is going to have to be skilled at bureaucracy in the best sense of the word. Jamie would say that's simply not his game. His successor would have to be up to speed on the nuances of committees in Whitehall and know the corridors of power and how it all works—almost like a diplomat.'

Whoever takes over the job come the time, and whatever the monarchy looks like in twenty years' time, barring accidents, one thing is certain: the partnership that William and Harry have built up during Jamie's tenure is likely to be the linchpin for its future. Diana joked that Harry was 'the spare', but he won't be a spare languishing in the wings as spares in recent times have. Harry pulled a blinder on his Diamond Jubilee tour of the Caribbean in March. Portia Simpson Miller,

Jamaica's prime minister, who had announced she wanted to get rid of the Queen as head of state, 'was reduced to a blushing, hugging schoolgirl at her first meet-and-greet with the Ginger One,' said the *Daily Mail*. The paper called him 'the Royal Family's secret weapon'.

Confessing himself to be an amateur historian, Jamie is known to compare the Princes to the fourteenth-century heir and spare, the Black Prince and John of Gaunt. One of the team concurs, 'in that you've got a really trusted sibling who is incredibly complementary to you in character as well as in outlook and belief and ideals and values and that sort of thing, which Harry undoubtedly is with William, who can share a lot of the burden and can apply different skills and talents at a very high strategic level to some of the issues you're going to have to face. And there may be things that might not be quite appropriate for the top man to do but the one down could do.

'For instance, Prince Harry's clearly proven area of focus is disadvantaged, forgotten children around the world. He's magnificent with young children, not far short of brilliant—you can see a lot of his mother in that. As everyone recognises now, you've got a huge problem brewing with disaffected youth, right down to when they first get excluded from school at the age of five, and somebody has got to address that. In some ways it's much easier for somebody who's not elected, or politically driven—somebody who has continuity and empathy and no angle on it, which is one of the strengths of monarchy. Harry would be perfectly suited to take that burden, or share it with the King and his Queen, both internationally and domestically. He could take his passions to a strategic level. It could be linked to an international organisation like Save the Children or the Red Cross.

'The Princess Royal's model is an interesting one, where she has been closely involved with Save the Children and travels around the world in a very non post-Imperial way, being a fantastic ambassador. Extrapolate that perhaps a bit more, and put a statesmanlike ring to it, and that's where I could see Harry ending up. If Prince William as King has got a younger brother who is doing that sort of thing, it could only be to his advantage and to the advantage of the country—particularly since they get on so well.'

The current Household's vision is a long way into the future. Right now, both Princes are serving officers with careers of indeterminate length ahead of them, and both fit in royal duties, foreign tours, charitable appearances and their private lives around their jobs. William's profile is higher than his brother's at the moment because of the feel-good wedding and because Kate is glamorous and wears fabulous clothes and has finally filled the gap left by Diana. They are a golden couple who, as their tour of North America proved, have the world at their feet. They are global superstars; they are what every A-list celebrity dreams of. Their fame gives them power that opens wallets and doors, their presence brings a sprinkling of fairy dust to every gathering. But there are dangers. Fame is seductive—and destructive—as Diana discovered. It is also notoriously fickle and this couple needs to be opening wallets and doors and sprinkling fairy dust long after the A-listers have been passed over for younger models or have sunk into wrinkled retirement.

William genuinely has no interest in celebrity. His knows, rightly, that the spotlight is on him because of who he happens to be, which was an accident of birth. But he knows he can use it to the nation's advantage. He has many of the best qualities of both parents in him, but the person he most seems to model himself on is his grandmother.

'She cares not for celebrity, that's for sure,' he told Robert Hardman. 'That's not what monarchy's about. It's about setting examples. It's about doing one's duty as she would say. It's about using your position for the good. It's about serving the country and that really is the crux of it.'

William spoke to Robert for his biography of the Queen because she specifically asked him to; he hates talking about himself, but his observations were very illuminating. Particularly one about her succession at the age of twenty-five.

'Back then,' he said, 'there was a very different attitude to women. Being a young lady at twenty-five—stepping in to do a job which many men thought they could probably do better—it must have been very daunting. And I think there was extra pressure for her to perform. You see the pictures of her and she looks so incredibly natural in the role. She's calm, she's poised, she's elegant, she's graceful and she's all the things she needs to be at twenty-five. And you think how loads of twenty-five-year-olds—myself, my brother and lots of people included—didn't have anything like that. And we didn't have that extra pressure put on us at that age. It's amazing that she didn't crack. She just carried on and kept going. And that's the thing about her. You present a challenge in front of her and she'll climb it. And I think that to be doing that for sixty years—it's incredible.

'There's a serenity about her. But I think if you are of an age, you have a pretty old-fashioned faith, you do your best every day and say your prayers every night—well, if you're criticised for it, you're not going to get much better whatever you do. What's the point of worrying?

'For her, it must be a relief to know that she has furrowed her own path and that she's done that successfully and that the decisions she's made have turned out to be correct. You make it up a lot as you go along. So to be proven right, when it's your decision-making, gives you a lot of confidence. You realise that the role you're doing—you're doing it well; that you're making a difference. That's what's key. It's about making a difference for the country.'

My guess is that one day William's grandchild might say much the same about him.

# DIAMOND JUBILEE

The news that Kate was expecting a baby, announced at the beginning of December 2012, was long awaited by the British public; but things were not as straightforward as everyone might have wished—and the news was temporarily overshadowed by tragedy. She was less than eight weeks pregnant when she made the announcement—a good month earlier than she would have chosen. The reason for going public so prematurely was that she had been admitted to hospital, suffering from acute morning sickness and dehydration, a rare condition that affects only one per cent of pregnant women called *hyperemesis gravidarum*. There was no way her admission to hospital could be kept under wraps, and she and William felt that while breaking the news before the twelve-week stage was risky, it was preferable to inevitable speculation about her health.

She had been spending the weekend with her parents in Bucklebury when the sickness became acute and her condition potentially serious. Two days earlier, she had been sick but not so sick she needed to change her plans. She had visited her former preparatory school, St Andrew's, in Pangbourne, to open a new hockey pitch, saying in her speech that her years at the school had been some of the happiest of her life. From the athletic way she wielded a hockey stick, albeit in Alexander McQueen and high-heeled boots, no one would have guessed she was unwell, but by the end of Sunday lunch she was badly dehydrated and was admitted that afternoon to King Edward VII Hospital in Central London.

*Hyperemesis gravidarum* is not generally life-threatening, but it's no fun for that one per cent who suffer. It causes relentless nausea and vomiting, which can quickly lead to dehydration and malnutrition, and in some cases it lasts throughout the pregnancy and involves repeated treatment in hospital. Kate was comparatively lucky, and after a few days she was sent home with doctors' orders for complete rest.

While she was still in hospital, however, a couple of young Australian radio presenters, Mel Grieg and Mike Christian, from 2Day FM in Sydney, made a hoax telephone call to King Edward VII's pretending to be the Queen and Prince of Wales inquiring about Kate's welfare. It was 5.30 in the morning in London and, because the switchboard was unmanned at that time of day, the call was taken by a nurse. Despite their giggles and absurdly plummy accents, Jacintha Saldanha took the pair at face value, and put the call through to a colleague who was on Kate's ward. The DJs had expected to be rumbled at the outset but instead, Jacintha's colleague gave them a genuine update on the Duchess's condition which was broadcast live across New South Wales.

What started out as a harmless prank turned into a catastrophe for which they were widely condemned. Although the hospital attached no blame to Jacintha Saldanha, and William and Kate made no complaint about the incident, this 46-year-old, Indian-born mother of two killed herself three days later in her nurses' quarters nearby, leaving three suicide notes. It later transpired that she had made two suicide attempts earlier in the year, while visiting her homeland; but it could not have been more tragic.

St James's Palace immediately released a statement expressing how 'deeply saddened' the Duke and Duchess of Cambridge had been to learn of Jacintha's death. 'They were looked after so wonderfully well by everybody at King Edward VII Hospital,' they said, 'and their thoughts and prayers are with Jacintha's family, friends and colleagues at this very sad time.'

The excitement at the news of Kate's pregnancy

brought 2012, a very good year for Britain, to a very happy conclusion. Despite the continuing economic situation and widespread hardship, the country rallied for the Queen's Diamond Jubilee. It was another excuse for giant parties and celebrations—just as William and Kate's wedding had been the year before—for strangers to connect with strangers and communities to pull together. In London, people again took to the streets in their hundreds of thousands, undeterred by everything the unseasonal June weather threw at them. They painted Union Jacks on their faces and wrapped themselves in flags; they camped, they waved banners and flags, they sang and cheered and partied to the rooftops; and their goodwill and affection for their monarch of sixty years—or 'Elizabeth the Great,' as one banner had it—was palpable.

There were four days of celebrations, beginning at the Epsom Derby in Surrey on June 2. As she is a passionate horserace-goer and bloodstock expert, it is one of the highlights of the Queen's calendar and was the perfect way to kick off these special celebrations. She and the Duke of Edinburgh arrived to an enthusiastic welcome and a rendition of 'God Save the Queen'—the first of many she would hear over the next three days—sung by classical singer Katherine Jenkins. Overhead, everyone was treated to a startling display from the Red Devils Parachute Team, who fell from the sky with giant Union Jack flags.

Sunday saw the largest river pageant ever staged in the world (according to the Guinness Book of Records) and the most spectacular to be seen on the Thames for 350 years. A thousand boats, from tugs, barges, steamers and pleasure cruisers to dragon boats and kayaks, slowly made their way through driving rain from Albert Bridge to Tower Bridge, a distance of seven miles. Amongst them was a collection of small ships used in the evacuation of stranded troops from the beaches of Dunkirk in 1940, and leading the procession, a £1 million 94 ft royal rowbarge, the *Gloriana*, specially commissioned for the Diamond Jubilee, the first to be built in over a century. It was powered by eighteen oarsmen including two Olympic gold medallists, Sir Steve Redgrave and Matthew Pinsent, three ex-servicemen who lost limbs in Afghanistan and Iraq, and the British Paralympic rowing hopeful Pamela Relph.

In the midst of the flotilla, following on from the rowing boats, was the Royal barge, the *Spirit of Chartwell*, lavishly and regally decorated in red, gold and purple, with ten thousand flowers from the royal estates. William and Kate joined the Queen, the Duke of Edinburgh, the Prince of Wales and Duchess of Cornwall, and Harry, while other members of the Royal Family and VIPs, including the Middleton family, were accommodated in other boats. The weather was miserable and prevented a 'Diamond Nine' flypast of Royal Navy helicopters led by a Swordfish bi-plane built in 1934, which was to have been a spectacular finale to the pageant. Looking at the Queen and her party, smiling broadly and enjoying the feast of sights and sounds, one would never have guessed how cold they all were. At one point, the Queen, sensing that her grandchildren were frozen, turned and said, 'Look warm! Wave and smile!'

And so they did. They stood out on deck for the full four hours and more, marvelling at everything around them, chatting cheerfully and waving at the cheering crowds on the river banks. Spectators were crammed onto every balcony, window and rooftop facing the river, most of them waving flags, and were said to number a million.

When, after nearly four hours, the barge pulled up and waited for forty-five minutes to allow the rest of the procession to pass it, everyone dashed below deck to warm up and revive themselves with a drink. Just as William was putting the glass to his lips, the music from a choir filtered down the stairs, at which the Queen's face lit up and she said, 'We've got to go hear this' and raced up on deck. Reluctantly, the younger members of the family, frozen to the bone, abandoned their glasses and followed their grandparents back into the pouring rain.

The following evening was party time. The Mall at the front of Buckingham Palace, one of the grandest thoroughfares in London, and the parks to either side were transformed into a vast open-air concert venue, teeming with humanity. Waving Union Jacks, people laughed, danced and sang along to the greatest collection of superstars spanning sixty years of popular music and entertainment that ever gathered under one sky. Amongst others there was Robbie Williams, Jessie J, will.i.am, Kylie Minogue, Annie Lennox and a quartet of knights: Cliff Richard, Tom Jones, Elton John and Paul McCartney, also Dame Shirley Bassey. There was an orchestra, the Kenyan Slum Drummers and the African Children's Choir; opera singer Alfie Boe, pianist Lang Lang; and comedians Lenny Henry and Jimmy Carr, who quipped that the Queen's sixty-year reign should serve as a warning that 'you've got to plan for your future and you've got to get a pension. She's eighty-six and she's had to rent out her driveway to Gary Barlow!' Gary Barlow, the singer from Take That, had masterminded the show and co-written, along with Sir Andrew Lloyd-Webber, the Jubilee song, 'Sing', that was the highlight of the evening. It was inspired by the Queen's love of the Commonwealth and performed by the Military Wives Choir and musicians that Gary Barlow had found on a trip to Kenya and other Commonwealth countries. It included a fourteen-year-old soloist called Lydia, whose voice sent shivers up the spine.

This massive extravaganza culminated in the Queen, who had arrived half way through and was wearing earplugs, taking to the stage alongside all the performers. Following a heart-warming tribute from the Prince of Wales, she lit the last of two thousand, two hundred and twelve beacons to have been lit across the United Kingdom in celebration of the Diamond Jubilee. The evening ended with a spectacular firework display that could have been seen and heard from many miles away.

'Your Majesty . . . Mummy,' Prince Charles began, to roars of approval from the crowd. 'I was three when my grandfather George VI died and suddenly, unexpectedly, you and my father's lives were irrevocably changed when you were only twenty-six. So as a nation this is our opportunity to thank you and my father for always being there for us. For inspiring us with your selfless duty and service and for making us proud to be British.' There were once again huge cheers from the crowd and from members of the Royal Family.

But that evening his father, always such a familiar sight by the Queen's side, was absent. To universal shock and dismay, the Duke of Edinburgh, just days short of his ninety-first birthday, was in hospital suffering from a bladder infection. He had unexpectedly fallen ill during the afternoon at Windsor Castle, possibly as a result of four hours in the cold and wet during the river pageant. A doctor had been called and he had been taken swiftly by ambulance to King Edward VII Hospital in Central London. This was the second time in a matter of months that he had been hospitalized. At Christmas it was a heart problem, and he had spent four nights in Papworth Hospital in Cambridge, where he had surgery to clear a blocked coronary artery.

William and Kate were having portrait photographs taken for their Foundation when the news come through, and William immediately cancelled the session, saying he must go to Buckingham Palace right away to be with the Queen. He was extremely upset and spent a good half hour with his grandmother before the start of the concert.

During his tribute from on stage, the Prince of Wales said, 'The only sad thing about this evening is that my father cannot be here with us because unfortunately he's been taken unwell. Ladies and gentlemen, if we shout loud enough he might just hear us in hospital.' At this the assembled multitude roared their approval, stamped their feet and chanted, 'Philip, Philip.' The shout-out had been William and Harry's idea.

The Duke's absence was felt all the more keenly on the final day of the celebrations when the Queen and other members of the family attended a national service of thanksgiving at St Paul's

Cathedral, lunch at Westminster Hall and an open carriage procession back to Buckingham Palace. The monarch struck a very lonely figure as she walked up the aisle of the Cathedral on her own, followed by Charles and Camilla, then William and Kate, then Harry. It was a stark reminder that the Queen and the Duke of Edinburgh will not be here for ever; but that there are others that will, in the fullness of time, follow in her footsteps.

That message was reinforced by their appearance on the balcony. For the first time, it was not the familiar scene of the extended Royal Family. Just six people stood on that vast balcony overlooking the Mall as an RAF flypast and a gun salute from the Queen's Guard brought a thrilling climax to four days of festivities. The Queen was flanked by her son and two grandsons, and Camilla and Kate. No explanation was offered by Buckingham Palace for this departure from the normal line-up, but the directive had come from the Queen herself, and no one was in any doubt that we were looking at the future: a scaled-down monarchy with a clear and secure line of succession.

The Queen waved and smiled broadly throughout the appearance, visibly delighted by the rapturous response from the throng of well-wishers below. While the Queen's Guard fired their rifles in a rare 'feu de joie,' the Band of the Irish Guards played the national anthem and everyone sang at the tops of their voices and waved their flags enthusiastically. Finally, the Queen's Guard gave three cheers, and each time, his 'hip, hip' was greeted with a deafening roar of 'hooray' that echoed down the Mall. It had been a triumphant and at times electrifying few days, and an unparalleled endorsement of the monarchy.

# LONDON 2012

Throughout her Diamond Jubilee tour, the Queen was met by ecstatic crowds. She confined her own travels to the British Isles, while the younger members of the family did the long-haul journeys to the Commonwealth on her behalf, but on several occasions the younger members joined her in the UK. She took Camilla and Kate to visit Fortnum and Mason's, the exclusive department store in Piccadilly, where all three seemed to be having very good fun. They were each given a Fortnums' wicker hamper that, winningly for three such dog lovers, included a pack of dog biscuits. Kate also travelled with the Queen to Leicester, where they were seen happily laughing together; but in Nottingham William came too— the first time the three had ever carried out an engagement of this sort together. The Duke of Edinburgh should have been with them but was recovering after his spell in hospital. William and Kate drove by car to Nottingham, where about twenty thousand people had turned out to see them, and the Queen arrived on the Royal Train. While they were waiting at the station, chatting to dignitaries on the platform, William called over to a group of people waving flags on the opposite side of the tracks, 'Are you waiting for the same train we are?'

It set the tone for a very relaxed and jolly day and after lunch, the three of them went to a Fields in Trust event at Vernon Park a few miles out of the city centre. William, as Patron of the Queen Elizabeth II Fields Challenge (to protect 2,012 open spaces as a memorial to the Jubilee) was due to make a speech and start a children's obstacle race, and the Queen was to unveil a plaque for the newly protected park. The good people of Nottingham, however, decided they didn't have a good enough view of the Royal trio from where they had been told to stand and so, taking matters into their own hands, simply started walking forwards towards the pavilion where the Royal party were sitting. Suddenly thousands of people were closing in, much to the anxiety of the Duke and Duchesses' security detail, but the crowds stopped, respectfully, about twenty feet from the pavilion and were no threat. William had to fight his way through them to get onto the field to fire the starting pistol and, according to one of their aides, 'the Queen was doubled up with laughter.'

The Queen seemed to have been more relaxed in

public during her Diamond Jubilee year, and shown more of her personality, than she had for the previous sixty years of her reign. Never more so than during the opening of the London 2012 Olympic Games on July 27, when she stunned and delighted thousands of people at the newly built Olympic Stadium at Stratford in east London, and the billion estimated to have been watching the event on television around the world. It was a spectacular, dizzying ceremony, three hours of glorious theatre and music, devised by the film director, Danny Boyle. In the midst of the show, called Isles of Wonder, which followed the progress of the British Isles from the early 19th century through the industrial revolution to the present day, the giant screens throughout the stadium suddenly cut to Daniel Craig, as 007, arriving at Buckingham Palace and making his way along the red-carpeted corridors to the Queen's study. Looking up from her desk, she turned to him and said cooly, 'Good evening, Mr Bond' before getting up and leaving the palace with him, Corgies at her heels, and heading towards a waiting helicopter. Moments later, there was the roar of a Westland hovering overhead and a figure, dressed identically to the Queen, jumped out and parachuted into the arena (closely followed by Mr Bond) to rapturous and incredulous gasps, not least from members of her own family who were as astonished and delighted as everyone else. No one knew, save the Queen's closest aides; not even the International Olympic Committee was in on the spoof.

Doom-mongers had forecast an organizational disaster, but the sceptics were proved wrong. The Olympic Games and the Paralympic Games that followed were a resounding success and generated extraordinary goodwill, not least of all, surprisingly, towards the Royal Family, who knew from the start, instinctively, that the whole thing was going to be a resounding success. The Queen's willingness to be part of such an elaborate stunt at the age of eighty-five won her nothing but praise and admiration; the Princess Royal, president of the British Olympic Association, was hailed by sports minister Hugh Robertson as 'one of the great unsung heroes of this whole process'; and Zara Phillips, her daughter, one-time Sports Personality of the Year, winning silver as part of the British equestrian team, became the first member of the Royal Family to win an Olympic medal. But William, Kate and Harry, as ambassadors for Team GB, had a significant part to play too. They were at the events day after day, most of the time dressed in the Team GB kit, supporting the athletes.

William had been cautious at the start. 'He didn't want to be seen to be freeloading when others were struggling to get tickets,' explains one of his aides, 'but he realizes that part of his role as a member of the Royal Family is to celebrate British and other Commonwealth success, and the reception he and others got from the public was so warm and welcoming that any reservations he had soon disappeared. It seemed to be a great fillip to the athletes that he, Kate, and Harry were there. They went up to the lounge where the athletes were relaxing and either commiserated with them or gave them a pat on the back. They really threw themselves into it. They love sport anyway and know a lot about it and who the players are; and they ended up seeing a lot more than they ever anticipated they would want to see.'

They just turned up at events and often sat in ordinary seats, or with the athletes; and they didn't stand on their dignity. At the velodrome one evening, rather than disturb other spectators, William gave Kate a helping hand so she could climb over the seats in the row behind to get to their own. So approving were the crowds that they started applauding the pair when they arrived at an event and applauding them when they left.

William and Harry were ecstatic when the male gymnasts won a bronze medal—the first Olympic medal for a British gymnastics team in a century—and William and Kate were so excited when Sir Chris Hoy, leading the men's spring cycling team, won the fifth gold medal of his career that they leapt from their seats and hugged and kissed each other with abandon. William was frightened they would be caught on a 'kiss cam.' 'I was absolutely dreading they were going to come and show myself and my wife and that would have been very embarrassing.'

They were rooting for British swimmers, British rowers, for British beach volleyball and hockey players; at the tennis they sat on the edge of their seats as Andy Murray fought his way through to the semi-finals, and they were there to cheer on their cousin, Zara, in the three-day eventing.

In an interview with the BBC sports commentator, Sue Barker, both Princes praised everyone involved in making the Games so slick and friendly, including the thousands of volunteers, the military, and buzz of the British public who have been getting behind the teams. After the 'wow factor' of the opening ceremony, William admitted that, 'Emotionally, our favourite moment of the Olympics so far was obviously Zara winning her medal, as we have that family connection. I got completely carried away in the moment. To actually be there when she got a medal and they've done so well as a team, and to see Team GB do brilliant so early on in the Olympics, I had goose-bumps on the back of my neck and I got far too carried away.'

They admitted their grandmother's stunt had been a surprise. William said: 'To be honest, we were kept completely in the dark about it, that's how big the secret was.' Then joked, 'She did such a good performance that she has now been asked to star in the next Bond film.'

In fact, there had been a rumour circulating at a family supper at Buckingham Palace the evening of the opening ceremony, after the reception for heads of state, and before they all made their way to the stadium. The rumour was that the Queen was going to jump out of a helicopter, but the idea was so outrageous and unthinkable that it was instantly dismissed. There had also been a story, some months earlier, that James Bond had been seen going into the Palace and that he'd been knighted by the Queen, but the family knew that this would never have happened and dismissed it. So that night, the surprise for them all was absolute.

'They thought it was absolutely amazing; they were absolutely blown away by it,' says one of their aides. 'The Queen's aides were on tenterhooks all evening because, of course, they had no idea how it was going to go down; it was a very unusual thing for the Queen to do and, remember, it was all done several months in advance. It's easy in hindsight so see how wonderful the Olympics were and it was all a great success, but even a month before the opening there was no considered sense that it was going to be a success. There was a lot of nervousness; but if ever there was a time to do it, it was then, in that most jubilant of jubilee years when the Queen was riding on such a high.'

# BREACH OF PRIVACY

A couple of days after attending the opening of the Paralympics, at the beginning of September, William and Kate flew to the South of France for a long weekend at David Linley's holiday home, Chateau d'Autet. Set amid six hundred and forty acres of woodland, near the medieval village of Viens in Provence, it is a former hunting lodge, where they had stayed before. It was ideal: sunny, comfortable and very private. The perfect place to spend lazy days swimming, reading and relaxing by the pool.

They had thought long and hard about going away while the Paralympics were on, afraid that it might be seen as disrespectful, but these few days were their only opportunity to have a holiday together for the rest of the year. The following week they were off on a hectic Diamond Jubilee tour of Southeast Asia and the South Pacific, and after that, William would be straight back to work.

The weather was glorious and the mini-break was everything they might have hoped for. What they didn't know, until they were in Malaysia a week later, was that a photographer had spied on them through the trees from a spot on the narrow winding road, half a mile away, and sold a series of intimate pictures to the French magazine *Closer*. They showed the pair sunbathing by the pool, Prince William in swimming trunks and his wife in nothing more than bikini bottoms.

The first person to get the news was their Press Secretary. He was staying in a separate hotel in Kuala Lumpur and immediately alerted their Private Secretary, who told the couple over breakfast. None of them, at that point, had seen the photos. William and Kate were clearly annoyed, but they didn't immediately appreciate the extent of their personal violation and were surprisingly sanguine about it as they carried out the morning's programme. Their hosts would never have guessed there was something wrong. But by lunchtime, the magazine had hit the streets of Paris and the photographs were scanned and emailed out to Malaysia.

It was only then that William and Kate realized the full extent of the intrusion. 'It was like a real punch in the stomach for both of them,' said one of their team. 'It was the angriest I've ever seen him. It was almost the angriest I've ever seen any human being, actually. It brought back home to him everything his mother had had to put up with. He was upset on his wife's behalf; and the Duchess was upset for him and upset that she'd got herself into that situation.'

The statement they issued that afternoon was as strongly worded as anything to have been issued by St James's Palace. It said,

'Their Royal Highnesses have been hugely

saddened to learn that a French publication and a photographer have invaded their privacy in such a grotesque and totally unjustifiable manner.

'The incident is reminiscent of the worst excesses of the press and paparazzi during the life of Diana, Princess of Wales, and all the more upsetting to the Duke and Duchess for being so.

'Their Royal Highnesses had every expectation of privacy in the remote house. It is unthinkable that anyone should take such photographs, let alone publish them.'

And then, as might have been expected from William, the statement went on to say, 'Officials acting on behalf of their Royal Highnesses are consulting with lawyers to consider what options may be available to the Duke and Duchess.'

This wasn't the first time in recent months that he had been provoked. Photographs of them holding hands on honeymoon in the Seychelles had been published in *Paris Match*. The British press, post-Leverson, had turned them down and also steered clear of a photo of the Royal pair walking their dog, Lupo, near their home in Anglesey. In both instances their aides had sent strongly worded letters to editors reminding them of the couple's right to privacy, but there had been no direct action from the couple themselves. They had been upset about the previous photographs, but this collection took the breach of privacy to an entirely different level.

William immediately discussed it with his advisors—and was pleased, as they all were, to have the reassuring presence of Sir David Manning on the trip. William also talked it through with Kate, and they were as one in the decision to take legal action. Kate was calm, as she always is, yet steely about the situation; William was typically level-headed and cautious about doing anything, but very stubborn and immoveable once he has determined a course of action.

Having made their decision and drafted their statement, said an aide, 'it was almost as if they collected themselves and got on with the rest of the day's events. They were there on behalf of the Queen and there was absolutely no way they were going to let her down and let this get in the way of what they were doing publicly there. I think they did themselves proud. The Duke said, "I want the Queen to be watching this at home and thinking, 'Well done; shoulders back, chest out, get on with it.'" They were so professional, and having seen the photographs, some of which were never published and were even more intrusive, they went out and were charming, laughing with people, relaxed, and the people they were with wouldn't have had a clue anything was going on.' They attended a garden party given in their honor by the British High Commissioner and stayed longer than they needed to. 'There was no sense of drama or panic at all, they were very contained in their anger, and they took a decision very early on that they were going to take action against this guy. He had crossed a red line. I say "guy," but at that point they didn't know whether it was one or two or more photographers. They were going to go after him and his publishers. They knew the photographs were going to go around the world, but they weren't going to chase after them like possessed lunatics. They were going to be dignified in what they did.'

The media, accompanying them on the tour, reported something a little different. The *Telegraph* reported that, 'as they boarded their plane at Kuala Lumpur airport, bound for the tour's next leg in Borneo, his thunderous mood was tangible. Teeth clenched and avoiding all eye contact with journalists, he ushered his wife, as quickly as diplomacy allowed, through the assembled dignitaries gathered to bid them farewell. Aware of her husband's barely concealed fury, the Duchess laid a placating hand on his back.'

Once in the air, however, according to one of those travelling with them, 'he was back to his old self, relaxed and joking and seemed to have rid the whole affair from his system very quickly. They arrived on the island of Borneo to a joyful, loud musical reception, with lots of dancing which was great for them; they really relaxed.' The next day, standing at the base of a tree deep in the rainforest, waiting to be hoisted up 130ft into the jungle canopy with his wife beside him, William turned to the small group of media. With a wicked smile, he asked, 'I don't suppose any journalists would like to go on up ahead of us?' The laughter continued when he pointed out the potential for 'wardrobe malfunctions' he was about to endure for the sake of a photo opportunity.

'Given the spotlight they had been under the day before, you couldn't have devised a better spot to put them in anywhere on earth the next day,' said one of their team. 'It was beautiful and they love that sort of environment; both of them love it. It was virgin forest as well, so unlike anywhere else in the world, just perfect for them, very quiet, relaxed, no one around and very few press.' While the Duke and Duchess were examining ants under a microscope, Kate's Assistant Private Secretary, Rebecca Deacon, showed one of her colleagues, who has a serious phobia about snakes, a photograph on her mobile phone of a cobra's head, pickled in a jar which she'd seen in a laboratory there. She knew about his phobia but hadn't realized how extreme it was. His instinctive reaction, in his terror, was to shout out an obscenity. His response rang out and William and Kate turned round as if to say, 'why on earth has our Press Secretary just told our Private Secretary what she can do with herself?' He had to leave the room, he was so mortified, and was convinced he was going to get the sack. He stood outside thinking, 'Oh my God, I can't believe I've done that at a public engagement,' and the two of them came out and the Duchess had her arm around the Prince and was kind of patting him, consoling him on the head, and I thought, it's obviously just hit them, they're really upset. And then I realized the Duke was crying with laughter, it was one of the funniest things he'd ever seen, and he said to us afterwards, any tension he had in his body from the day before evaporated and the rest of the tour, you wouldn't know anything bad had happened to them. 'I've never seen them quite so happy, relaxed, enjoying themselves. The pictures of them dancing to this amazing music they put on for them in Tuvalu . . . I've never seen the two of them like it. This is conjecture here, but if you'd asked the Duke what is one of the worse things that can happen to your wife, this would have been it. And it had happened and they'd survived it, and they'd been so dignified. They were such professionals and we were all so, so proud of them.'

The French court banned *Closer* from selling or re-using the photographs and demanded that the original images be returned to the Duke and Duchess within twenty-four hours or face a daily fine of 10,000 euros. William and Kate also filed a separate criminal complaint under France's strict privacy laws. Initially there was no name on their complaint because the magazine had refused to name the photographer, but the pair refused to give up. In April 2013, after six months of persistent pressure, the boss of the company that publishes *Closer*, Ernesto Mauri, and a local French photographer, Valerie Suau, were under formal investigation for invasion of privacy.

Their persistence is maybe a marker for the future; that no intrusion into their child's privacy will go unpunished.

# THIRD IN LINE

HRH Prince George Alexander Louis of Cambridge was born at 4.24 on the afternoon of Monday July 22 in the private Lindo Wing of St Mary's Hospital in Paddington, weighing a healthy 8lb 6oz. The announcement that the Duchess 'was safely delivered of a son,' came four hours later at 8.29, delivered by the couple's new Press Secretary, Ed Perkins, to the hundreds of news crews, journalists and photographers, penned into enclosures opposite the entrance to the Lindo Wing. The country was in the grip of Royal baby fever; also a rare heatwave and that Monday had been the hottest day of the year, a sweltering 33 degrees in Central London; the media had been rooted to their patch of pavement for the last three weeks, desperately waiting for something to tell their readers and viewers that was not just wild speculation, guesswork or waffle. Finally, the news that the Duchess had been admitted to the hospital came at 7.28 that morning; she and William had arrived by car shortly before 6.00 and had slipped in through a door in a side street, accompanied by their protection officers. For the next thirteen hours, until Ed Perkins appeared with something concrete, the nation had waited on tenterhooks, and the 24-hour rolling news presenters, so close but still so far, had resorted to filming each other. Something momentous was going on inside the building but for the time being there was no news to report and nothing new to say.

The original plan had been for the birth to be announced in the traditional manner, as William's own birth had been, with a notice posted on the forecourt of Buckingham Palace, but mindful that the newspapers were holding their front pages for the news, a decision was taken to speed up the process. Thus came the facts: 'The Duke of Cambridge was present for the birth,' Her Royal Highness and her child were both doing well and would remain in hospital overnight, and both families had been informed and were delighted by the news. And, as if anyone had needed to be reminded, 'The baby is third in the line of Succession after His Royal Highness The Prince of Wales and His Royal Highness The Duke of Cambridge.'

William and Kate had spent the precious hours between their baby's birth and the announcement, alone with him, enjoying having him to themselves before the inevitable and no doubt daunting obligation to share him with the world; and telephoning their families. William's first call was to the Queen, who later said, 'The first born is very special.' He then spoke to his father and his brother. Prince Charles, who was on a visit to Yorkshire with Camilla, was the only member of the family to be out and about in public on the Tuesday, and was visibly elated by the news. He said he and his wife were 'overjoyed' and 'thrilled. Grandparenthood is a unique moment in anyone's life, as countless kind people have told me in recent months, so I am enormously proud and happy to be a grandfather for the first time and we are eagerly looking forward to seeing the baby in the near future.' William later released a statement himself, saying, 'We could not be happier.'

While messages of congratulations began to pour in from celebrities, church leaders, politicians and statesmen from across the world—starting with the Obamas, who wished 'them all the happiness and blessings parenthood brings'— William and Kate settled down with their baby to a night at the hospital. And Britain, parts of the Commonwealth and a surprising number of other countries too, that had been talking about little else for weeks, started cracking open the champagne. All but the most curmudgeonly seemed to have a smile on their face. The following morning's newspapers reflected the mood, most of them devoting several pages plus special supplements to the news. The *Sun*, famous for its witty headlines, changed its masthead for the day to The Son. Apocalyptic thunder storms were forecast but they were no match for the noise of a forty-one-gun salute fired by the King's Troop Royal Horse Artillery in Green Park, the Royal Artillery Company's sixty-two-gun salvo from the Tower of London and three-hours of peeling bells at Westminster Abbey. Fountains and prominent buildings in the capitol and across the Commonwealth turned blue, and before the Changing of the Guard at Buckingham Palace, the Guardsmen played 'Congratulations'. Thousands of people had flocked to the Palace to see the official notice of the birth for themselves—forming, in true British fashion, an orderly, if very long, queue. The notice, written on crested Buckingham Palace notepaper and displayed on an easel in the forecourt, said, 'Her Royal Highness The Duchess of Cambridge was safely delivered of a son at 4.24pm today. Her Royal Highness and her child are both doing well.' It was signed and dated by the Duchess's medical team: Mr Marcus Setchell, Surgeon-Gynaecologist, Mr Guy Thorpe-Beeston, Obstetrician and Dr

Sunit Godambe, Consultant Neonatologist at St Mary's Hospital.

At 11.55 on that Tuesday—after what seemed like a very long morning for those who had camped out at the hospital—William and Kate put out another statement. 'We would like to thank the staff at the Lindo Wing and the whole hospital for the tremendous care the three of us have received. We know it has been a very busy period for the hospital and we would like to thank everyone—staff, patients and visitors—for their understanding during this time.'

Did that mean they would be leaving soon? The media were very much hoping so; this was the picture and the story they had waited so interminably for; but they were disappointed. There wasn't even a visitor to break the monotony. Then shortly after 3.00, some excitement. A black taxi drew up carrying Carole and Michael Middleton. About forty-five minutes later the new grandparents came out beaming, Carole saying of her first cuddle, 'Amazing; it's all coming back. They are both doing really well and we are so thrilled.' The baby was 'absolutely beautiful,' the parents were coping 'fabulously', and no, she had not suggested a name, 'Absolutely not, but thank you.'

Next to arrive were Charles and Camilla, whose limousine pulled up two hours later. They had been on their way from Yorkshire to Wales for a further day of engagements and taken a last minute decision to divert to London. While still in Yorkshire, Camilla had said, 'It's very exciting and it's wonderful for the grandfather—he's brilliant with children.' They too stayed for about forty-five minutes, during which three future kings were in the same room for the first time in more than a hundred years of British royal history; and they too emerged beaming. While Camilla jumped straight into the waiting car, Charles was happy to share his excitement. The baby was 'Marvelous, absolutely marvelous,' he said. 'You wait and see—you'll see in a minute.'

It was the first indication that the long wait might be nearing a close. Finally, at 7.15 that evening, the trio appeared to a mad frenzy of flashbulbs and deafening cheers, with their son cradled in his mother's arms. She was wearing a blue and white polka dot Jenny Packham dress, he was in an open-necked blue and white striped shirt and the baby was swaddled in a white shawl. Kate looked radiant and amazingly calm, as did William. The pair were clearly feeling euphoric. They stood for a moment or two on the steps to the hospital smiling and waving; Kate then carefully handed the baby over to William and they walked towards the crowds and seemed happy to answer questions fired at them. 'He's got a good pair of lungs on him, that's for sure,' said William. 'He's a big boy, he's quite heavy. We're still working on a name so we'll have that as soon as we can. It's the first time that we've seen him really, so we're having a proper chance to catch up.' Kate said, 'It's very emotional, it's such a special time. I think any parent will know what this feeling feels like.' William concurred, 'It's very special.' Would it be George, someone asked? William laughed. 'Wait and see, wait and see . . .' (It was in the early evening of the following day that his names were announced: George Alexander Louis.) William was typically jovial. 'He's got her looks, fortunately,' he said. 'No no, I'm not sure about that,' said Kate. Nodding to his son's covering of fine dark hair, he added, 'He's got way more than me, thank God.' How about nappy-changing someone asked? 'We've done that already,' said William breezily. 'He's done the first one already,' she added. 'He was very good.' William confirmed that the birth was overdue. 'It was,' he said, 'and I'll remind him of his tardiness when he's a bit older because I know how long you've all been sat out here. Hopefully the hospital and you guys can all go back to normal now and we're going to look after him.'

They retreated inside for a few minutes and then reemerged with their son in a baby car seat which William strapped into the back of a waiting Range Rover while Kate got into the back seat alongside him. William then jumped into the driving seat, his protection officer beside him and with more smiles and waves they were off to Kensington Palace, where Kate's sister, Pippa, and her boyfriend were waiting to greet them.

When Diana was due to give birth to William at the same hospital wing thirty-one years earlier, she had misled the public into thinking her due date was her own birthday, July 1, so when she and Charles made the dash to the hospital at 5 am on the morning of June 21, there were neither photographers nor well wishers waiting.

Thirty one years on, the media had been determined not to be duped a second time. The Palace had said the baby was due in the middle of July but someone, somewhere started a rumour that July 13 was the date. The panic started, and the world's media flocked in their hundreds to Paddington, just to be on the safe side, two weeks in advance of that date. They staked out good vantage points for their ladders and equipment and set up camp on the pavement opposite the Lindo Wing, in the normally quiet road that runs along the back of the hospital. And as the longest heatwave in seven years left them sweltering, two weeks turned into three and still they sat there, day after boring day, and waited.

Meanwhile, Kate had kept a low profile. She had last been seen in public at the Trooping the Colour in June and since then, she had divided her time between their cottage at Kensington Palace and her parents' house in Bucklebury. Last year the Middletons had moved into a Georgian manor house in the village which is bigger, has more land and is more secluded, than their previous house, and therefore more secure. While William was on duty in Anglesey, he had had a small helicopter standing by, lent to him by a friend, to whisk him to London should Kate suddenly go into labour, but he couldn't and didn't put life on hold. The weekend before George's birth, he was calmly playing polo in charity matches alongside his brother, the first, on the Saturday, in Kent, sixty miles from London, the other in Cirencester, a hundred miles away. For all the calm, there were contingency plans in place to get him to Paddington on a sixpence if the call came through, but it never did. It so happened that he was on leave in the days before the birth and having been at Bucklebury, they headed to London less than a week before Kate went into labour.

For all William's modernity and use of social media, he has more than a streak of the traditional in him. The news of his engagement first broke on Twitter, but he had felt that the birth of the third in line to the throne was a rather different matter and had asked his team to find out how the news of his own birth had been handled so that he could emulate it. Hence the easel at Buckingham Palace although the timing made it preferable on the day to announce the news verbally and electronically first. All along he had been wanting to preserve as much of the magic as possible; and to juggle what for him and Kate was a very private and personal event, with the historical importance of this baby and the entirely justifiable public interest in it.

Home at Kensington Palace was still the little two-bedroom cottage, where the next morning, the Queen went to visit her great-grandson. She had told a guest at a reception at Buckingham Palace the night before that she was 'thrilled' about the baby and certainly seemed so. 'The first born is very special,' she had said.

Their staff had already moved to their new offices at Kensington Palace but their own apartment, 1A, Princess Margaret's former home, which needed extensive renovation, would not be ready until the autumn. By that time, William will have completed the final months of his tour of duty at Anglesey. After months of indecision about his future, whether to leave the Armed Forces and take up Royal duties full time, or sign up for another three years, he had finally opted to stay. Rather than continuing with Search and Rescue, which would mean another remote location, possibly Lossiemouth in Scotland, it seems probable that he will return to his regiment, the Blues and Royals and possibly join the Cavalry division at Knightsbridge Barracks. It would be close to home and allow him more time with his family and to be the hands-on father that he would like.

Charles doted on his sons but he didn't spend enough time with them. They adore him and they enjoy a very easy relationship with him nowadays with plenty of banter and teasing, but Charles didn't get the work/life balance right when they were growing up. He ensured that excellent people were in place to look after William and Harry and those people remain close friends, but however good, other people are no substitute for the real thing. William may very well want to do things differently.

His parents had been determined that he should have a normal childhood and it was certainly more normal than his father's but it was still unmistakably royal. Sadly, as it turned out, it was also chaotic and traumatic. William is unlikely to want for his own son the experience of growing up in the nursery, as he did, where he ate, played and slept; in homes run by liveried butlers, footmen, valets, housekeepers and cooks. Kate's upbringing, of course, was normal, albeit privileged. It was also happy and secure and that is what he will want, above all, for his own child.

In Anglesey they looked after themselves, with no more than a cleaning lady to help; and so far the only staff to have been taken on in preparation for the move to the new apartment, is a housekeeper with a very flexible job description. The chances are she will be asked to walk the dog and mind the baby from time to time, as well as polishing the silver and organizing receptions. They did not take on a maternity nurse and have no plans to have a full-time nanny, at least for the time being. That may have to change, of course, when Kate goes back to work, but it seems probable that they will do most of the child care themselves and it's unlikely that their household will be as formal as the one in which William was brought up.

There is also every likelihood that the Middletons will do some babysitting; Carole, after all, is his only grandmother and William knows just how valuable the relationship with grand-mothers can be—and indeed with grandfathers too. There is little doubt Carole and Michael, also their two other children, Pippa and James, will play a significant role in George's life, making him the first royal heir to have a genuine understanding of how ordinary people live—a valuable asset for a modern day monarch. They all went down to Bucklebury to stay with Kate's parents the day after they left hospital. There is no doubt George will spend time at Bucklebury as the years go by and the families will almost certainly carry on holidaying together and spending Christmases together. William and Kate were at Bucklebury last Christmas. It was the first time William had ever missed the Royal Family gathering at Sandringham, and he needed to seek the Queen's permission to be absent; but she gave it immediately. In future, they might choose to alternate Christmases between Sandringham and Bucklebury and will no doubt join the annual Royal Family sojourn at Balmoral, where George will presumably learn to ride, fish and shoot, like his father and grandfather before him.

Those Royal gatherings will be important because the fact is Prince George of Cambridge is not a normal, middle-class boy whose life is his own. He will have a wonderfully carefree childhood, one hopes, with friends from far and wide, but beyond that he has a lifetime of discipline, duty and service ahead of him and there is no place to understand that better than surrounded by others who are in the same situation.

Prince Charles will doubtless be a doting and indulgent grandfather. He has had step-grandchildren to practice on, but the arrival of his own was clearly a unique sensation. Shortly before the birth, in a very relaxed visit to Wales he had asked members of a ladies' circle if they had 'any hints on grandparenthood'? When someone volunteered that you tend to have more time for your grandchildren than you had for your children, he agreed, saying, 'Yes, it's a different part of your life. The great thing is to encourage them. Show them things to take their interest. My grandmother did that, she was wonderful.'

'Oh, yes,' he was looking forward to the baby,

he said. 'It is very important to create a bond when they are very young.' Adding, 'The great thing is to try and pull their legs before they pull yours.'

The difficulty with any plans that William and Kate undoubtedly have to allow their child the freedom that normal people enjoy, is privacy and hence security. This baby is the first direct heir to be born in the internet age. Lord Justice Leveson went a long way to taming the tabloids in his lengthy report on the culture and ethics of the British media that was finally published in November 2012, but he scarcely mentioned the elephant in the room, the internet, which is largely unpoliced and uncontrollable. As Prince Harry discovered in Las Vegas, anyone with a mobile phone can take a photo and post it on the internet.

The challenge will be to persuade the public to let the young prince be as carefree as other children so that he is not constantly marked out as different. Photographers were the bane of William's childhood, but in recent years he has been able to move around at will, and the communities in which he has lived have liked him and therefore been pleased and been proud, almost, to protect him. The hope must be that this child will grow up to be equally polite, charming and unassuming so that when people come across George Cambridge endeavouring to enjoy a moment of normality like anyone else, they let him.

# ACKNOWLEDGEMENTS

A book like this is only as good as the people one speaks to and I would like to thank all those who were so generous with their time and trusting enough to talk to me about Prince William and share their memories and experiences. Some are named in the book, some are not but each one of them played a vital part in helping me build what I hope is an accurate and fair portrait of the Prince. I did not speak to him directly about his life—he hates talking about himself—but he did allow several of those who are close to him to talk to me, including members of his Household, and for that I am immensely grateful. They are a very impressive and likeable group of people, utterly dedicated both to the Princes they work for and to the institution of monarchy—and there's not a trace of pomposity amongst them. Their guidance and their input have been invaluable.

I am also grateful to those people who painstakingly checked the manuscript to ensure that I had faithfully reported what they told me. I hope, between us, we have weeded out all the errors. If not, my apologies.

Top of the list of the others I must thank is Fenella Bates at Hodder & Stoughton, who thought of the idea and asked me to write the book. She has been a complete delight to work with, as have her colleagues Rowena Webb, Kerry Hood, Ciara Foley, Jason Bartholomew, Susan Spratt and Camilla Dowse who put together some wonderful photographs.

I also owe special thanks to Martin Seager, consultant clinical psychologist and adult psychotherapist, for his insights. He has been a wise and invaluable sounding board.

As is Jane Turnbull, who has always been so much more than an agent. I would be lost without her. Ditto my husband James, who yet again took over all things domestic while I wrote—and annoyingly does them better than me.

Thank you all.

# BIBLIOGRAPHY

Most of the books I have drawn from have been my own, written over the last thirty years:

*Diana, Princess of Wales* (Sidgwick & Jackson, 1982)
*Charles* (Sidgwick & Jackson, 1987)
*Charles and Diana, Portrait of a Marriage* (Headline, 1991)
*Charles, Victim or Villain?* (HarperCollins, 1998)
*The Firm: The Troubled Life of the House of Windsor* (HarperCollins, 2005)

Other books consulted:

Bradford, Sarah, *Diana* (Viking Adult, 2006)
Brandryth, Giles, *Philip and Elizabeth: Portrait of a Marriage* (Century, 2004)
Dimbleby, Jonathan, *The Prince of Wales: A Biography* (Little Brown, 1994)
Geldof, Bob, *Is That It?* (Sidgwick & Jackson, 1986)
Goldsmith, Lady Annabel, *Annabel: An Unconventional Life* (Weidenfeld & Nicolson, 2004)
Hardman, Robert, *Our Queen* (Random House, 2011)
Jephson, P.D., *Shadows of a Princess* (HarperCollins, 2000)

Jobson, Robert, *William & Kate* (John Blake, 2010)

Junor, John, *Listening for a Midnight Tram* (Chapmans, 1990)

Morton, Andrew, *Diana—Her True Story/In Her Own Words* (Michael O'Mara Books, 1997)

Nicholl, Katie, *William and Harry* (Preface, 2010)

Prochaska, Frank, *Royal Bounty: The Making of a Welfare Monarchy* (YUP, 1995)

Seward, Ingrid, *William & Harry* (Headline, 2003)

Shawcross, William, *Queen Elizabeth, the Queen Mother* (Macmillan, 2009)

Wales, HRH the Prince of and Charles Clover, *Highgrove: Portrait of an Estate* (Chapmans, 1993)

I am very grateful to their authors and publishers. While every effort has been made to acknowledge the copyright holders of extracts used in this book, full acknowledgement will gladly be made in future editions.

# PICTURE ACKNOWLEDGEMENTS

© Camera Press London: 299 (bottom), 300 (top)/photo Louis Jaques, 300 (bottom)/photo *The Times*, 301 (top)/photo Arthur Edwards, 301 (bottom left)/photo Spen/AL, 302 (top)/photo Mike Anthony, 306 (top)/photo Jim Bennet, 307 (middle), 309 (bottom) & 310 (top)/photos Glenn Harvey, 319 (bottom)/photo Richard Stonehouse, 326 (top & bottom left), 336 (top & bottom) & 343 (top)/photos Mark Stewart. © Getty Images: 299 (top)/photo Terry Disney/Central Press, 305 (top)/photo Bob Thomas, 305 (bottom)/photo Terry Fincher, 307 (top), 308 (top), 313 (top & bottom), 314 (bottom), 316 (bottom) & 324 (bottom)/photos Tim Graham, 312 (top)/photo Jayne Fincher, 325 (middle)/photo Anwar Hussein Collection, 328 (bottom)/photo Paul Ellis, 330 (top)/photo Stefan Rousseau, 333 (bottom)/photo Mark Taylor, 335 (top)/photo George Pimentel, 339 (top)/photo Geoff Robins. © Ian Jones: 317, 318, 321 (top), 323 (middle & bottom), 325 (bottom), 327 (top), 328 (top), 329 (middle), 330 (bottom), 332 (bottom), 335 (bottom), 338 (top), 340 (top), 342 (bottom), 343 (bottom), 344 (top). © Mirrorpix: 303 (top)/photo *Daily Record*, 304 (top), 309 (top), 310 (bottom), 316 (top)/photo Jeremy Williams, 331 (top)/

photo Ian Vogler, 334 (bottom)/photo Phil Harris. © NI Syndication: 322(right)/photo *The Sun*. © Press Association Images: 301 (bottom right), 304 (middle & bottom), 306 (bottom)/photo David Caulkin, 307 (bottom), 315 (top), 319 (top), 320 (bottom), 323 (top right) & 341 (bottom)/photos Julian Parker, 324 (top)/photo Mark Cuthbert, 327 (bottom), 331 (bottom), 334 (top)/photo Oli Scarff, 337 (bottom)/photo Jonathan Short, 338 (bottom left)/photo Chris Jackson, 338 (bottom right)/photo Toby Melville, 339 (bottom), 340 (bottom)/photos *The Canadian Press*/Fred Chartrand, 342 (middle)/ photo Arthur Edwards, 341 (top), 342 (top)/ photos *The Canadian Press*/Nathan Denette, 345/photo Andrew Milligan. © Rex Features: 302 (bottom)/photo Keith Butcher, 303 (bottom)/ photo Mike Charity, 308 (bottom)/photo Brendan Beirne, 311/photo David Hartley, 312 (bottom)/photo Cassidy and Leigh, 314 (top), 315 (bottom), 320 (top)/photo Carl De Souza, 321 (middle), 321 (bottom)/photo *Evening Standard*/ Jeremy Selwyn, 322 (left)/photo *Daily Mail*/ Malcolm Clarke, 325 (top), 326 (bottom right), 329 (top)/photo Associated Newspapers/Mark Large, 329 (bottom) & 333 (top)/photos Tim Rooke, 332 (top), 337 (top), 344 (middle & bottom).

Every reasonable effort has been made to contact the copyright holders of material reproduced in this book. But if there are any errors or omissions, Hodder & Stoughton will be pleased to insert the appropriate acknowledgement in any subsequent printing of this publication.

**Center Point Large Print**
600 Brooks Road / PO Box 1
Thorndike ME 04986-0001 USA

**(207) 568-3717**

**US & Canada:**
**1 800 929-9108**
**www.centerpointlargeprint.com**